CONTENTS

THE DARWIN INCIDENT

Shun Umezawa

02

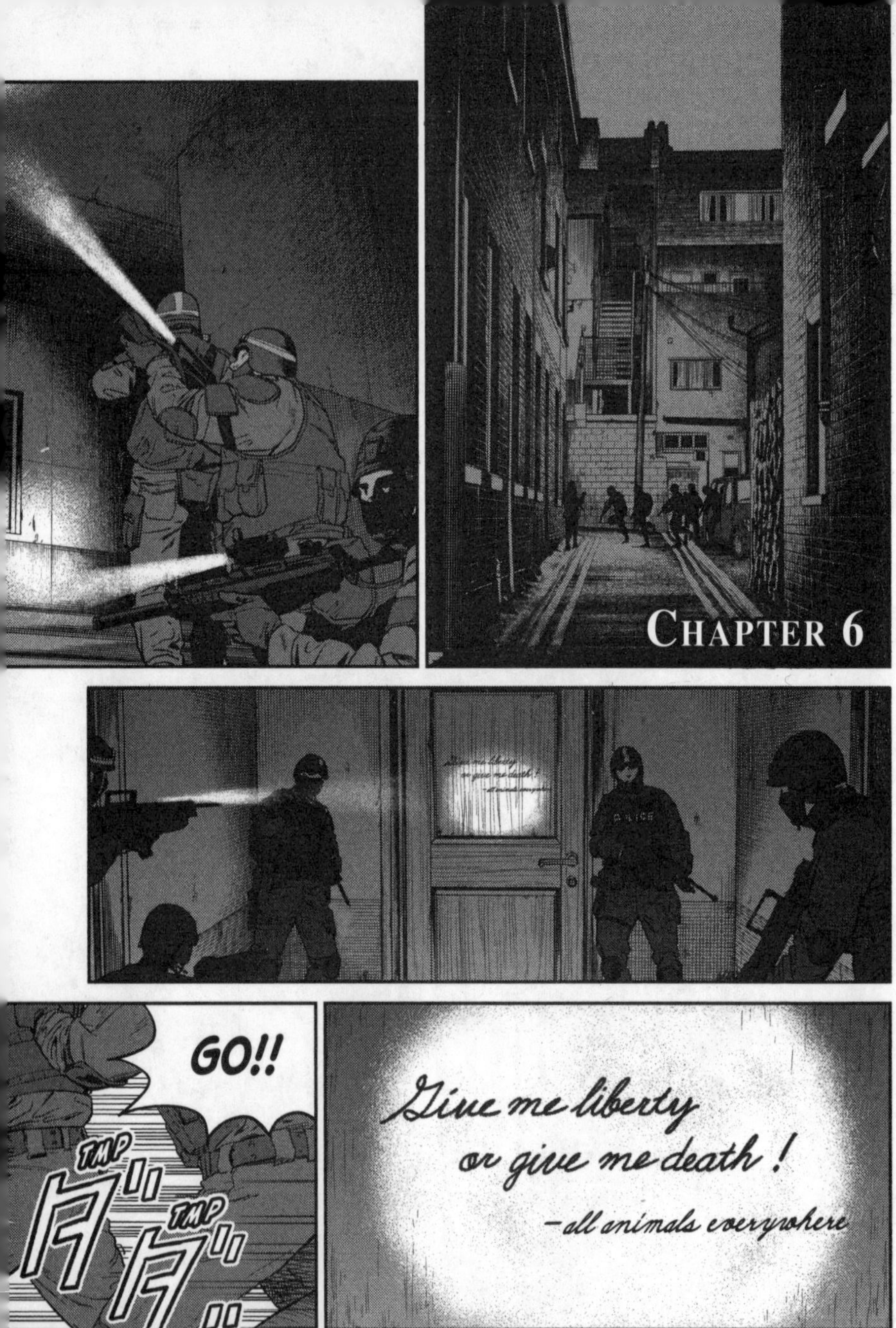
CHAPTER 6
Give me liberty or give me death!
—all animals everywhere
GO!!
TMP
TMP

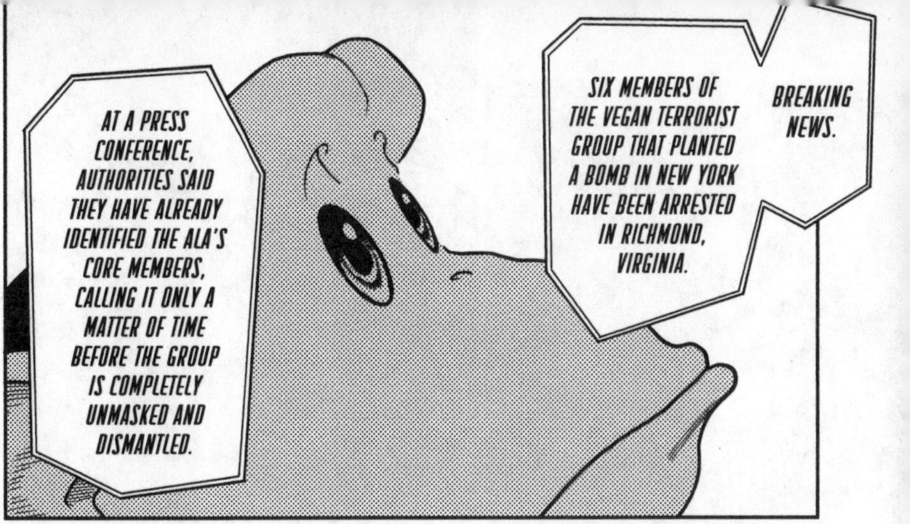
BREAKING NEWS.
SIX MEMBERS OF THE VEGAN TERRORIST GROUP THAT PLANTED A BOMB IN NEW YORK HAVE BEEN ARRESTED IN RICHMOND, VIRGINIA.
AT A PRESS CONFERENCE, AUTHORITIES SAID THEY HAVE ALREADY IDENTIFIED THE ALA'S CORE MEMBERS, CALLING IT ONLY A MATTER OF TIME BEFORE THE GROUP IS COMPLETELY UNMASKED AND DISMANTLED.

CHAPTER 6 / A GAP IN THE LAW

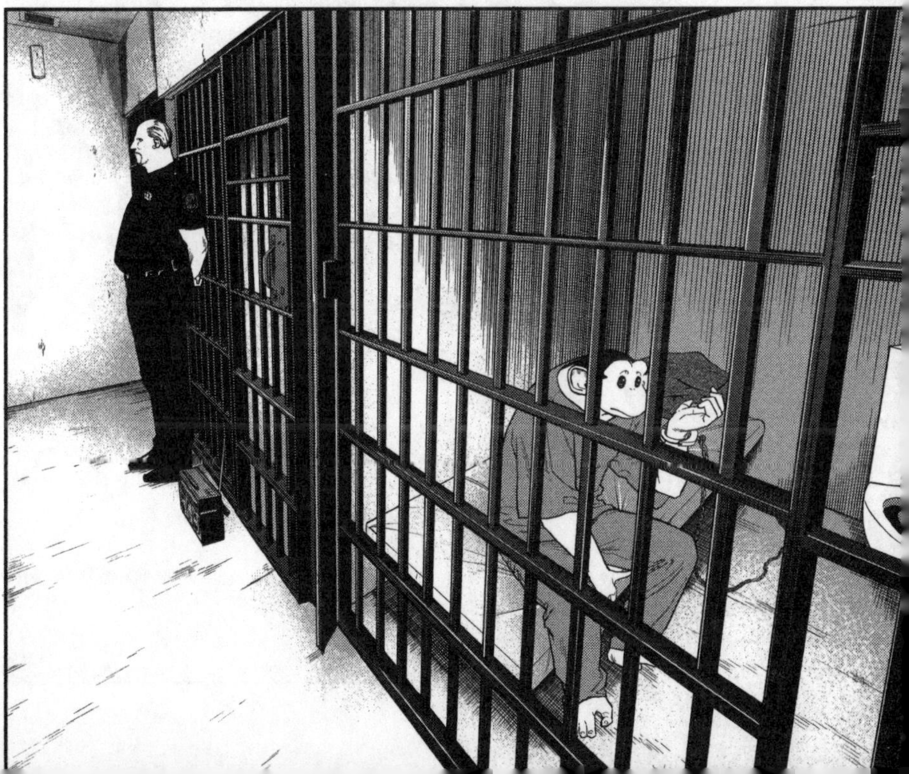

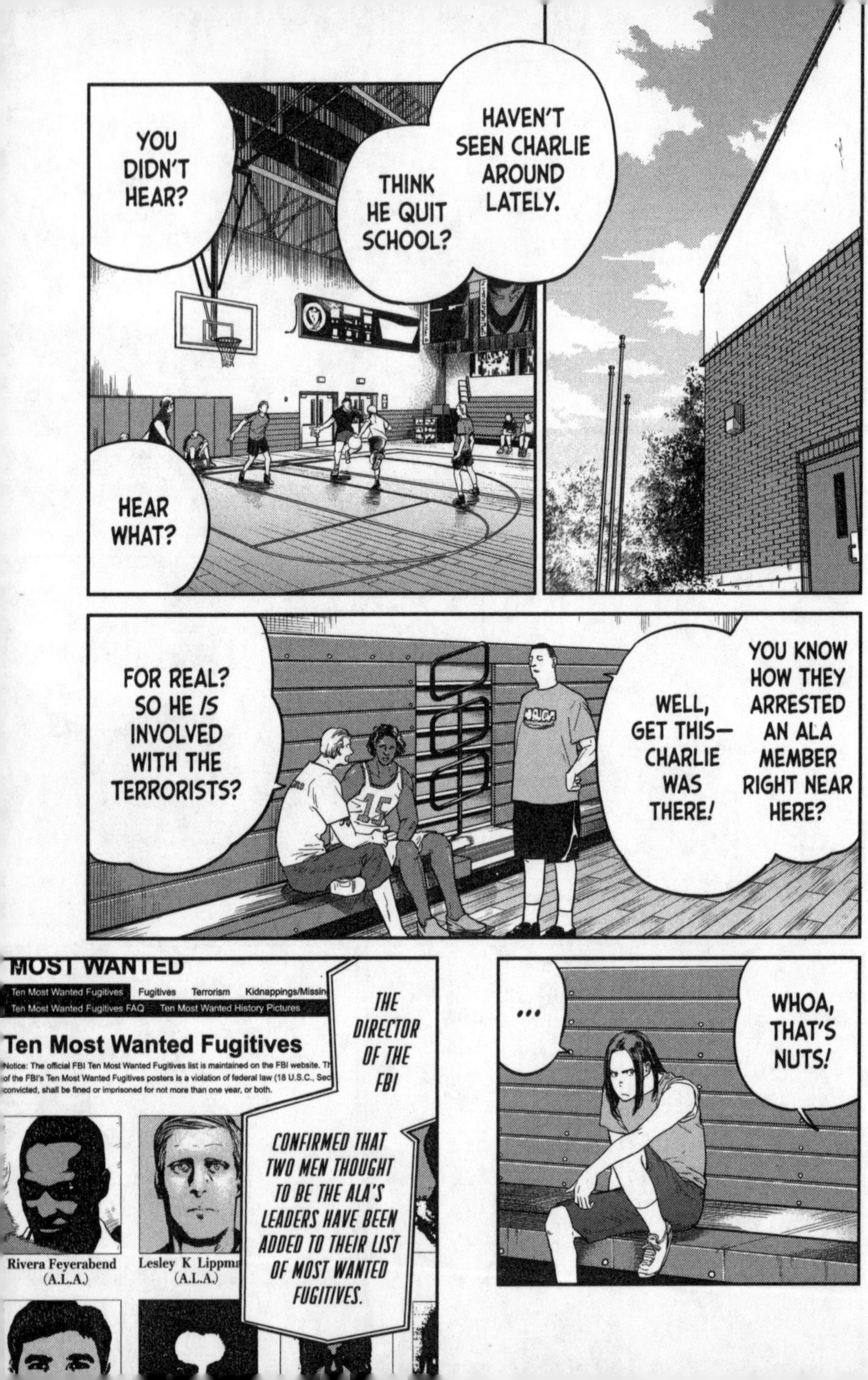
HAVEN'T SEEN CHARLIE AROUND LATELY.
THINK HE QUIT SCHOOL?
YOU DIDN'T HEAR?
HEAR WHAT?
YOU KNOW HOW THEY ARRESTED AN ALA MEMBER RIGHT NEAR HERE?
WELL, GET THIS—CHARLIE WAS THERE!
FOR REAL? SO HE *IS* INVOLVED WITH THE TERRORISTS?
WHOA, THAT'S NUTS!
...
MOST WANTED
Ten Most Wanted Fugitives Fugitives Terrorism Kidnappings/Missin
Ten Most Wanted Fugitives FAQ Ten Most Wanted History Pictures
Ten Most Wanted Fugitives
Notice: The official FBI Ten Most Wanted Fugitives list is maintained on the FBI website. Th
of the FBI's Ten Most Wanted Fugitives posters is a violation of federal law (18 U.S.C., Sec
convicted, shall be fined or imprisoned for not more than one year, or both.
Rivera Feyerabend (A.L.A.)
Lesley K Lippma (A.L.A.)
THE DIRECTOR OF THE FBI
CONFIRMED THAT TWO MEN THOUGHT TO BE THE ALA'S LEADERS HAVE BEEN ADDED TO THEIR LIST OF MOST WANTED FUGITIVES.

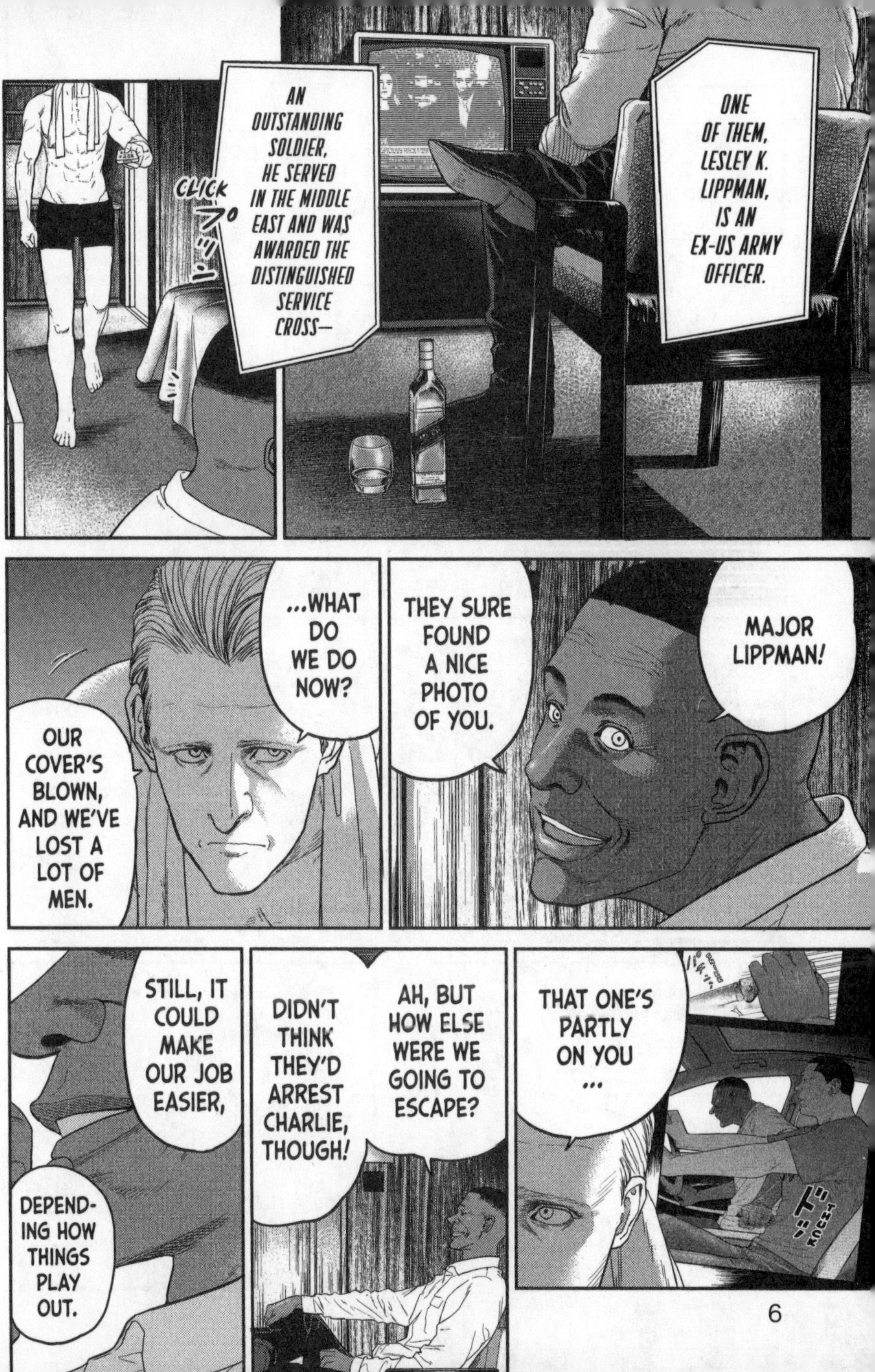
ONE OF THEM, LESLEY K. LIPPMAN, IS AN EX-US ARMY OFFICER.
AN OUTSTANDING SOLDIER, HE SERVED IN THE MIDDLE EAST AND WAS AWARDED THE DISTINGUISHED SERVICE CROSS—
CLICK
MAJOR LIPPMAN!
THEY SURE FOUND A NICE PHOTO OF YOU.
...WHAT DO WE DO NOW?
OUR COVER'S BLOWN, AND WE'VE LOST A LOT OF MEN.
THAT ONE'S PARTLY ON YOU ...
AH, BUT HOW ELSE WERE WE GOING TO ESCAPE?
DIDN'T THINK THEY'D ARREST CHARLIE, THOUGH!
STILL, IT COULD MAKE OUR JOB EASIER,
DEPENDING HOW THINGS PLAY OUT.

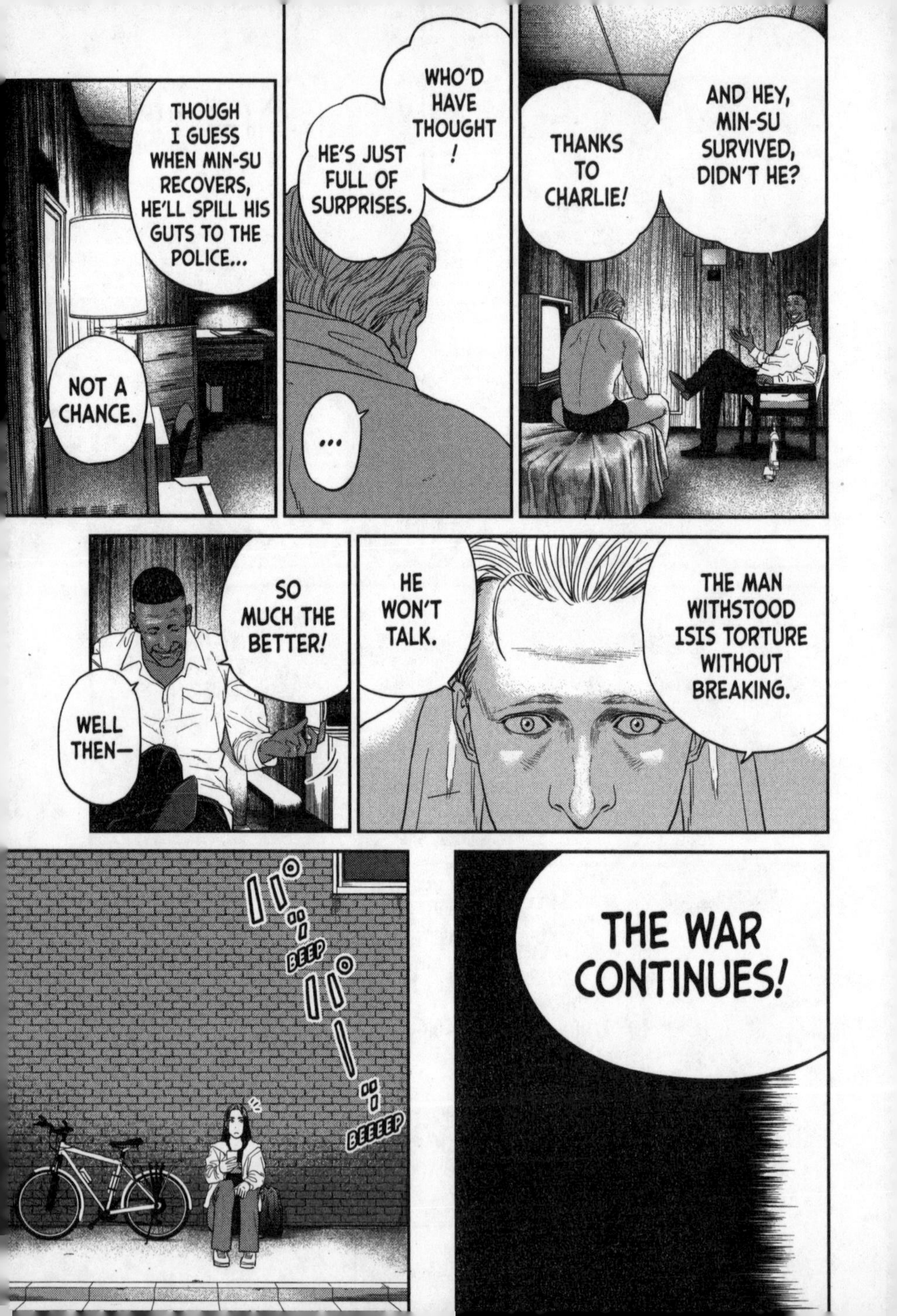
AND HEY, MIN-SU SURVIVED, DIDN'T HE?
THANKS TO CHARLIE!
WHO'D HAVE THOUGHT!
HE'S JUST FULL OF SURPRISES.
...
THOUGH I GUESS WHEN MIN-SU RECOVERS, HE'LL SPILL HIS GUTS TO THE POLICE...
NOT A CHANCE.
THE MAN WITHSTOOD ISIS TORTURE WITHOUT BREAKING.
HE WON'T TALK.
SO MUCH THE BETTER!
WELL THEN—
THE WAR CONTINUES!
BEEP
BEEEEP

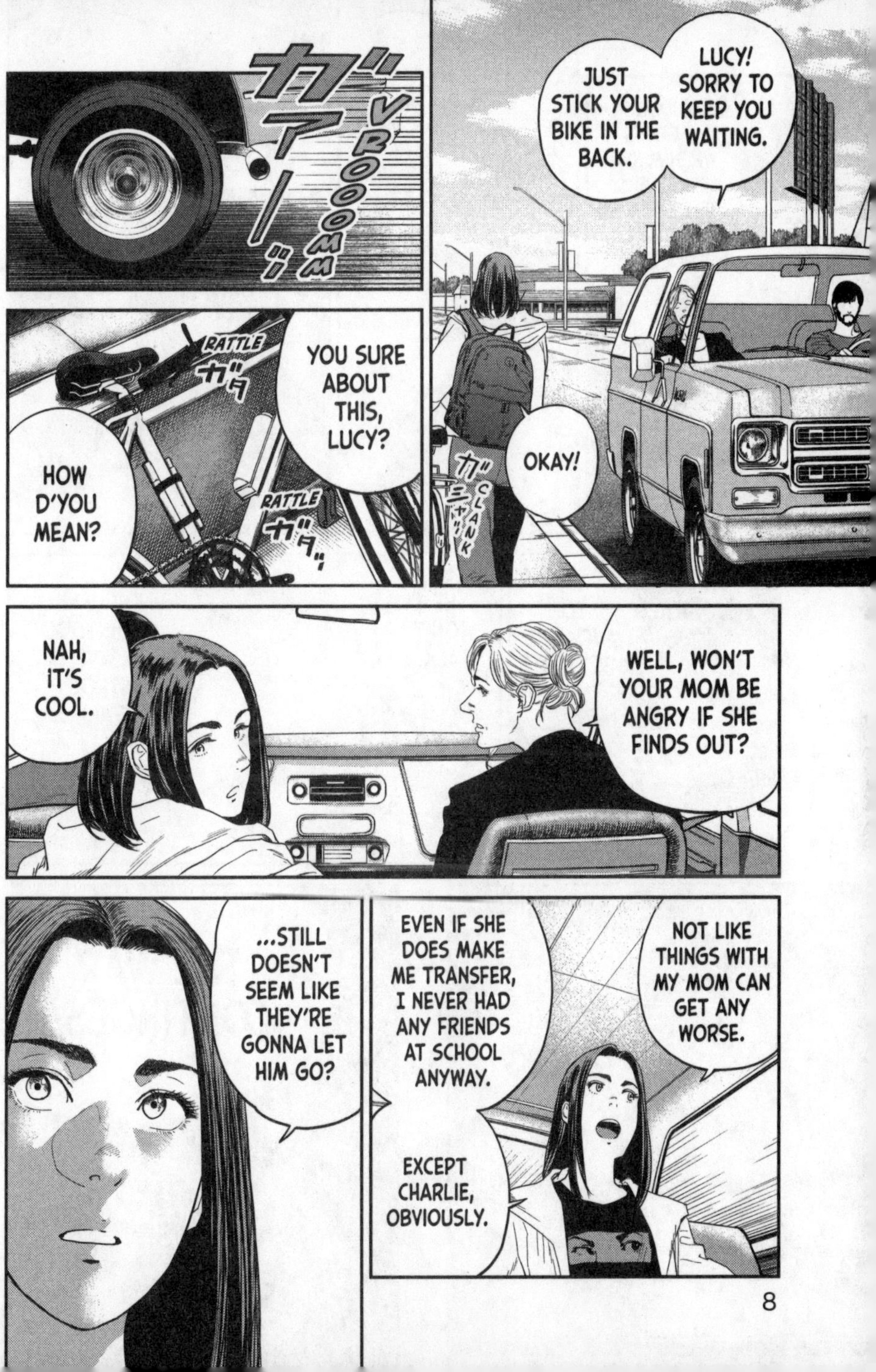
LUCY! SORRY TO KEEP YOU WAITING.
JUST STICK YOUR BIKE IN THE BACK.
OKAY!
CLANK
VROOOOOMM
YOU SURE ABOUT THIS, LUCY?
RATTLE
ガタ
HOW D'YOU MEAN?
RATTLE
WELL, WON'T YOUR MOM BE ANGRY IF SHE FINDS OUT?
NAH, IT'S COOL.
NOT LIKE THINGS WITH MY MOM CAN GET ANY WORSE.
EVEN IF SHE DOES MAKE ME TRANSFER, I NEVER HAD ANY FRIENDS AT SCHOOL ANYWAY.
EXCEPT CHARLIE, OBVIOUSLY.
...STILL DOESN'T SEEM LIKE THEY'RE GONNA LET HIM GO?

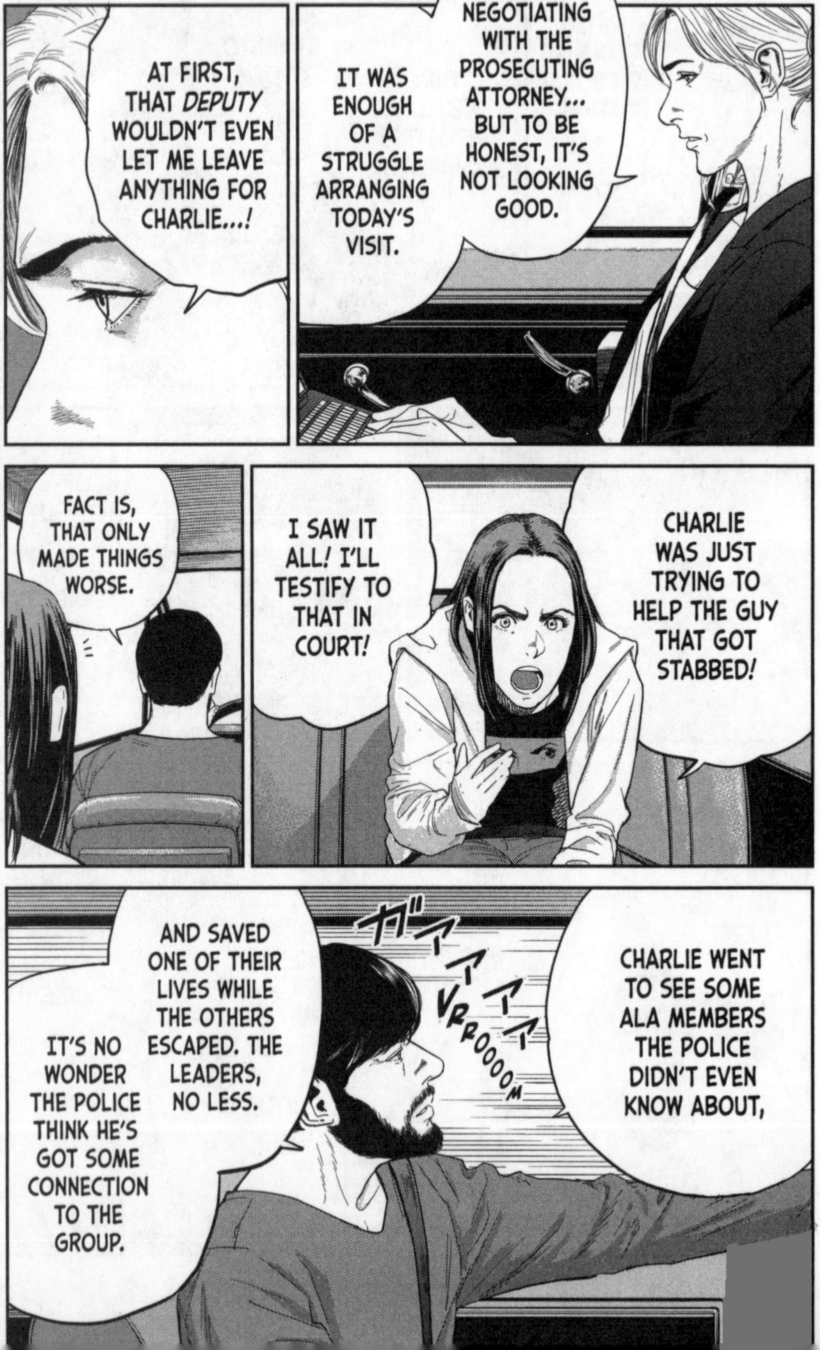
WE'RE NEGOTIATING WITH THE PROSECUTING ATTORNEY... BUT TO BE HONEST, IT'S NOT LOOKING GOOD.
IT WAS ENOUGH OF A STRUGGLE ARRANGING TODAY'S VISIT.
AT FIRST, THAT *DEPUTY* WOULDN'T EVEN LET ME LEAVE ANYTHING FOR CHARLIE...!
CHARLIE WAS JUST TRYING TO HELP THE GUY THAT GOT STABBED!
I SAW IT ALL! I'LL TESTIFY TO THAT IN COURT!
FACT IS, THAT ONLY MADE THINGS WORSE.
CHARLIE WENT TO SEE SOME ALA MEMBERS THE POLICE DIDN'T EVEN KNOW ABOUT,
VRROOOOM
AND SAVED ONE OF THEIR LIVES WHILE THE OTHERS ESCAPED. THE LEADERS, NO LESS.
IT'S NO WONDER THE POLICE THINK HE'S GOT SOME CONNECTION TO THE GROUP.

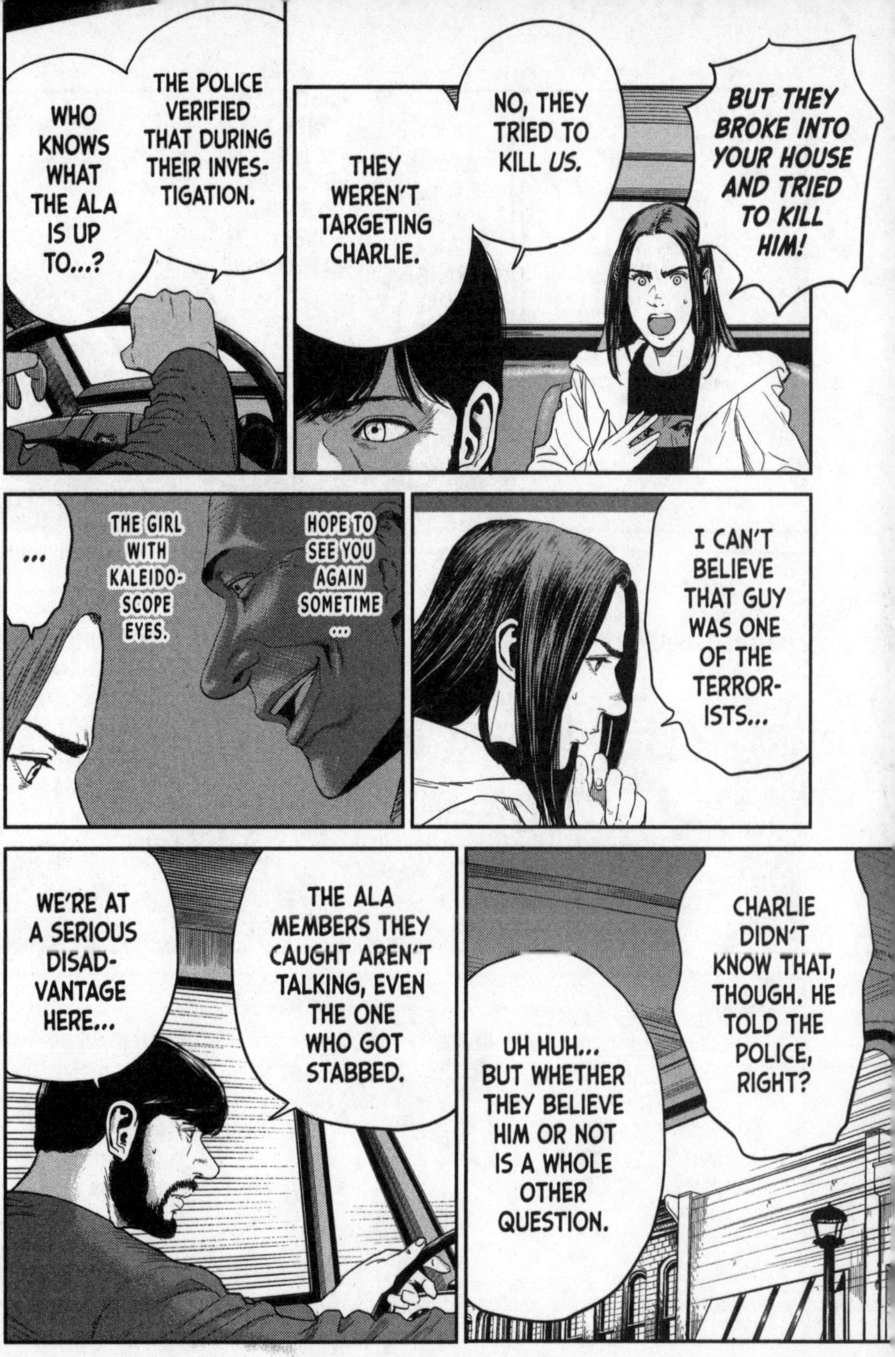
BUT THEY BROKE INTO YOUR HOUSE AND TRIED TO KILL HIM!
NO, THEY TRIED TO KILL *US.*
THEY WEREN'T TARGETING CHARLIE.
THE POLICE VERIFIED THAT DURING THEIR INVESTIGATION.
WHO KNOWS WHAT THE ALA IS UP TO...?
I CAN'T BELIEVE THAT GUY WAS ONE OF THE TERRORISTS...
HOPE TO SEE YOU AGAIN SOMETIME...
THE GIRL WITH KALEIDOSCOPE EYES.
...
CHARLIE DIDN'T KNOW THAT, THOUGH. HE TOLD THE POLICE, RIGHT?
UH HUH... BUT WHETHER THEY BELIEVE HIM OR NOT IS A WHOLE OTHER QUESTION.
THE ALA MEMBERS THEY CAUGHT AREN'T TALKING, EVEN THE ONE WHO GOT STABBED.
WE'RE AT A SERIOUS DISADVANTAGE HERE...

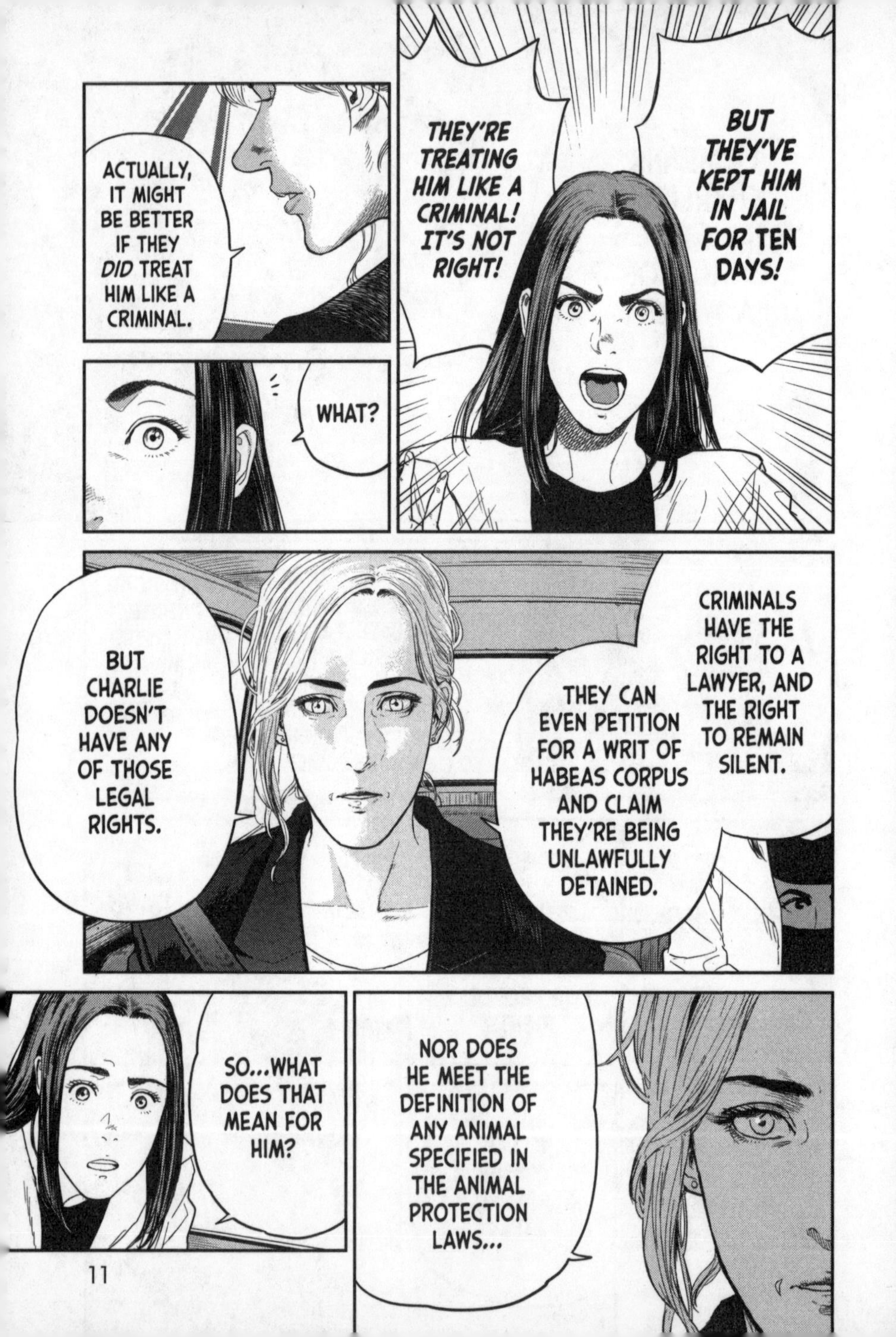
BUT THEY'VE KEPT HIM IN JAIL FOR TEN DAYS!
THEY'RE TREATING HIM LIKE A CRIMINAL! IT'S NOT RIGHT!
ACTUALLY, IT MIGHT BE BETTER IF THEY *DID* TREAT HIM LIKE A CRIMINAL.
WHAT?
CRIMINALS HAVE THE RIGHT TO A LAWYER, AND THE RIGHT TO REMAIN SILENT.
THEY CAN EVEN PETITION FOR A WRIT OF HABEAS CORPUS AND CLAIM THEY'RE BEING UNLAWFULLY DETAINED.
BUT CHARLIE DOESN'T HAVE ANY OF THOSE LEGAL RIGHTS.
NOR DOES HE MEET THE DEFINITION OF ANY ANIMAL SPECIFIED IN THE ANIMAL PROTECTION LAWS...
SO...WHAT DOES THAT MEAN FOR HIM?

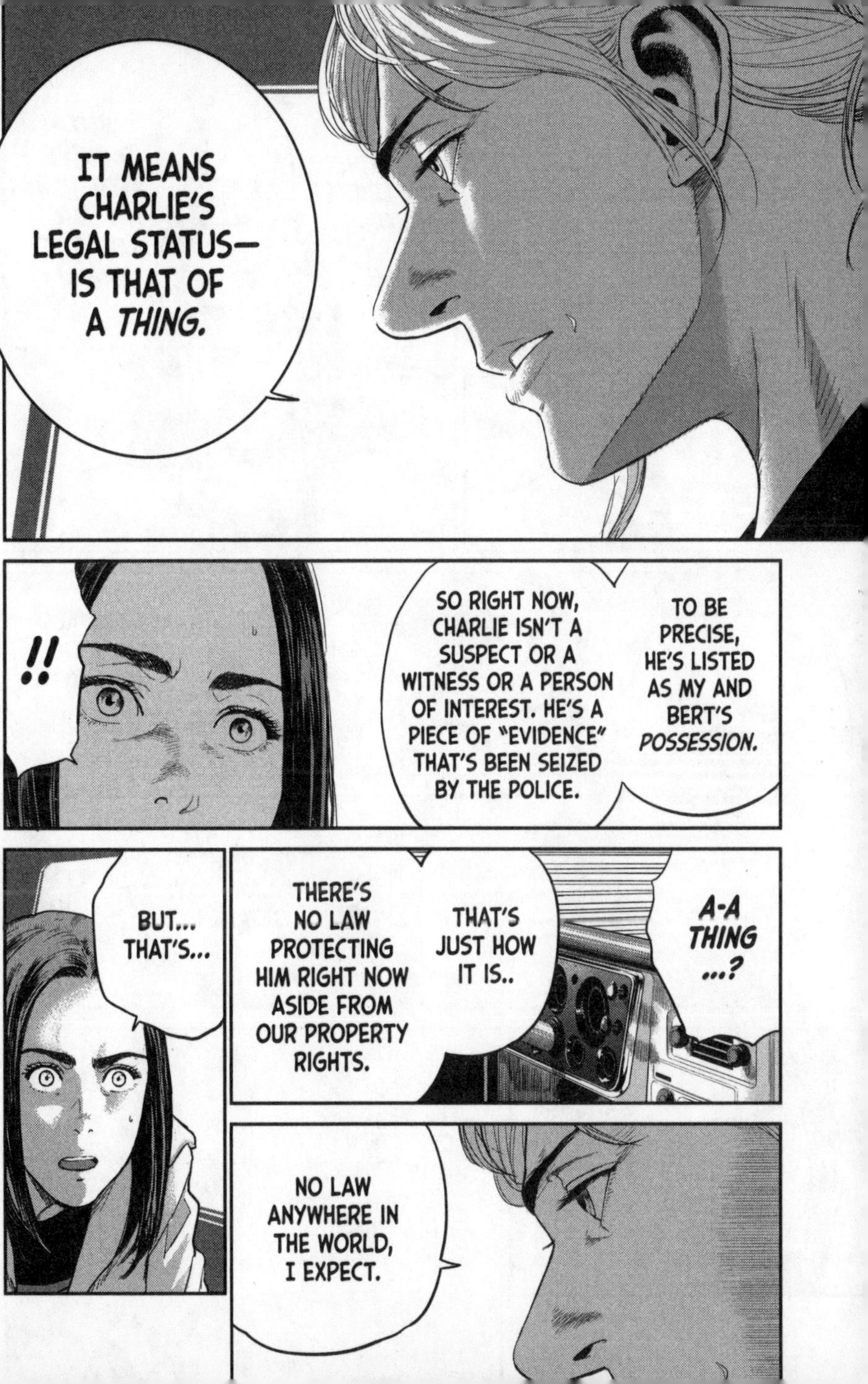
IT MEANS CHARLIE'S LEGAL STATUS—IS THAT OF A *THING.*
SO RIGHT NOW, CHARLIE ISN'T A SUSPECT OR A WITNESS OR A PERSON OF INTEREST. HE'S A PIECE OF "EVIDENCE" THAT'S BEEN SEIZED BY THE POLICE.
TO BE PRECISE, HE'S LISTED AS MY AND BERT'S *POSSESSION.*
!!
A-A THING ...?
THAT'S JUST HOW IT IS..
THERE'S NO LAW PROTECTING HIM RIGHT NOW ASIDE FROM OUR PROPERTY RIGHTS.
NO LAW ANYWHERE IN THE WORLD, I EXPECT.
BUT... THAT'S...

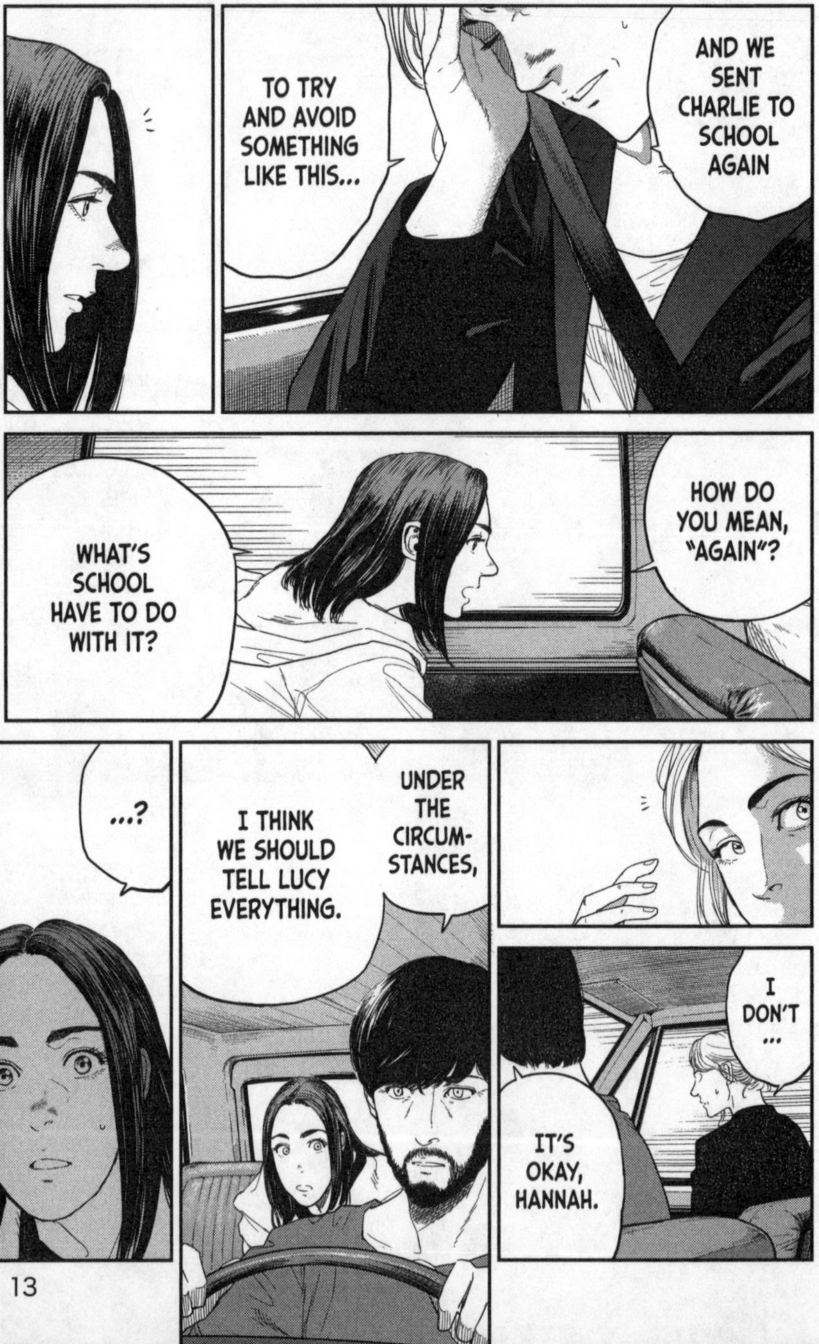
AND WE SENT CHARLIE TO SCHOOL AGAIN
TO TRY AND AVOID SOMETHING LIKE THIS...
HOW DO YOU MEAN, "AGAIN"?
WHAT'S SCHOOL HAVE TO DO WITH IT?
I DON'T ...
IT'S OKAY, HANNAH.
UNDER THE CIRCUM-STANCES,
I THINK WE SHOULD TELL LUCY EVERYTHING.
...?

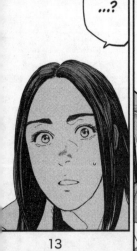

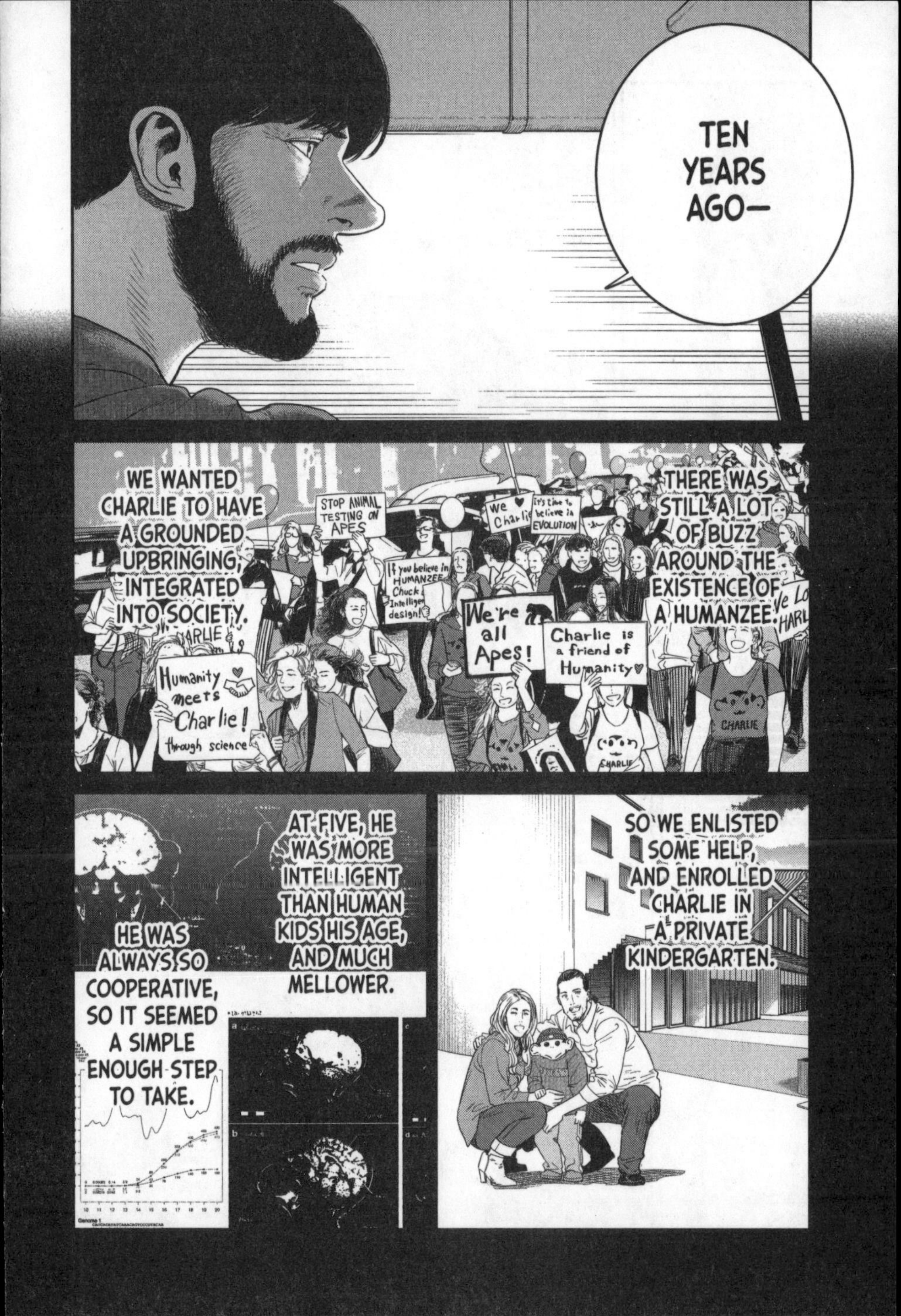

TEN YEARS AGO—
THERE WAS STILL A LOT OF BUZZ AROUND THE EXISTENCE OF A HUMANZEE.
WE WANTED CHARLIE TO HAVE A GROUNDED UPBRINGING, INTEGRATED INTO SOCIETY.
We ♥ Charlie
It's time to believe in EVOLUTION
STOP ANIMAL TESTING ON APES
We're all Apes!
Charlie is a friend of Humanity♥
Humanity ♥ meets Charlie! through science
CHARLIE
SO WE ENLISTED SOME HELP, AND ENROLLED CHARLIE IN A PRIVATE KINDERGARTEN.
AT FIVE, HE WAS MORE INTELLIGENT THAN HUMAN KIDS HIS AGE, AND MUCH MELLOWER.
HE WAS ALWAYS SO COOPERATIVE, SO IT SEEMED A SIMPLE ENOUGH STEP TO TAKE.

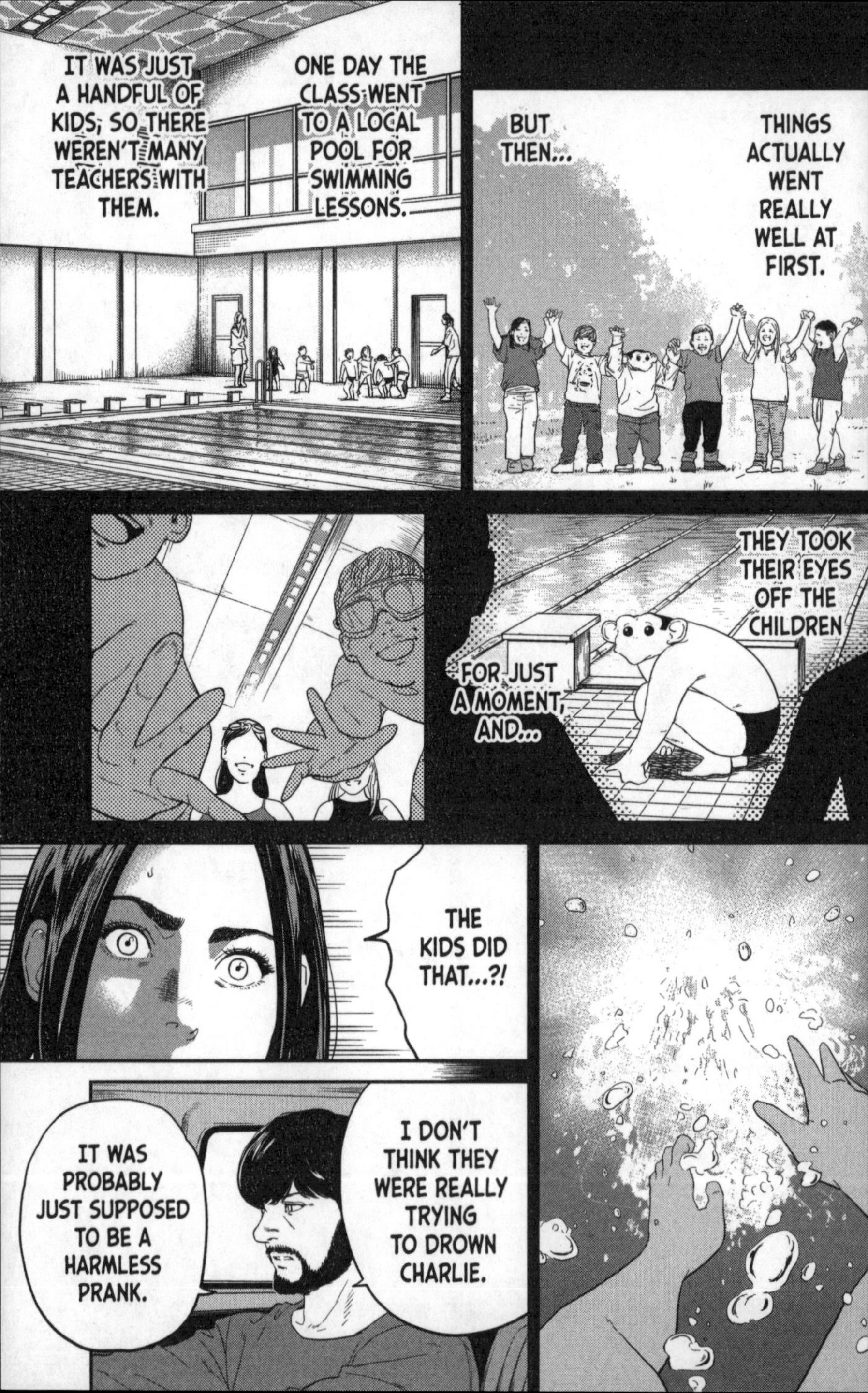
THINGS ACTUALLY WENT REALLY WELL AT FIRST.
BUT THEN...
ONE DAY THE CLASS WENT TO A LOCAL POOL FOR SWIMMING LESSONS.
IT WAS JUST A HANDFUL OF KIDS, SO THERE WEREN'T MANY TEACHERS WITH THEM.
THEY TOOK THEIR EYES OFF THE CHILDREN
FOR JUST A MOMENT, AND...
THE KIDS DID THAT...?!
I DON'T THINK THEY WERE REALLY TRYING TO DROWN CHARLIE.
IT WAS PROBABLY JUST SUPPOSED TO BE A HARMLESS PRANK.

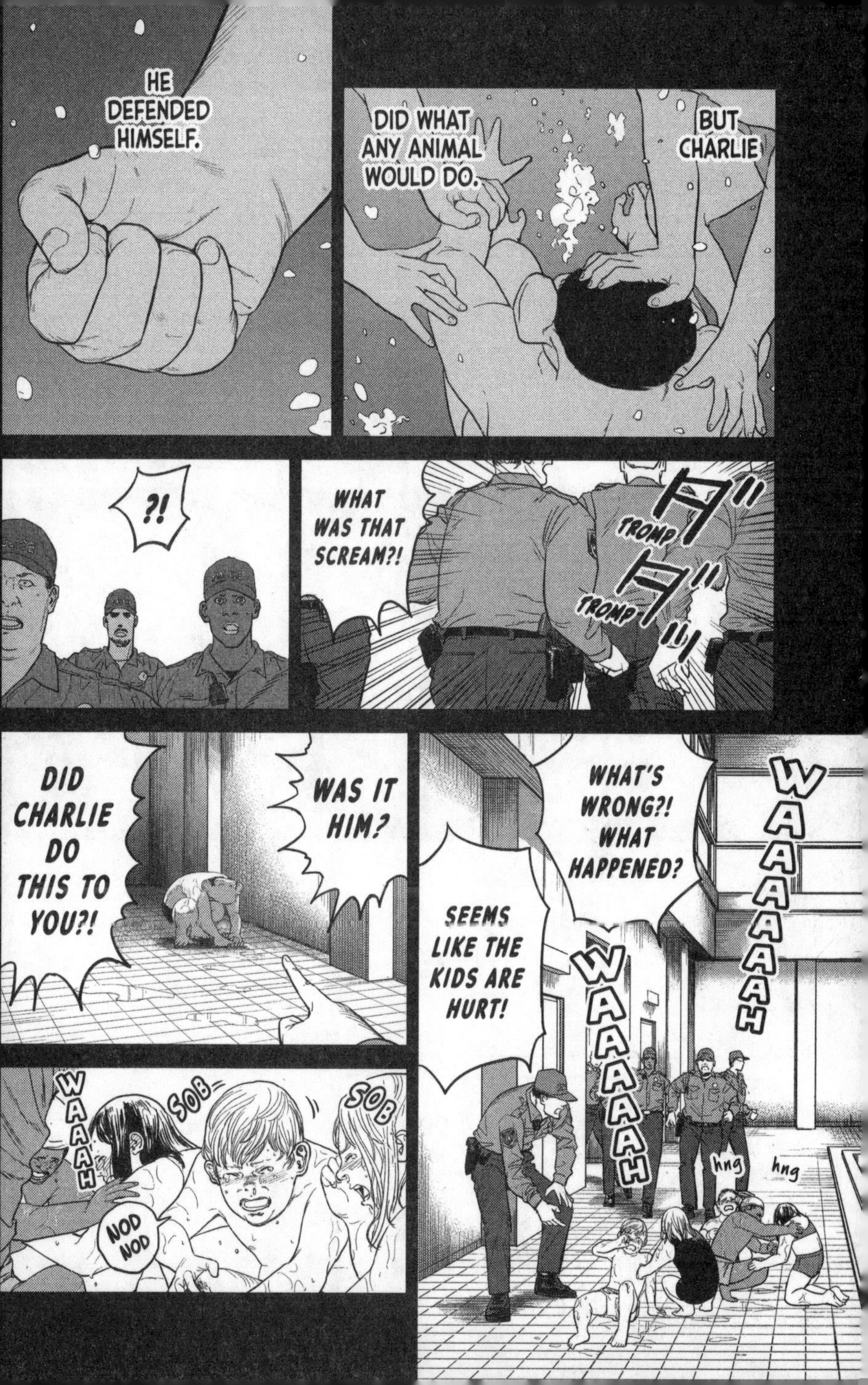
BUT CHARLIE
DID WHAT ANY ANIMAL WOULD DO.
HE DEFENDED HIMSELF.
TROMP
WHAT WAS THAT SCREAM?!
TROMP
?!
WAAAAAAAH
WHAT'S WRONG?! WHAT HAPPENED?
WAAAAAAAH
SEEMS LIKE THE KIDS ARE HURT!
hng
hng
WAS IT HIM?
DID CHARLIE DO THIS TO YOU?!
SOB
SOB
WAAAH
NOD NOD

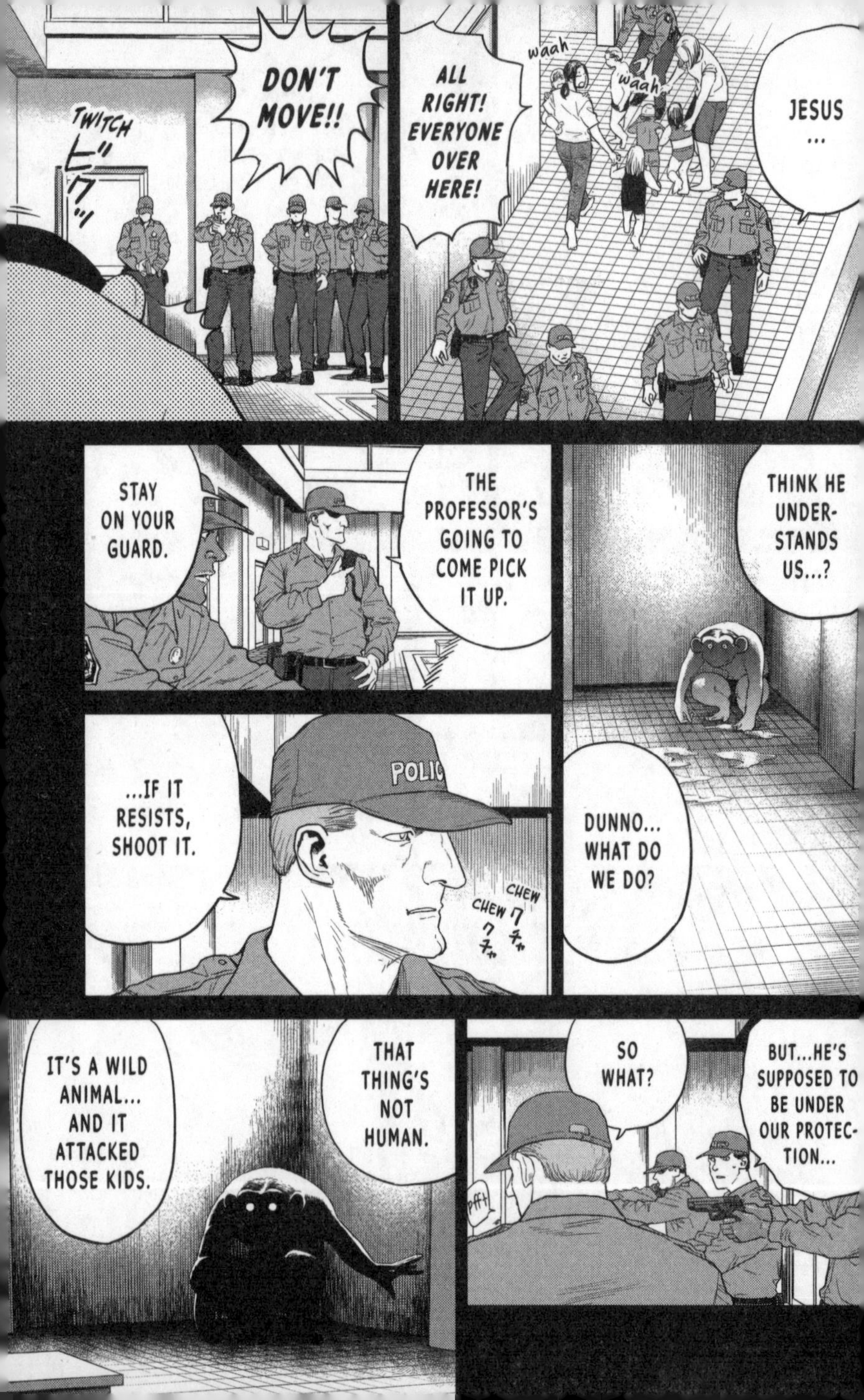
JESUS ...
waah
waah
ALL RIGHT! EVERYONE OVER HERE!
DON'T MOVE!!
TWITCH
ビクッ
THINK HE UNDER-STANDS US...?
DUNNO... WHAT DO WE DO?
THE PROFESSOR'S GOING TO COME PICK IT UP.
STAY ON YOUR GUARD.
POLIC
...IF IT RESISTS, SHOOT IT.
CHEW CHEW
クチャクチャ
BUT...HE'S SUPPOSED TO BE UNDER OUR PROTEC-TION...
SO WHAT?
pfft
THAT THING'S NOT HUMAN.
IT'S A WILD ANIMAL... AND IT ATTACKED THOSE KIDS.

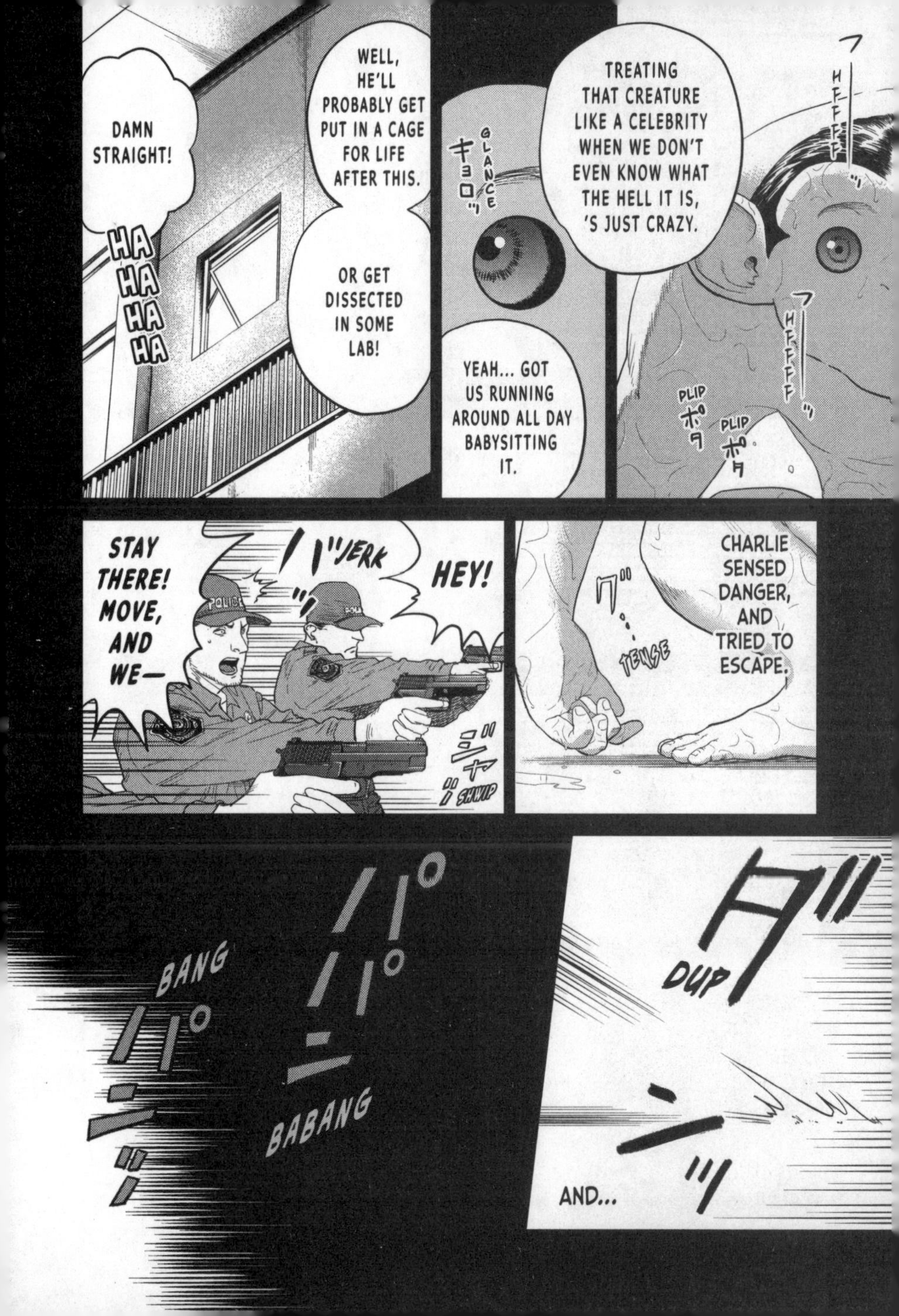
HFFFFF
HFFFFF
PLIP
PLIP
TREATING THAT CREATURE LIKE A CELEBRITY WHEN WE DON'T EVEN KNOW WHAT THE HELL IT IS, 'S JUST CRAZY.
GLANCE
YEAH... GOT US RUNNING AROUND ALL DAY BABYSITTING IT.
WELL, HE'LL PROBABLY GET PUT IN A CAGE FOR LIFE AFTER THIS.
OR GET DISSECTED IN SOME LAB!
DAMN STRAIGHT!
HA HA HA HA
CHARLIE SENSED DANGER, AND TRIED TO ESCAPE.
TENSE
HEY!
JERK
STAY THERE! MOVE, AND WE—
SHWIP
DUP
AND...
BANG
BABANG

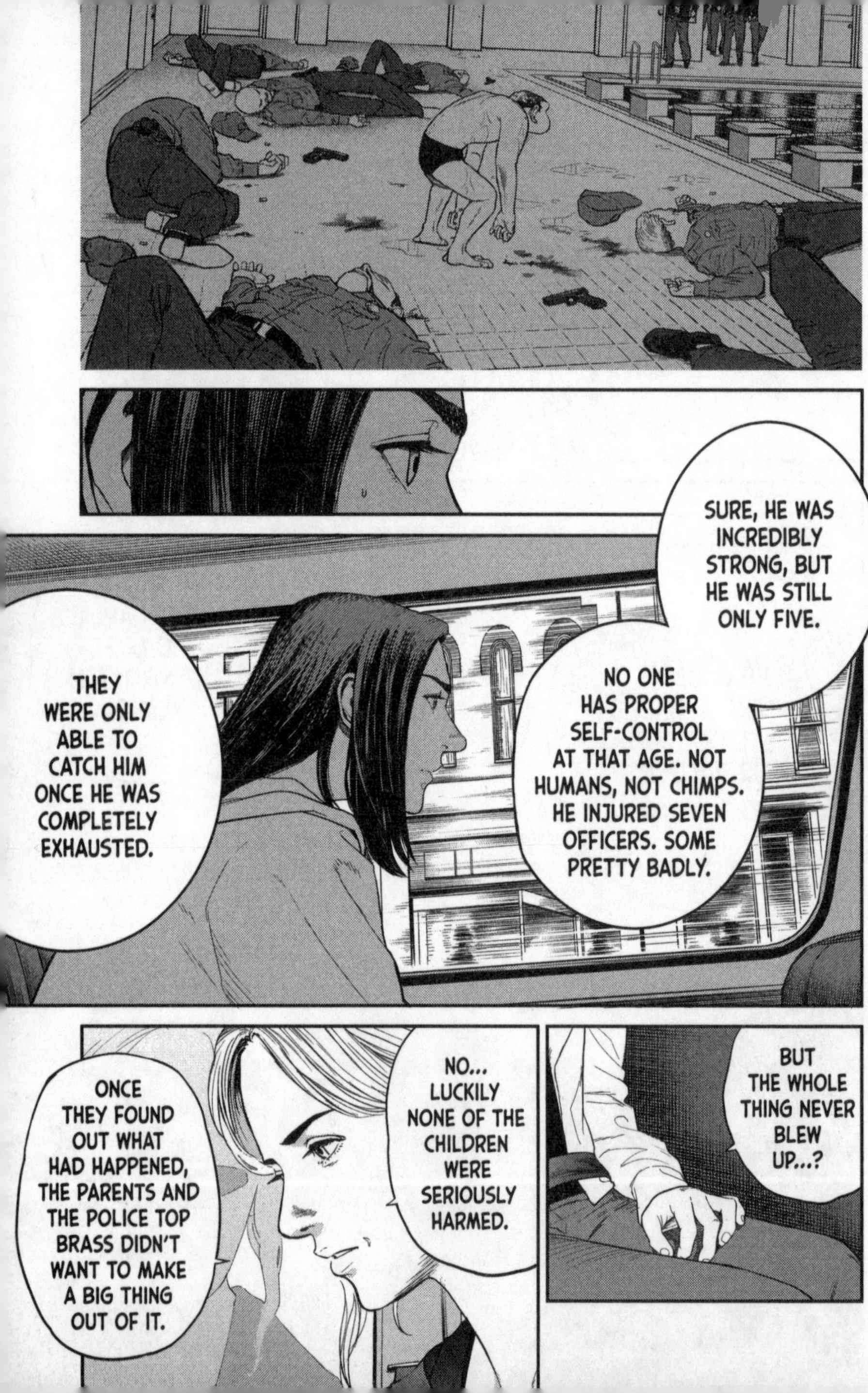
SURE, HE WAS INCREDIBLY STRONG, BUT HE WAS STILL ONLY FIVE.
NO ONE HAS PROPER SELF-CONTROL AT THAT AGE. NOT HUMANS, NOT CHIMPS. HE INJURED SEVEN OFFICERS. SOME PRETTY BADLY.
THEY WERE ONLY ABLE TO CATCH HIM ONCE HE WAS COMPLETELY EXHAUSTED.
BUT THE WHOLE THING NEVER BLEW UP...?
NO... LUCKILY NONE OF THE CHILDREN WERE SERIOUSLY HARMED.
ONCE THEY FOUND OUT WHAT HAD HAPPENED, THE PARENTS AND THE POLICE TOP BRASS DIDN'T WANT TO MAKE A BIG THING OUT OF IT.

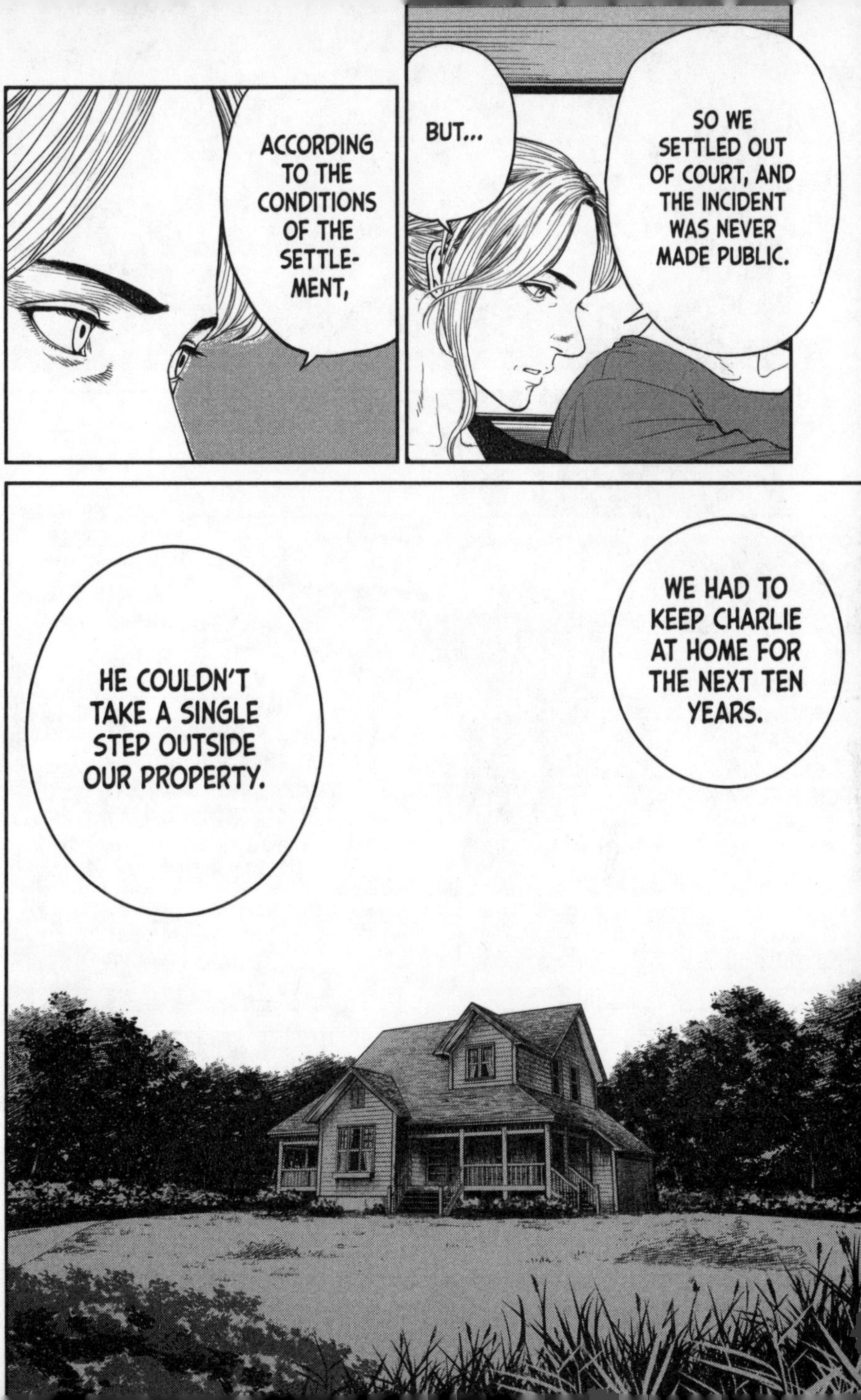
SO WE SETTLED OUT OF COURT, AND THE INCIDENT WAS NEVER MADE PUBLIC.
BUT...
ACCORDING TO THE CONDITIONS OF THE SETTLE-MENT,
WE HAD TO KEEP CHARLIE AT HOME FOR THE NEXT TEN YEARS.
HE COULDN'T TAKE A SINGLE STEP OUTSIDE OUR PROPERTY.

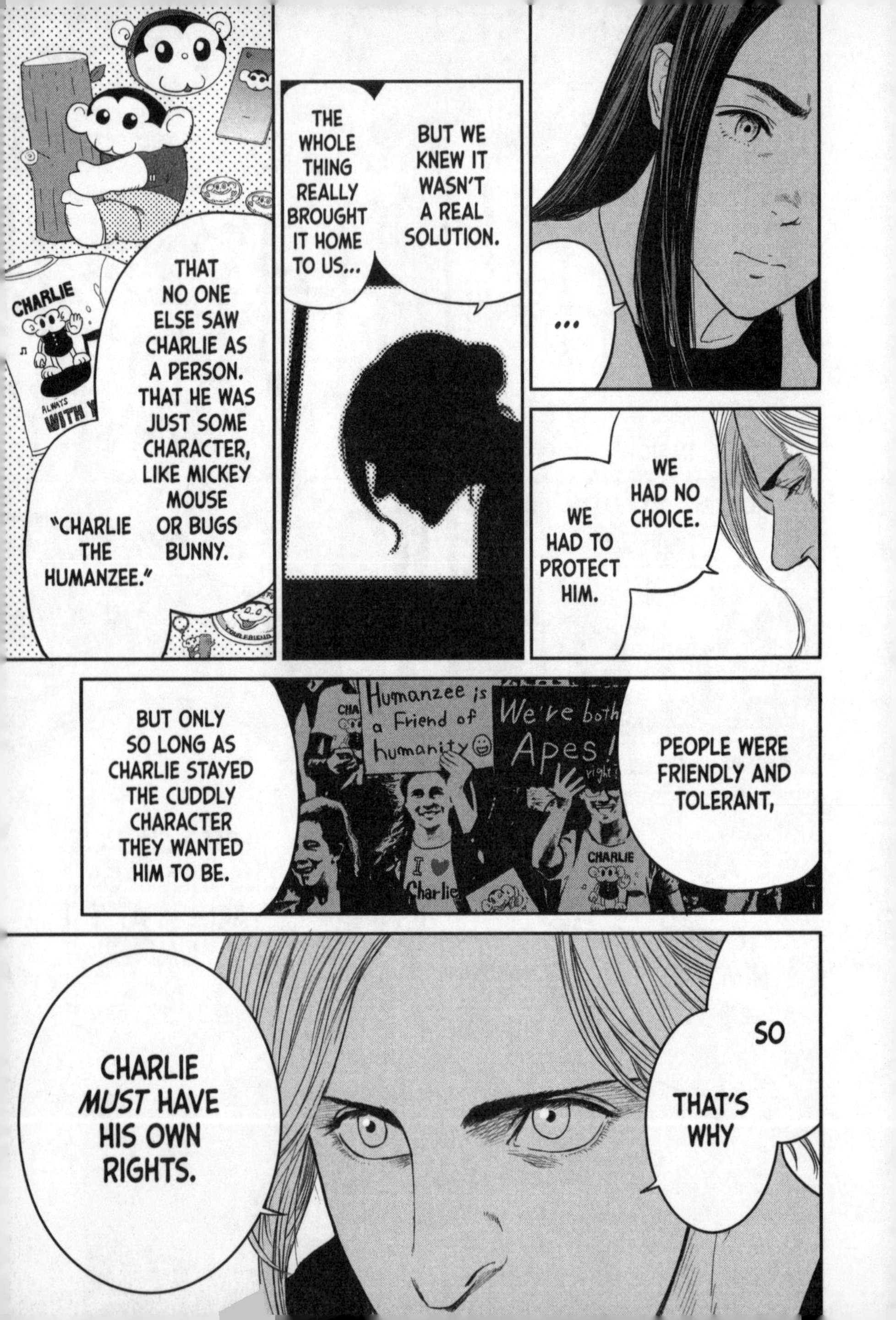
...
WE HAD NO CHOICE.
WE HAD TO PROTECT HIM.
BUT WE KNEW IT WASN'T A REAL SOLUTION.
THE WHOLE THING REALLY BROUGHT IT HOME TO US...
CHARLIE
THAT NO ONE ELSE SAW CHARLIE AS A PERSON. THAT HE WAS JUST SOME CHARACTER, LIKE MICKEY MOUSE OR BUGS BUNNY.
"CHARLIE THE HUMANZEE."
PEOPLE WERE FRIENDLY AND TOLERANT,
We're both Apes! right?
Humanzee is a Friend of humanity
CHARLIE
I ♥ Charlie
BUT ONLY SO LONG AS CHARLIE STAYED THE CUDDLY CHARACTER THEY WANTED HIM TO BE.
SO THAT'S WHY
CHARLIE *MUST* HAVE HIS OWN RIGHTS.

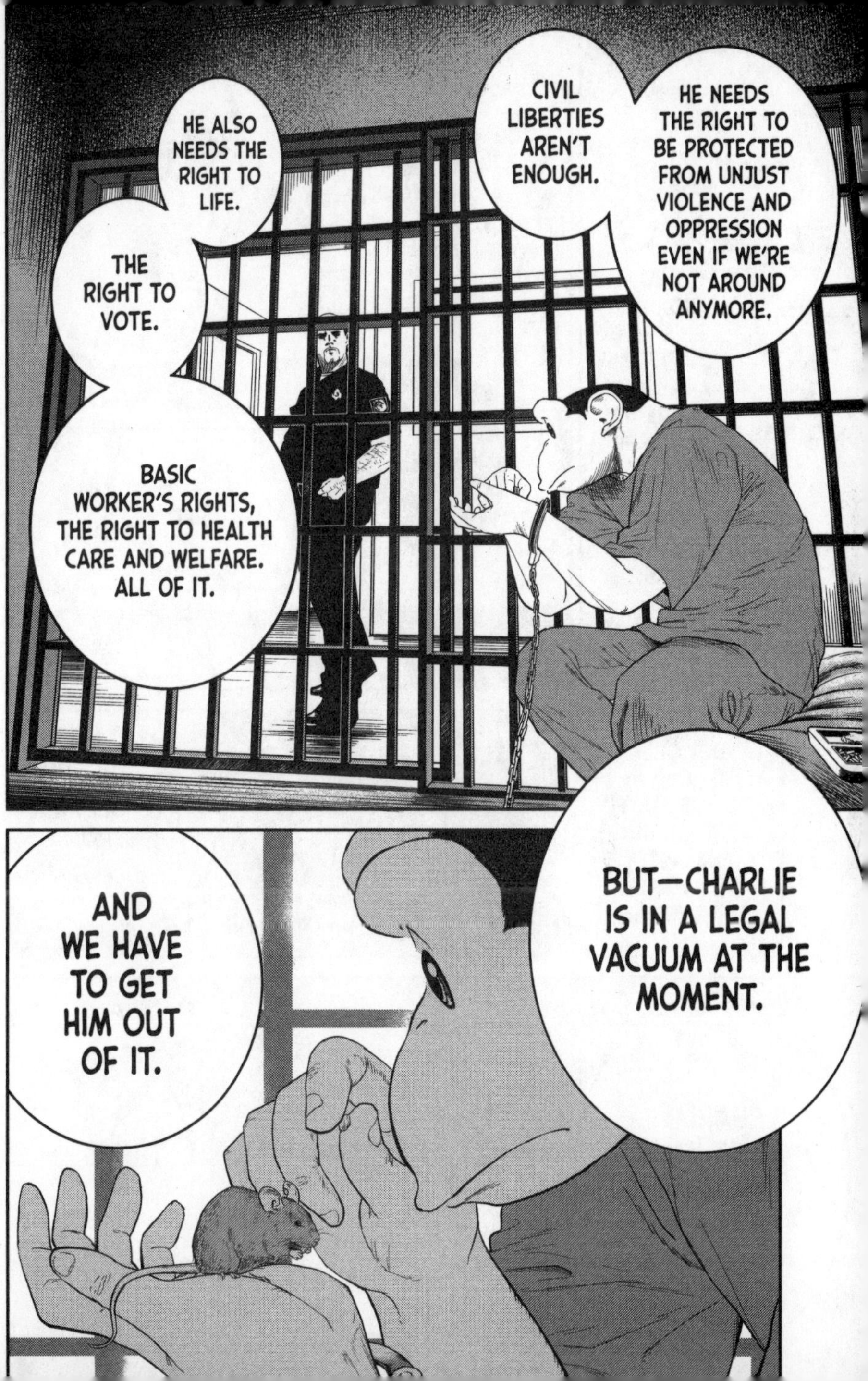
HE NEEDS THE RIGHT TO BE PROTECTED FROM UNJUST VIOLENCE AND OPPRESSION EVEN IF WE'RE NOT AROUND ANYMORE.
CIVIL LIBERTIES AREN'T ENOUGH.
HE ALSO NEEDS THE RIGHT TO LIFE.
THE RIGHT TO VOTE.
BASIC WORKER'S RIGHTS, THE RIGHT TO HEALTH CARE AND WELFARE. ALL OF IT.
BUT—CHARLIE IS IN A LEGAL VACUUM AT THE MOMENT.
AND WE HAVE TO GET HIM OUT OF IT.

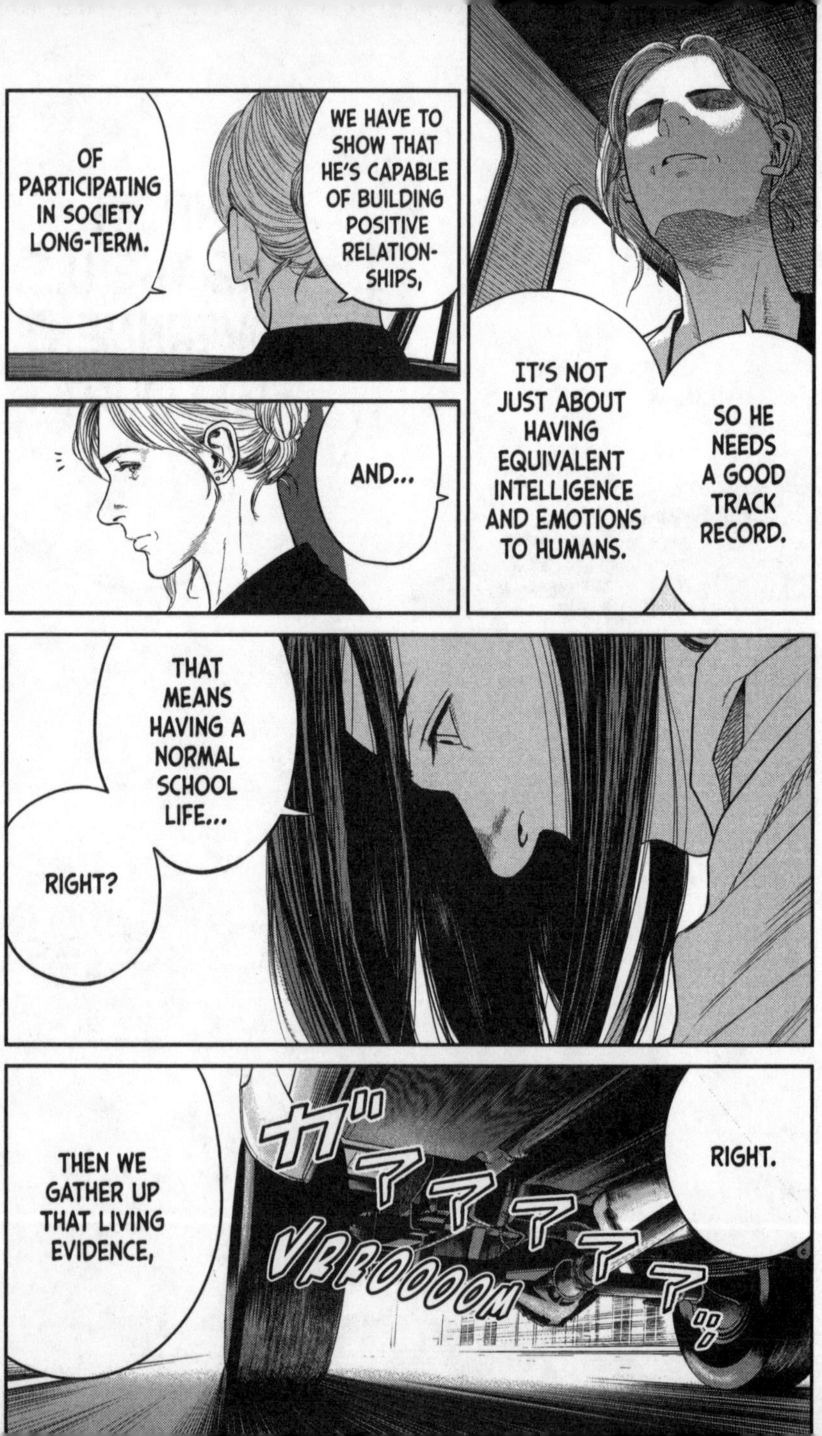
IT'S NOT JUST ABOUT HAVING EQUIVALENT INTELLIGENCE AND EMOTIONS TO HUMANS.
SO HE NEEDS A GOOD TRACK RECORD.
WE HAVE TO SHOW THAT HE'S CAPABLE OF BUILDING POSITIVE RELATION-SHIPS,
OF PARTICIPATING IN SOCIETY LONG-TERM.
AND...
THAT MEANS HAVING A NORMAL SCHOOL LIFE...
RIGHT?
RIGHT.
ガァァァァァッ
VRROOOOM
THEN WE GATHER UP THAT LIVING EVIDENCE,

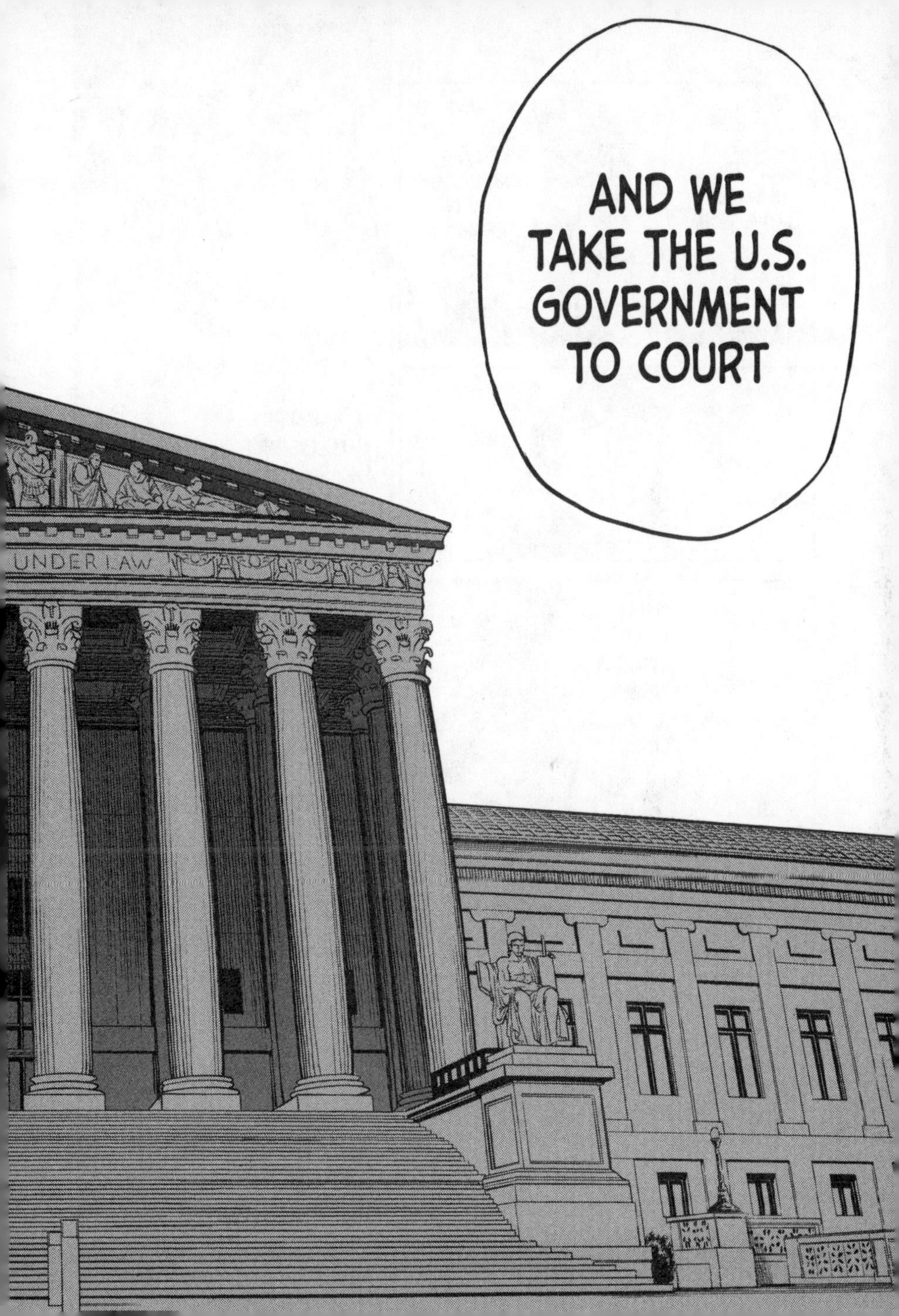
AND WE TAKE THE U.S. GOVERNMENT TO COURT
UNDER LAW

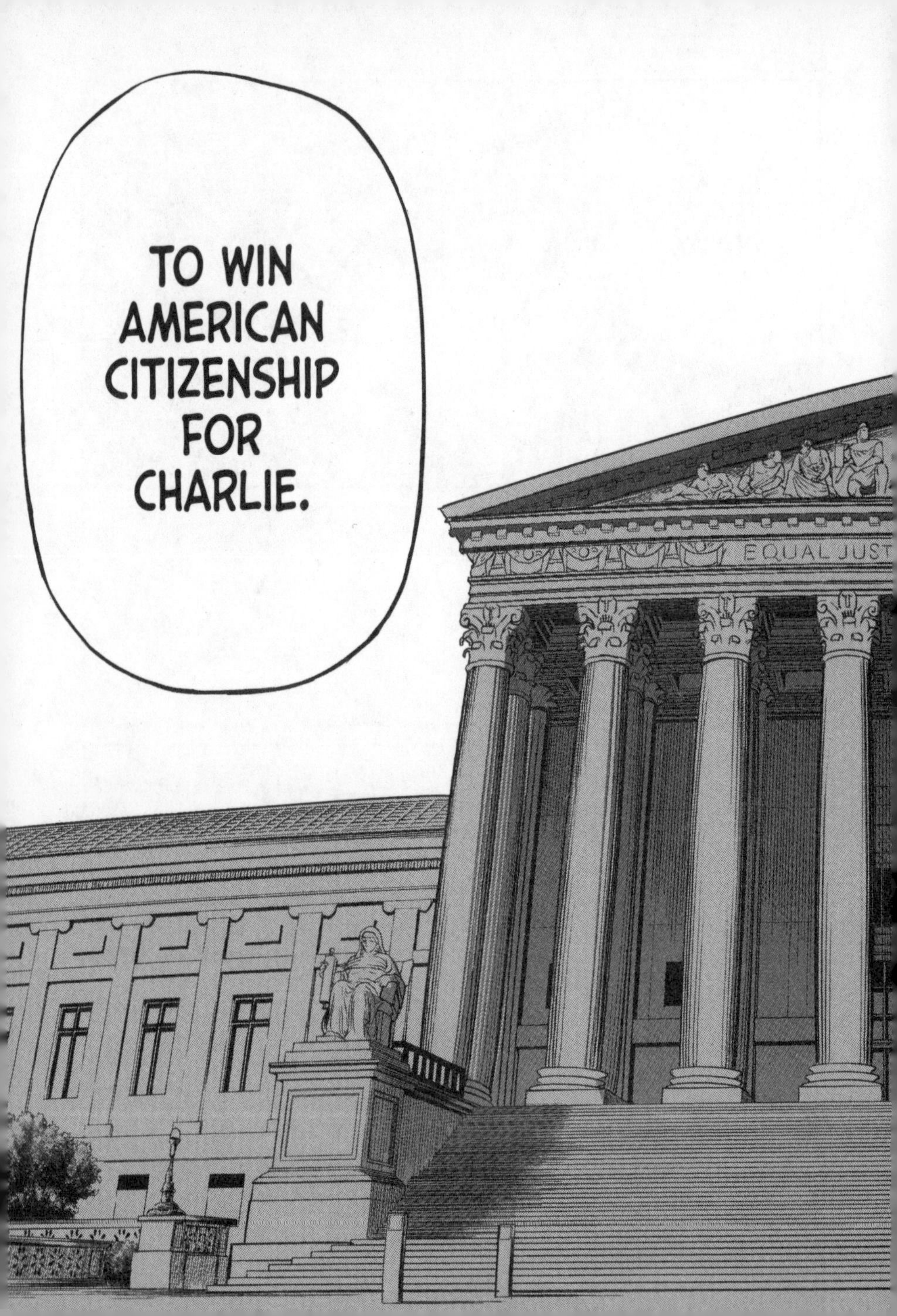
TO WIN AMERICAN CITIZENSHIP FOR CHARLIE.
EQUAL JUST

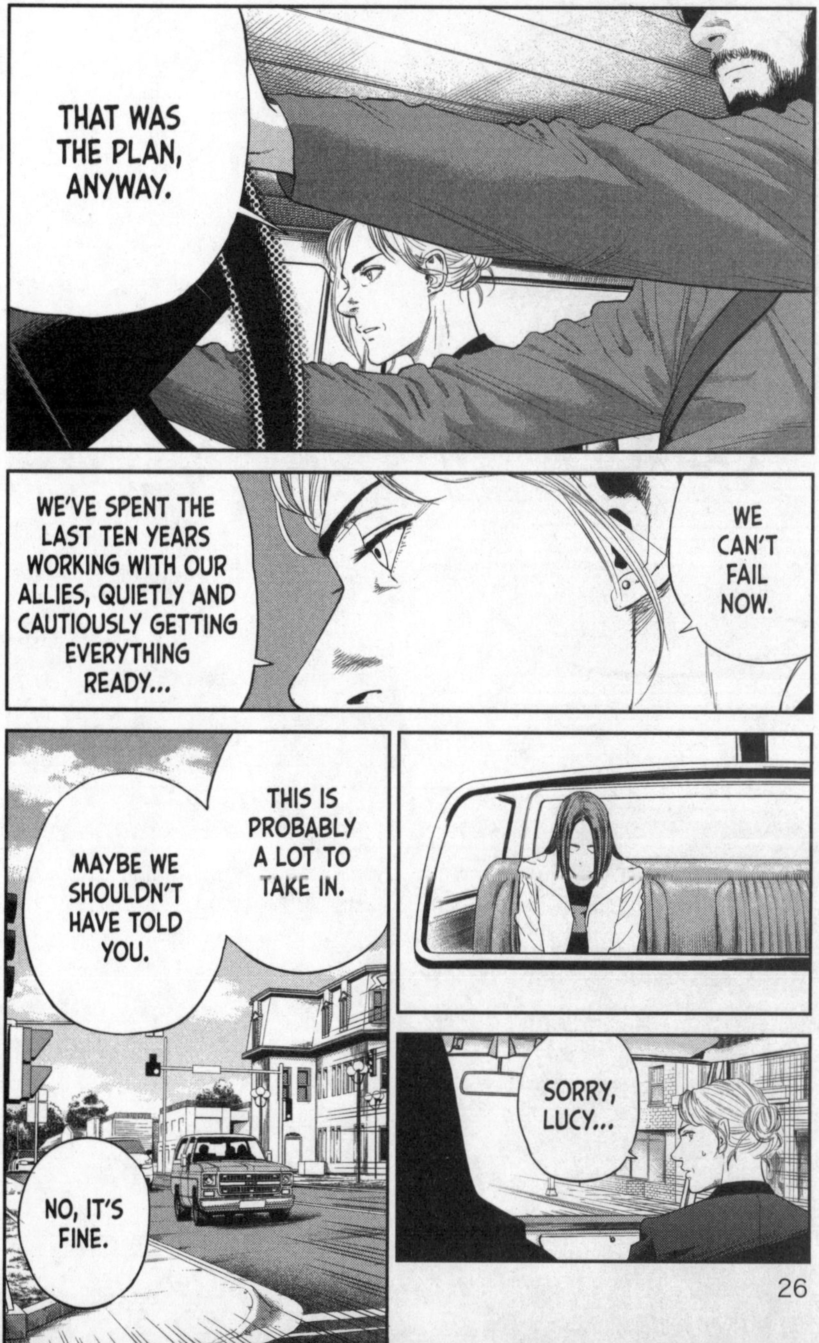
THAT WAS THE PLAN, ANYWAY.
WE CAN'T FAIL NOW.
WE'VE SPENT THE LAST TEN YEARS WORKING WITH OUR ALLIES, QUIETLY AND CAUTIOUSLY GETTING EVERYTHING READY...
SORRY, LUCY...
THIS IS PROBABLY A LOT TO TAKE IN.
MAYBE WE SHOULDN'T HAVE TOLD YOU.
NO, IT'S FINE.

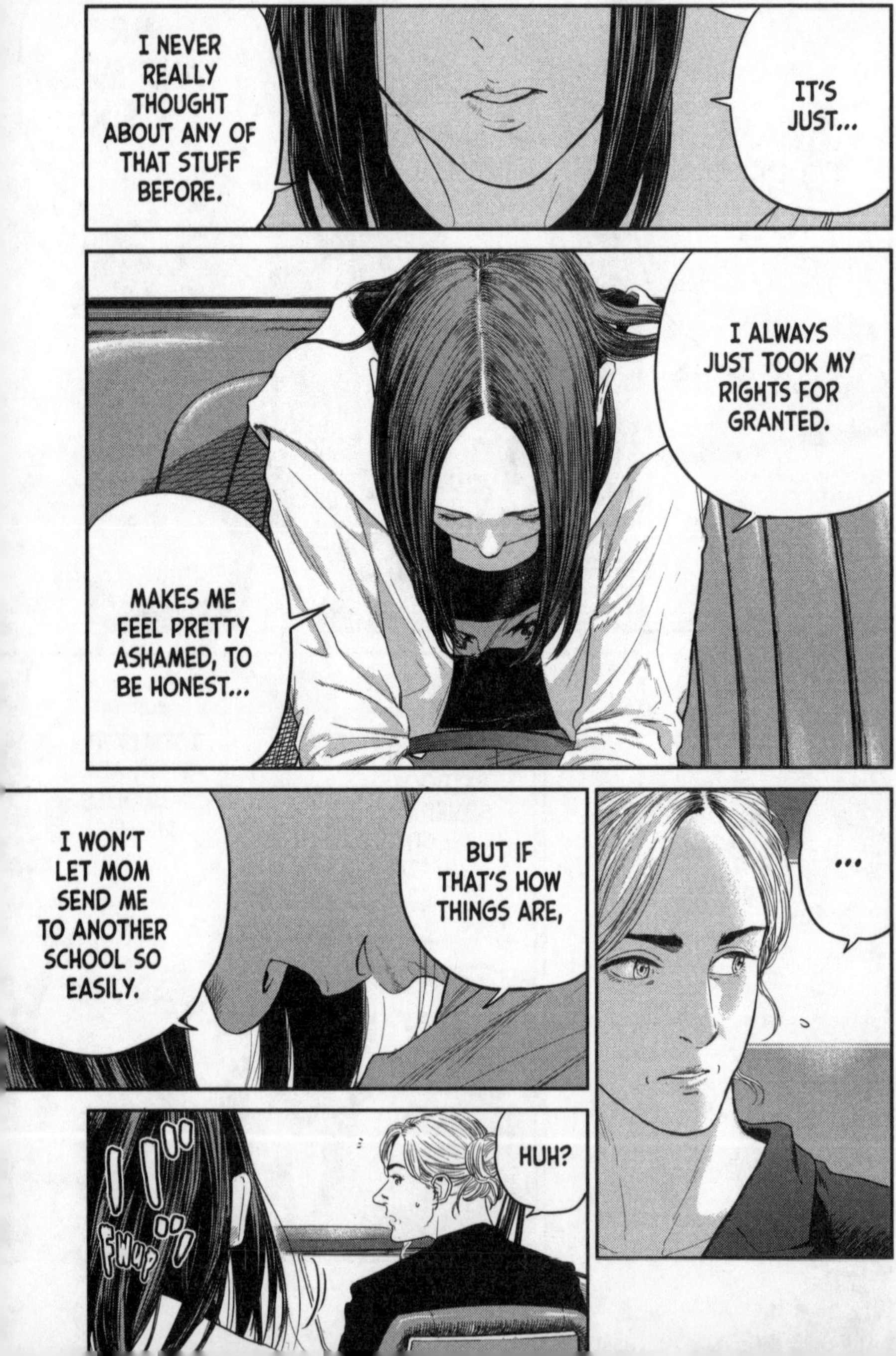
IT'S JUST...
I NEVER REALLY THOUGHT ABOUT ANY OF THAT STUFF BEFORE.
I ALWAYS JUST TOOK MY RIGHTS FOR GRANTED.
MAKES ME FEEL PRETTY ASHAMED, TO BE HONEST...
...
BUT IF THAT'S HOW THINGS ARE,
I WON'T LET MOM SEND ME TO ANOTHER SCHOOL SO EASILY.
HUH?
FWUP

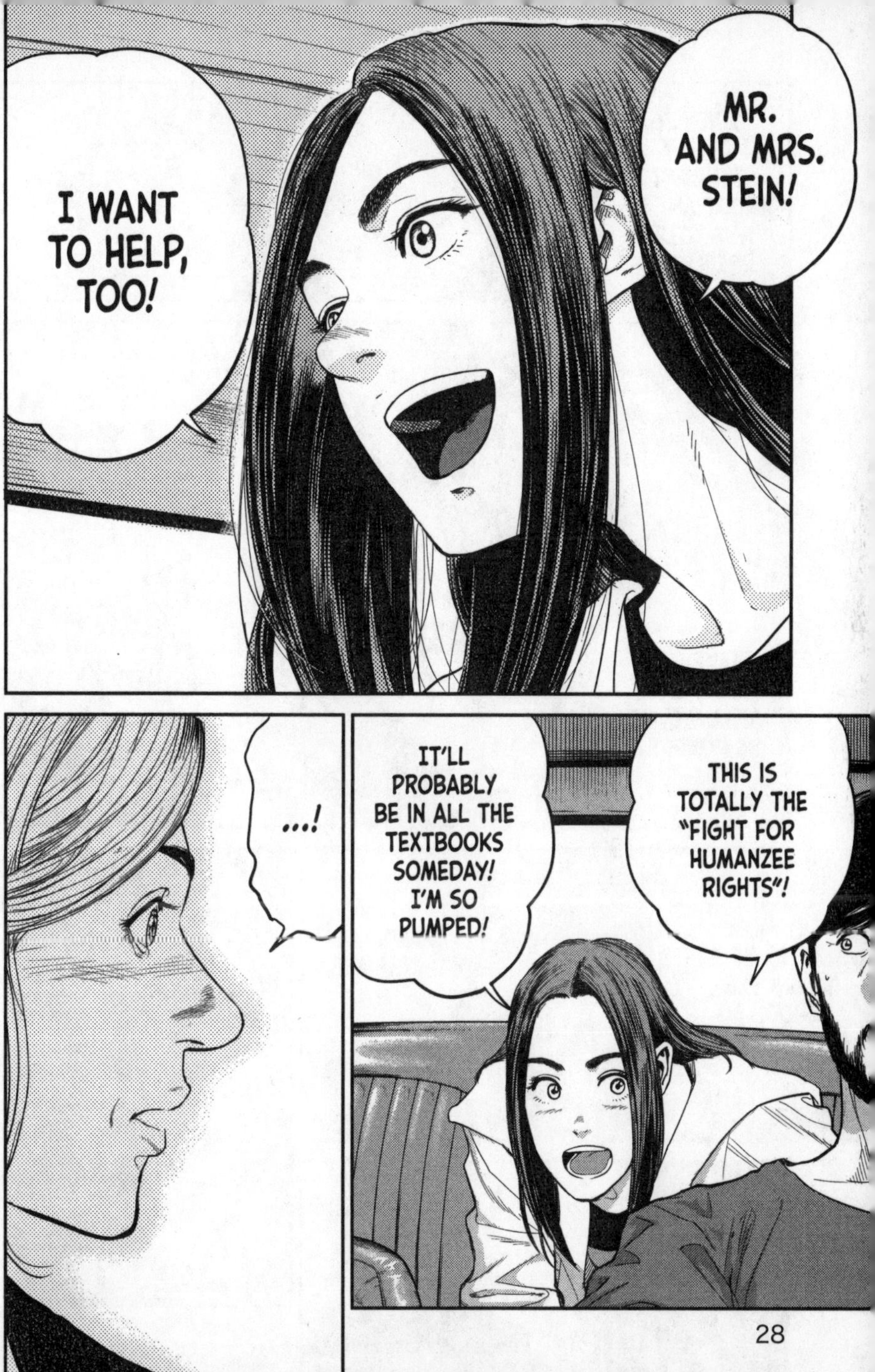
MR. AND MRS. STEIN!
I WANT TO HELP, TOO!
THIS IS TOTALLY THE "FIGHT FOR HUMANZEE RIGHTS"!
IT'LL PROBABLY BE IN ALL THE TEXTBOOKS SOMEDAY! I'M SO PUMPED!
...!

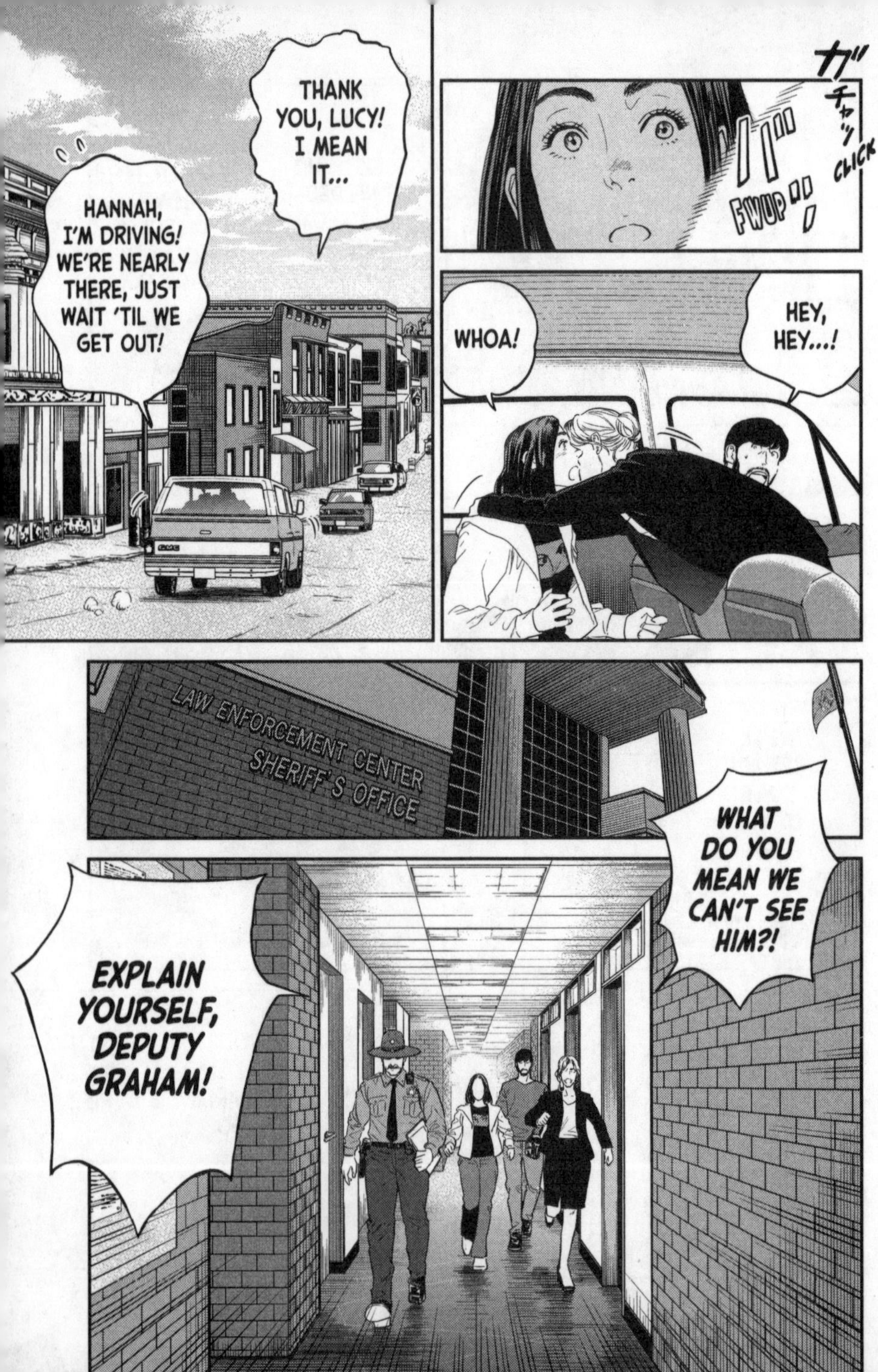
ガチャッ
CLICK
バッ
FWUP!!
HEY, HEY...!
WHOA!
THANK YOU, LUCY! I MEAN IT...
HANNAH, I'M DRIVING! WE'RE NEARLY THERE, JUST WAIT 'TIL WE GET OUT!
LAW ENFORCEMENT CENTER
SHERIFF'S OFFICE
WHAT DO YOU MEAN WE CAN'T SEE HIM?!
EXPLAIN YOURSELF, DEPUTY GRAHAM!

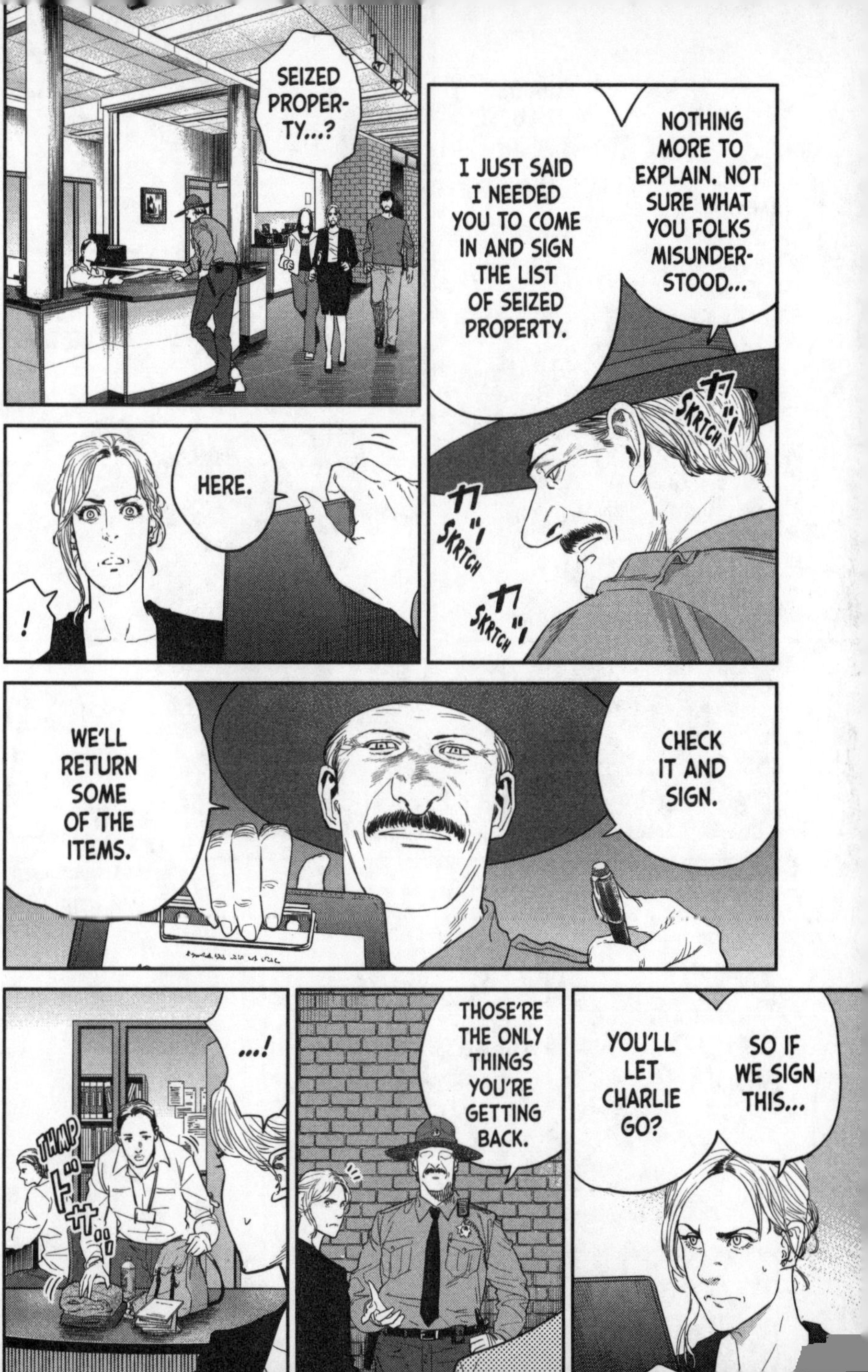
NOTHING MORE TO EXPLAIN. NOT SURE WHAT YOU FOLKS MISUNDER-STOOD...
I JUST SAID I NEEDED YOU TO COME IN AND SIGN THE LIST OF SEIZED PROPERTY.
SKRTCH
SKRTCH
SKRTCH
SEIZED PROPER-TY...?
HERE.
!
CHECK IT AND SIGN.
WE'LL RETURN SOME OF THE ITEMS.
SO IF WE SIGN THIS...
YOU'LL LET CHARLIE GO?
THOSE'RE THE ONLY THINGS YOU'RE GETTING BACK.
...!
THMP

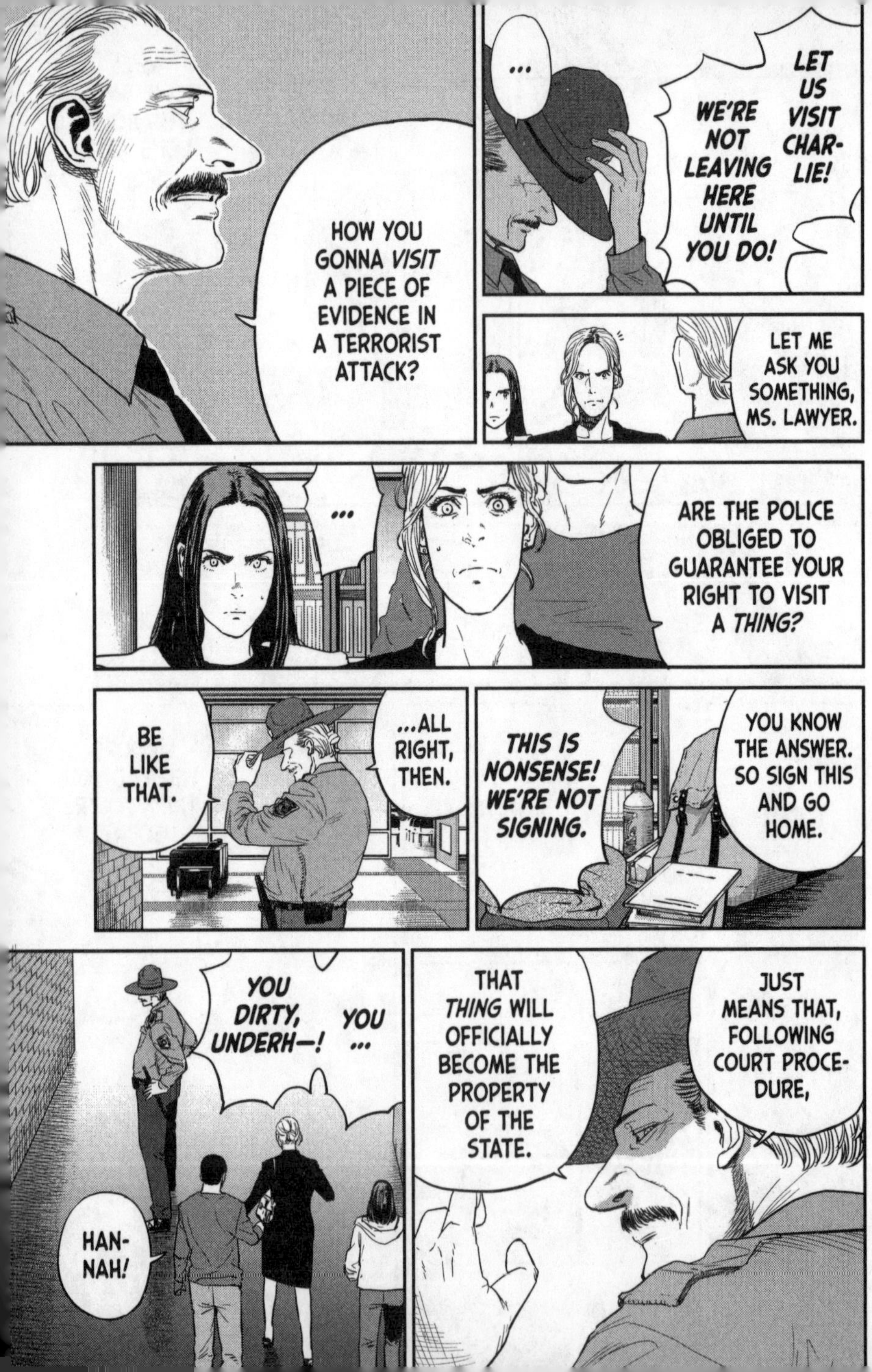
LET US VISIT CHAR-LIE!
WE'RE NOT LEAVING HERE UNTIL YOU DO!
...
LET ME ASK YOU SOMETHING, MS. LAWYER.
HOW YOU GONNA VISIT A PIECE OF EVIDENCE IN A TERRORIST ATTACK?
ARE THE POLICE OBLIGED TO GUARANTEE YOUR RIGHT TO VISIT A THING?
...
YOU KNOW THE ANSWER. SO SIGN THIS AND GO HOME.
THIS IS NONSENSE! WE'RE NOT SIGNING.
...ALL RIGHT, THEN.
BE LIKE THAT.
JUST MEANS THAT, FOLLOWING COURT PROCE-DURE,
THAT THING WILL OFFICIALLY BECOME THE PROPERTY OF THE STATE.
YOU ...
YOU DIRTY, UNDERH—!
HAN-NAH!

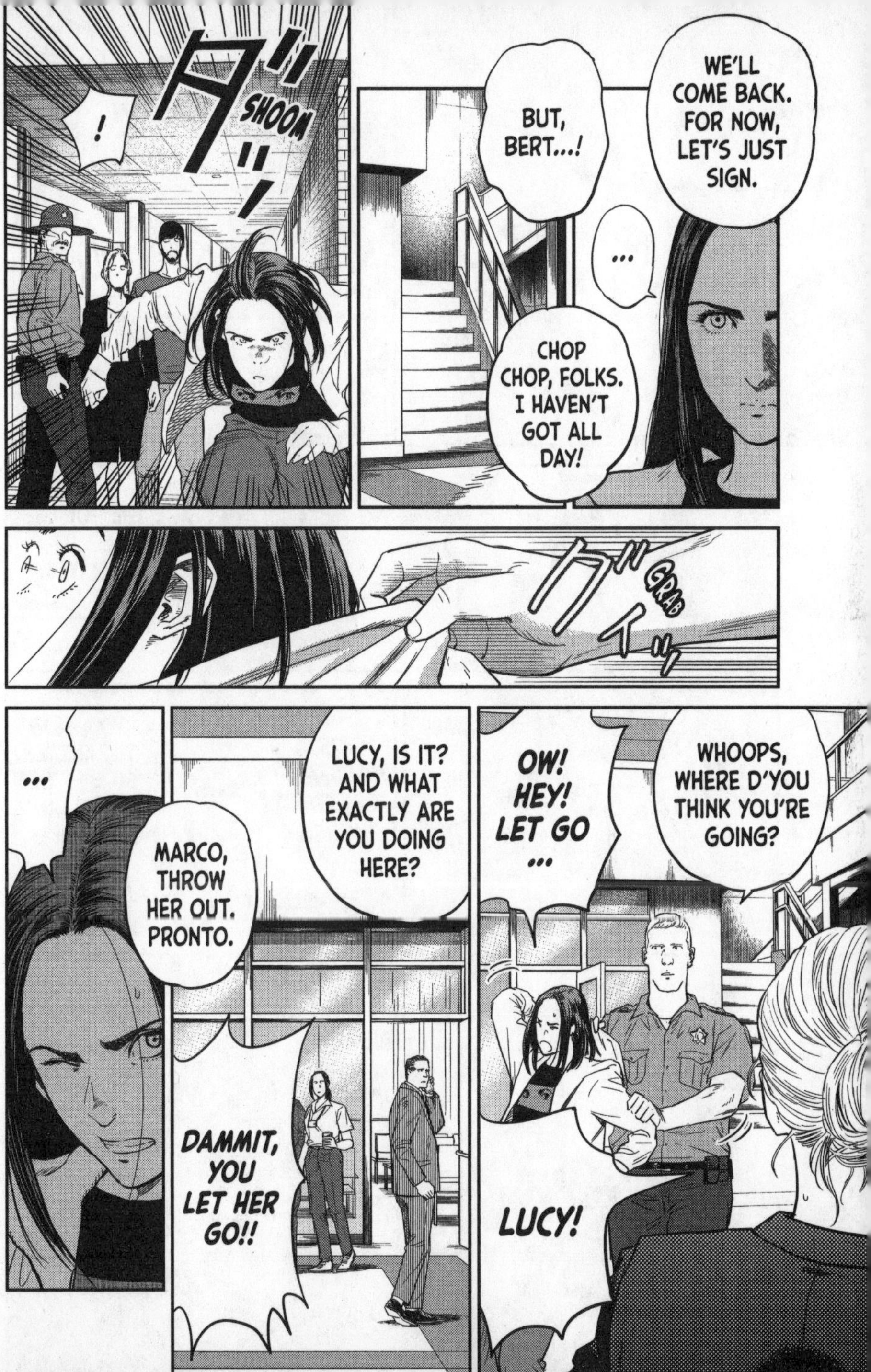
WE'LL COME BACK. FOR NOW, LET'S JUST SIGN.
BUT, BERT...!
...
CHOP CHOP, FOLKS. I HAVEN'T GOT ALL DAY!
SHOOM
!
GRAB
WHOOPS, WHERE D'YOU THINK YOU'RE GOING?
OW! HEY! LET GO ...
LUCY!
LUCY, IS IT? AND WHAT EXACTLY ARE YOU DOING HERE?
DAMMIT, YOU LET HER GO!!
...
MARCO, THROW HER OUT. PRONTO.

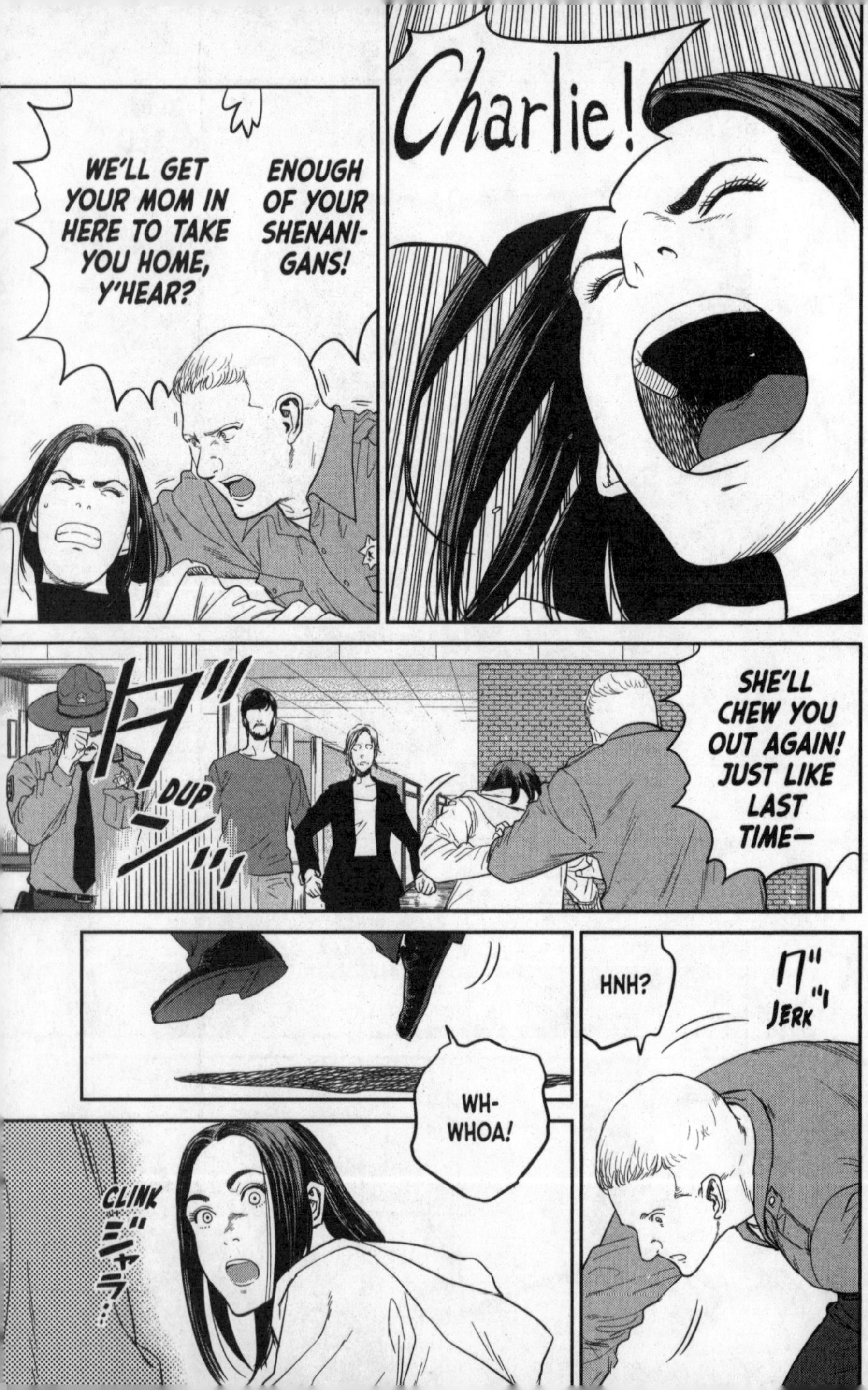
Charlie!
ENOUGH OF YOUR SHENANIGANS!
WE'LL GET YOUR MOM IN HERE TO TAKE YOU HOME, Y'HEAR?
SHE'LL CHEW YOU OUT AGAIN! JUST LIKE LAST TIME—
ダッ
DUP
HNH?
ガッ
JERK
WH-WHOA!
CLINK
ジャラ…

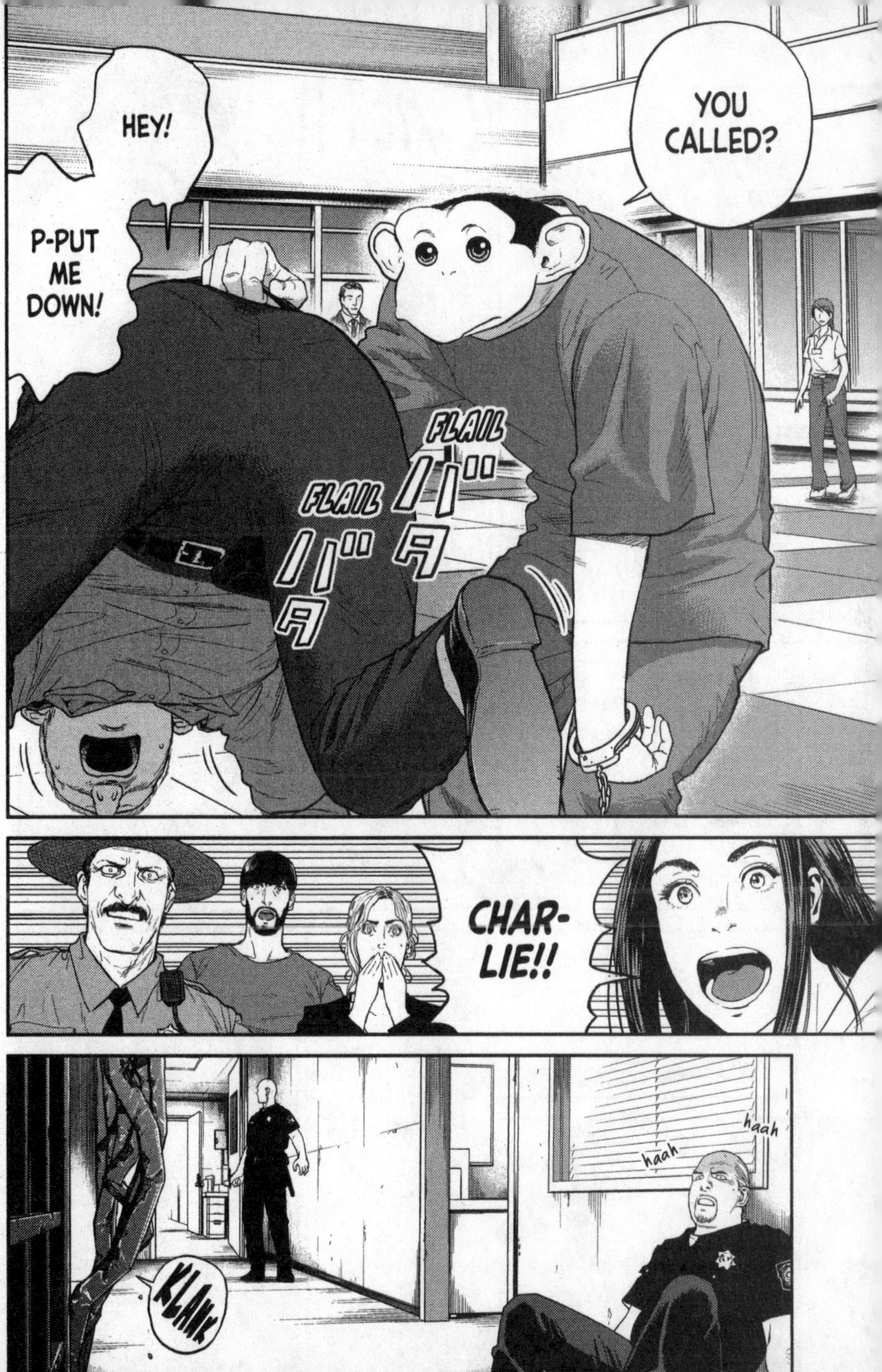
YOU CALLED?
HEY!
P-PUT ME DOWN!
FLAIL
バタ
FLAIL
バタ
CHAR-LIE!!
haah
haah
KLANK

CHAPTER 6 / END

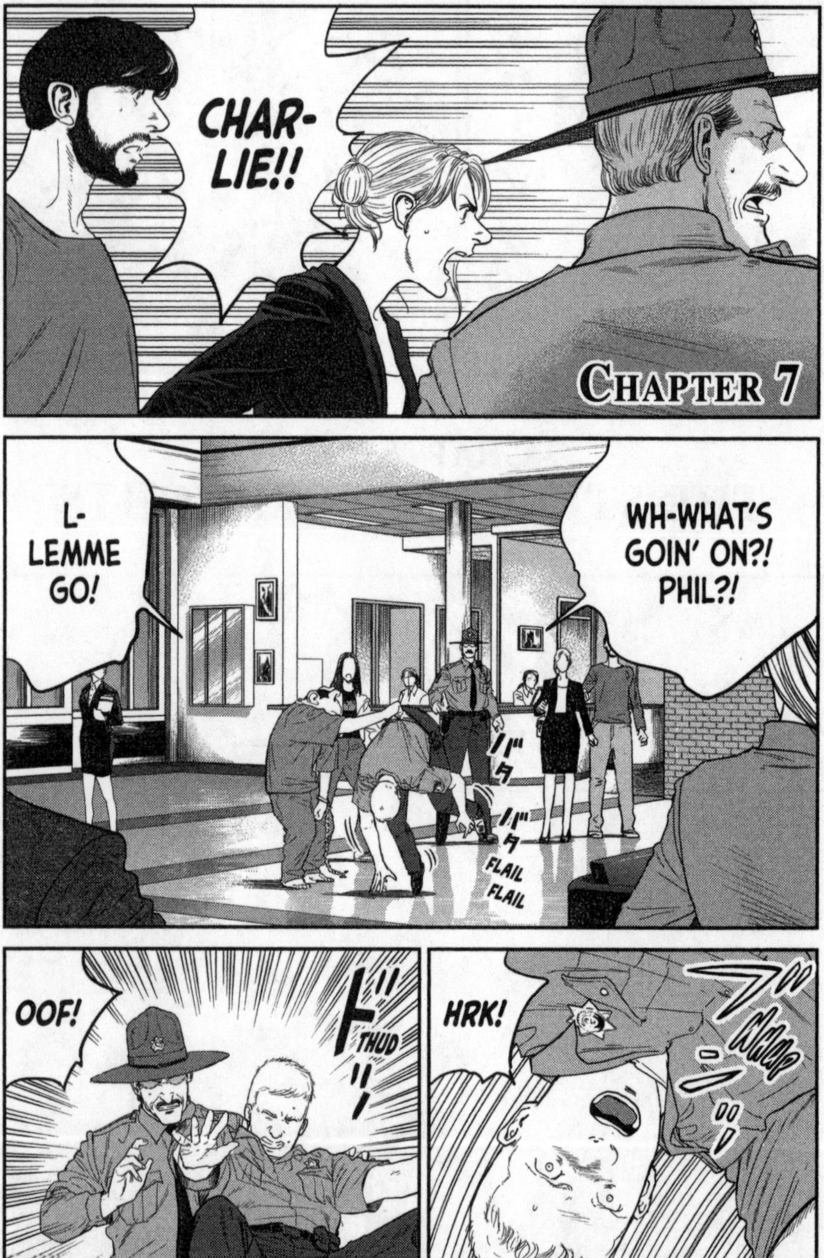
CHAR-LIE!!
CHAPTER 7
WH-WHAT'S GOIN' ON?! PHIL?!
L-LEMME GO!
バタ
バタ
FLAIL FLAIL
HRK!
OOF!
ドッ
THUD

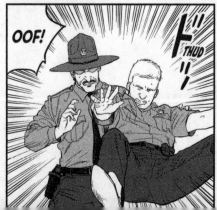

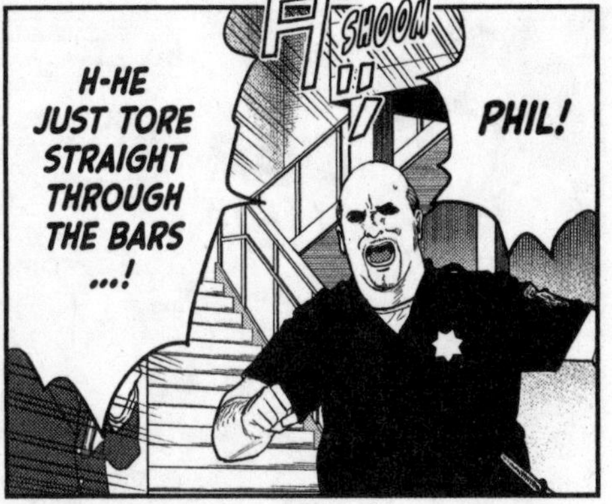
SHOOM
PHIL!
H-HE JUST TORE STRAIGHT THROUGH THE BARS ...!

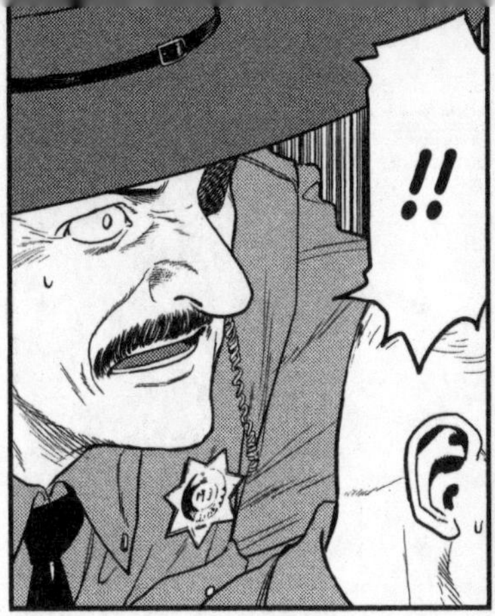
!!

CHAPTER 7 / THE STRUGGLE FOR RIGHTS

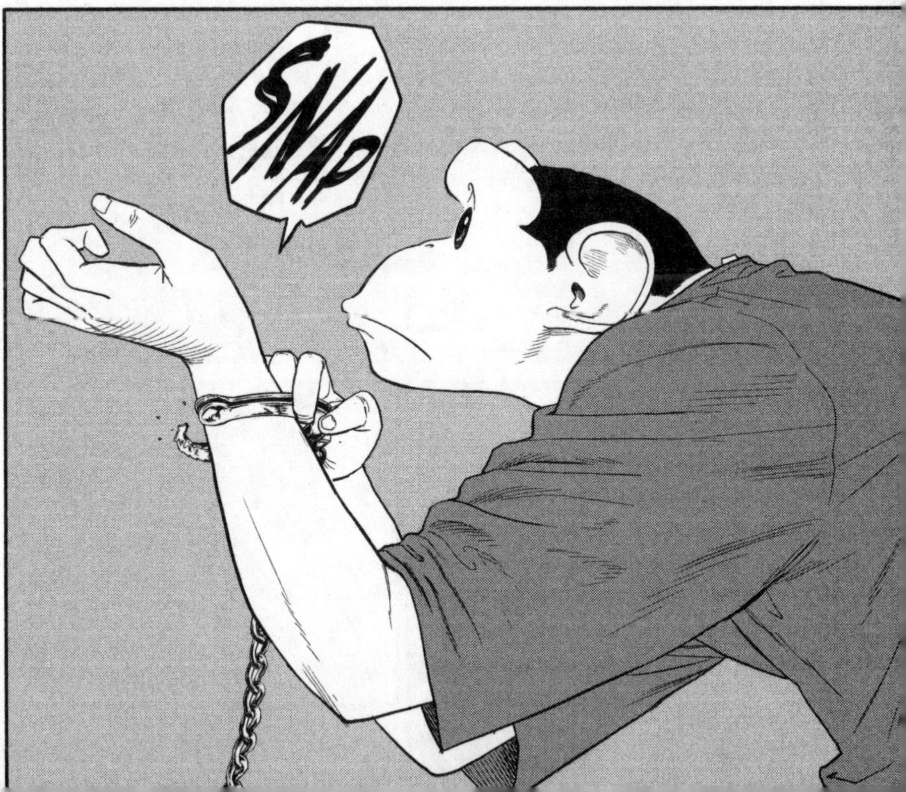
SNAP

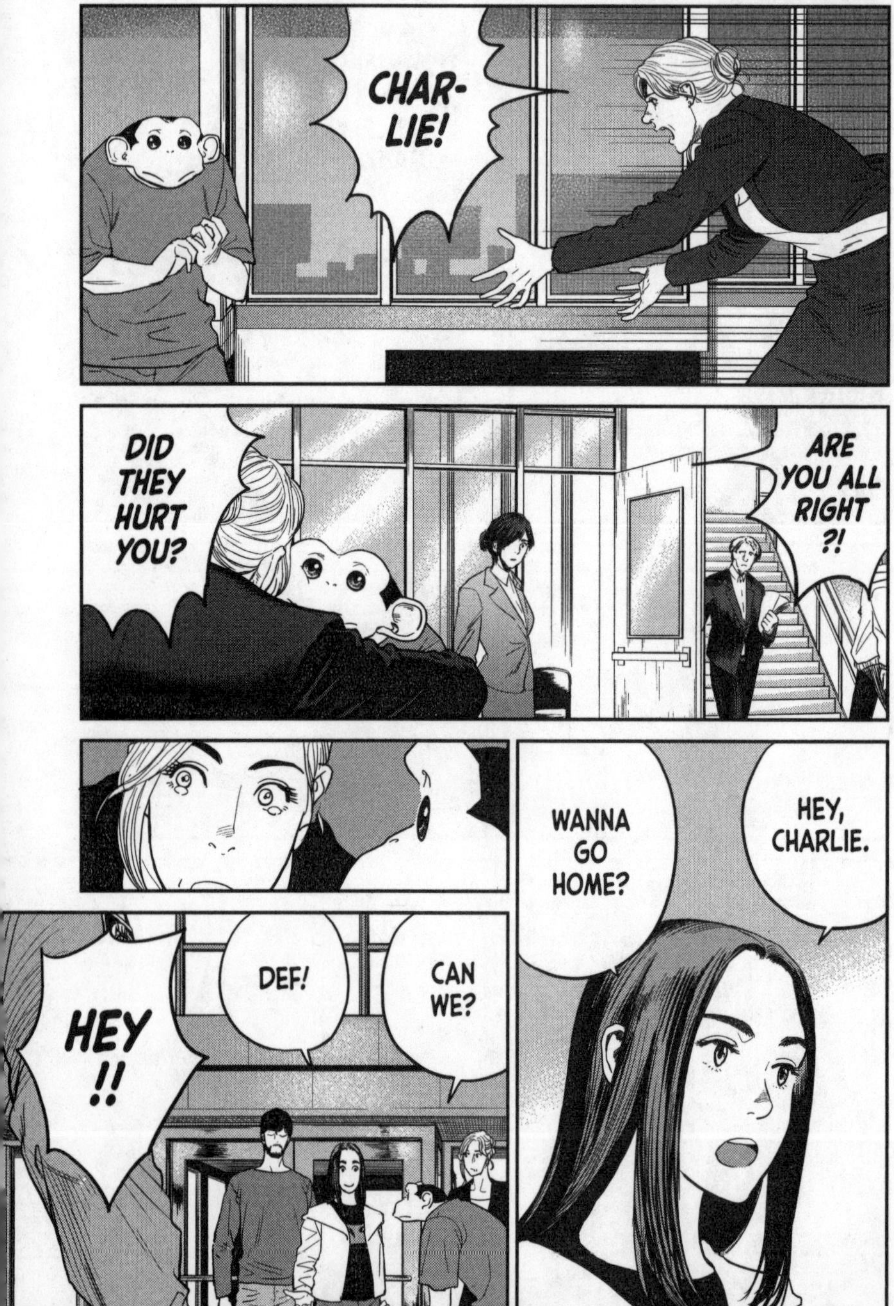
CHAR-LIE!
ARE YOU ALL RIGHT ?!
DID THEY HURT YOU?
HEY, CHARLIE.
WANNA GO HOME?
CAN WE?
DEF!
HEY !!

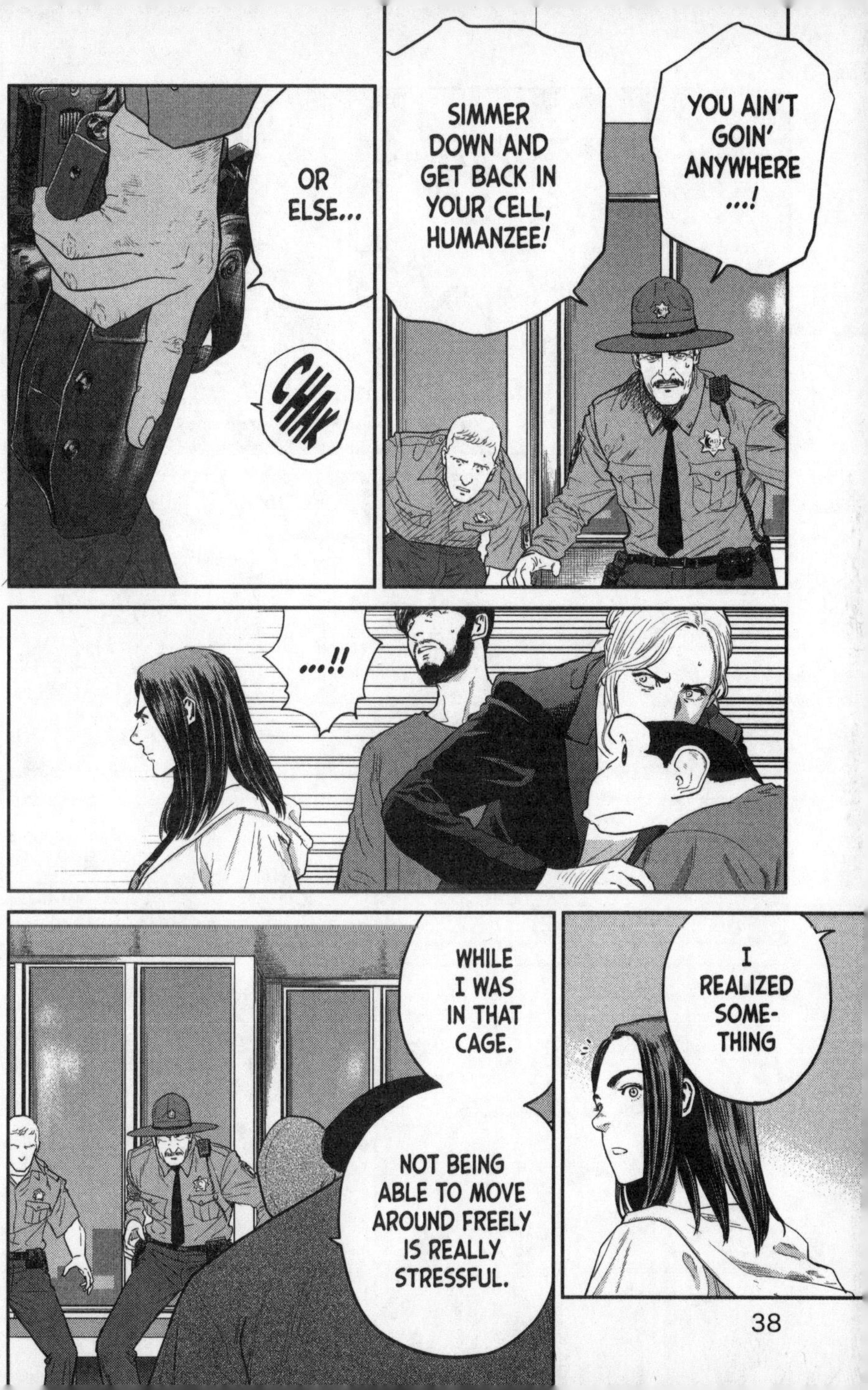
YOU AIN'T GOIN' ANYWHERE ...!
SIMMER DOWN AND GET BACK IN YOUR CELL, HUMANZEE!
OR ELSE...
CHAK
...!!
I REALIZED SOME-THING
WHILE I WAS IN THAT CAGE.
NOT BEING ABLE TO MOVE AROUND FREELY IS REALLY STRESSFUL.

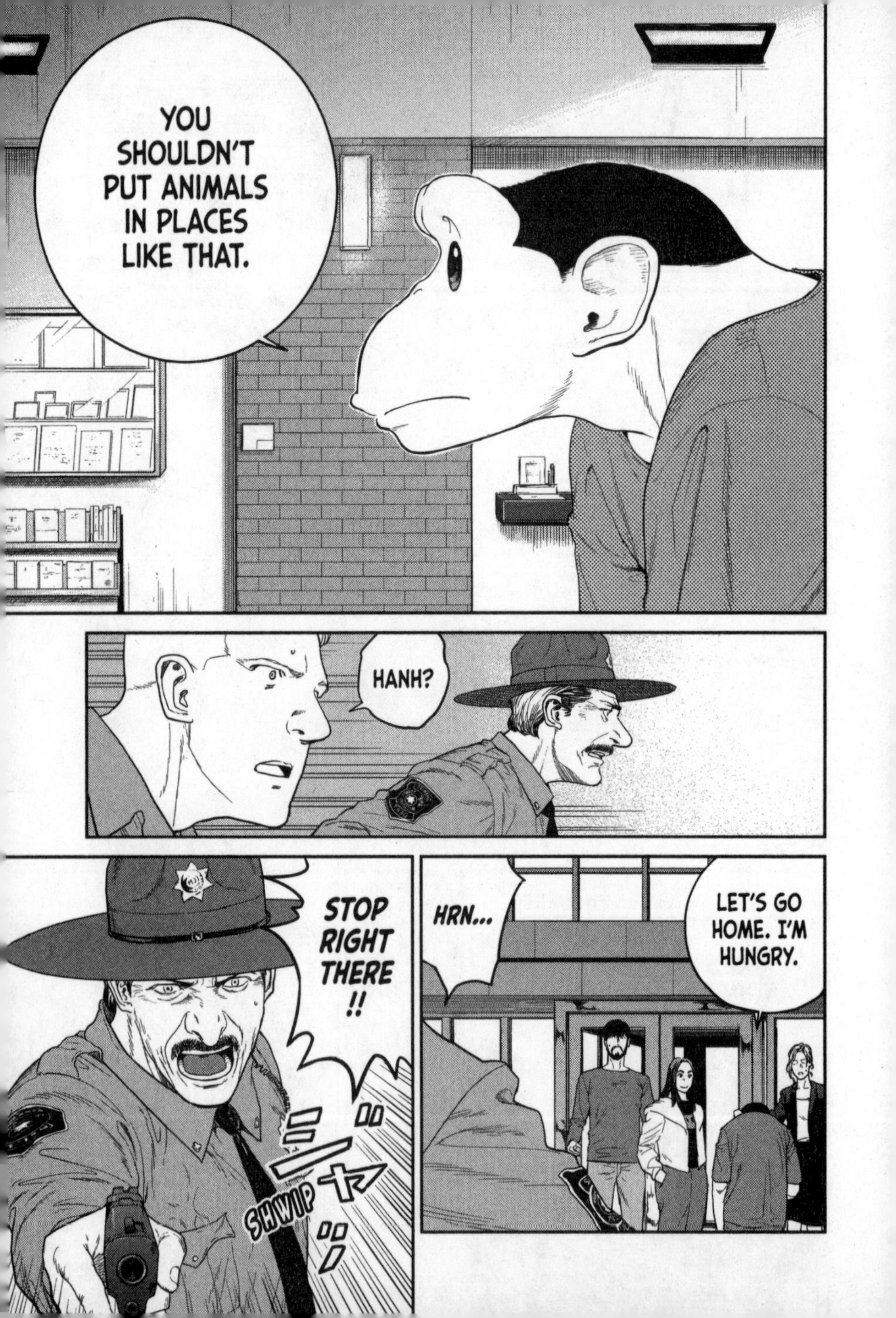
YOU SHOULDN'T PUT ANIMALS IN PLACES LIKE THAT.
HANH?
LET'S GO HOME. I'M HUNGRY.
HRN...
STOP RIGHT THERE !!
SHWIP

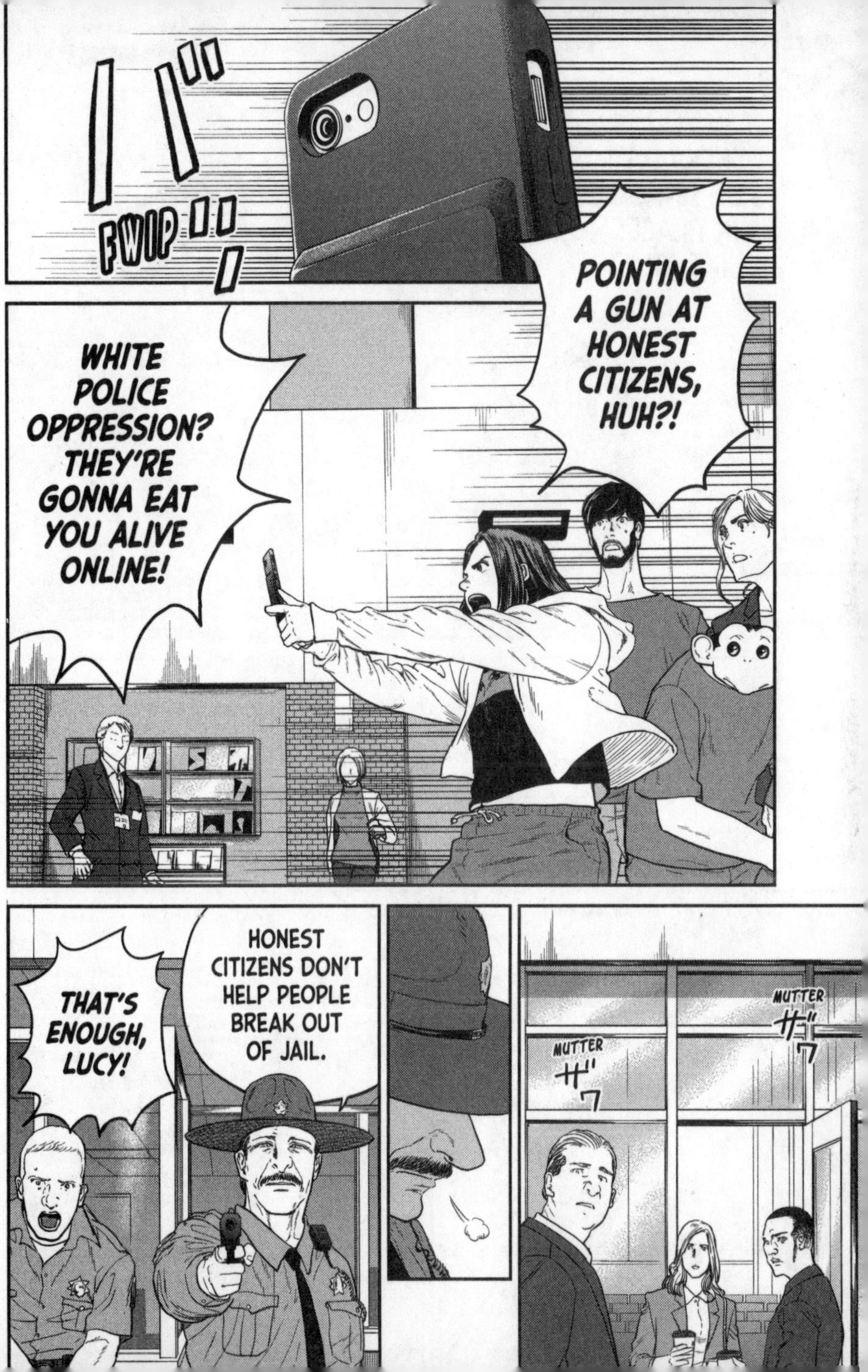
FWIP
POINTING A GUN AT HONEST CITIZENS, HUH?!
WHITE POLICE OPPRESSION? THEY'RE GONNA EAT YOU ALIVE ONLINE!
MUTTER ザワ
MUTTER ザワ
HONEST CITIZENS DON'T HELP PEOPLE BREAK OUT OF JAIL.
THAT'S ENOUGH, LUCY!

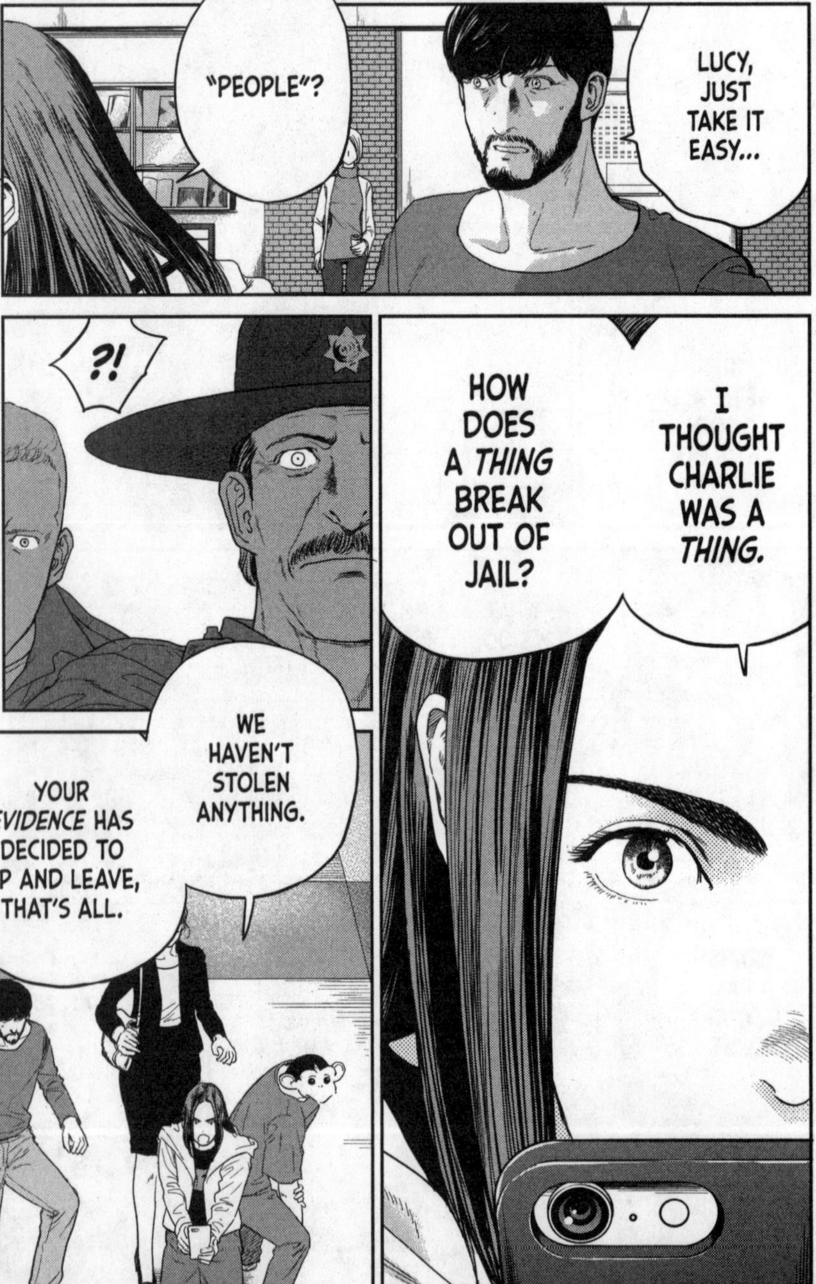
LUCY, JUST TAKE IT EASY...
"PEOPLE"?
I THOUGHT CHARLIE WAS A *THING.*
HOW DOES A *THING* BREAK OUT OF JAIL?
?!
WE HAVEN'T STOLEN ANYTHING.
YOUR *EVIDENCE* HAS DECIDED TO UP AND LEAVE, THAT'S ALL.

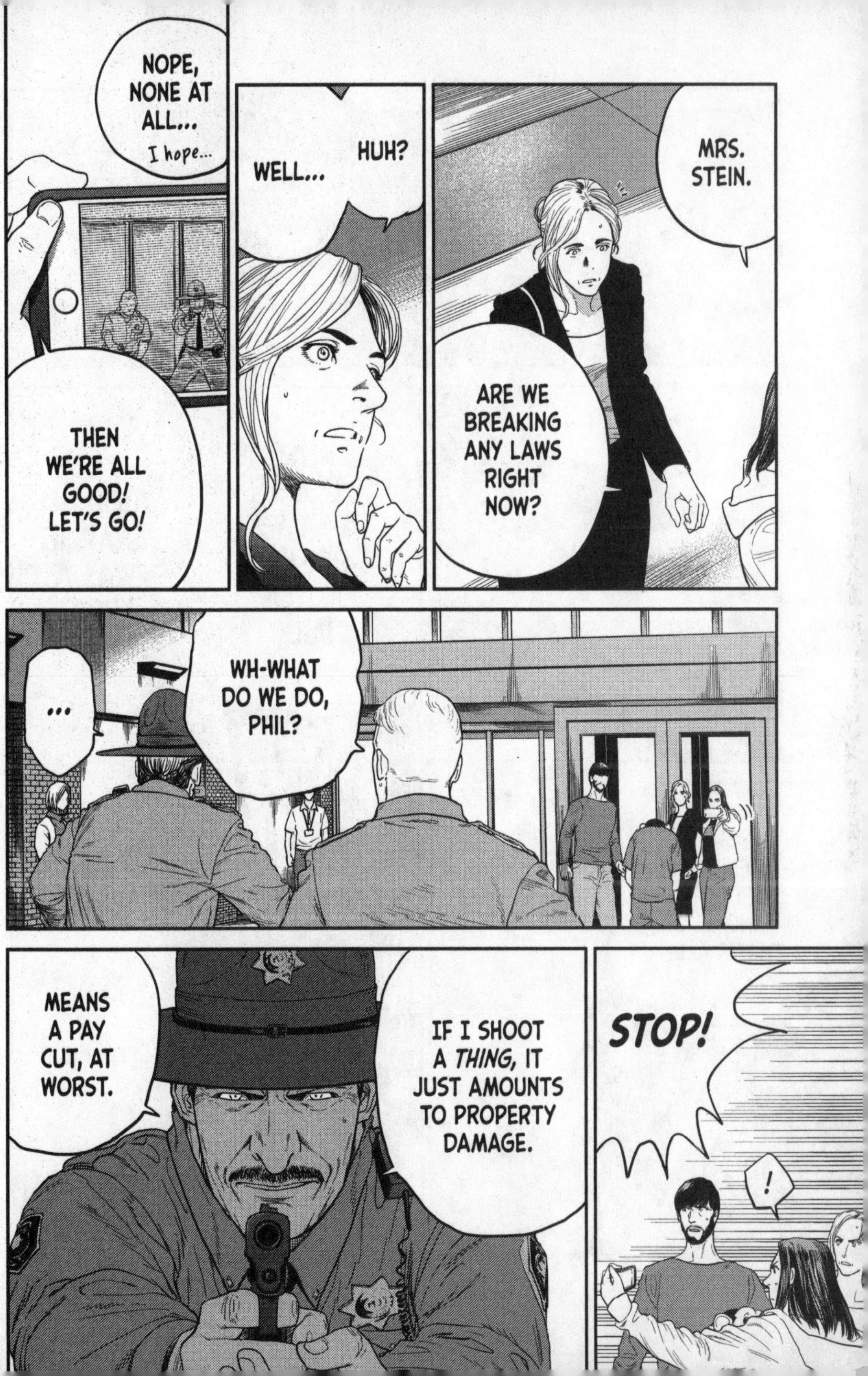
MRS. STEIN.
ARE WE BREAKING ANY LAWS RIGHT NOW?
HUH?
WELL...
NOPE, NONE AT ALL...
I hope...
THEN WE'RE ALL GOOD! LET'S GO!
WH-WHAT DO WE DO, PHIL?
...
STOP!
!
IF I SHOOT A *THING*, IT JUST AMOUNTS TO PROPERTY DAMAGE.
MEANS A PAY CUT, AT WORST.

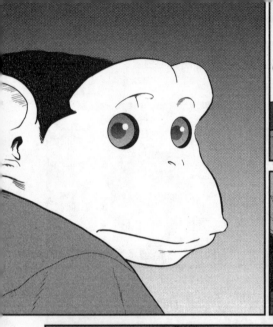
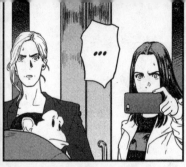
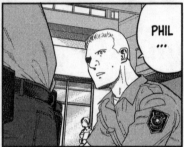

PHIL
...

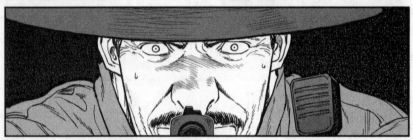

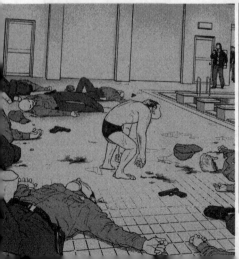
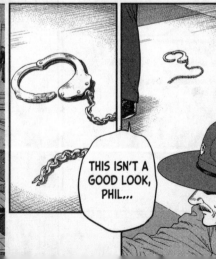

THIS ISN'T A GOOD LOOK, PHIL...

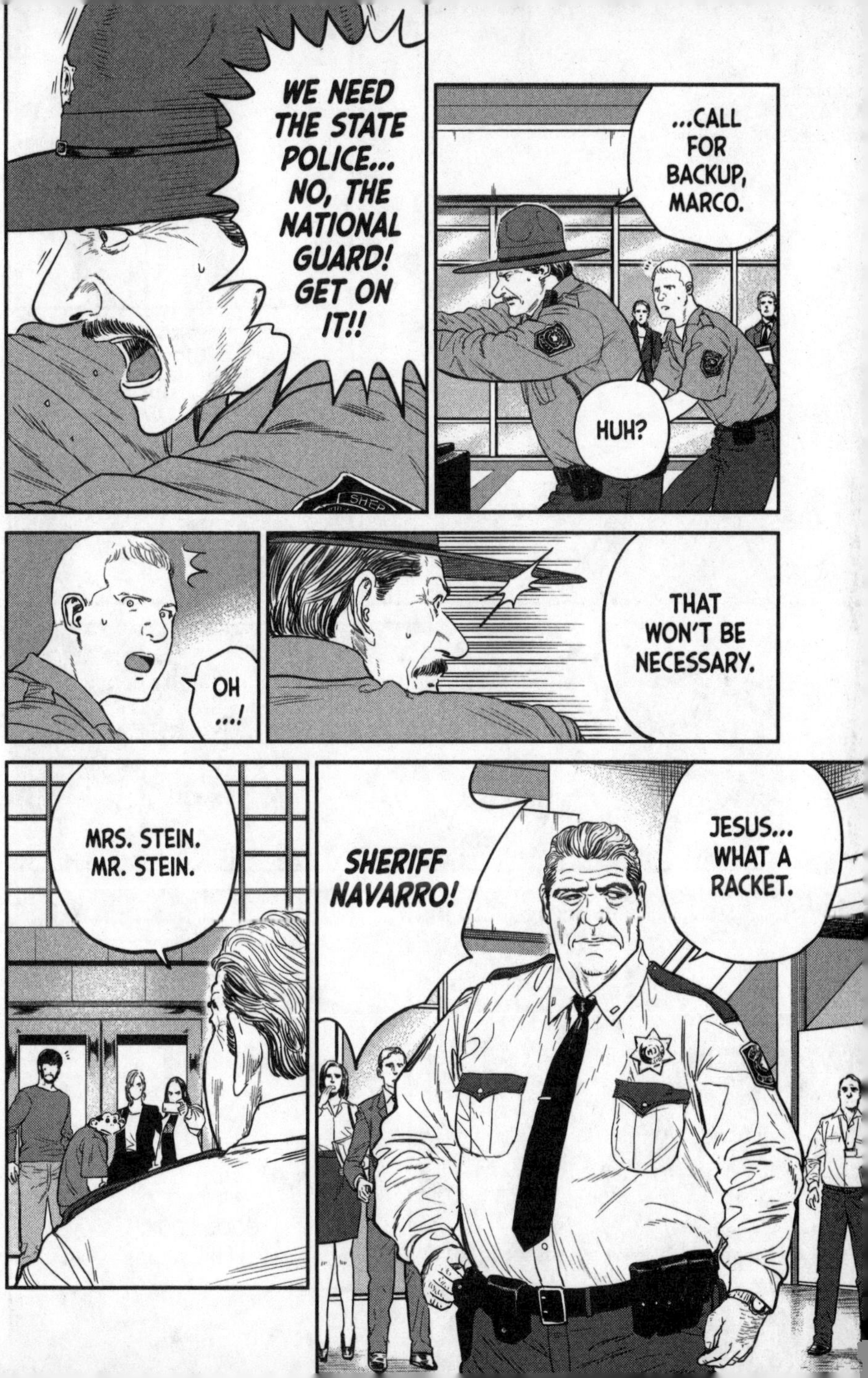
...CALL FOR BACKUP, MARCO.
HUH?
WE NEED THE STATE POLICE... NO, THE NATIONAL GUARD! GET ON IT!!
THAT WON'T BE NECESSARY.
OH ...!
JESUS... WHAT A RACKET.
SHERIFF NAVARRO!
MRS. STEIN. MR. STEIN.

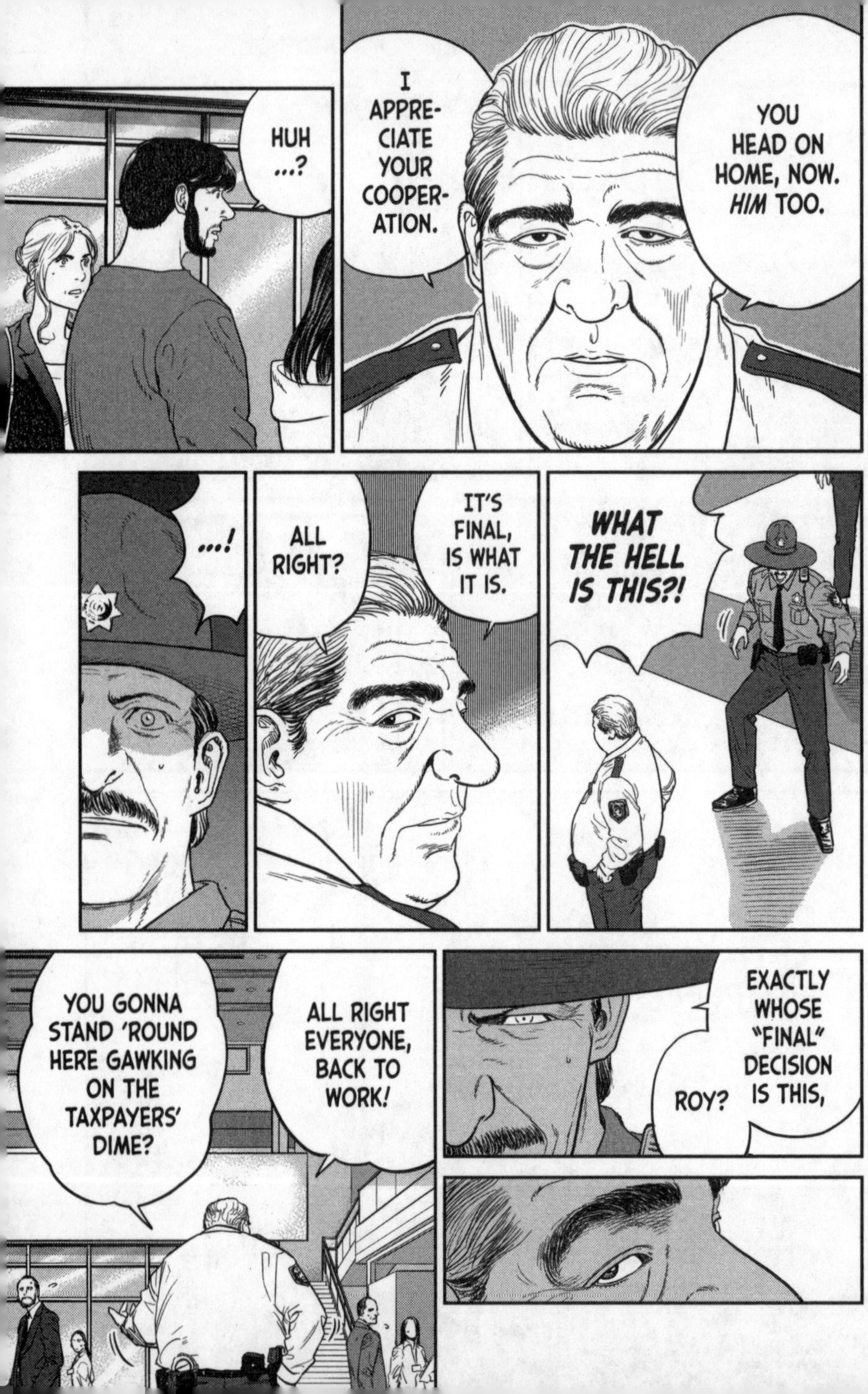
YOU HEAD ON HOME, NOW. *HIM* TOO.
I APPRECIATE YOUR COOPERATION.
HUH ...?
WHAT THE HELL IS THIS?!
IT'S FINAL, IS WHAT IT IS.
ALL RIGHT?
...!
EXACTLY WHOSE "FINAL" DECISION IS THIS,
ROY?
ALL RIGHT EVERYONE, BACK TO WORK!
YOU GONNA STAND 'ROUND HERE GAWKING ON THE TAXPAYERS' DIME?

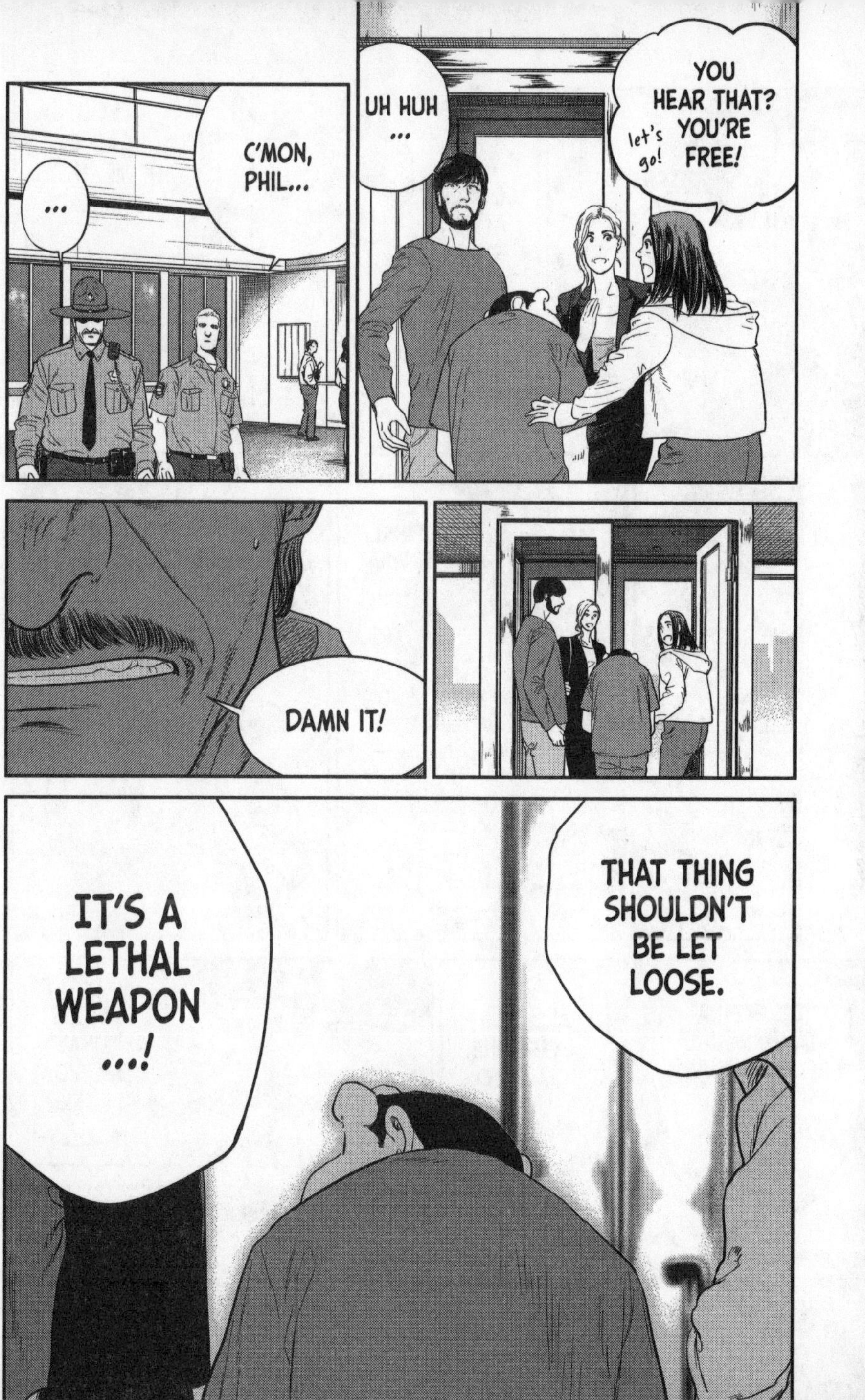
YOU HEAR THAT? YOU'RE FREE!
let's go!
UH HUH ...
C'MON, PHIL...
...
DAMN IT!
THAT THING SHOULDN'T BE LET LOOSE.
IT'S A LETHAL WEAPON ...!

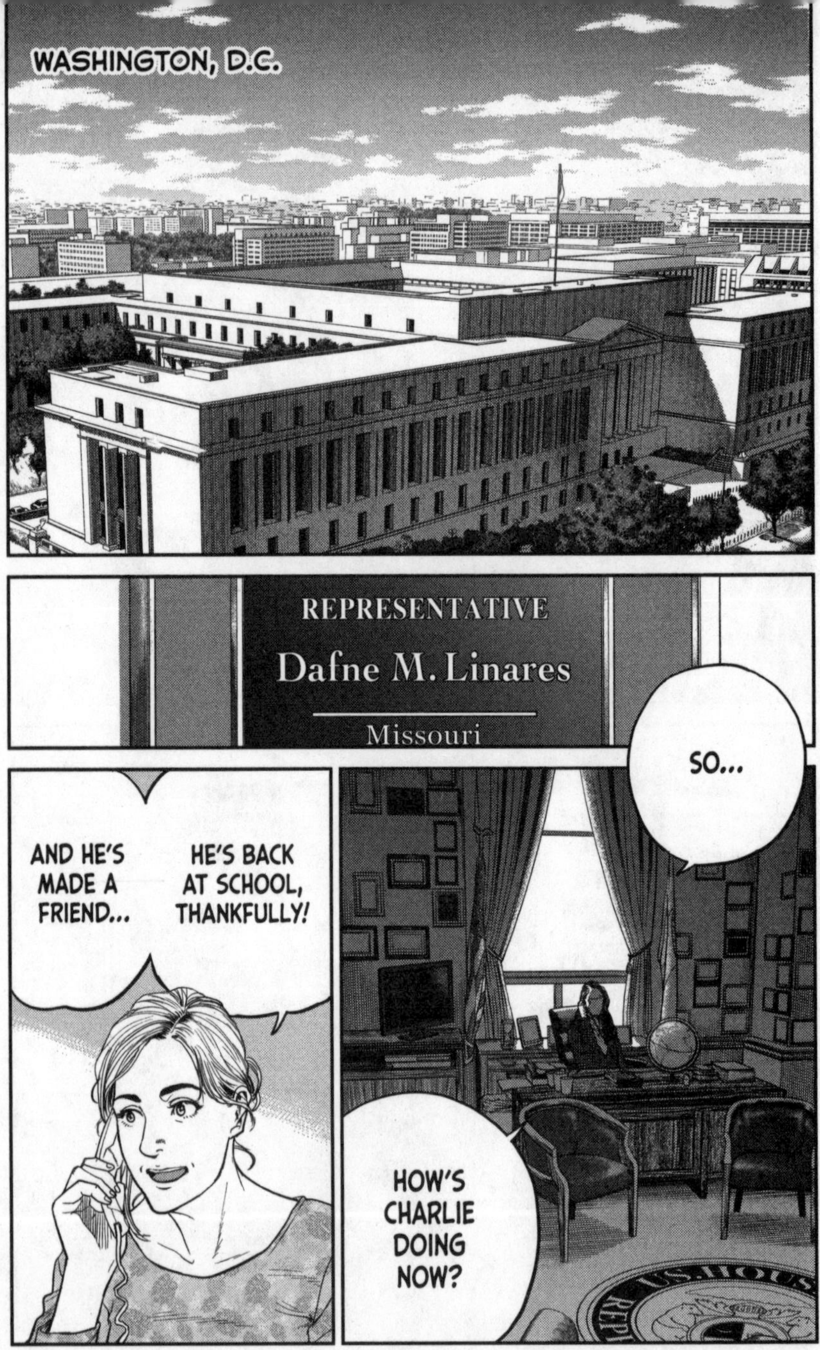
WASHINGTON, D.C.
REPRESENTATIVE
Dafne M. Linares
Missouri
SO...
HOW'S CHARLIE DOING NOW?
HE'S BACK AT SCHOOL, THANKFULLY!
AND HE'S MADE A FRIEND...

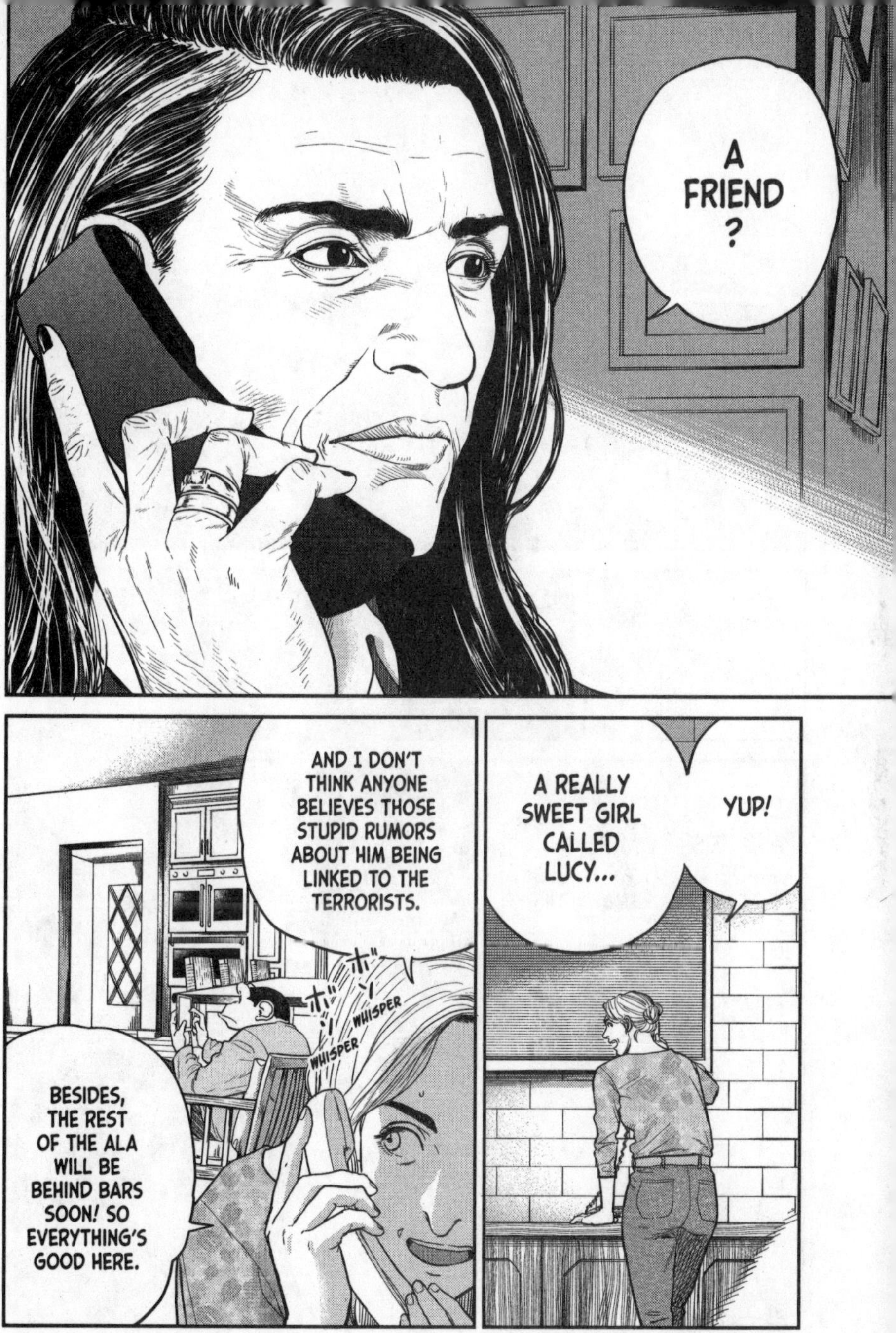
A FRIEND ?
YUP!
A REALLY SWEET GIRL CALLED LUCY...
AND I DON'T THINK ANYONE BELIEVES THOSE STUPID RUMORS ABOUT HIM BEING LINKED TO THE TERRORISTS.
ボソ WHISPER
ボソ WHISPER
BESIDES, THE REST OF THE ALA WILL BE BEHIND BARS SOON! SO EVERYTHING'S GOOD HERE.

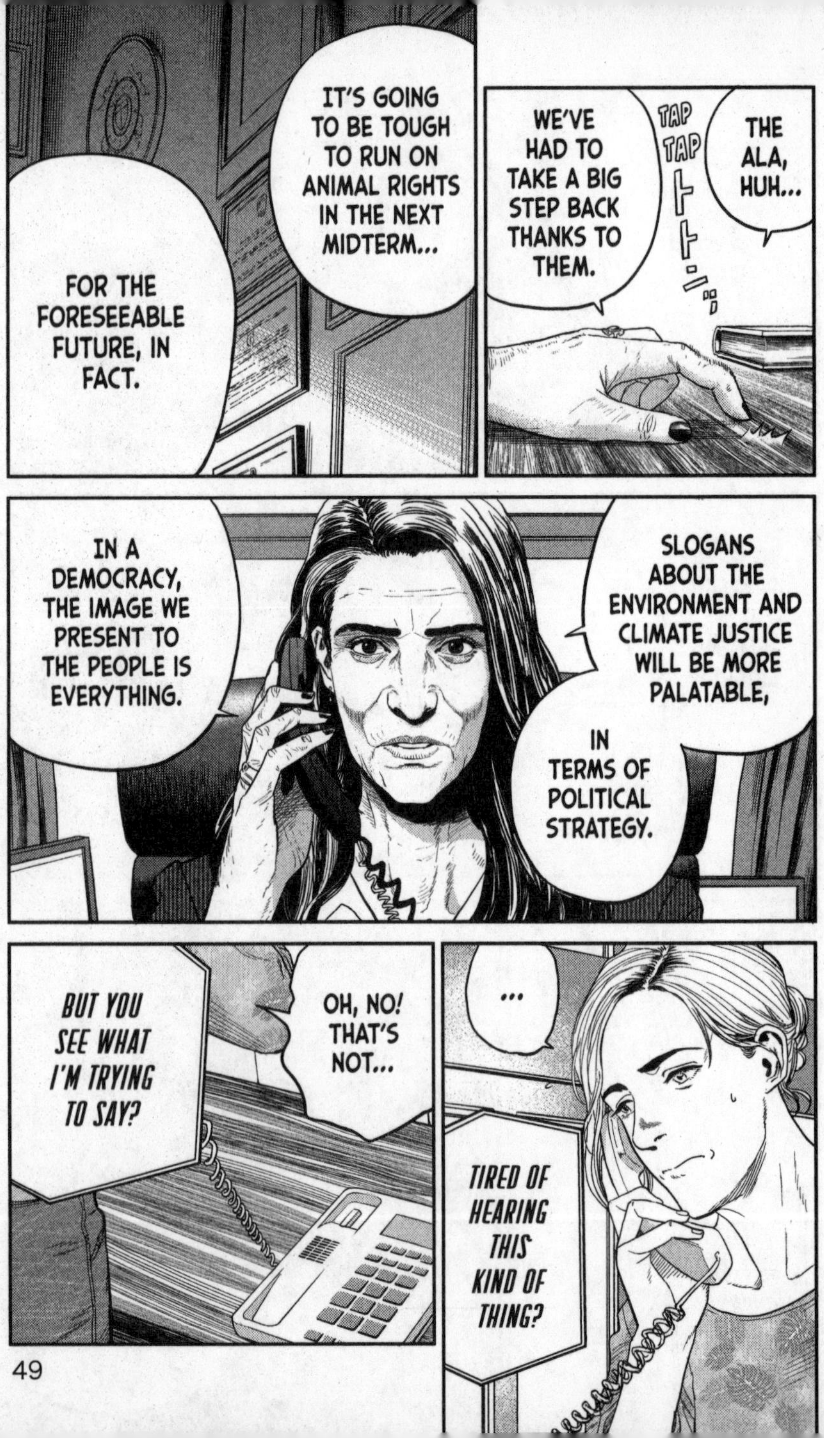

THE ALA, HUH...
TAP TAP
WE'VE HAD TO TAKE A BIG STEP BACK THANKS TO THEM.
IT'S GOING TO BE TOUGH TO RUN ON ANIMAL RIGHTS IN THE NEXT MIDTERM...
FOR THE FORESEEABLE FUTURE, IN FACT.
SLOGANS ABOUT THE ENVIRONMENT AND CLIMATE JUSTICE WILL BE MORE PALATABLE,
IN TERMS OF POLITICAL STRATEGY.
IN A DEMOCRACY, THE IMAGE WE PRESENT TO THE PEOPLE IS EVERYTHING.
...
TIRED OF HEARING THIS KIND OF THING?
OH, NO! THAT'S NOT...
BUT YOU SEE WHAT I'M TRYING TO SAY?

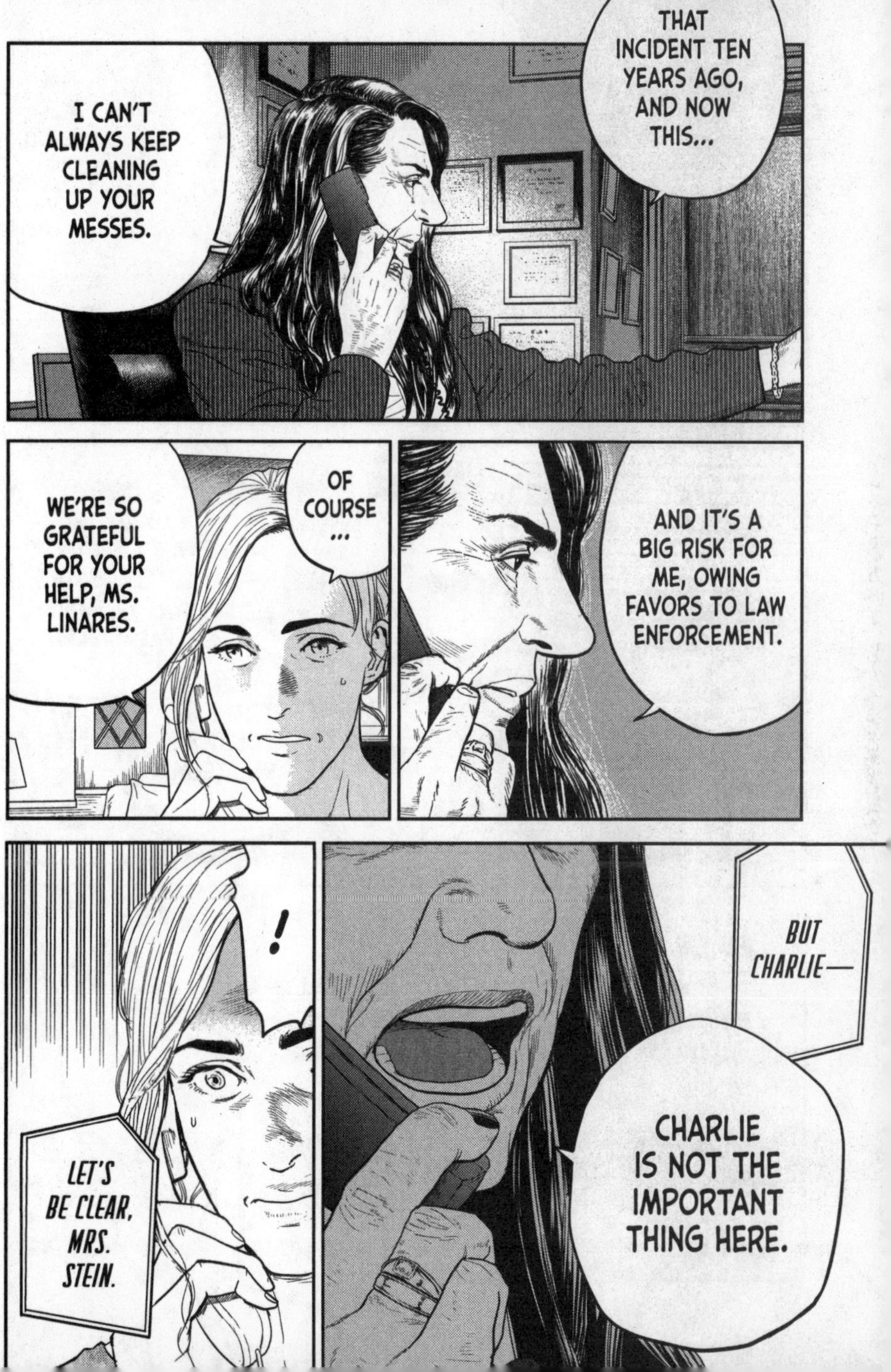
THAT INCIDENT TEN YEARS AGO, AND NOW THIS...
I CAN'T ALWAYS KEEP CLEANING UP YOUR MESSES.
AND IT'S A BIG RISK FOR ME, OWING FAVORS TO LAW ENFORCEMENT.
OF COURSE ...
WE'RE SO GRATEFUL FOR YOUR HELP, MS. LINARES.
BUT CHARLIE—
CHARLIE IS NOT THE IMPORTANT THING HERE.
!
LET'S BE CLEAR, MRS. STEIN.

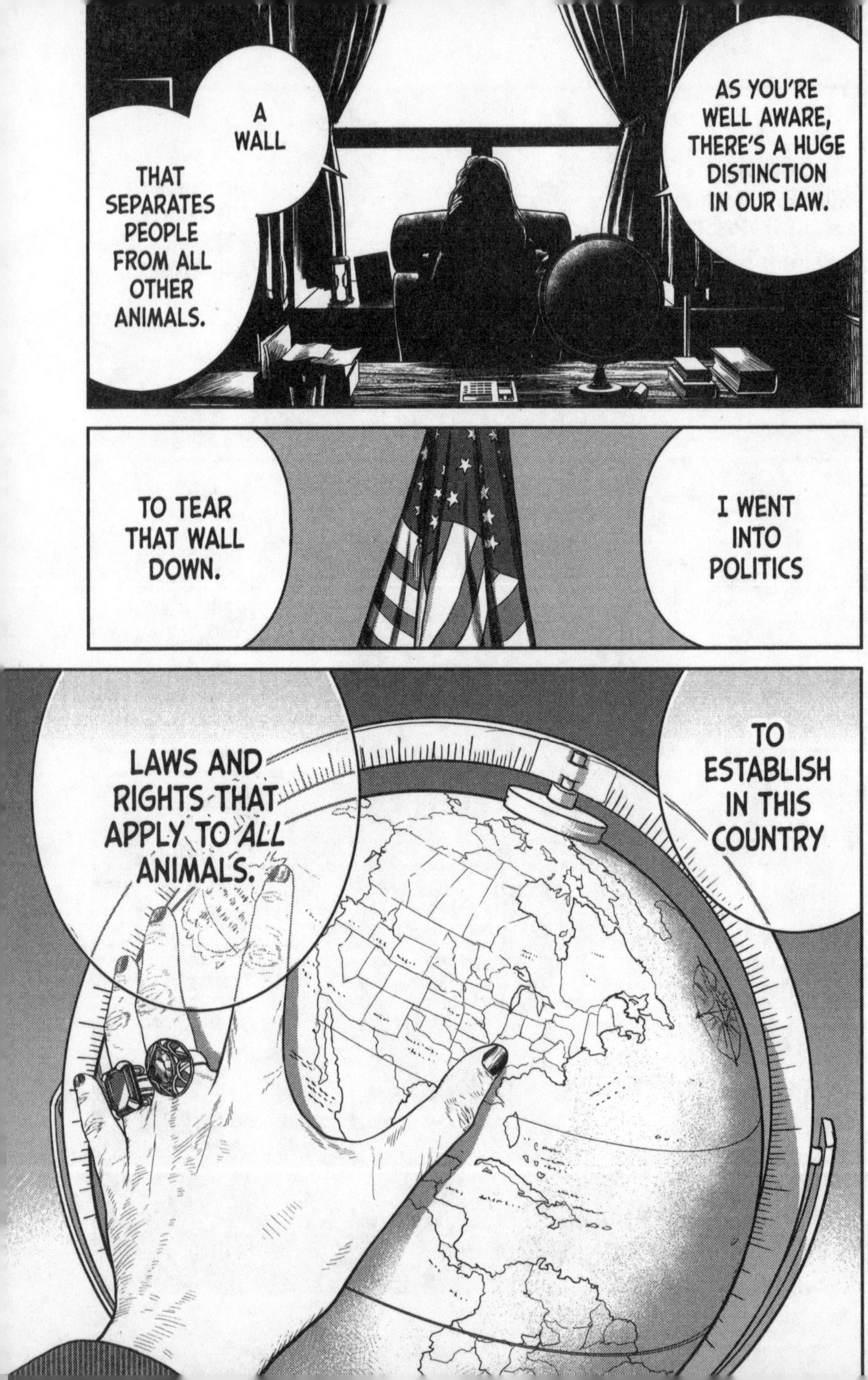
AS YOU'RE WELL AWARE, THERE'S A HUGE DISTINCTION IN OUR LAW.
A WALL
THAT SEPARATES PEOPLE FROM ALL OTHER ANIMALS.
I WENT INTO POLITICS
TO TEAR THAT WALL DOWN.
TO ESTABLISH IN THIS COUNTRY
LAWS AND RIGHTS THAT APPLY TO *ALL* ANIMALS.

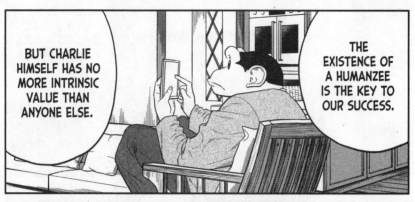

THE EXISTENCE OF A HUMANZEE IS THE KEY TO OUR SUCCESS.
BUT CHARLIE HIMSELF HAS NO MORE INTRINSIC VALUE THAN ANYONE ELSE.
ANYWAY, IF THERE ARE ANY MORE ISSUES, KEEPING HIM THERE ISN'T GOING TO BE EASY.
DON'T FORGET THAT.
...
I'LL KEEP THAT IN MIND... REPRESEN-TATIVE LINARES.

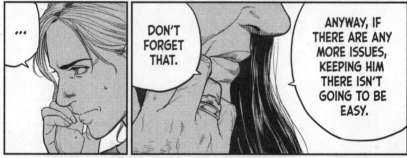

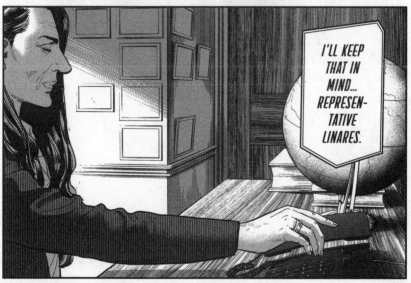

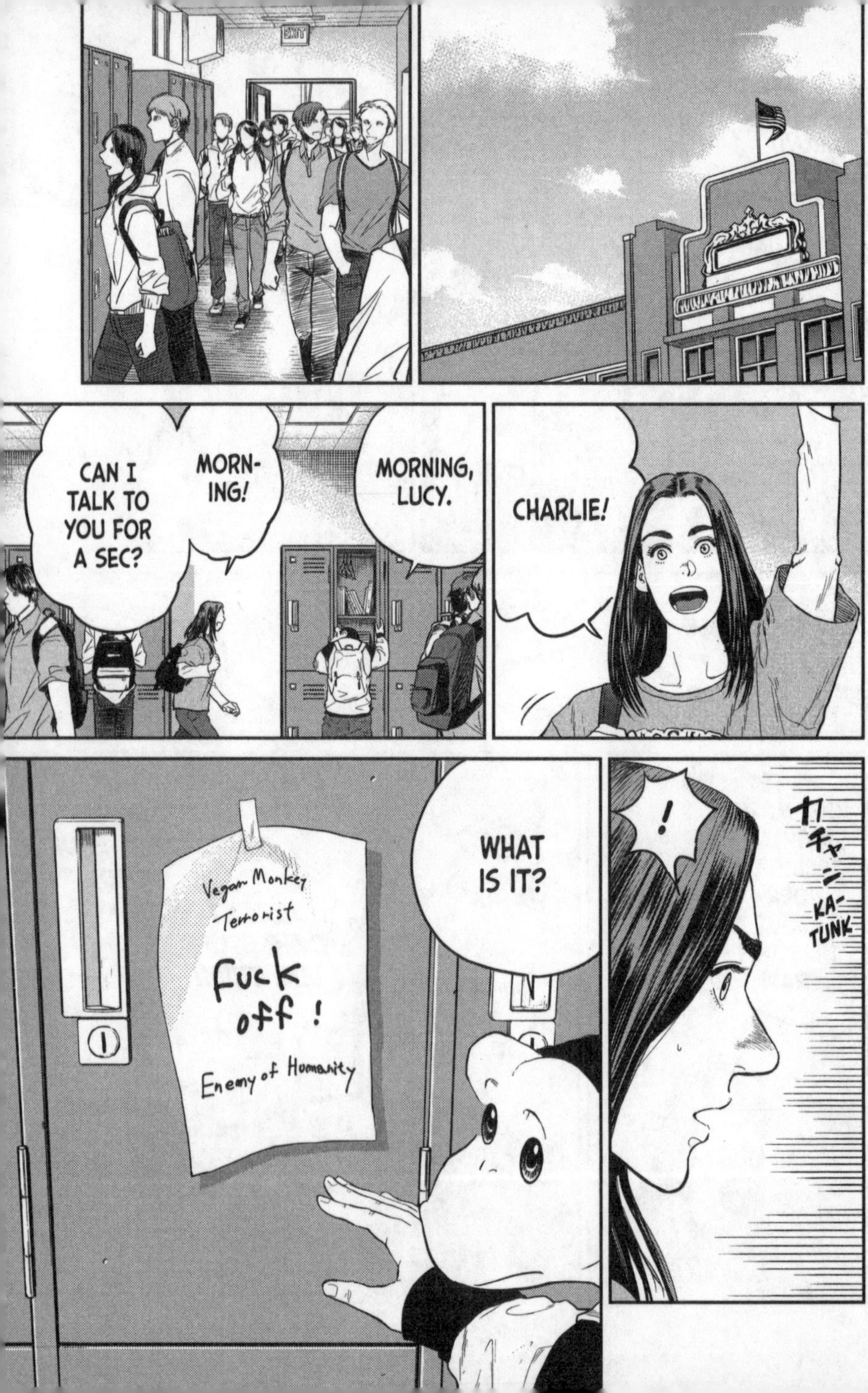
CHARLIE!
MORNING, LUCY.
MORNING!
CAN I TALK TO YOU FOR A SEC?
!
カチャン
KA-TUNK
WHAT IS IT?
Vegan Monkey
Terrorist
fuck off !
Enemy of Humanity

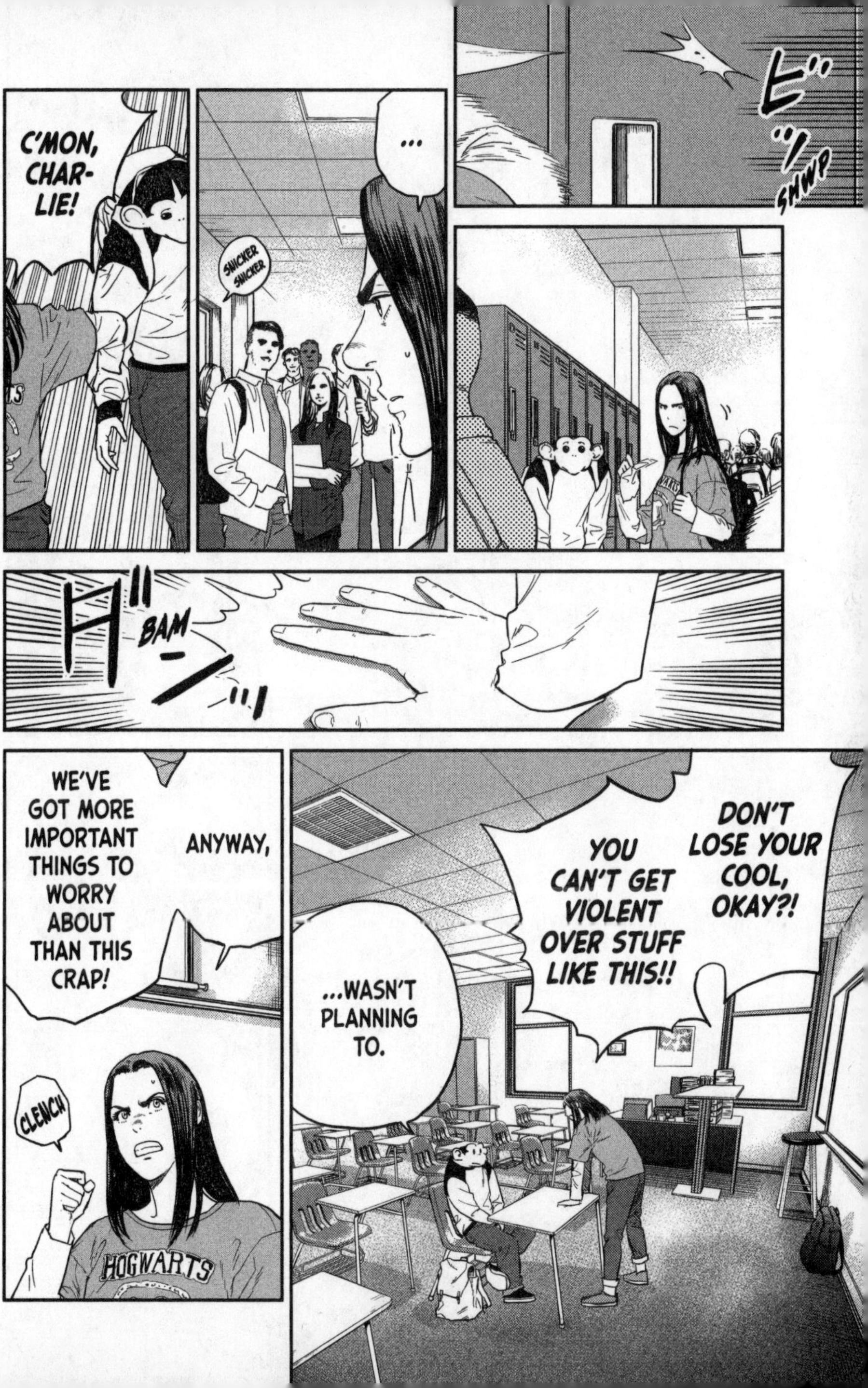
SHWP
...
SNICKER SNICKER
C'MON, CHAR-LIE!
BAM
DON'T LOSE YOUR COOL, OKAY?!
YOU CAN'T GET VIOLENT OVER STUFF LIKE THIS!!
...WASN'T PLANNING TO.
ANYWAY,
WE'VE GOT MORE IMPORTANT THINGS TO WORRY ABOUT THAN THIS CRAP!
CLENCH
HOGWARTS

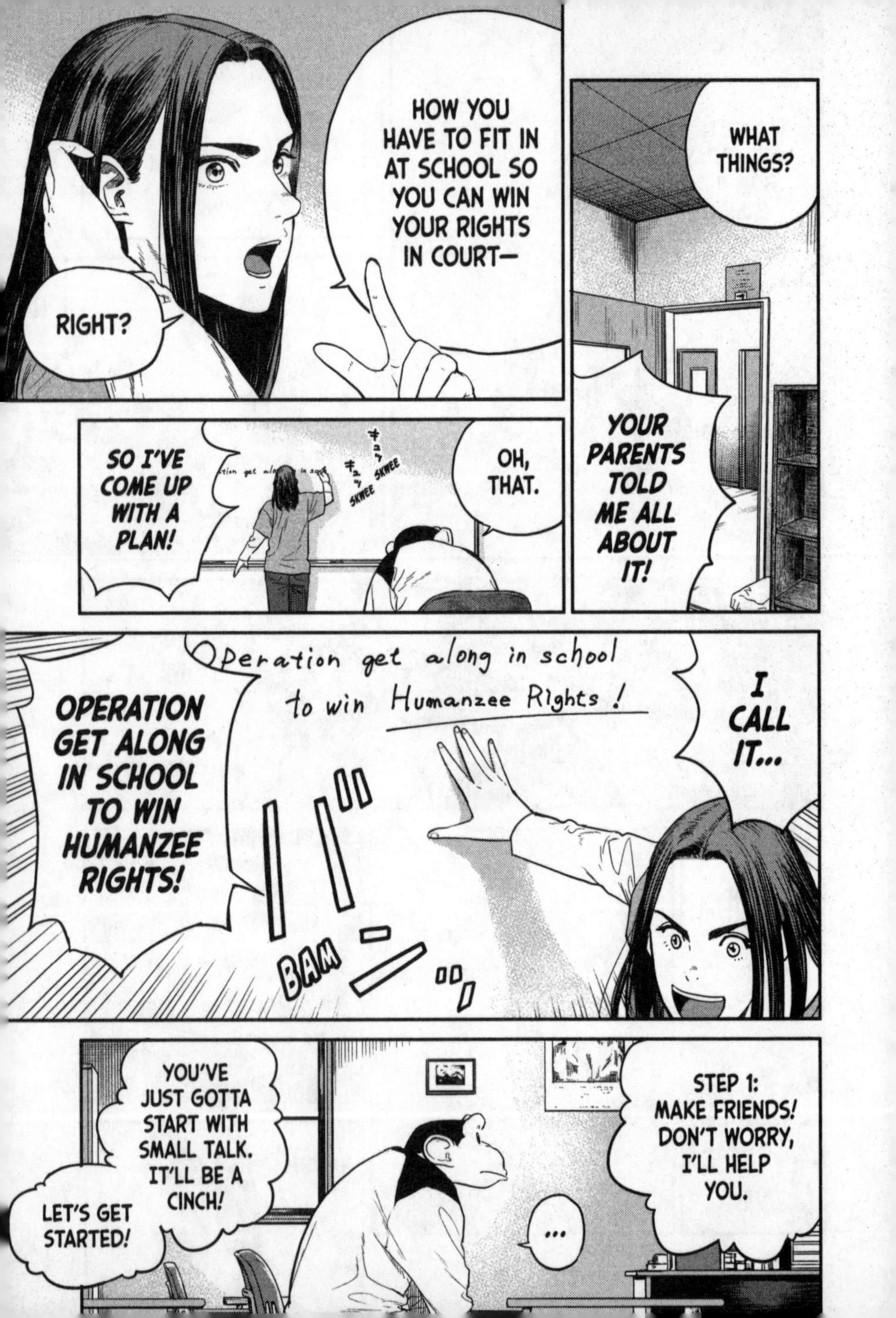
WHAT THINGS?
YOUR PARENTS TOLD ME ALL ABOUT IT!
HOW YOU HAVE TO FIT IN AT SCHOOL SO YOU CAN WIN YOUR RIGHTS IN COURT—
RIGHT?
OH, THAT.
SKWEE
SKWEE
SO I'VE COME UP WITH A PLAN!
I CALL IT...
Operation get along in school to win Humanzee Rights!
OPERATION GET ALONG IN SCHOOL TO WIN HUMANZEE RIGHTS!
BAM
STEP 1: MAKE FRIENDS! DON'T WORRY, I'LL HELP YOU.
...
YOU'VE JUST GOTTA START WITH SMALL TALK. IT'LL BE A CINCH!
LET'S GET STARTED!

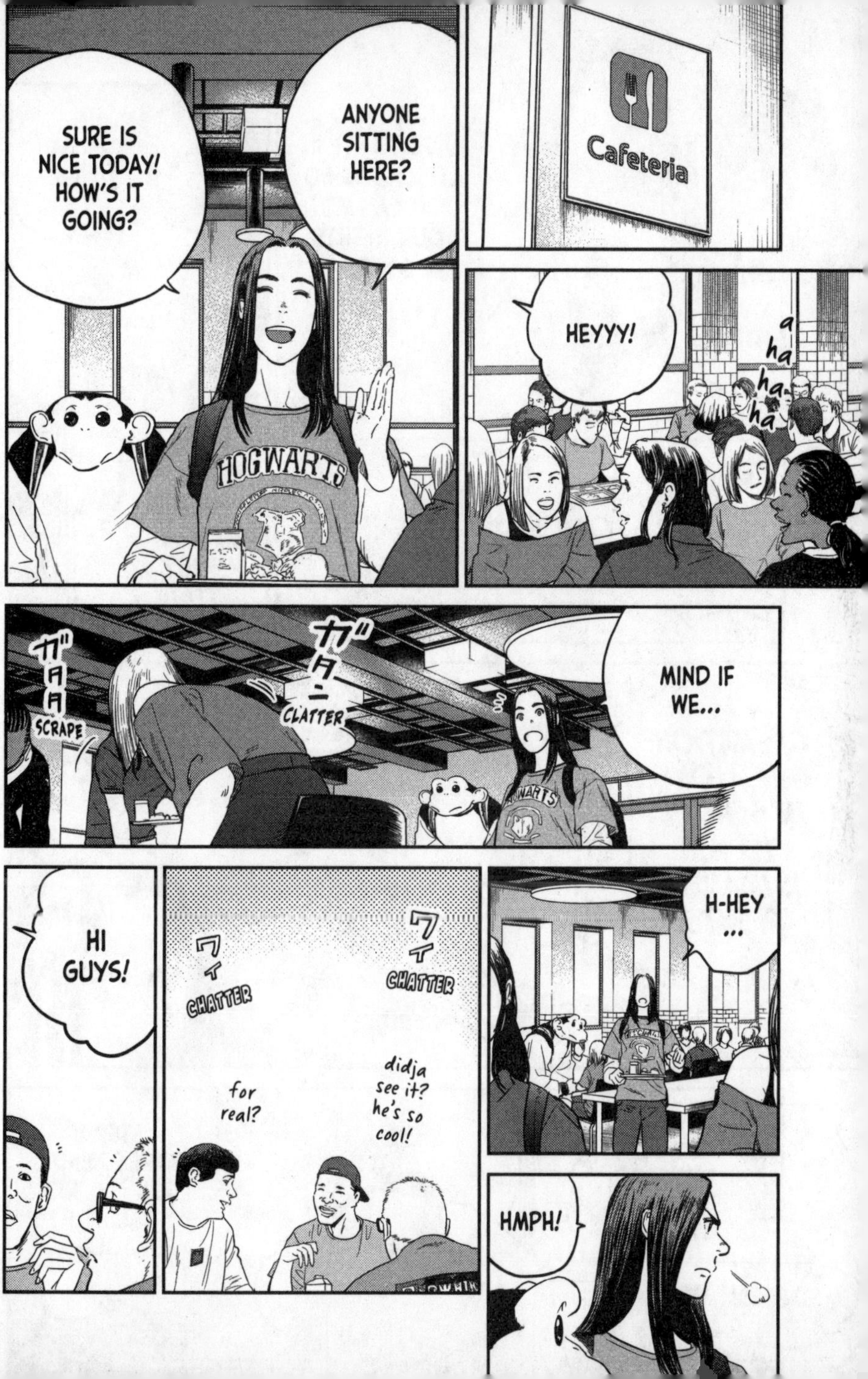
Cafeteria
HEYYY!
a ha ha ha ha
ANYONE SITTING HERE?
SURE IS NICE TODAY! HOW'S IT GOING?
HOGWARTS
MIND IF WE...
CLATTER
ガタタ
SCRAPE
H-HEY ...
HMPH!
ワイ
CHATTER
ワイ
CHATTER
didja see it? he's so cool!
for real?
HI GUYS!

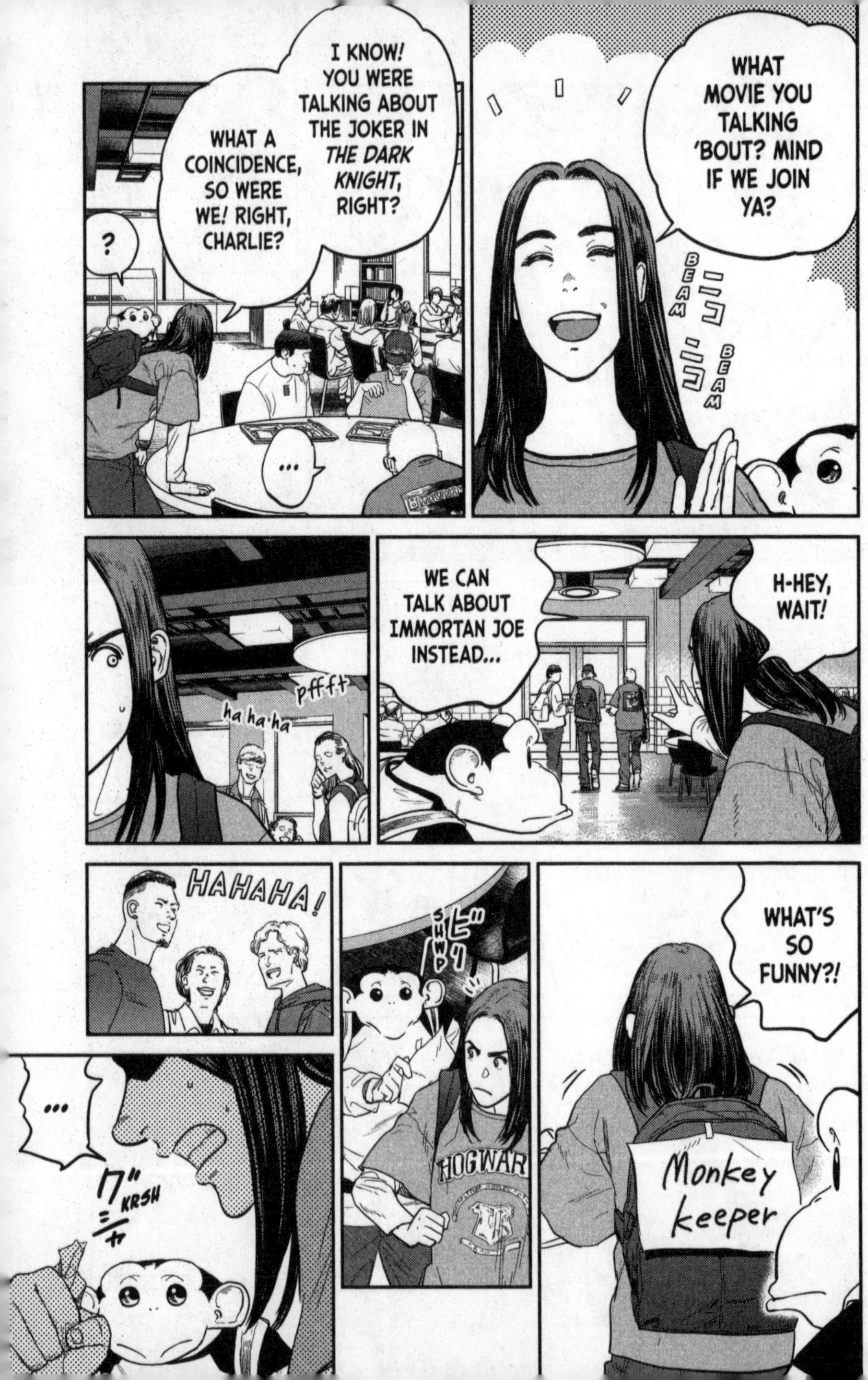
WHAT MOVIE YOU TALKING 'BOUT? MIND IF WE JOIN YA?
BEAM
BEAM
I KNOW! YOU WERE TALKING ABOUT THE JOKER IN THE DARK KNIGHT, RIGHT?
WHAT A COINCIDENCE, SO WERE WE! RIGHT, CHARLIE?
?
...
H-HEY, WAIT!
WE CAN TALK ABOUT IMMORTAN JOE INSTEAD...
pfffft
ha ha ha
WHAT'S SO FUNNY?!
Monkey keeper
SHWD
HAHAHA!
...
KRSH

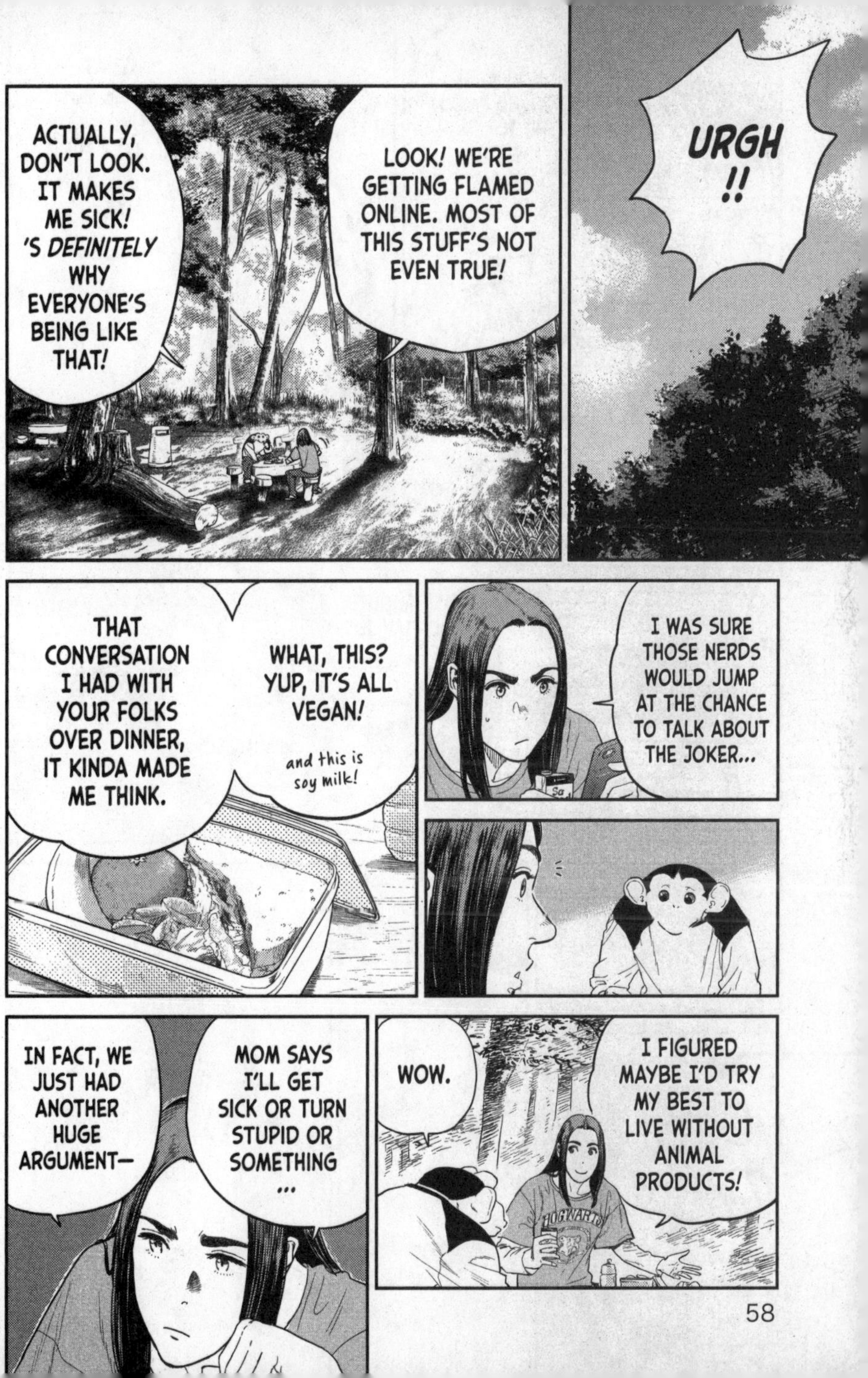
URGH !!
LOOK! WE'RE GETTING FLAMED ONLINE. MOST OF THIS STUFF'S NOT EVEN TRUE!
ACTUALLY, DON'T LOOK. IT MAKES ME SICK! 'S *DEFINITELY* WHY EVERYONE'S BEING LIKE THAT!
I WAS SURE THOSE NERDS WOULD JUMP AT THE CHANCE TO TALK ABOUT THE JOKER...
WHAT, THIS? YUP, IT'S ALL VEGAN!
and this is soy milk!
THAT CONVERSATION I HAD WITH YOUR FOLKS OVER DINNER, IT KINDA MADE ME THINK.
I FIGURED MAYBE I'D TRY MY BEST TO LIVE WITHOUT ANIMAL PRODUCTS!
WOW.
MOM SAYS I'LL GET SICK OR TURN STUPID OR SOMETHING ...
IN FACT, WE JUST HAD ANOTHER HUGE ARGUMENT—

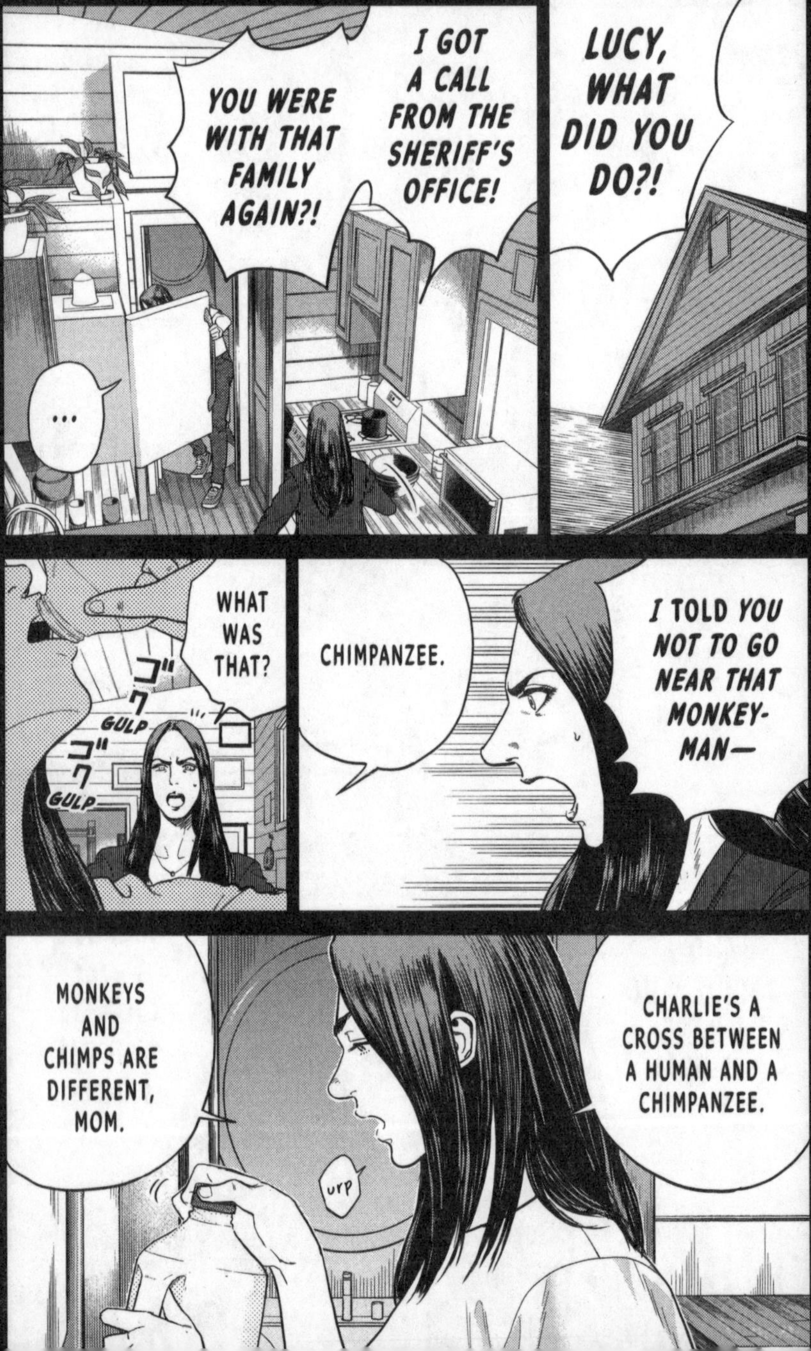
LUCY, WHAT DID YOU DO?!
I GOT A CALL FROM THE SHERIFF'S OFFICE!
YOU WERE WITH THAT FAMILY AGAIN?!
...
I TOLD YOU NOT TO GO NEAR THAT MONKEY-MAN—
CHIMPANZEE.
WHAT WAS THAT?
ゴク GULP
ゴク GULP
CHARLIE'S A CROSS BETWEEN A HUMAN AND A CHIMPANZEE.
MONKEYS AND CHIMPS ARE DIFFERENT, MOM.
urp

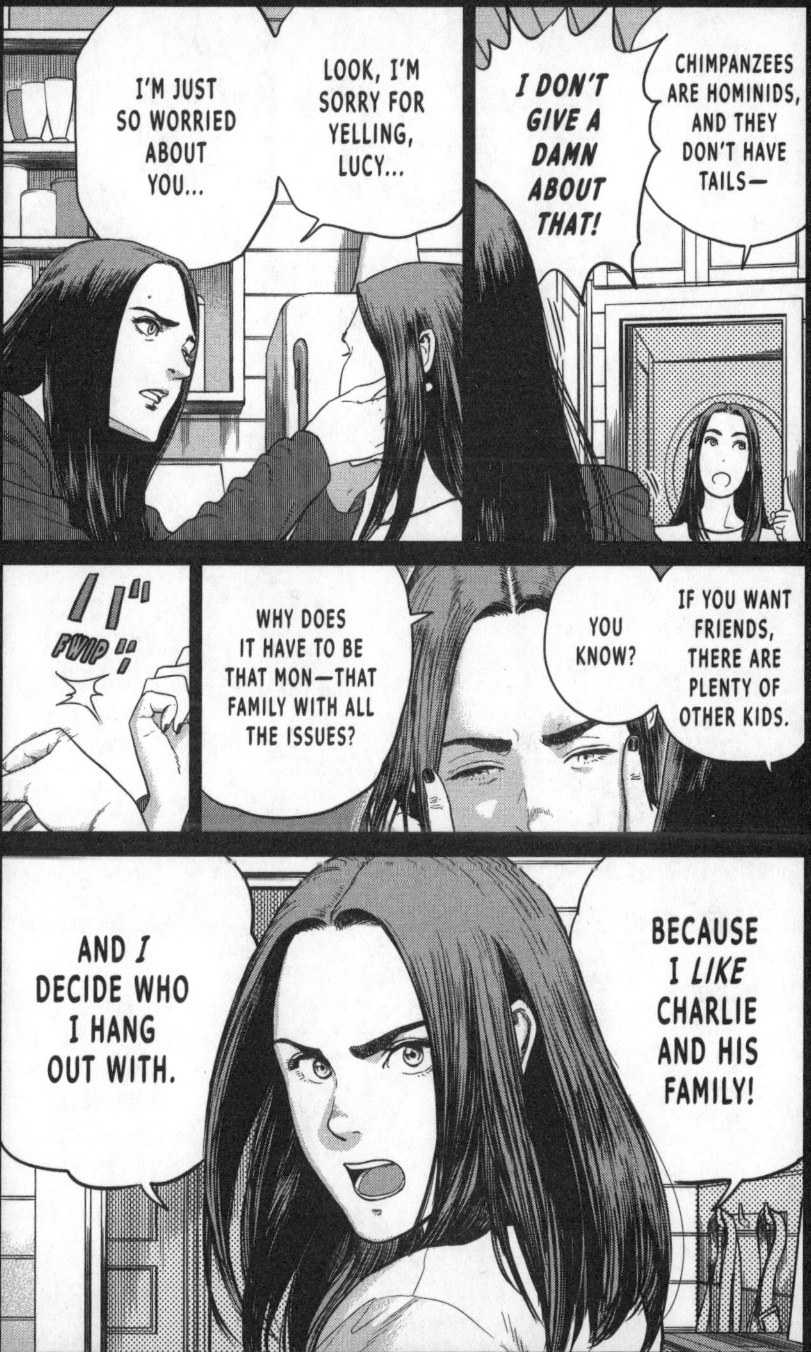
CHIMPANZEES ARE HOMINIDS, AND THEY DON'T HAVE TAILS—
I DON'T GIVE A DAMN ABOUT THAT!
LOOK, I'M SORRY FOR YELLING, LUCY...
I'M JUST SO WORRIED ABOUT YOU...
IF YOU WANT FRIENDS, THERE ARE PLENTY OF OTHER KIDS.
YOU KNOW?
WHY DOES IT HAVE TO BE THAT MON—THAT FAMILY WITH ALL THE ISSUES?
FWIP
BECAUSE I LIKE CHARLIE AND HIS FAMILY!
AND I DECIDE WHO I HANG OUT WITH.

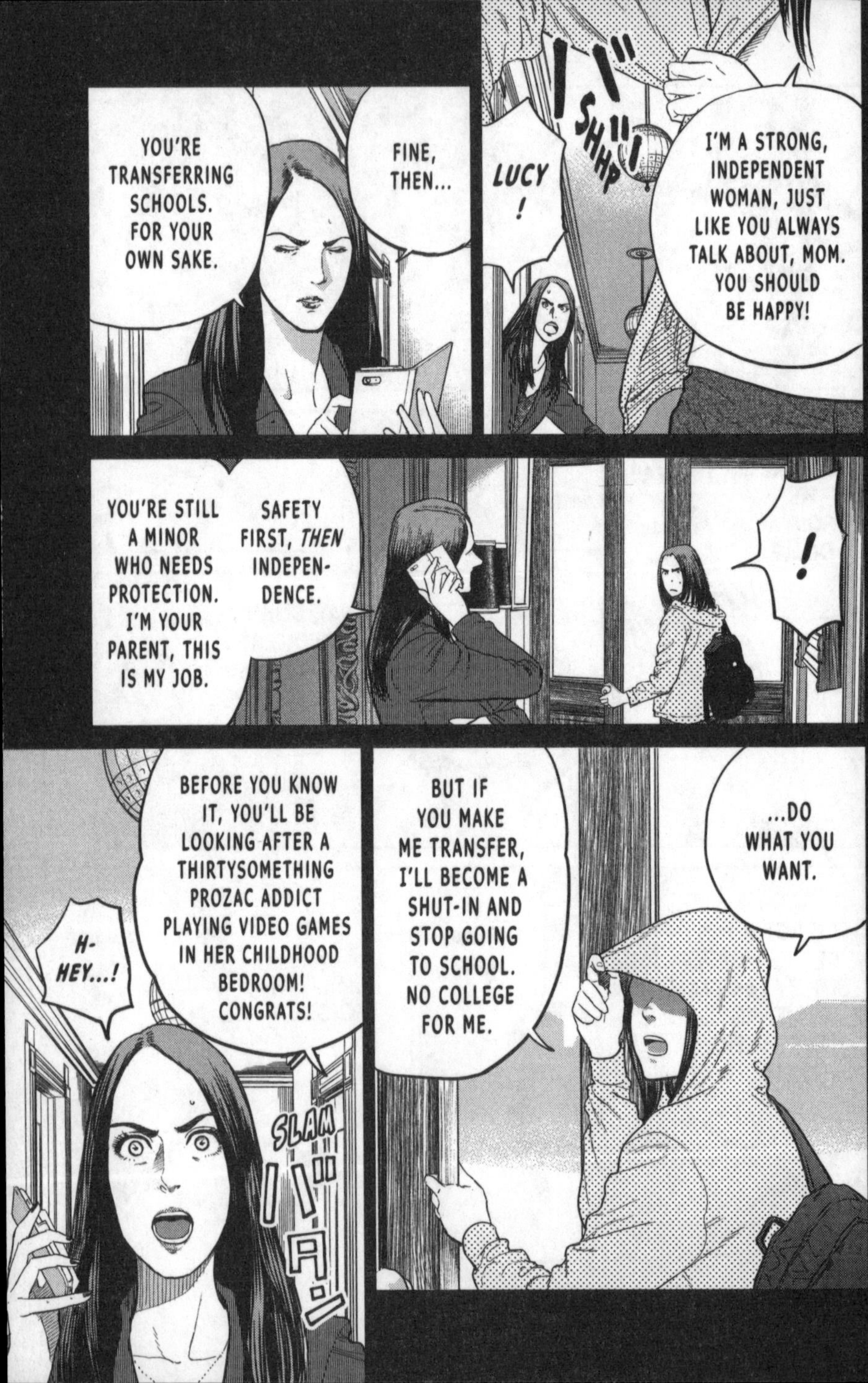
SHHP
I'M A STRONG, INDEPENDENT WOMAN, JUST LIKE YOU ALWAYS TALK ABOUT, MOM. YOU SHOULD BE HAPPY!
LUCY!
FINE, THEN...
YOU'RE TRANSFERRING SCHOOLS. FOR YOUR OWN SAKE.
!
SAFETY FIRST, *THEN* INDEPENDENCE.
YOU'RE STILL A MINOR WHO NEEDS PROTECTION. I'M YOUR PARENT, THIS IS MY JOB.
...DO WHAT YOU WANT.
BUT IF YOU MAKE ME TRANSFER, I'LL BECOME A SHUT-IN AND STOP GOING TO SCHOOL. NO COLLEGE FOR ME.
BEFORE YOU KNOW IT, YOU'LL BE LOOKING AFTER A THIRTYSOMETHING PROZAC ADDICT PLAYING VIDEO GAMES IN HER CHILDHOOD BEDROOM! CONGRATS!
H-HEY...!
SLAM

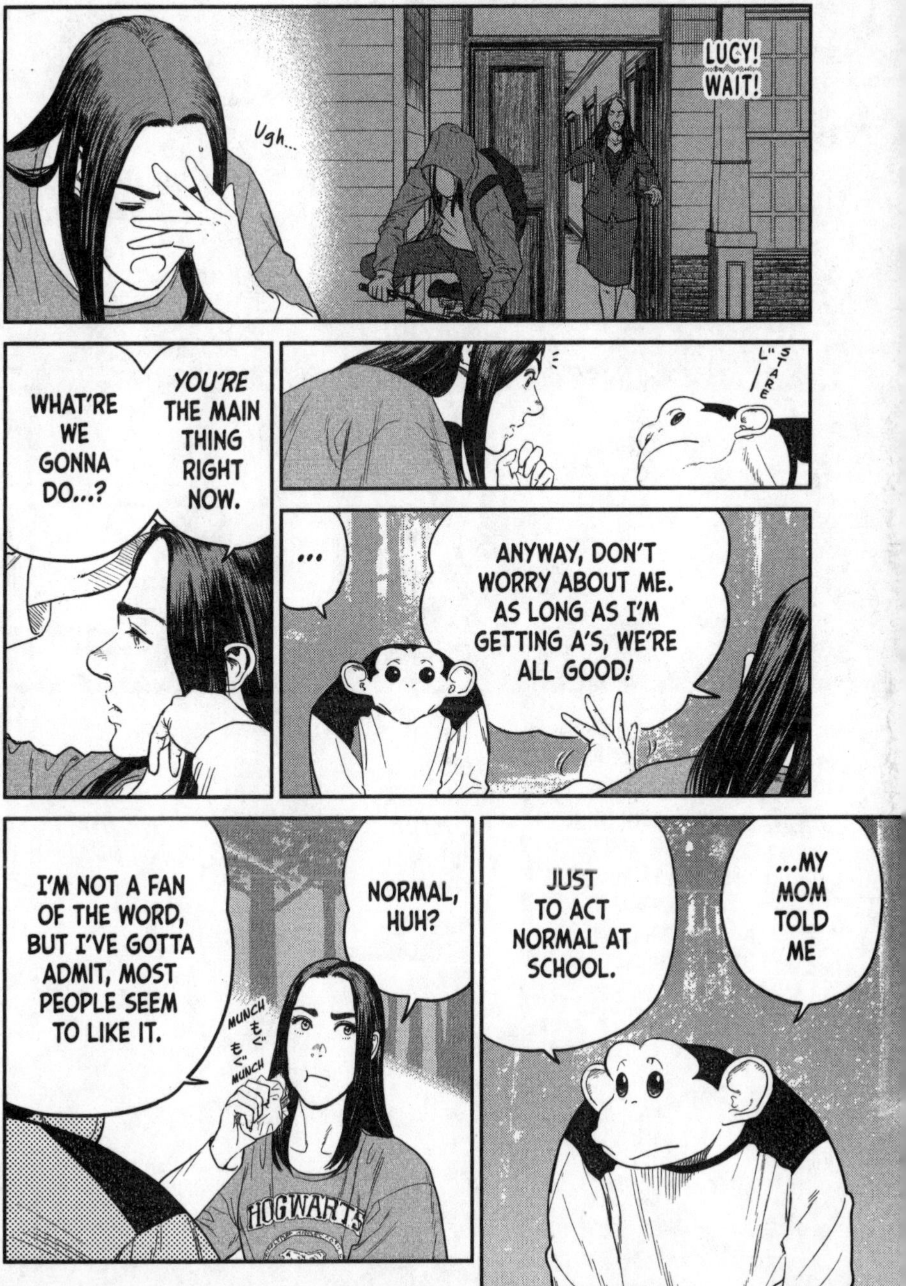
LUCY! WAIT!
Ugh...
じー STARE
ANYWAY, DON'T WORRY ABOUT ME. AS LONG AS I'M GETTING A'S, WE'RE ALL GOOD!
...
YOU'RE THE MAIN THING RIGHT NOW.
WHAT'RE WE GONNA DO...?
...MY MOM TOLD ME
JUST TO ACT NORMAL AT SCHOOL.
NORMAL, HUH?
I'M NOT A FAN OF THE WORD, BUT I'VE GOTTA ADMIT, MOST PEOPLE SEEM TO LIKE IT.
MUNCH もぐ もぐ MUNCH
HOGWARTS

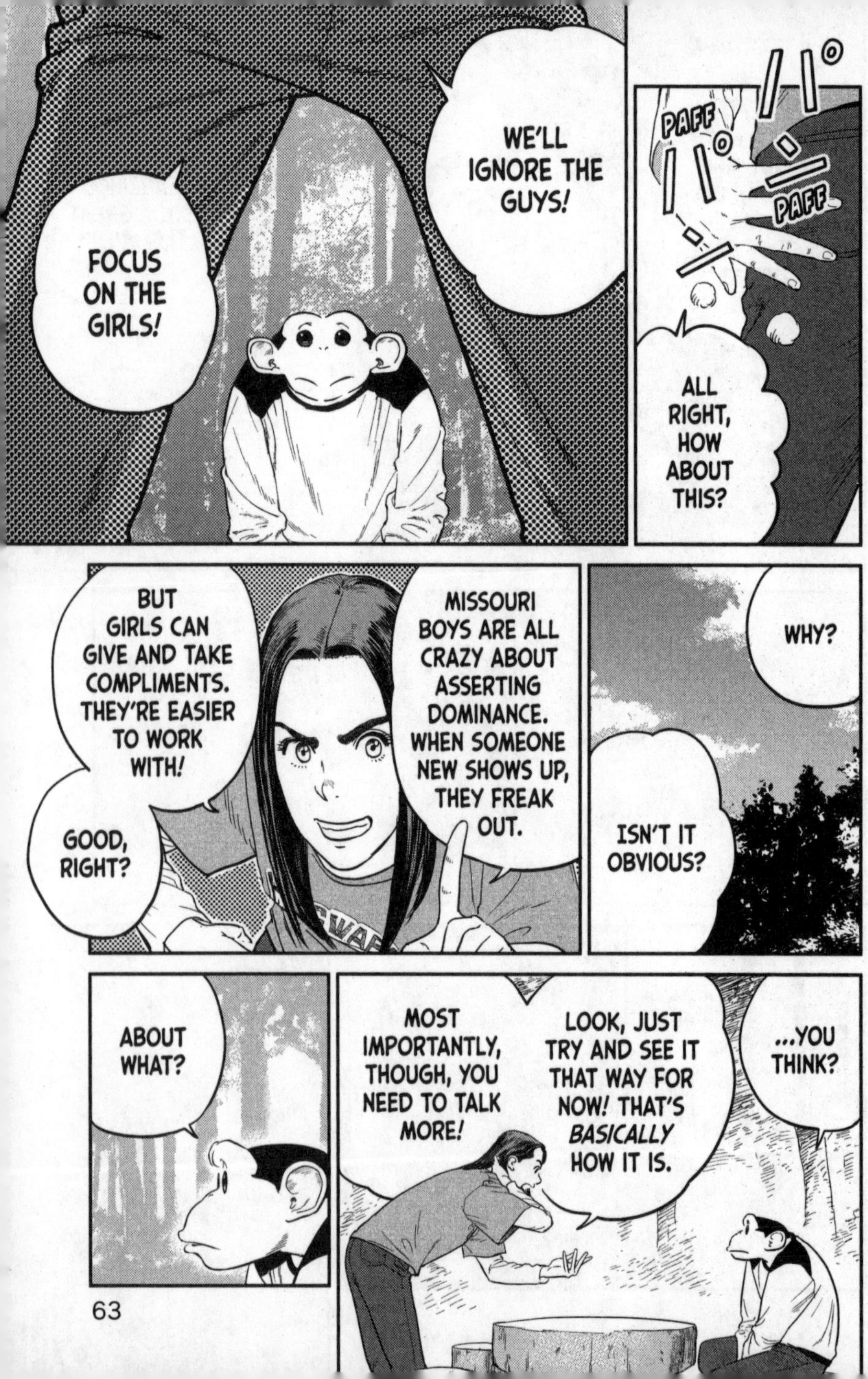
PAFF
PAFF
ALL RIGHT, HOW ABOUT THIS?
WE'LL IGNORE THE GUYS!
FOCUS ON THE GIRLS!
WHY?
ISN'T IT OBVIOUS?
MISSOURI BOYS ARE ALL CRAZY ABOUT ASSERTING DOMINANCE. WHEN SOMEONE NEW SHOWS UP, THEY FREAK OUT.
BUT GIRLS CAN GIVE AND TAKE COMPLIMENTS. THEY'RE EASIER TO WORK WITH!
GOOD, RIGHT?
...YOU THINK?
LOOK, JUST TRY AND SEE IT THAT WAY FOR NOW! THAT'S *BASICALLY* HOW IT IS.
MOST IMPORTANTLY, THOUGH, YOU NEED TO TALK MORE!
ABOUT WHAT?

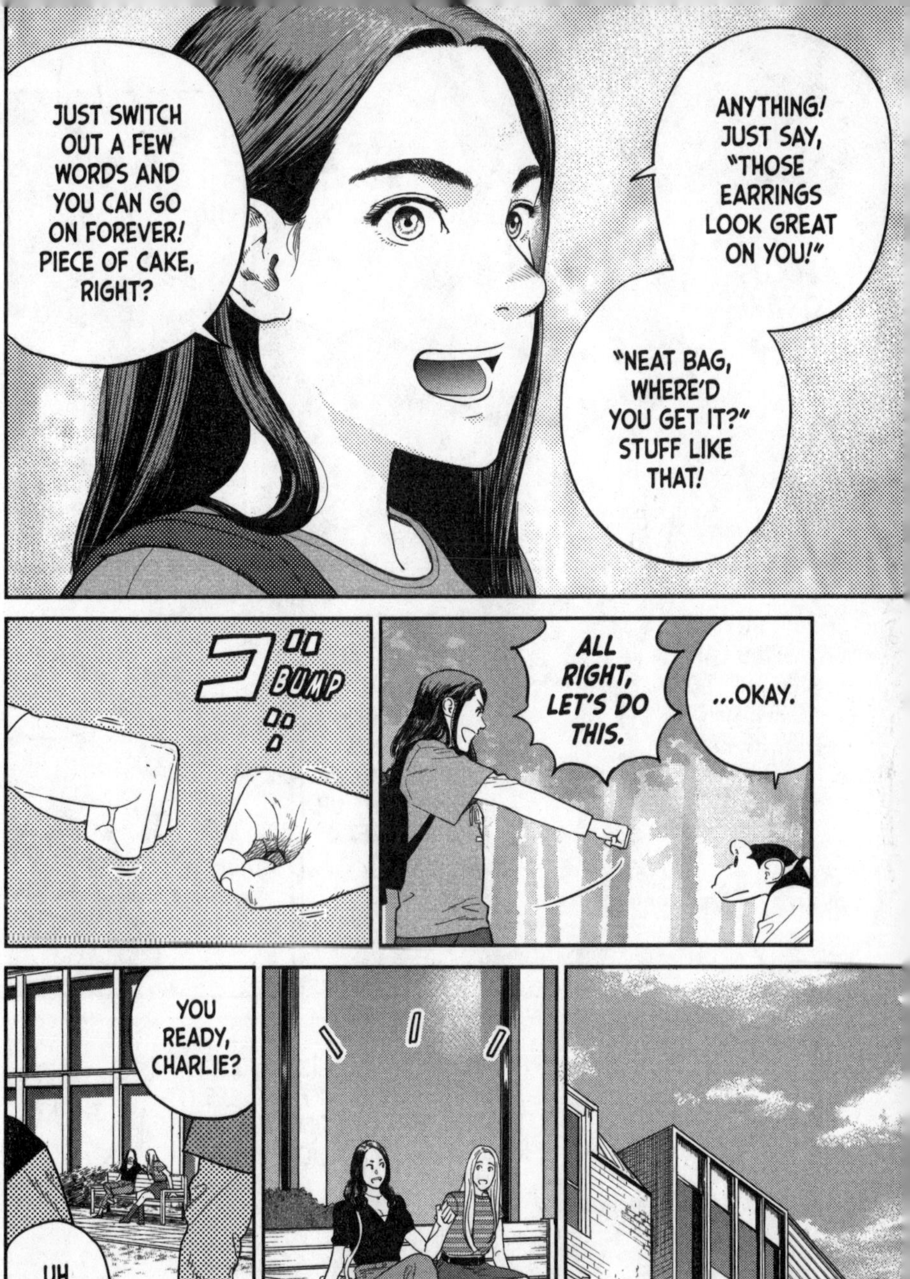
ANYTHING! JUST SAY, "THOSE EARRINGS LOOK GREAT ON YOU!"
"NEAT BAG, WHERE'D YOU GET IT?" STUFF LIKE THAT!
JUST SWITCH OUT A FEW WORDS AND YOU CAN GO ON FOREVER! PIECE OF CAKE, RIGHT?
...OKAY.
ALL RIGHT, LET'S DO THIS.
BUMP
YOU READY, CHARLIE?
UH HUH.

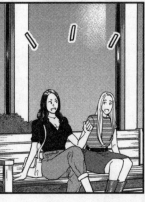

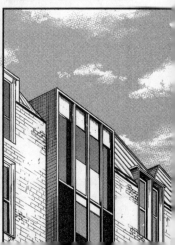

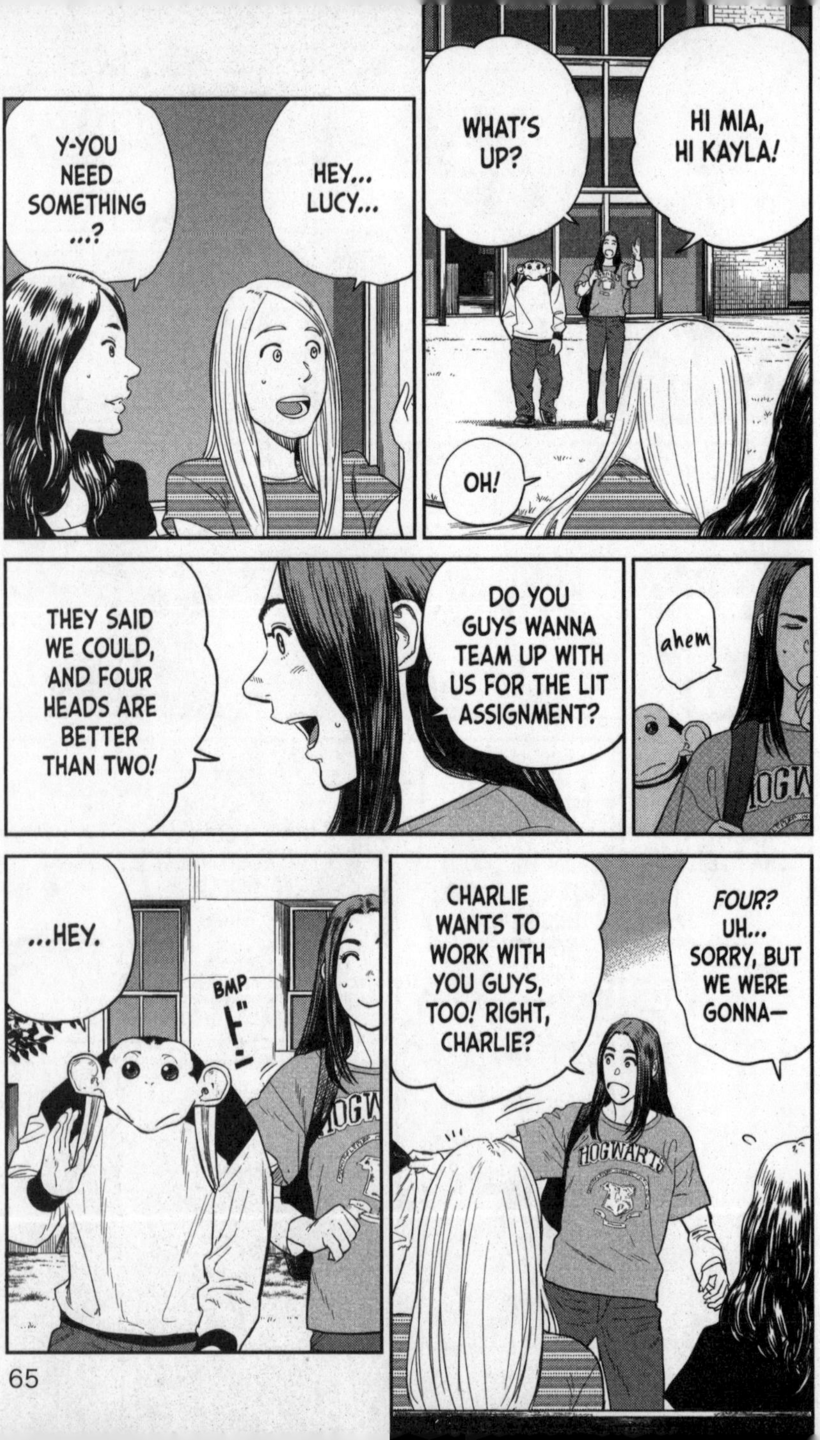
HI MIA, HI KAYLA!
WHAT'S UP?
OH!
HEY... LUCY...
Y-YOU NEED SOMETHING ...?
ahem
DO YOU GUYS WANNA TEAM UP WITH US FOR THE LIT ASSIGNMENT?
THEY SAID WE COULD, AND FOUR HEADS ARE BETTER THAN TWO!
FOUR? UH... SORRY, BUT WE WERE GONNA—
CHARLIE WANTS TO WORK WITH YOU GUYS, TOO! RIGHT, CHARLIE?
...HEY.
BMP

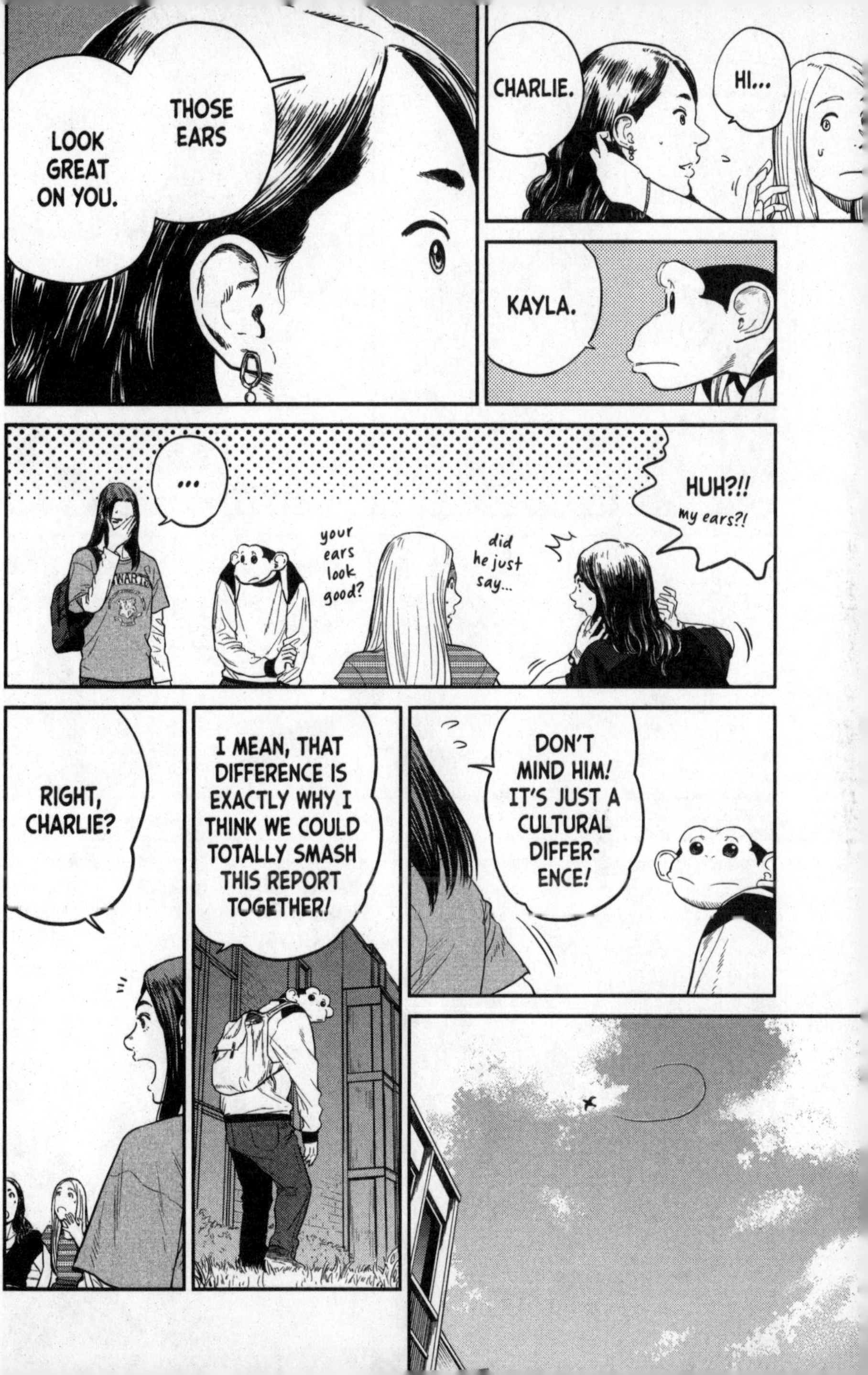
HI...
CHARLIE.
KAYLA.
THOSE EARS LOOK GREAT ON YOU.
HUH?!!
my ears?!
did he just say...
your ears look good?
...
DON'T MIND HIM! IT'S JUST A CULTURAL DIFFER-ENCE!
I MEAN, THAT DIFFERENCE IS EXACTLY WHY I THINK WE COULD TOTALLY SMASH THIS REPORT TOGETHER!
RIGHT, CHARLIE?

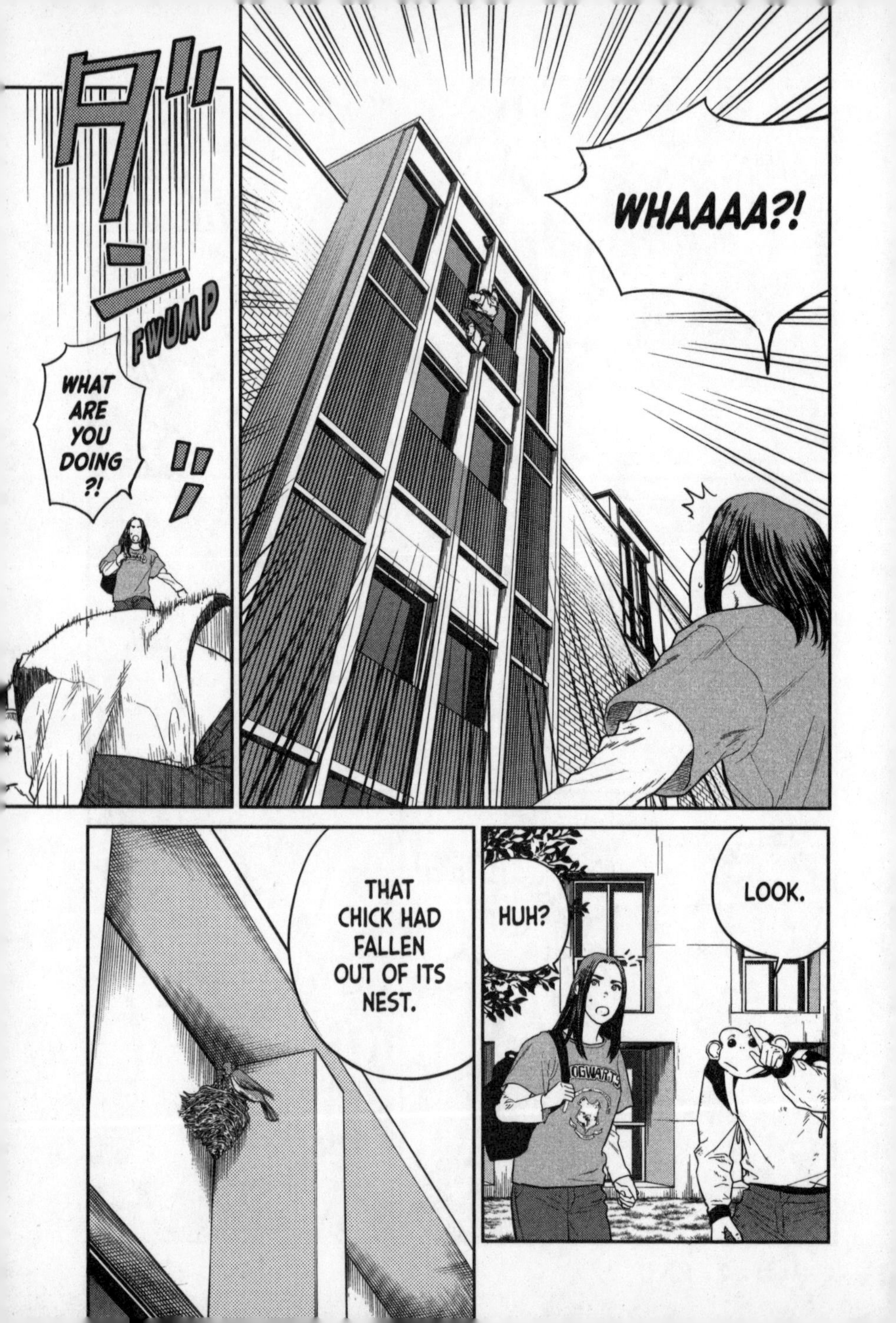
WHAAAA?!
FWUMP
WHAT ARE YOU DOING ?!
LOOK.
HUH?
THAT CHICK HAD FALLEN OUT OF ITS NEST.

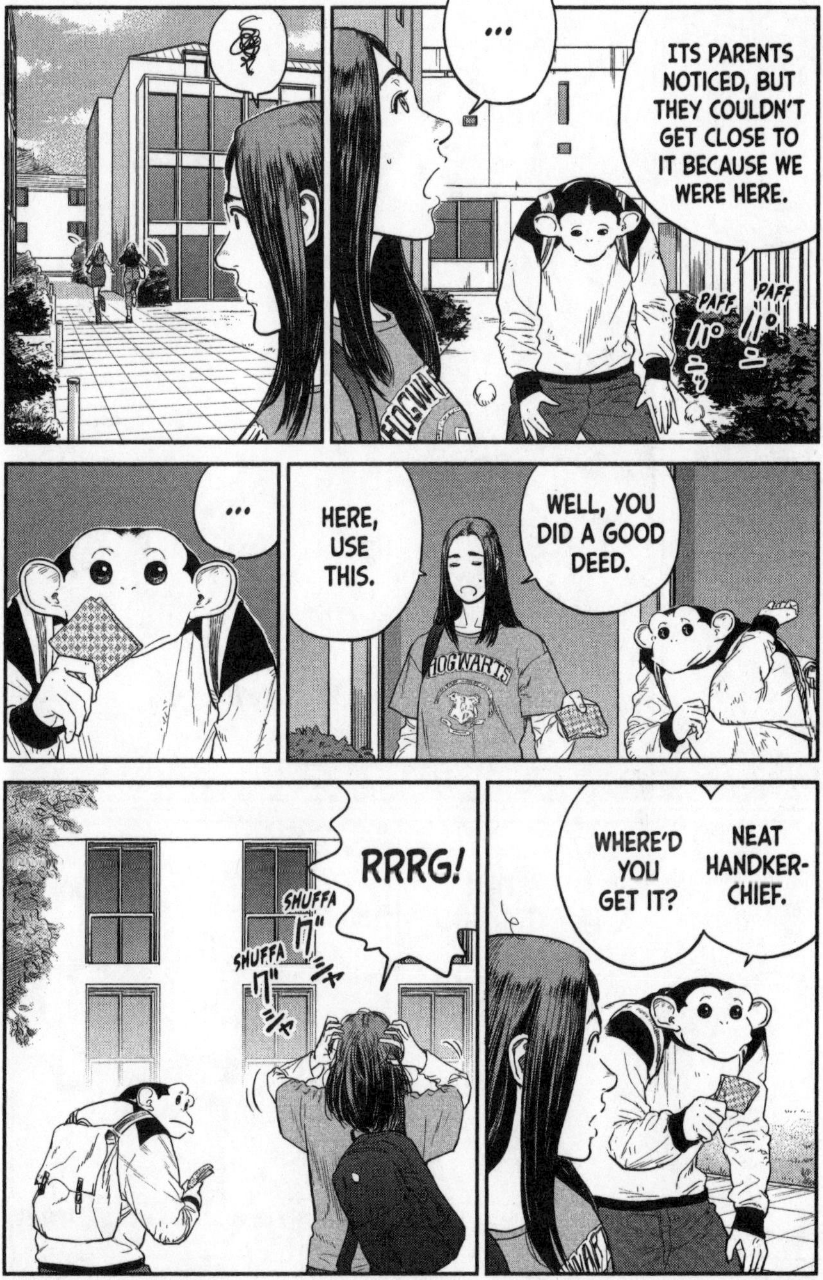
ITS PARENTS NOTICED, BUT THEY COULDN'T GET CLOSE TO IT BECAUSE WE WERE HERE.
...
PAFF
PAFF
WELL, YOU DID A GOOD DEED.
HERE, USE THIS.
...
NEAT HANDKER-CHIEF.
WHERE'D YOU GET IT?
RRRG!
SHUFFA
SHUFFA

CHAPTER 7 / END

CHAPTER 8

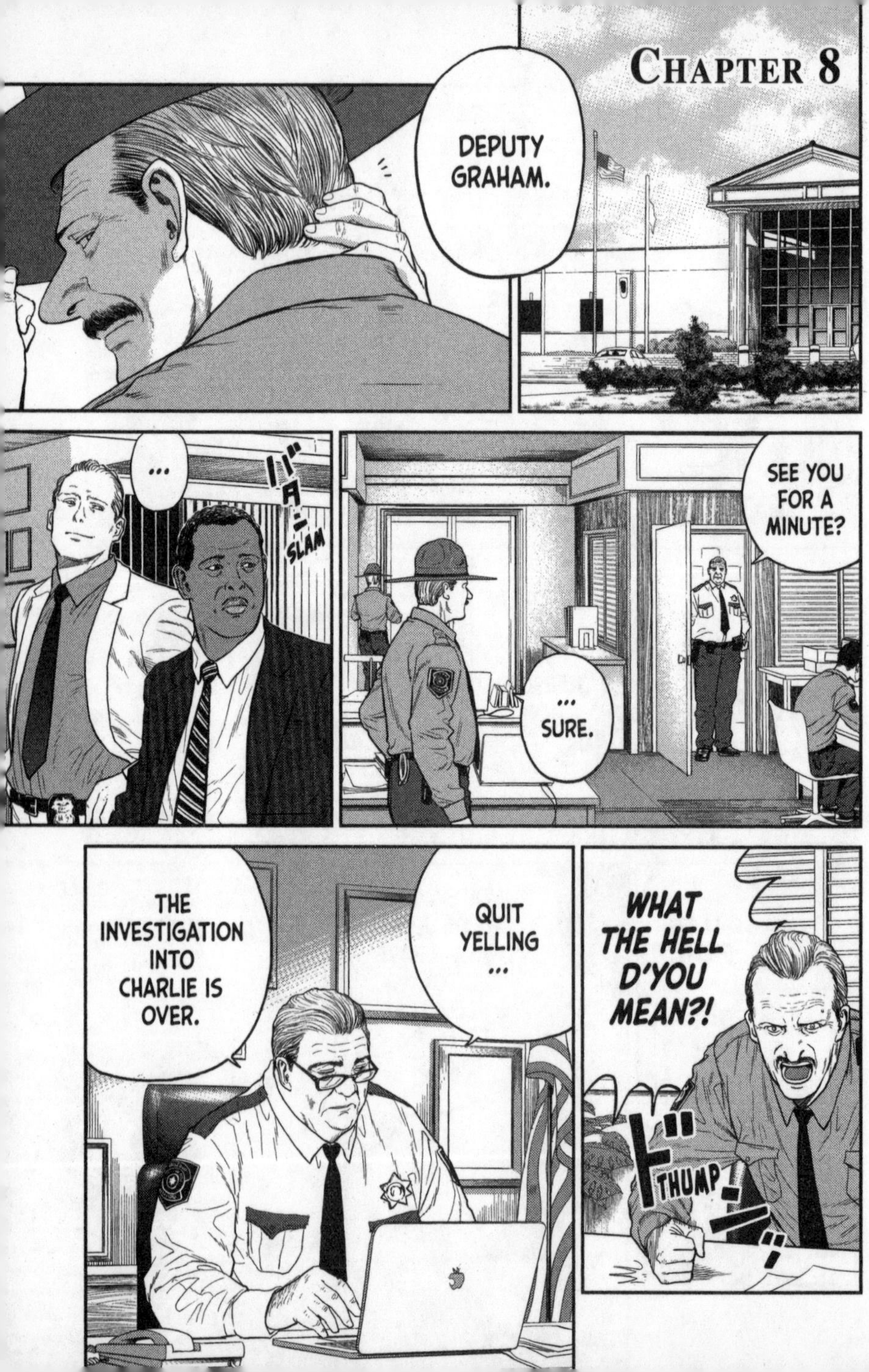
DEPUTY GRAHAM.
SEE YOU FOR A MINUTE?
... SURE.
...
SLAM
WHAT THE HELL D'YOU MEAN?!
THUMP
QUIT YELLING ...
THE INVESTIGATION INTO CHARLIE IS OVER.

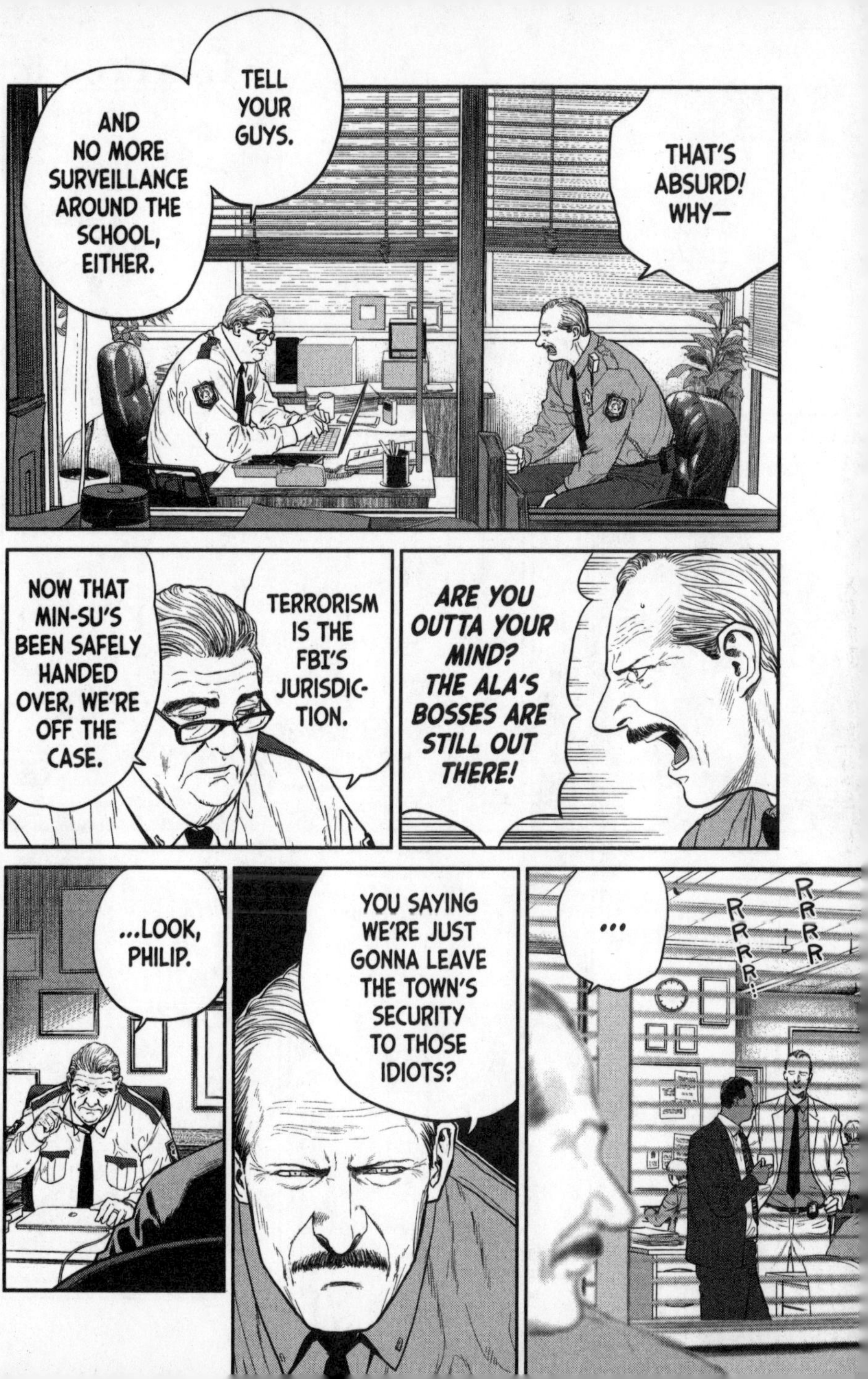
TELL YOUR GUYS.
AND NO MORE SURVEILLANCE AROUND THE SCHOOL, EITHER.
THAT'S ABSURD! WHY—
ARE YOU OUTTA YOUR MIND? THE ALA'S BOSSES ARE STILL OUT THERE!
TERRORISM IS THE FBI'S JURISDICTION.
NOW THAT MIN-SU'S BEEN SAFELY HANDED OVER, WE'RE OFF THE CASE.
RRRR
RRRR!
...
YOU SAYING WE'RE JUST GONNA LEAVE THE TOWN'S SECURITY TO THOSE IDIOTS?
...LOOK, PHILIP.

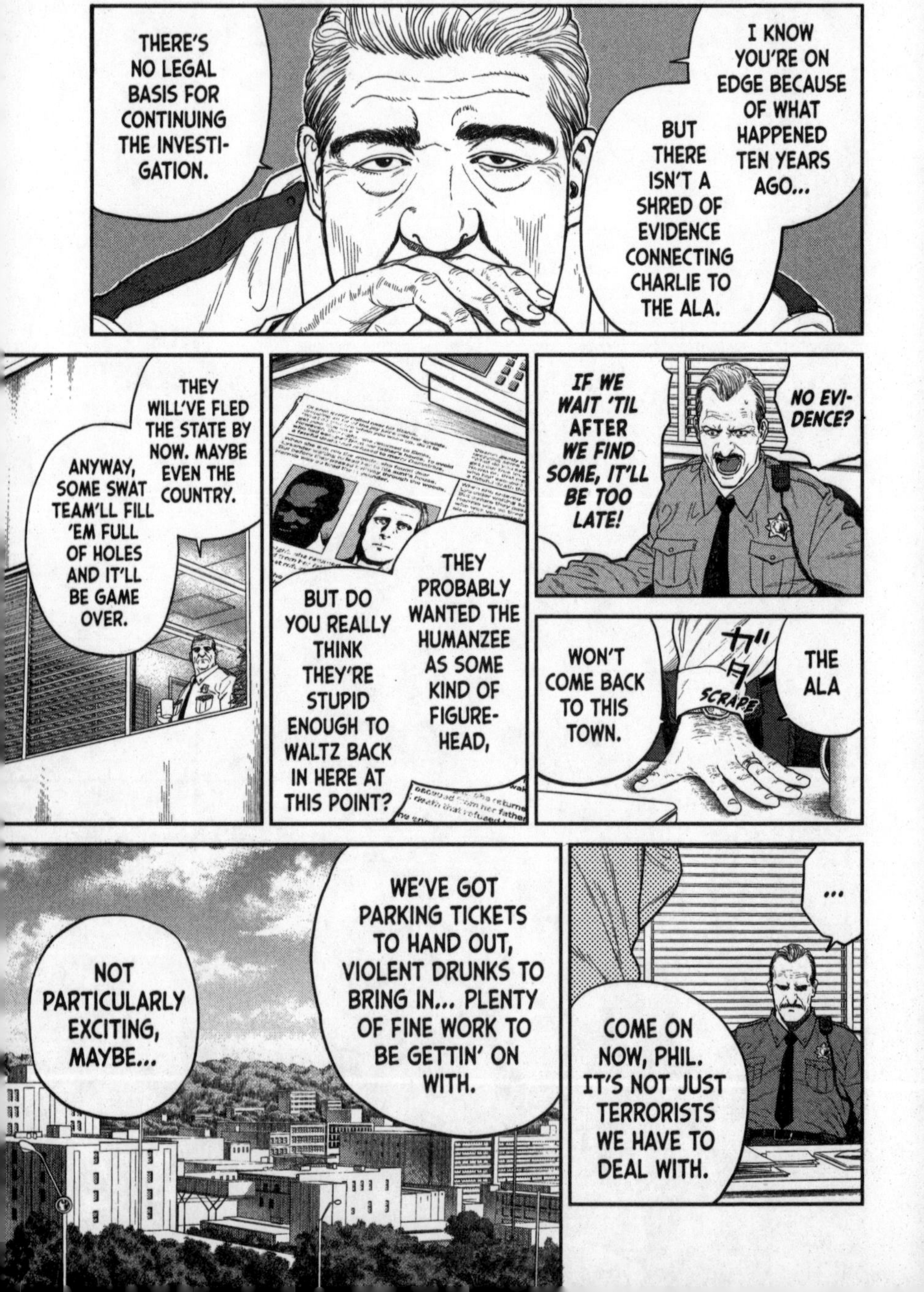

I KNOW YOU'RE ON EDGE BECAUSE OF WHAT HAPPENED TEN YEARS AGO...
BUT THERE ISN'T A SHRED OF EVIDENCE CONNECTING CHARLIE TO THE ALA.
THERE'S NO LEGAL BASIS FOR CONTINUING THE INVESTI-GATION.
NO EVI-DENCE?
IF WE WAIT 'TIL AFTER WE FIND SOME, IT'LL BE TOO LATE!
THE ALA
ガタ
SCRAPE
WON'T COME BACK TO THIS TOWN.
THEY PROBABLY WANTED THE HUMANZEE AS SOME KIND OF FIGURE-HEAD,
BUT DO YOU REALLY THINK THEY'RE STUPID ENOUGH TO WALTZ BACK IN HERE AT THIS POINT?
THEY WILL'VE FLED THE STATE BY NOW. MAYBE EVEN THE COUNTRY.
ANYWAY, SOME SWAT TEAM'LL FILL 'EM FULL OF HOLES AND IT'LL BE GAME OVER.
...
COME ON NOW, PHIL. IT'S NOT JUST TERRORISTS WE HAVE TO DEAL WITH.
WE'VE GOT PARKING TICKETS TO HAND OUT, VIOLENT DRUNKS TO BRING IN... PLENTY OF FINE WORK TO BE GETTIN' ON WITH.
NOT PARTICULARLY EXCITING, MAYBE...

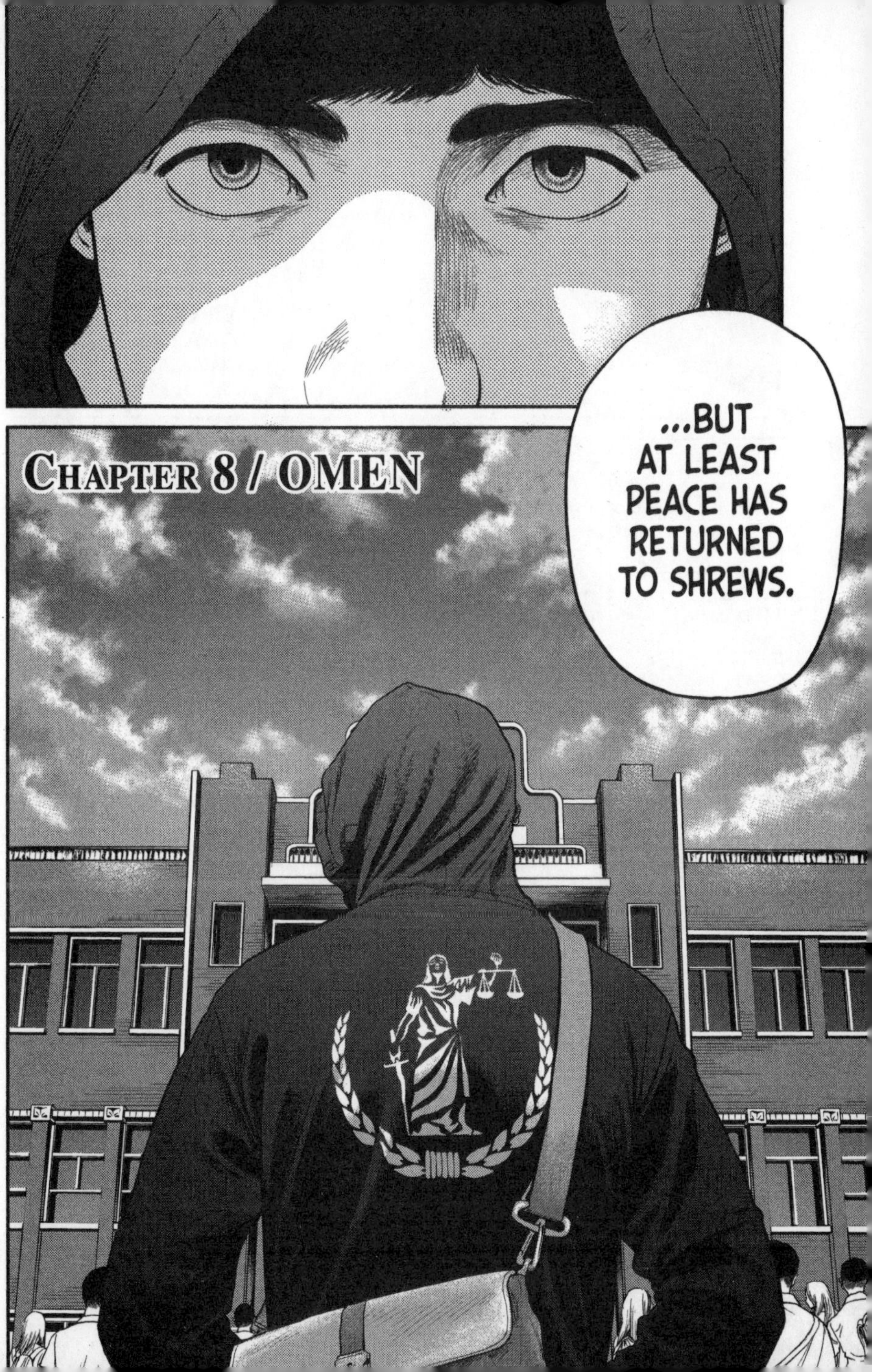
...BUT AT LEAST PEACE HAS RETURNED TO SHREWS.
CHAPTER 8 / OMEN

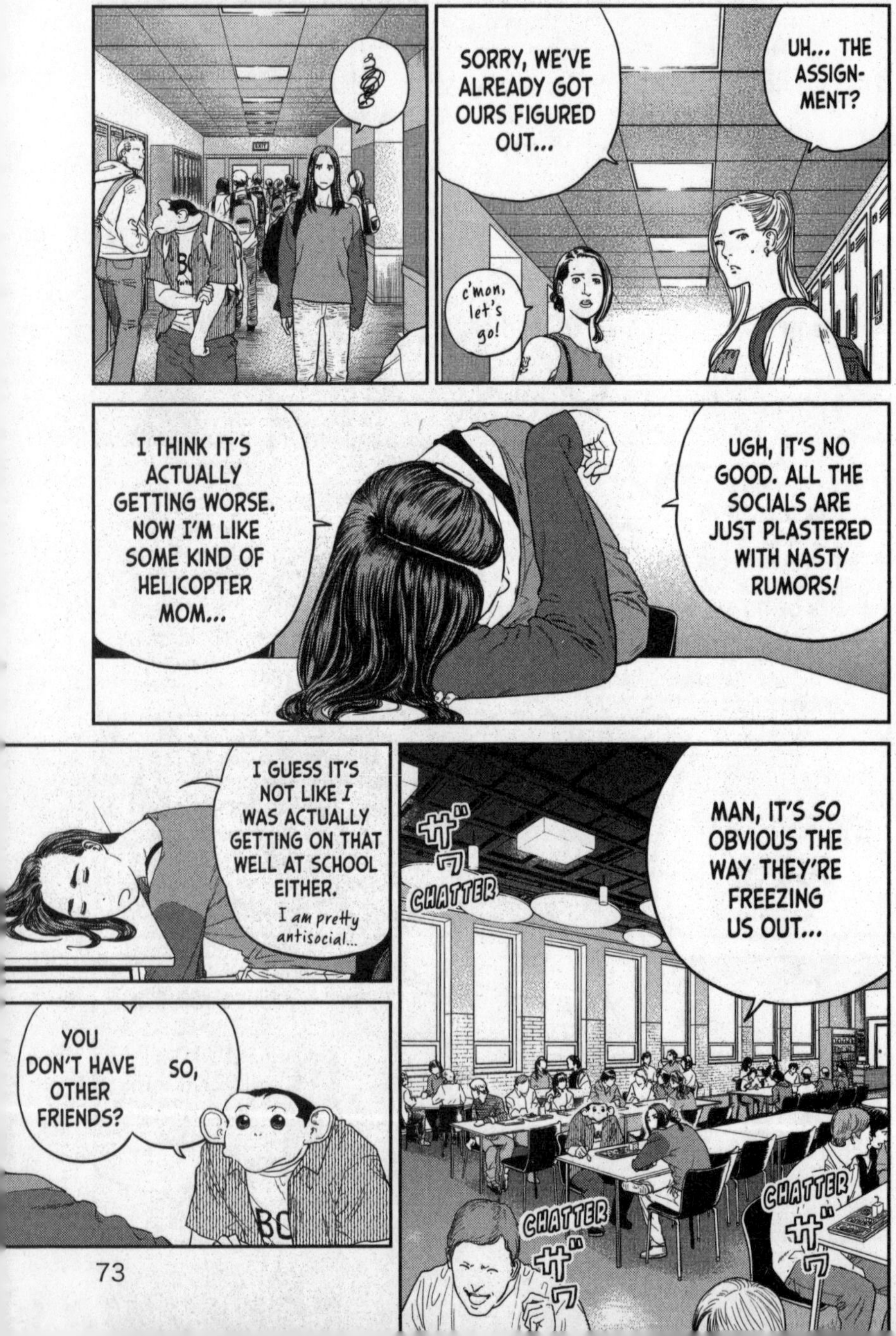
UH... THE ASSIGN-MENT?
SORRY, WE'VE ALREADY GOT OURS FIGURED OUT...
c'mon, let's go!
UGH, IT'S NO GOOD. ALL THE SOCIALS ARE JUST PLASTERED WITH NASTY RUMORS!
I THINK IT'S ACTUALLY GETTING WORSE. NOW I'M LIKE SOME KIND OF HELICOPTER MOM...
MAN, IT'S *SO* OBVIOUS THE WAY THEY'RE FREEZING US OUT...
CHATTER
CHATTER
CHATTER
CHATTER
I GUESS IT'S NOT LIKE *I* WAS ACTUALLY GETTING ON THAT WELL AT SCHOOL EITHER.
I am pretty antisocial...
SO,
YOU DON'T HAVE OTHER FRIENDS?

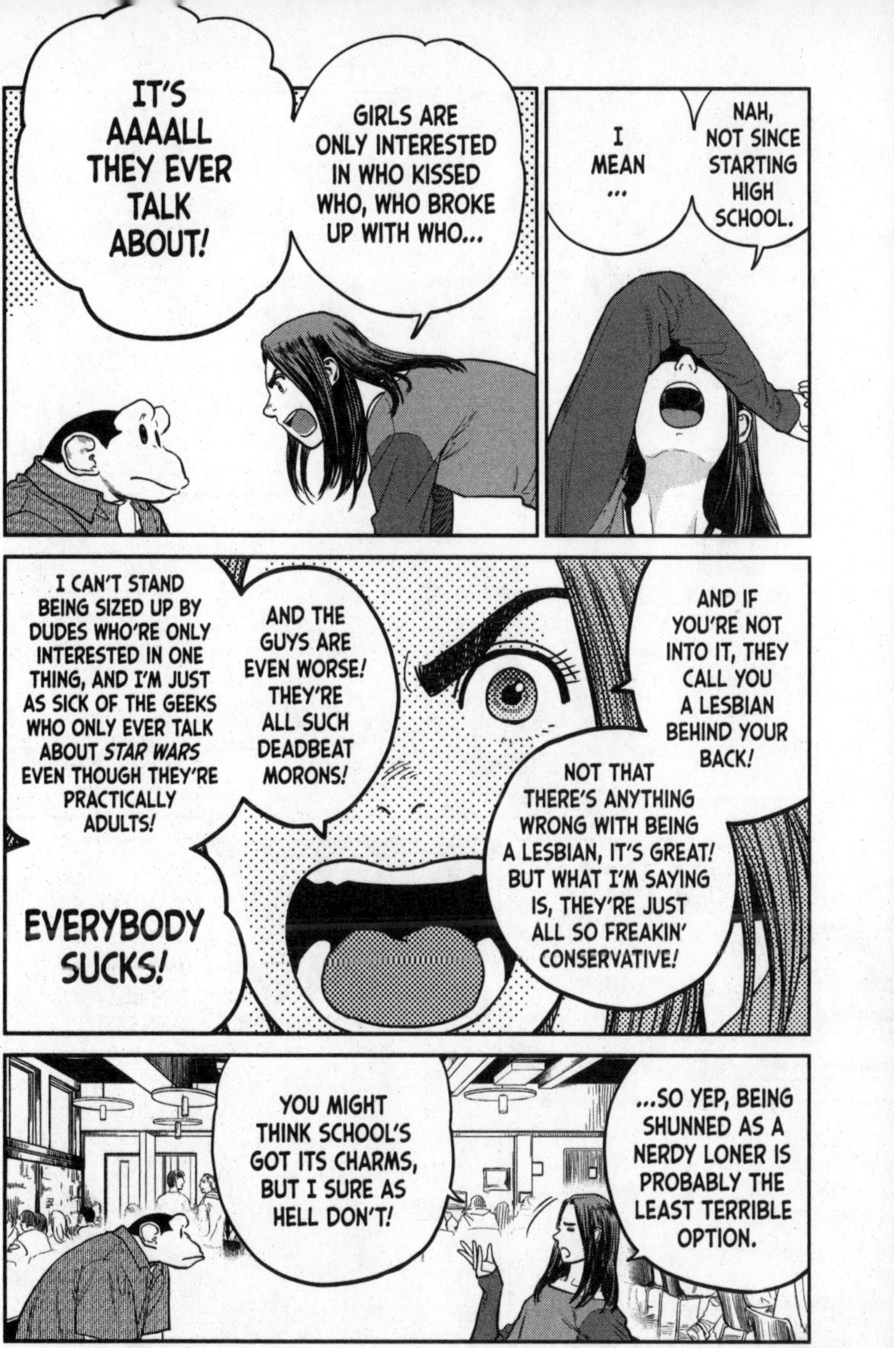
NAH, NOT SINCE STARTING HIGH SCHOOL.
I MEAN ...
GIRLS ARE ONLY INTERESTED IN WHO KISSED WHO, WHO BROKE UP WITH WHO...
IT'S AAAALL THEY EVER TALK ABOUT!
AND IF YOU'RE NOT INTO IT, THEY CALL YOU A LESBIAN BEHIND YOUR BACK!
NOT THAT THERE'S ANYTHING WRONG WITH BEING A LESBIAN, IT'S GREAT! BUT WHAT I'M SAYING IS, THEY'RE JUST ALL SO FREAKIN' CONSERVATIVE!
AND THE GUYS ARE EVEN WORSE! THEY'RE ALL SUCH DEADBEAT MORONS!
I CAN'T STAND BEING SIZED UP BY DUDES WHO'RE ONLY INTERESTED IN ONE THING, AND I'M JUST AS SICK OF THE GEEKS WHO ONLY EVER TALK ABOUT *STAR WARS* EVEN THOUGH THEY'RE PRACTICALLY ADULTS!
EVERYBODY SUCKS!
...SO YEP, BEING SHUNNED AS A NERDY LONER IS PROBABLY THE LEAST TERRIBLE OPTION.
YOU MIGHT THINK SCHOOL'S GOT ITS CHARMS, BUT I SURE AS HELL DON'T!

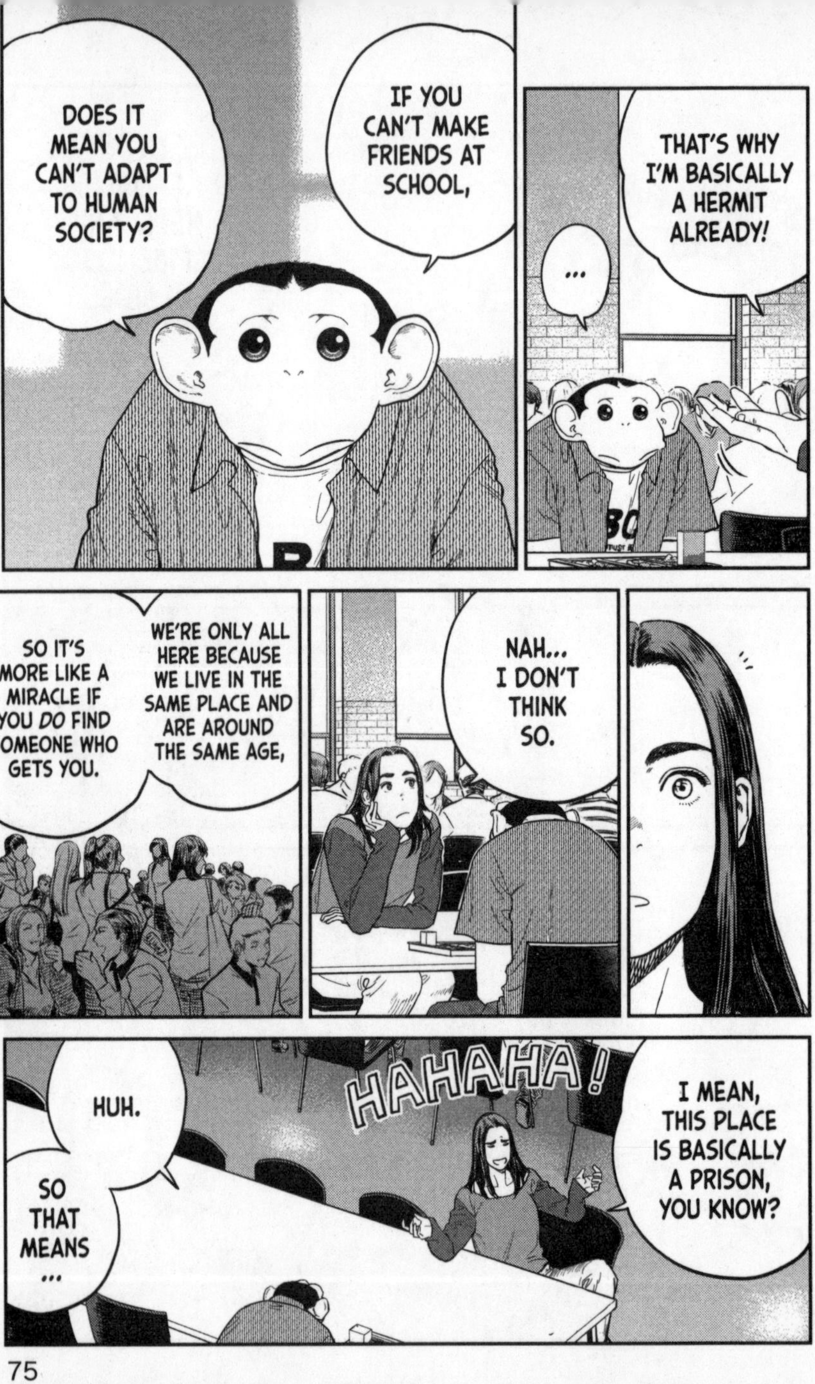
THAT'S WHY I'M BASICALLY A HERMIT ALREADY!
...
IF YOU CAN'T MAKE FRIENDS AT SCHOOL,
DOES IT MEAN YOU CAN'T ADAPT TO HUMAN SOCIETY?
NAH... I DON'T THINK SO.
WE'RE ONLY ALL HERE BECAUSE WE LIVE IN THE SAME PLACE AND ARE AROUND THE SAME AGE,
SO IT'S MORE LIKE A MIRACLE IF YOU *DO* FIND SOMEONE WHO GETS YOU.
I MEAN, THIS PLACE IS BASICALLY A PRISON, YOU KNOW?
HAHAHA!
HUH.
SO THAT MEANS ...

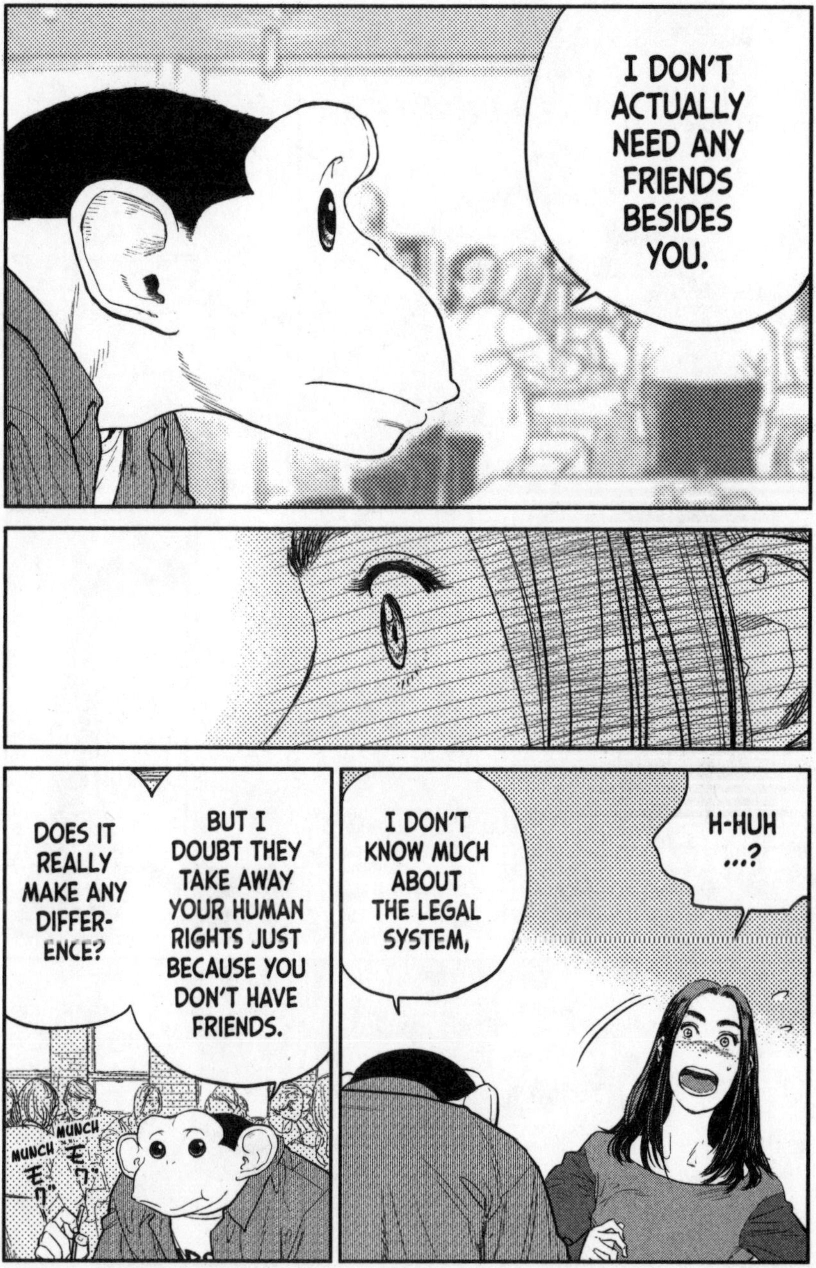
I DON'T ACTUALLY NEED ANY FRIENDS BESIDES YOU.
H-HUH ...?
I DON'T KNOW MUCH ABOUT THE LEGAL SYSTEM,
BUT I DOUBT THEY TAKE AWAY YOUR HUMAN RIGHTS JUST BECAUSE YOU DON'T HAVE FRIENDS.
DOES IT REALLY MAKE ANY DIFFER-ENCE?
MUNCH モグ
MUNCH モグ

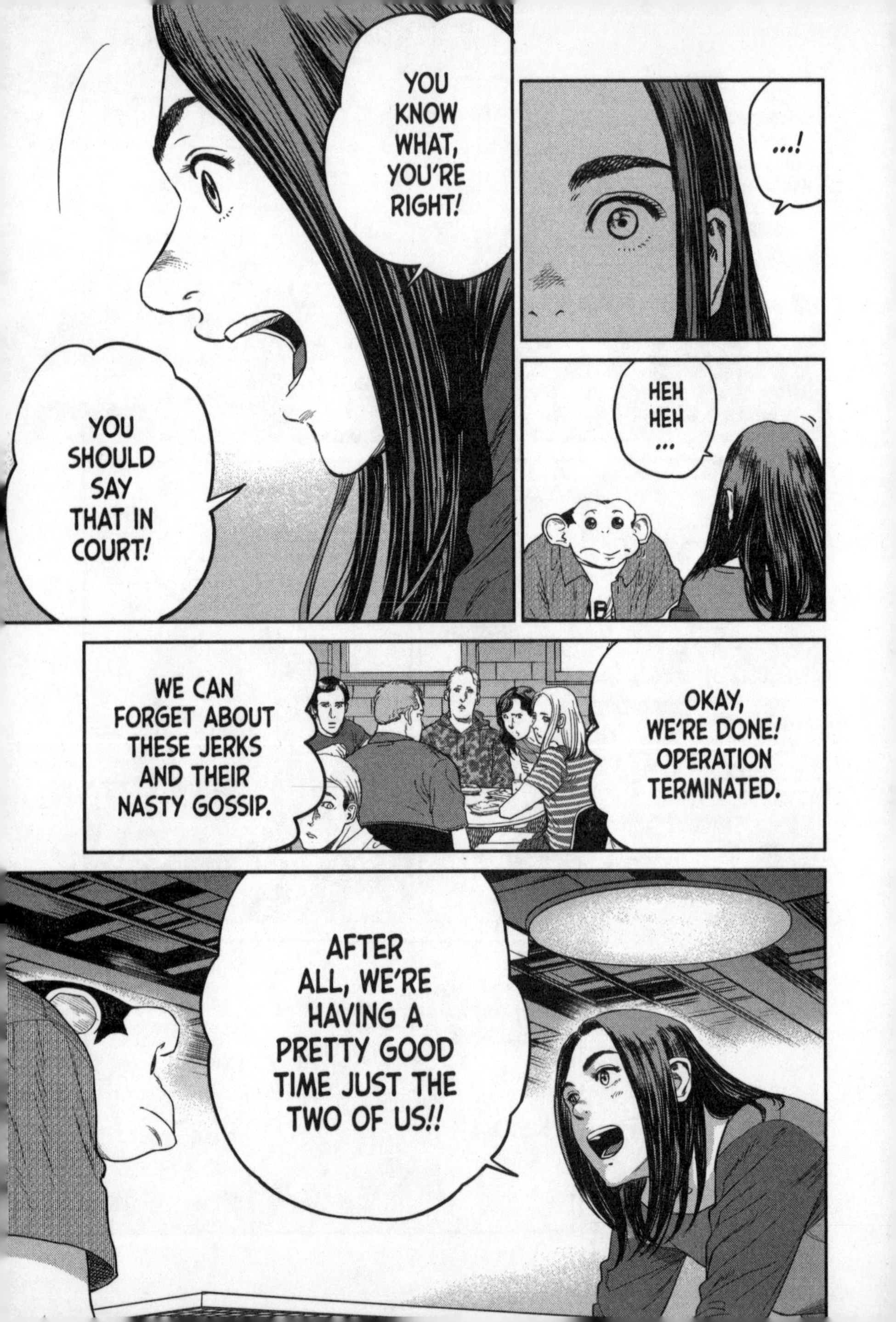
...!
HEH HEH ...
YOU KNOW WHAT, YOU'RE RIGHT!
YOU SHOULD SAY THAT IN COURT!
OKAY, WE'RE DONE! OPERATION TERMINATED.
WE CAN FORGET ABOUT THESE JERKS AND THEIR NASTY GOSSIP.
AFTER ALL, WE'RE HAVING A PRETTY GOOD TIME JUST THE TWO OF US!!

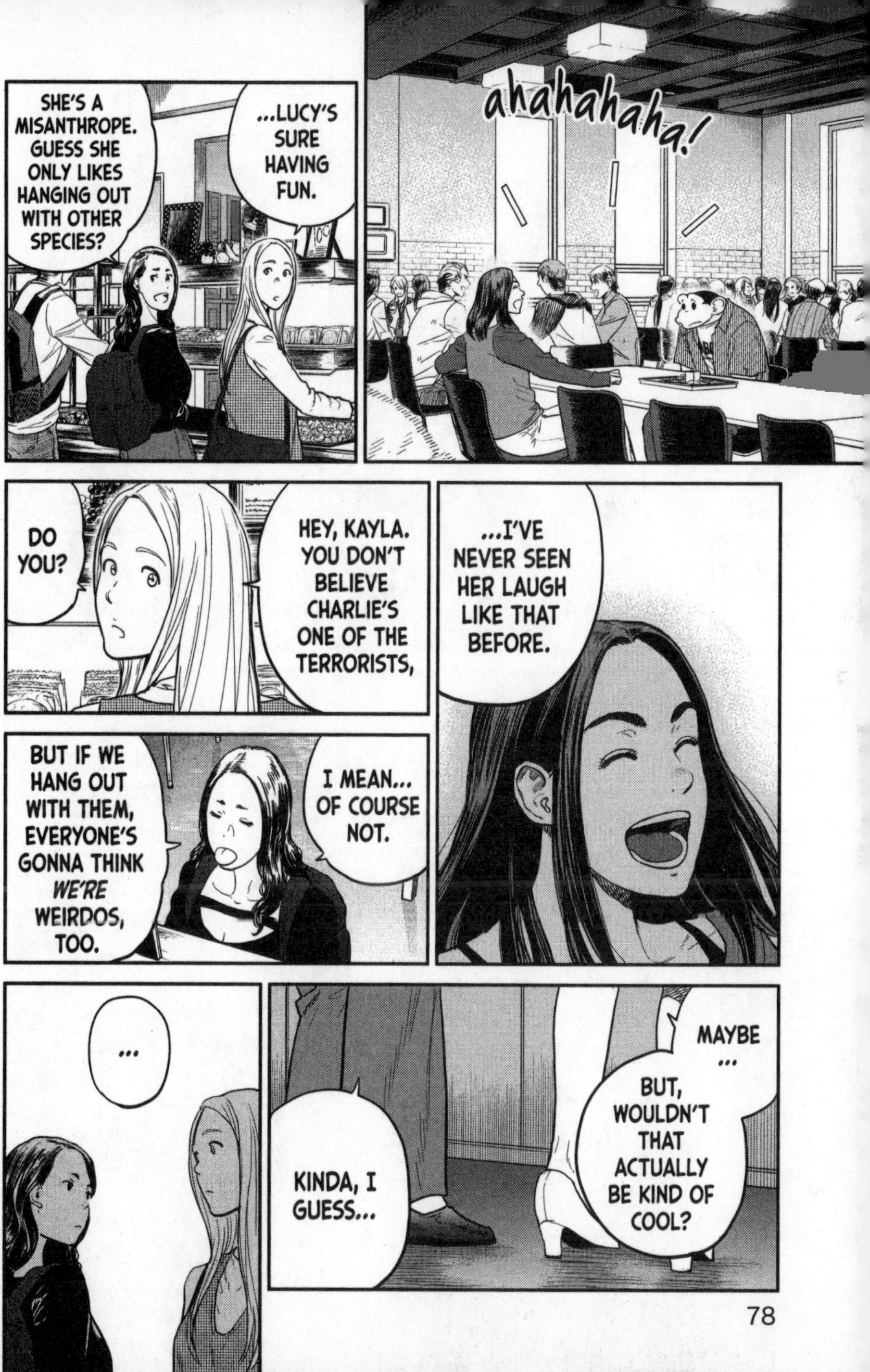
ahahahahaha!
...LUCY'S SURE HAVING FUN.
SHE'S A MISANTHROPE. GUESS SHE ONLY LIKES HANGING OUT WITH OTHER SPECIES?
...I'VE NEVER SEEN HER LAUGH LIKE THAT BEFORE.
HEY, KAYLA. YOU DON'T BELIEVE CHARLIE'S ONE OF THE TERRORISTS,
DO YOU?
I MEAN... OF COURSE NOT.
BUT IF WE HANG OUT WITH THEM, EVERYONE'S GONNA THINK *WE'RE* WEIRDOS, TOO.
MAYBE ...
BUT, WOULDN'T THAT ACTUALLY BE KIND OF COOL?
KINDA, I GUESS...
...

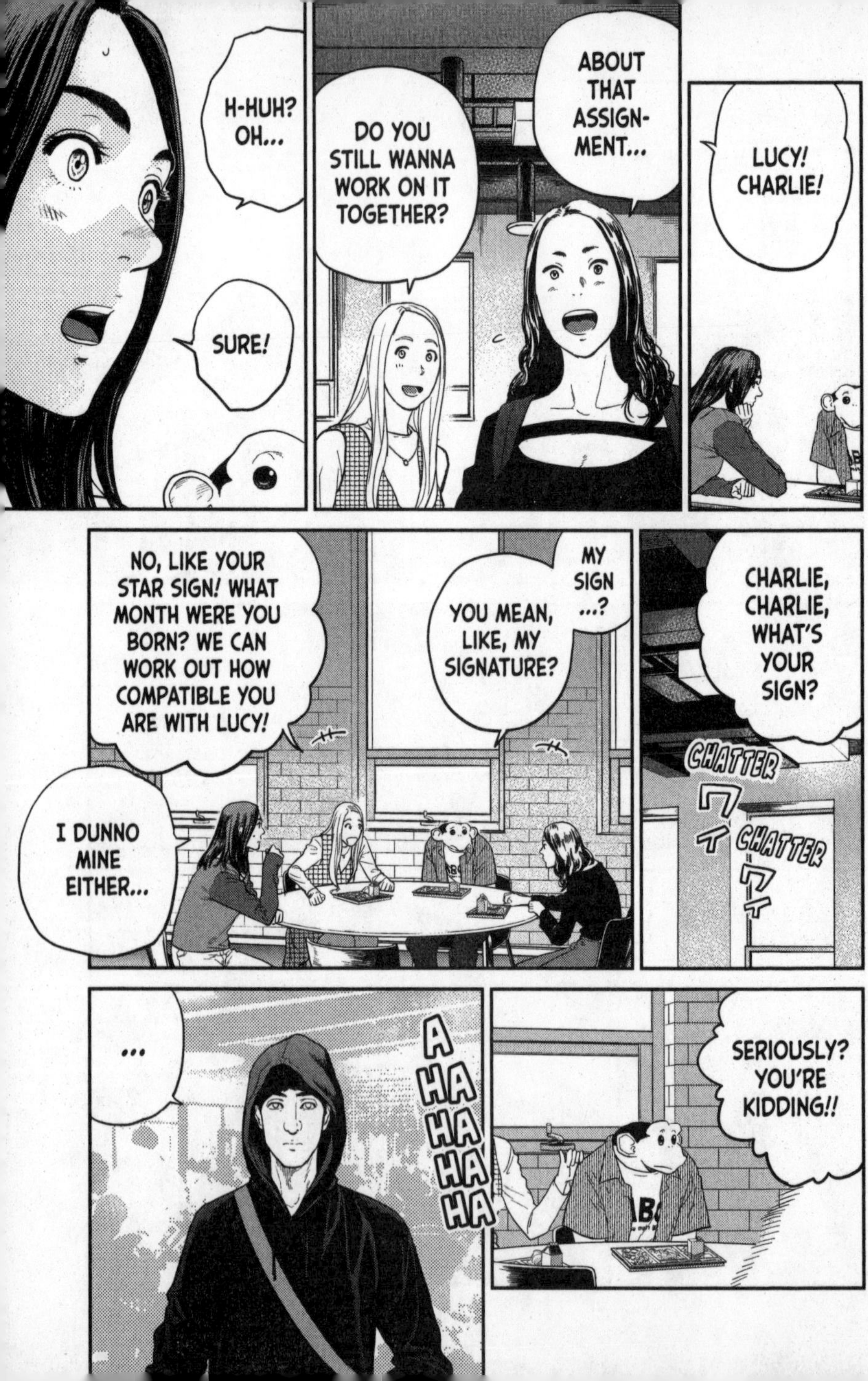
LUCY! CHARLIE!
ABOUT THAT ASSIGNMENT...
DO YOU STILL WANNA WORK ON IT TOGETHER?
H-HUH? OH...
SURE!
CHARLIE, CHARLIE, WHAT'S YOUR SIGN?
CHATTER
ワイ
CHATTER
ワイ
MY SIGN ...?
YOU MEAN, LIKE, MY SIGNATURE?
NO, LIKE YOUR STAR SIGN! WHAT MONTH WERE YOU BORN? WE CAN WORK OUT HOW COMPATIBLE YOU ARE WITH LUCY!
I DUNNO MINE EITHER...
SERIOUSLY? YOU'RE KIDDING!!
AHAHAHAHAHA
...

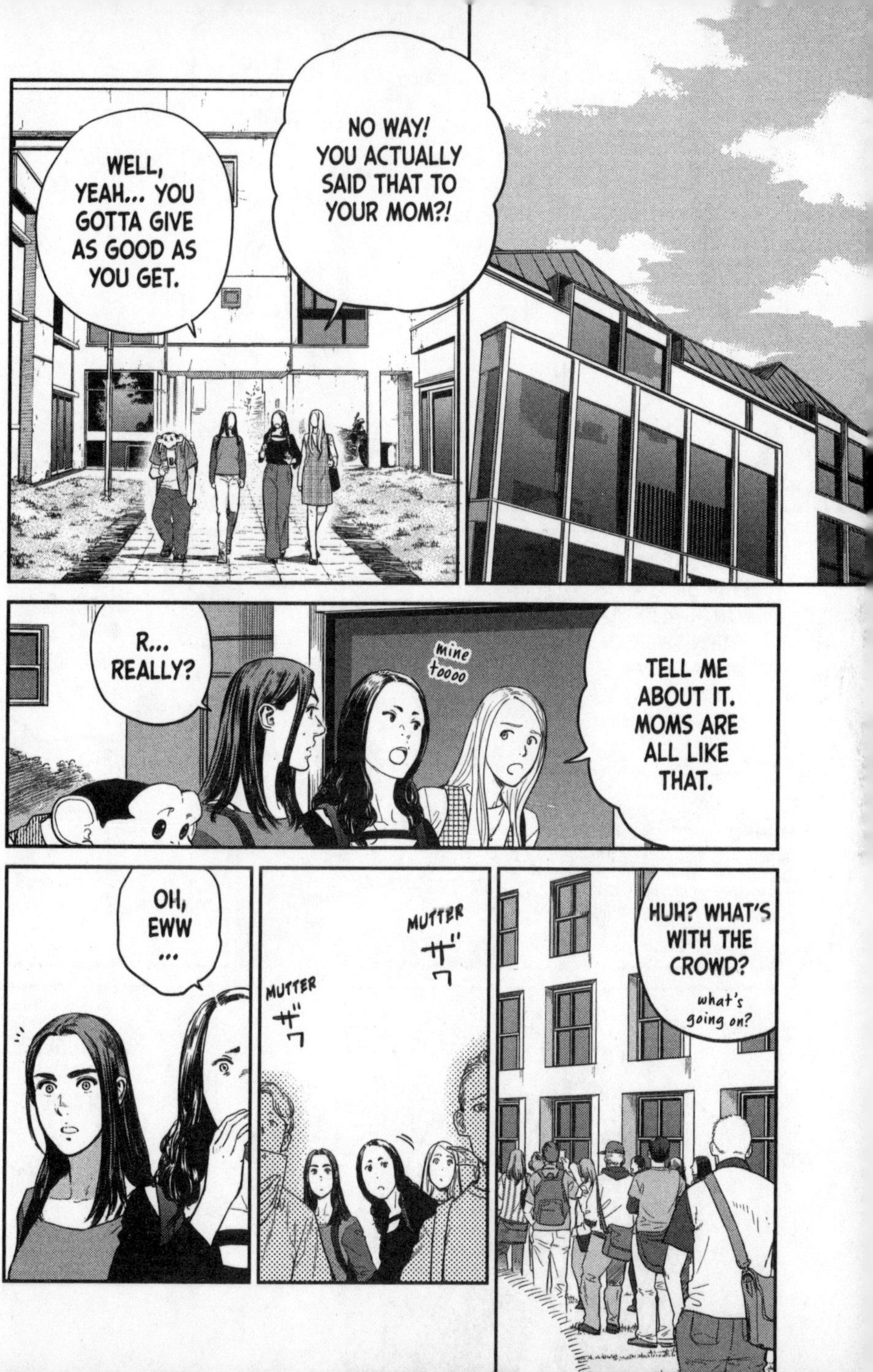
NO WAY! YOU ACTUALLY SAID THAT TO YOUR MOM?!
WELL, YEAH... YOU GOTTA GIVE AS GOOD AS YOU GET.
TELL ME ABOUT IT. MOMS ARE ALL LIKE THAT.
mine toooo
R... REALLY?
HUH? WHAT'S WITH THE CROWD?
what's going on?
MUTTER
ザワ
MUTTER
ザワ
OH, EWW ...

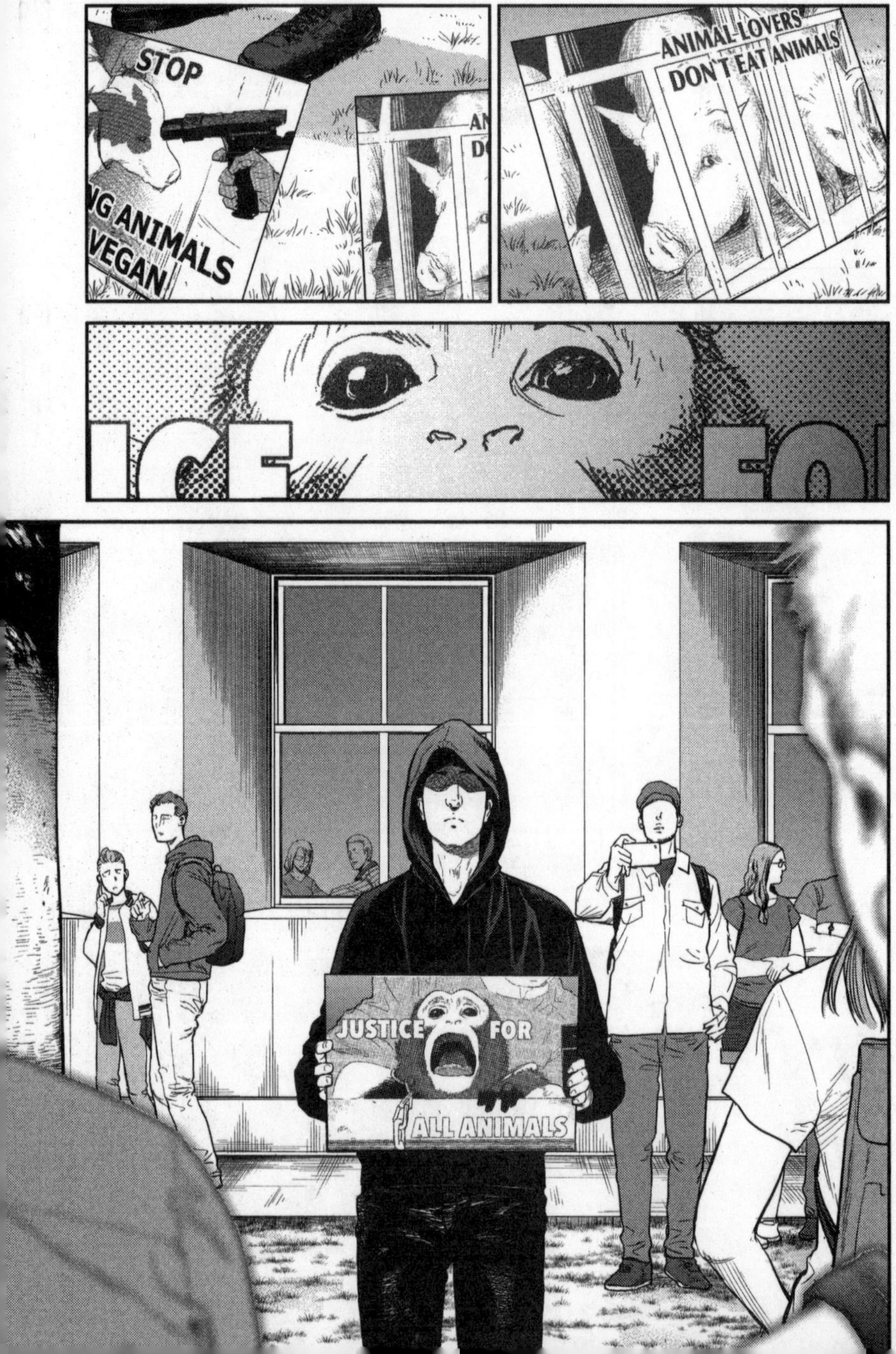
ANIMAL LOVERS DON'T EAT ANIMALS
STOP
NG ANIMALS
VEGAN
JUSTICE FOR
ALL ANIMALS

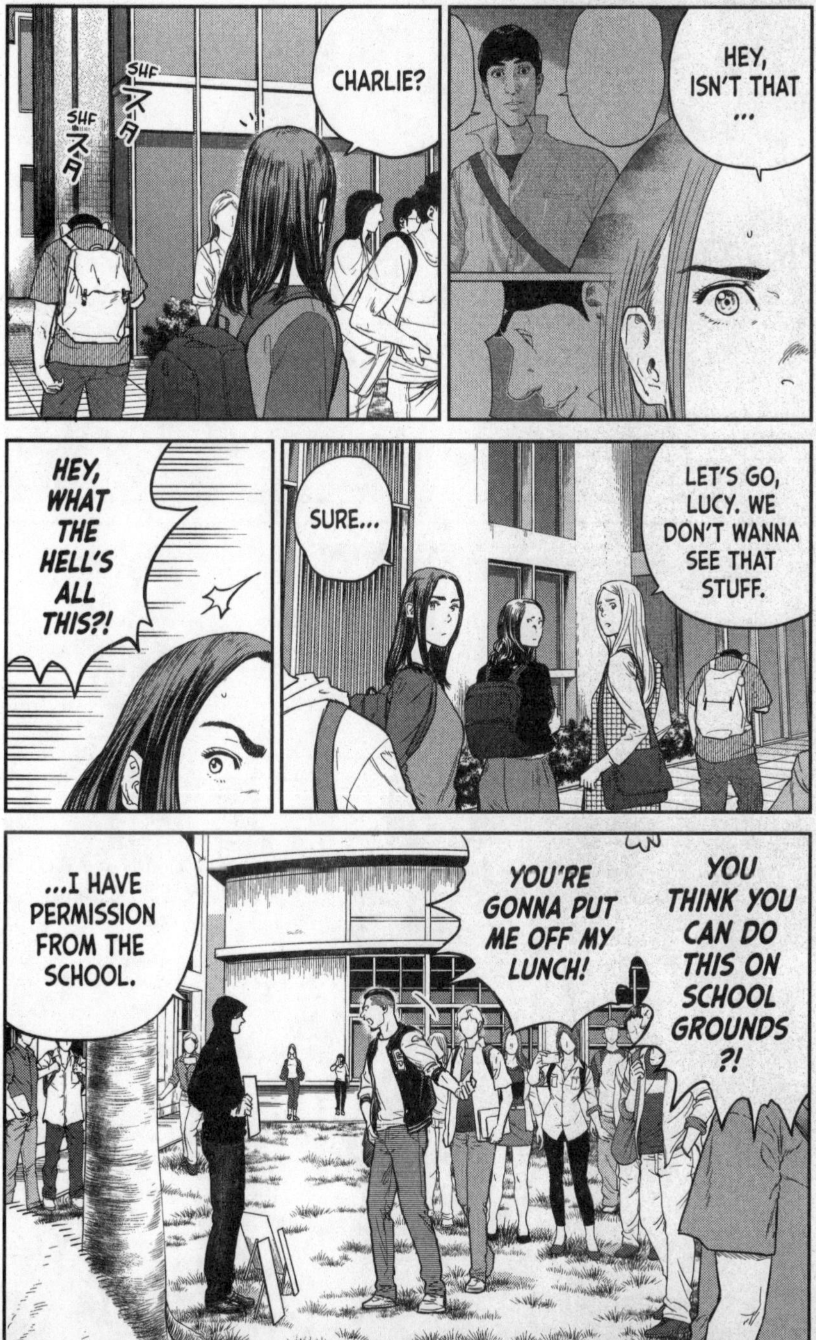

HEY, ISN'T THAT ...
CHARLIE?
SHF スタ
SHF スタ
LET'S GO, LUCY. WE DON'T WANNA SEE THAT STUFF.
SURE...
HEY, WHAT THE HELL'S ALL THIS?!
YOU THINK YOU CAN DO THIS ON SCHOOL GROUNDS?!
YOU'RE GONNA PUT ME OFF MY LUNCH!
...I HAVE PERMISSION FROM THE SCHOOL.

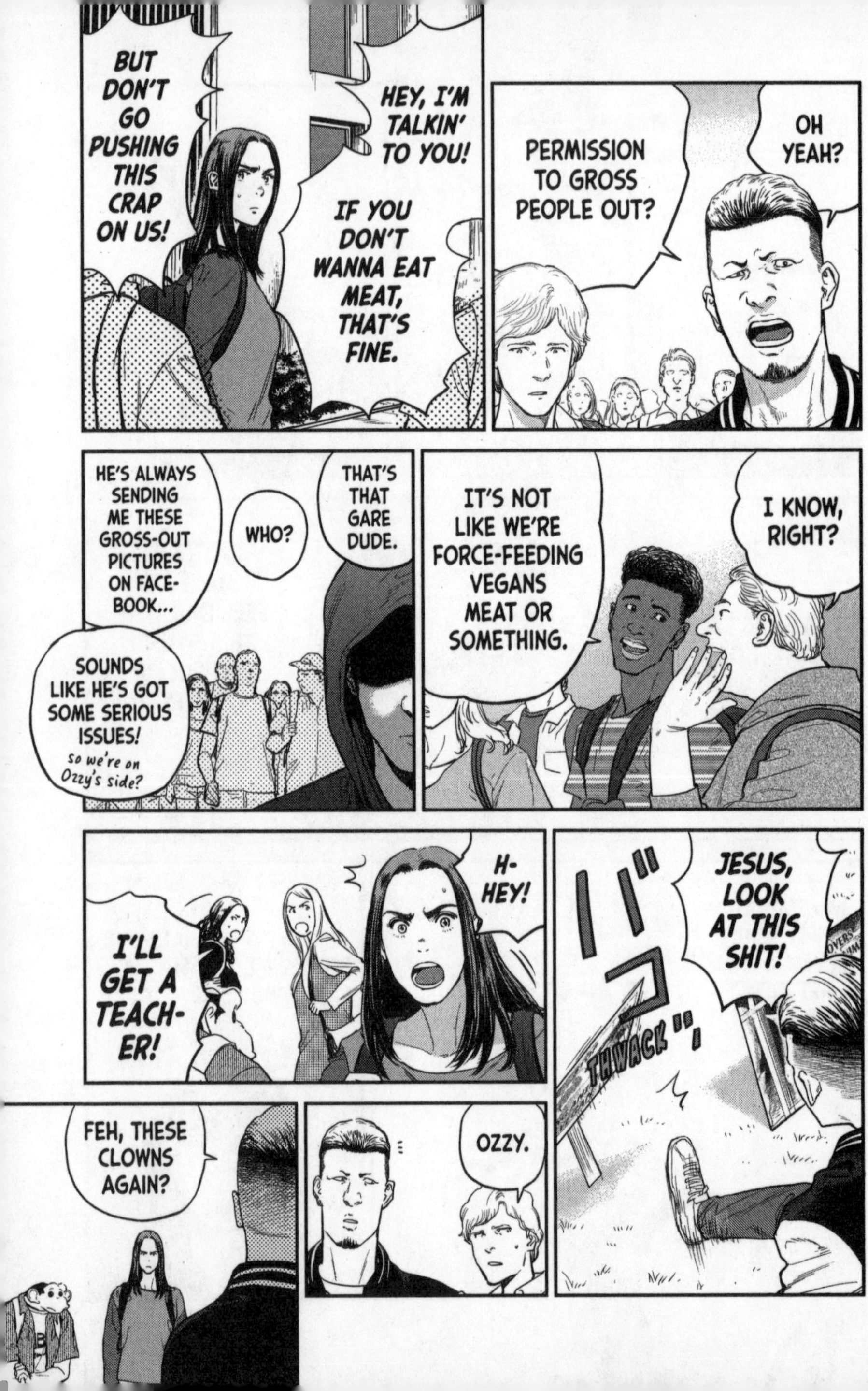
OH YEAH?
PERMISSION TO GROSS PEOPLE OUT?
HEY, I'M TALKIN' TO YOU!
IF YOU DON'T WANNA EAT MEAT, THAT'S FINE.
BUT DON'T GO PUSHING THIS CRAP ON US!
I KNOW, RIGHT?
IT'S NOT LIKE WE'RE FORCE-FEEDING VEGANS MEAT OR SOMETHING.
THAT'S THAT GARE DUDE.
WHO?
HE'S ALWAYS SENDING ME THESE GROSS-OUT PICTURES ON FACE-BOOK...
SOUNDS LIKE HE'S GOT SOME SERIOUS ISSUES!
so we're on Ozzy's side?
JESUS, LOOK AT THIS SHIT!
THWACK
H-HEY!
I'LL GET A TEACH-ER!
OZZY.
FEH, THESE CLOWNS AGAIN?

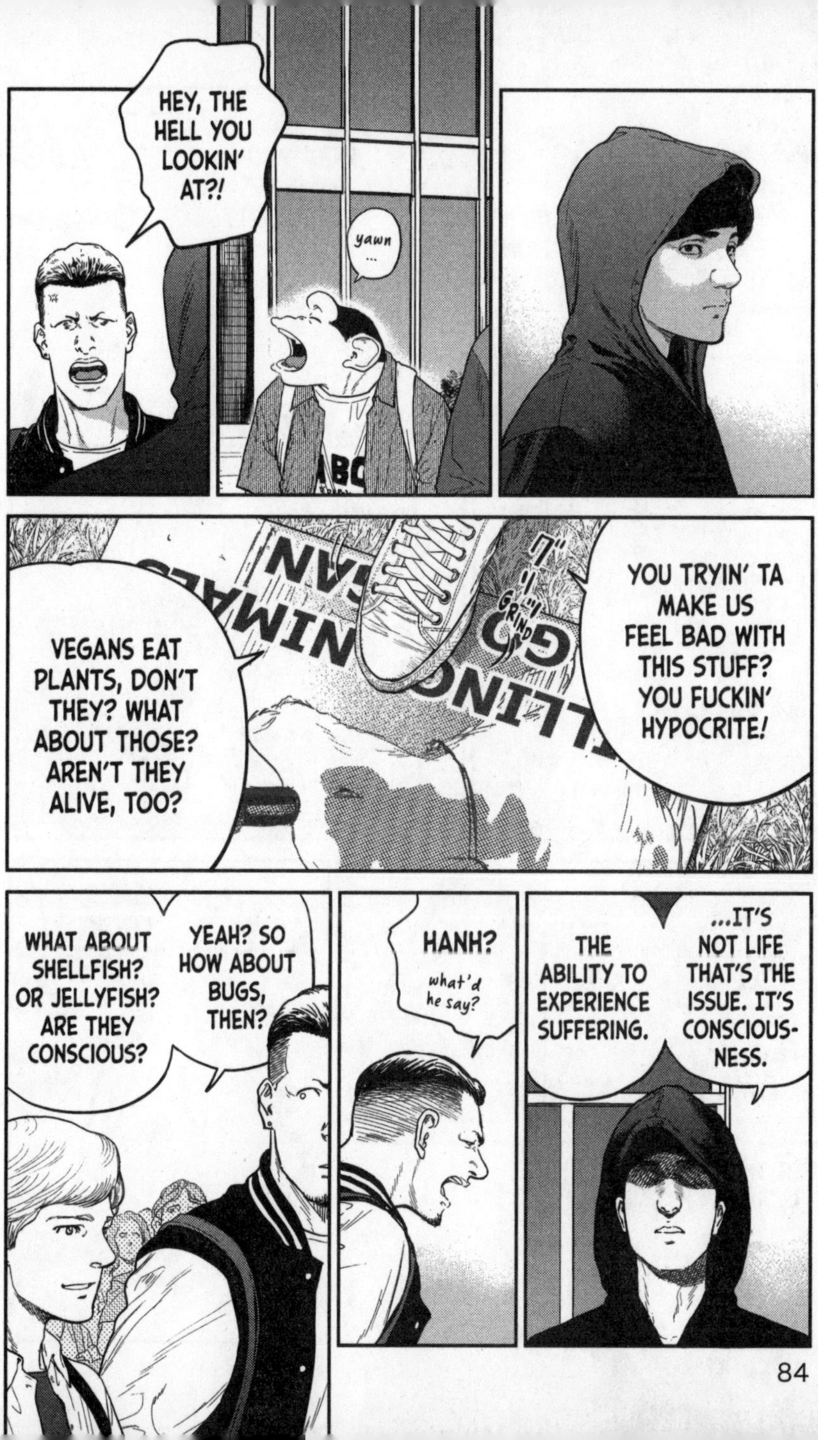
yawn ...
HEY, THE HELL YOU LOOKIN' AT?!
YOU TRYIN' TA MAKE US FEEL BAD WITH THIS STUFF? YOU FUCKIN' HYPOCRITE!
GRIND
VEGANS EAT PLANTS, DON'T THEY? WHAT ABOUT THOSE? AREN'T THEY ALIVE, TOO?
...IT'S NOT LIFE THAT'S THE ISSUE. IT'S CONSCIOUS-NESS.
THE ABILITY TO EXPERIENCE SUFFERING.
HANH?
what'd he say?
YEAH? SO HOW ABOUT BUGS, THEN?
WHAT ABOUT SHELLFISH? OR JELLYFISH? ARE THEY CONSCIOUS?

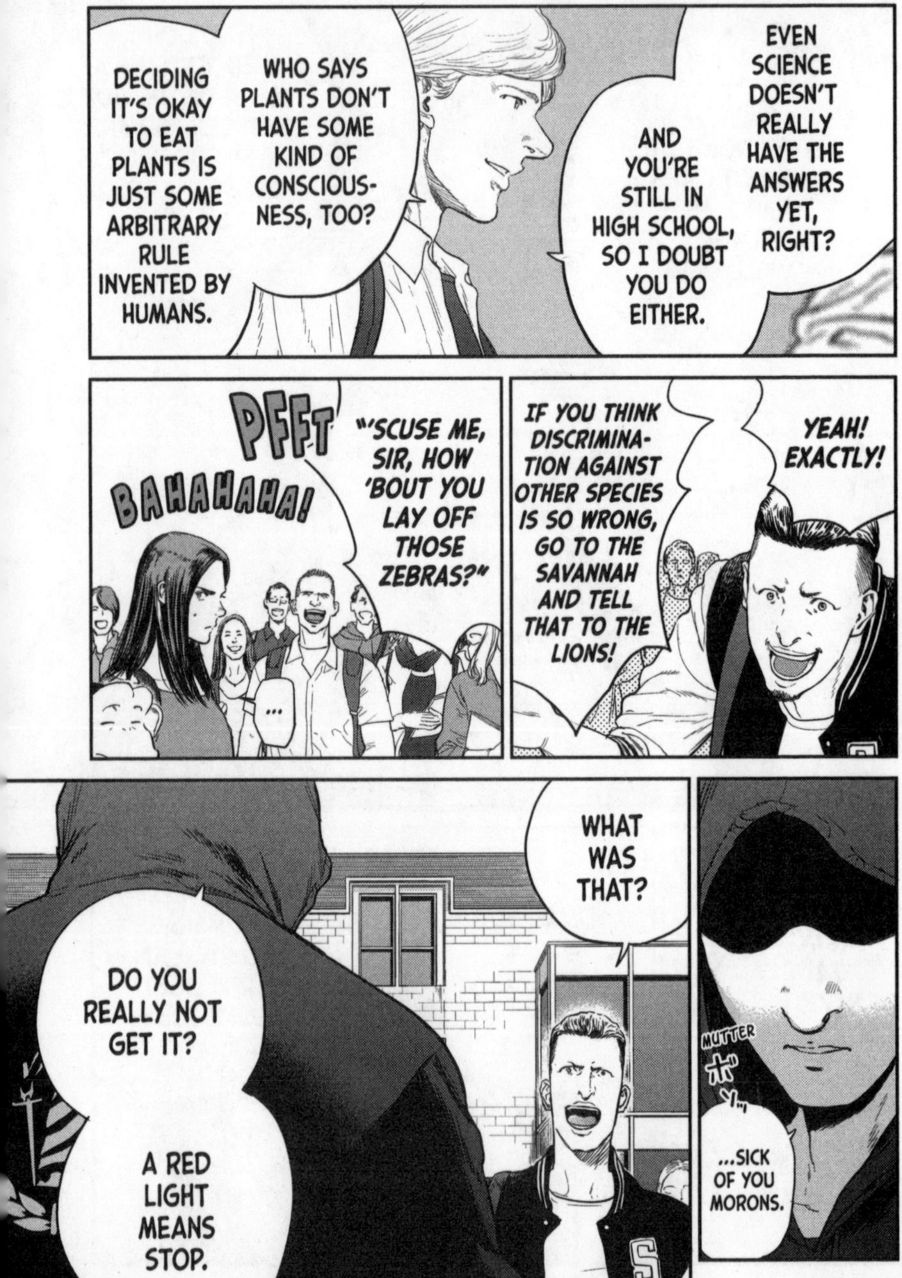
EVEN SCIENCE DOESN'T REALLY HAVE THE ANSWERS YET, RIGHT?
AND YOU'RE STILL IN HIGH SCHOOL, SO I DOUBT YOU DO EITHER.
WHO SAYS PLANTS DON'T HAVE SOME KIND OF CONSCIOUS-NESS, TOO?
DECIDING IT'S OKAY TO EAT PLANTS IS JUST SOME ARBITRARY RULE INVENTED BY HUMANS.
YEAH! EXACTLY!
IF YOU THINK DISCRIMINA-TION AGAINST OTHER SPECIES IS SO WRONG, GO TO THE SAVANNAH AND TELL THAT TO THE LIONS!
"'SCUSE ME, SIR, HOW 'BOUT YOU LAY OFF THOSE ZEBRAS?"
PFFT
BAHAHAHA!
...
MUTTER
...SICK OF YOU MORONS.
WHAT WAS THAT?
DO YOU REALLY NOT GET IT?
A RED LIGHT MEANS STOP.

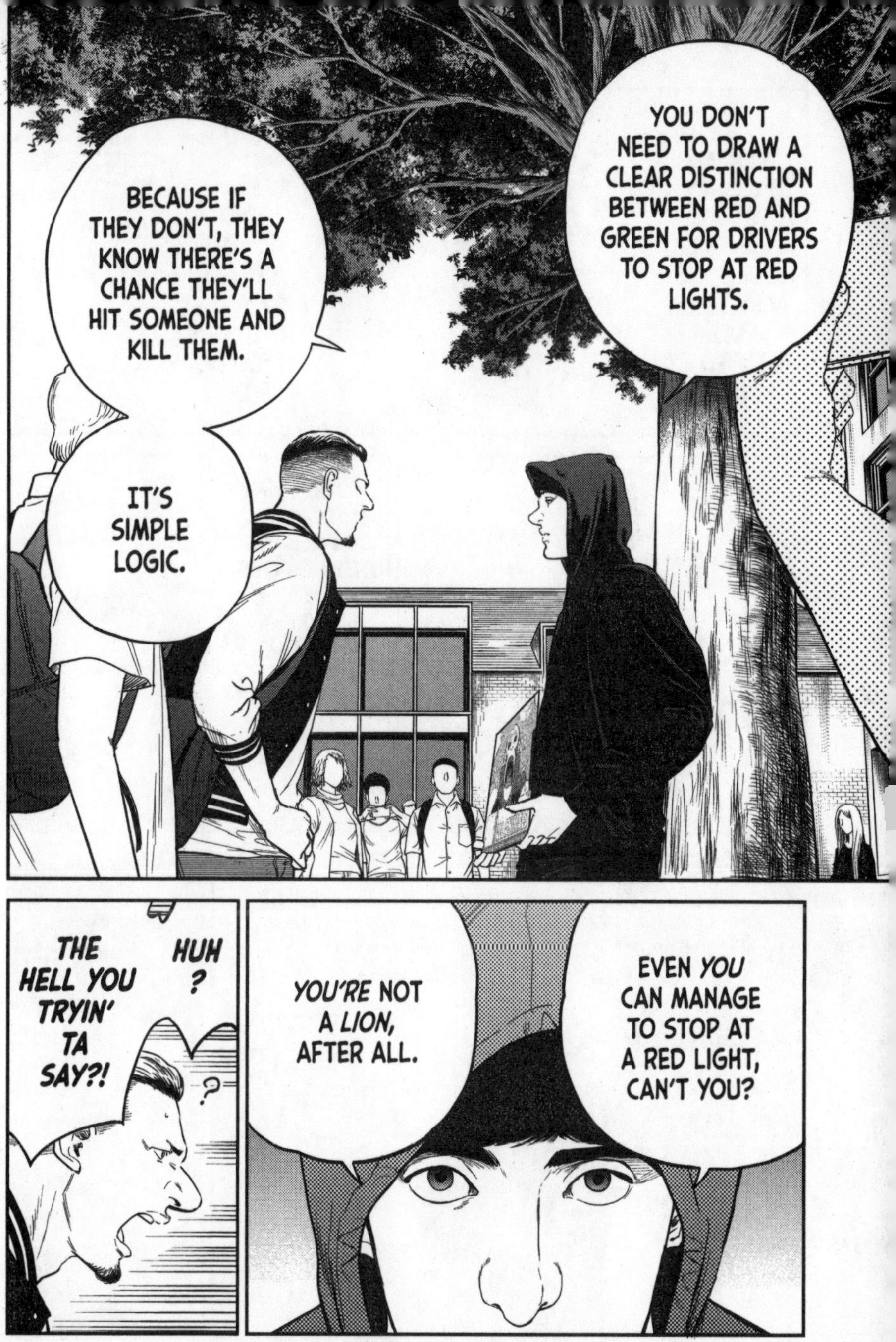
YOU DON'T NEED TO DRAW A CLEAR DISTINCTION BETWEEN RED AND GREEN FOR DRIVERS TO STOP AT RED LIGHTS.
BECAUSE IF THEY DON'T, THEY KNOW THERE'S A CHANCE THEY'LL HIT SOMEONE AND KILL THEM.
IT'S SIMPLE LOGIC.
EVEN *YOU* CAN MANAGE TO STOP AT A RED LIGHT, CAN'T YOU?
YOU'RE NOT A *LION*, AFTER ALL.
HUH?
THE HELL YOU TRYIN' TA SAY?!
?

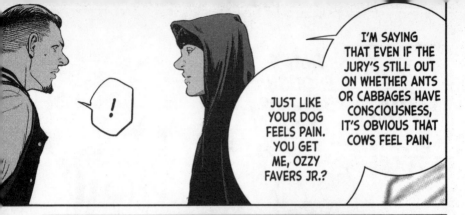

I'M SAYING THAT EVEN IF THE JURY'S STILL OUT ON WHETHER ANTS OR CABBAGES HAVE CONSCIOUSNESS, IT'S OBVIOUS THAT COWS FEEL PAIN.
JUST LIKE YOUR DOG FEELS PAIN. YOU GET ME, OZZY FAVERS JR.?
!
SURELY YOU DON'T THINK
YOUR PRECIOUS PUP WOULDN'T SUFFER IF HE WAS STRUNG UP OR CHOPPED TO BITS?
TWITCH
YANK
!
GRAB

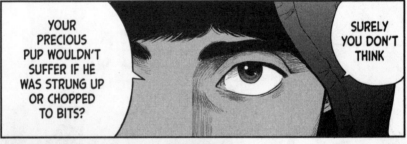

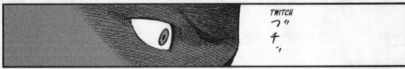

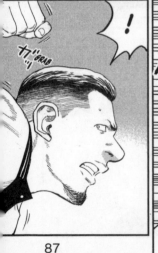

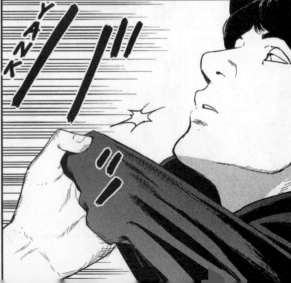

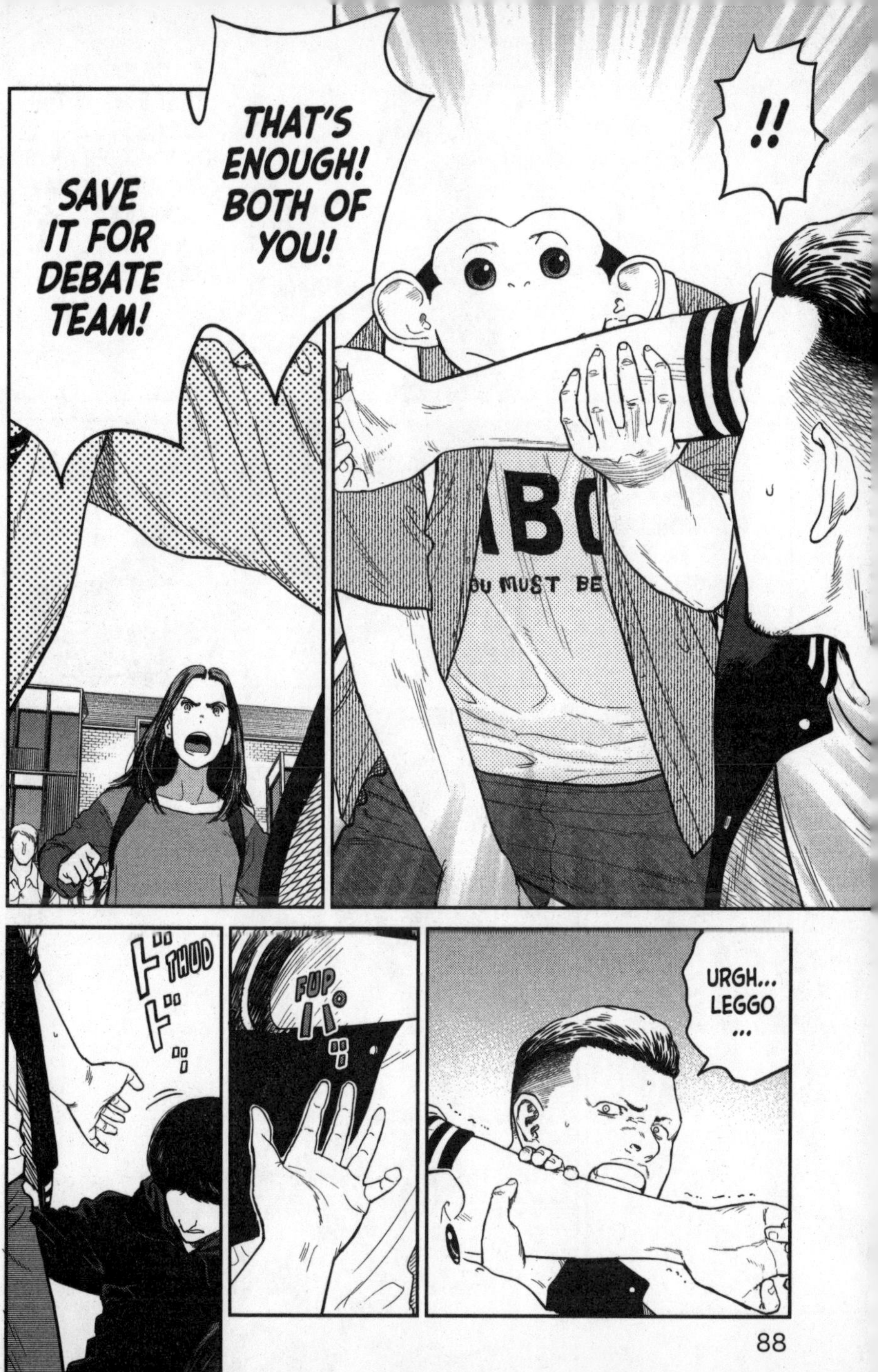
!!
THAT'S ENOUGH! BOTH OF YOU!
SAVE IT FOR DEBATE TEAM!
URGH... LEGGO ...
FUP
THUD

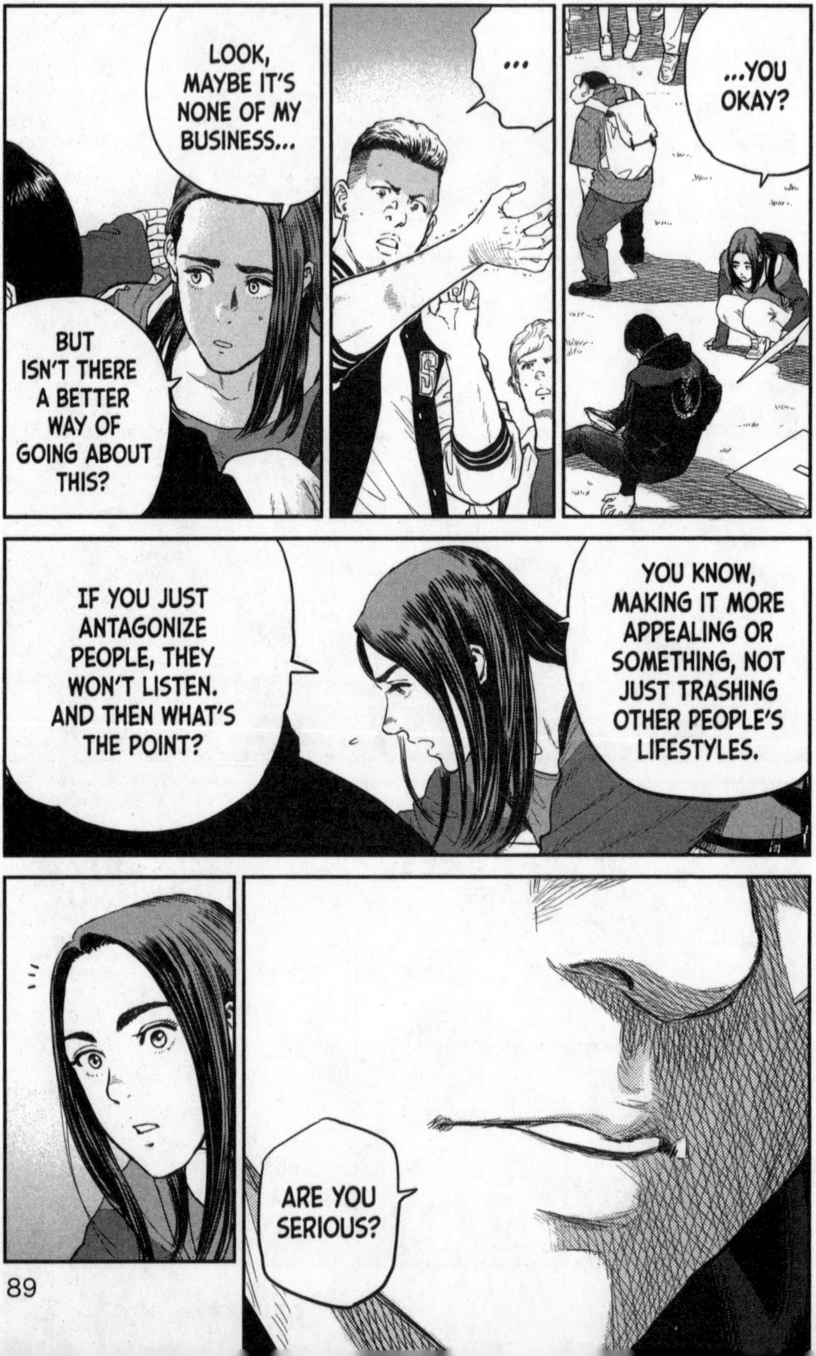
...YOU OKAY?
...
LOOK, MAYBE IT'S NONE OF MY BUSINESS...
BUT ISN'T THERE A BETTER WAY OF GOING ABOUT THIS?
YOU KNOW, MAKING IT MORE APPEALING OR SOMETHING, NOT JUST TRASHING OTHER PEOPLE'S LIFESTYLES.
IF YOU JUST ANTAGONIZE PEOPLE, THEY WON'T LISTEN. AND THEN WHAT'S THE POINT?
ARE YOU SERIOUS?

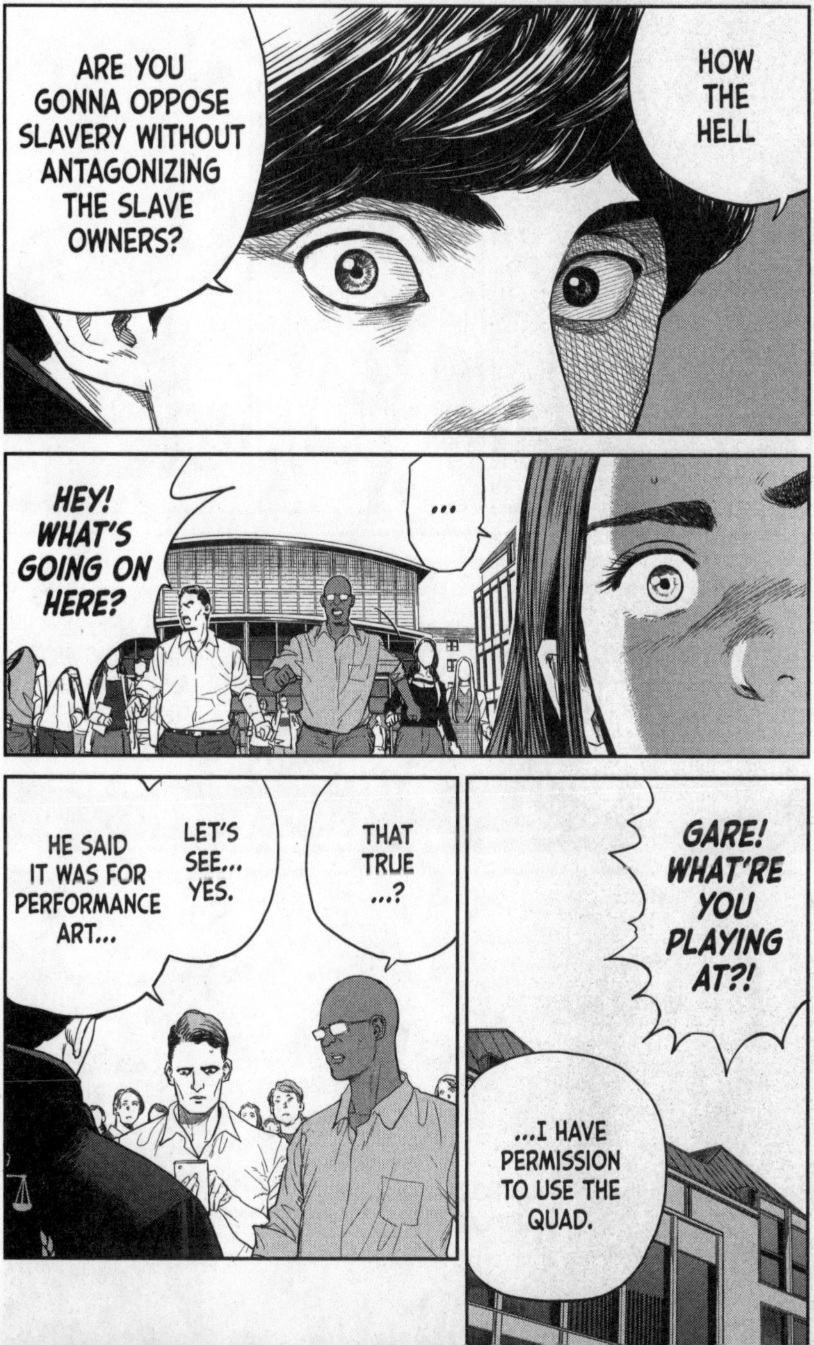
HOW THE HELL
ARE YOU GONNA OPPOSE SLAVERY WITHOUT ANTAGONIZING THE SLAVE OWNERS?
...
HEY! WHAT'S GOING ON HERE?
GARE! WHAT'RE YOU PLAYING AT?!
...I HAVE PERMISSION TO USE THE QUAD.
THAT TRUE ...?
LET'S SEE... YES.
HE SAID IT WAS FOR PERFORMANCE ART...

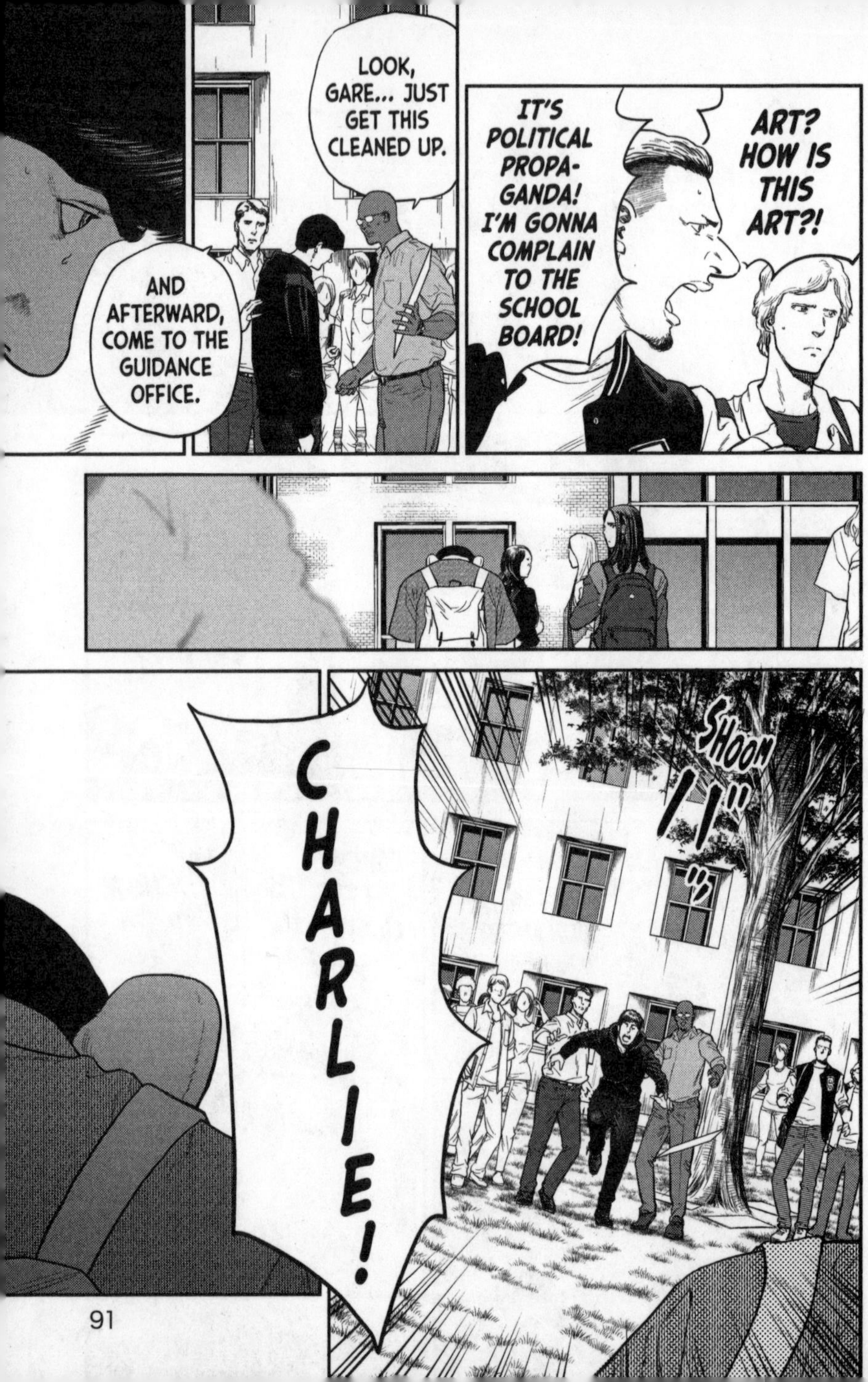
ART? HOW IS THIS ART?!
IT'S POLITICAL PROPAGANDA! I'M GONNA COMPLAIN TO THE SCHOOL BOARD!
LOOK, GARE... JUST GET THIS CLEANED UP.
AND AFTERWARD, COME TO THE GUIDANCE OFFICE.
SHOOM
CHARLIE!

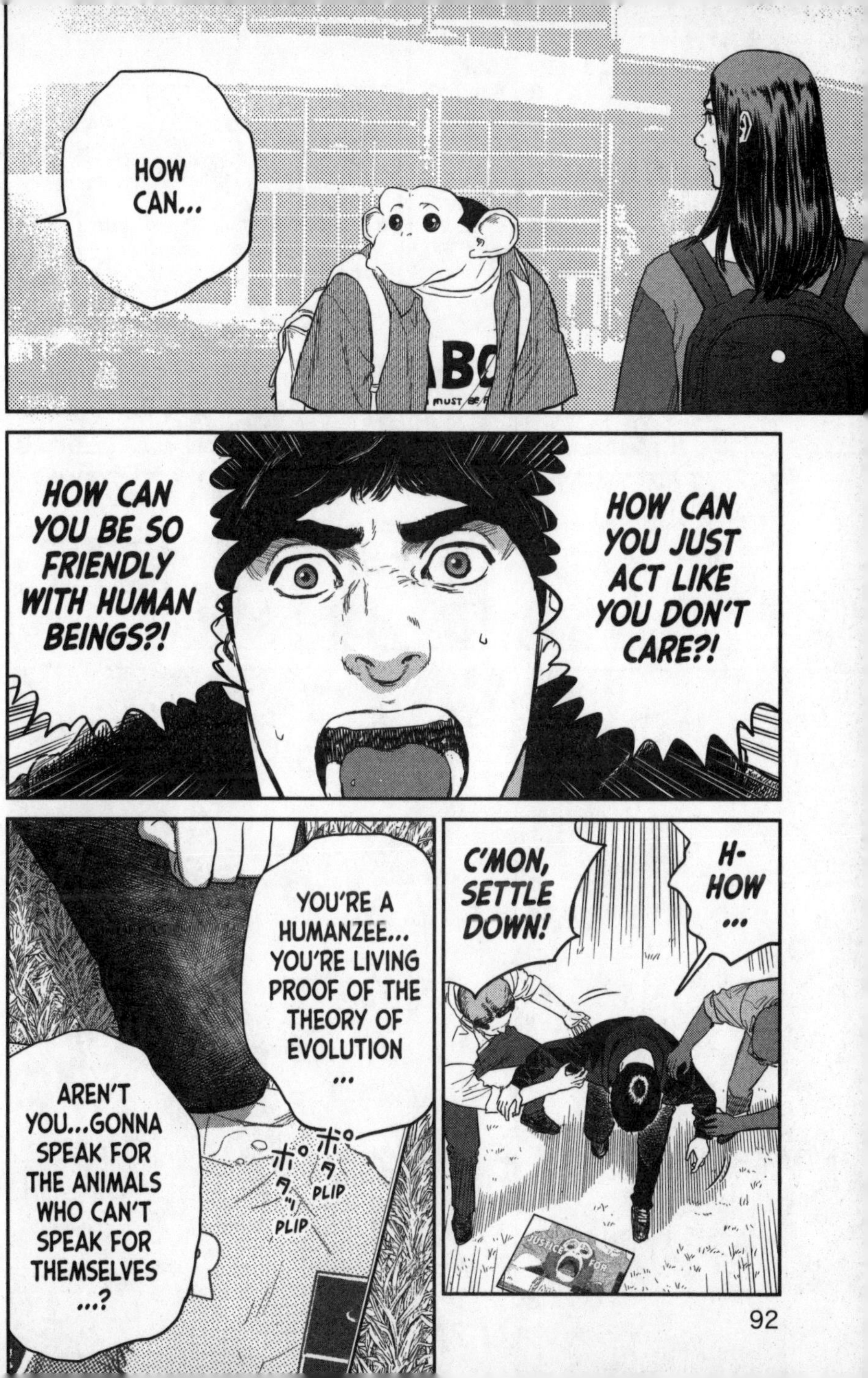
HOW CAN...
HOW CAN YOU JUST ACT LIKE YOU DON'T CARE?!
HOW CAN YOU BE SO FRIENDLY WITH HUMAN BEINGS?!
H- HOW ...
C'MON, SETTLE DOWN!
JUSTICE FOR
YOU'RE A HUMANZEE... YOU'RE LIVING PROOF OF THE THEORY OF EVOLUTION ...
ポタ PLIP
ポタッ PLIP
AREN'T YOU...GONNA SPEAK FOR THE ANIMALS WHO CAN'T SPEAK FOR THEMSELVES ...?

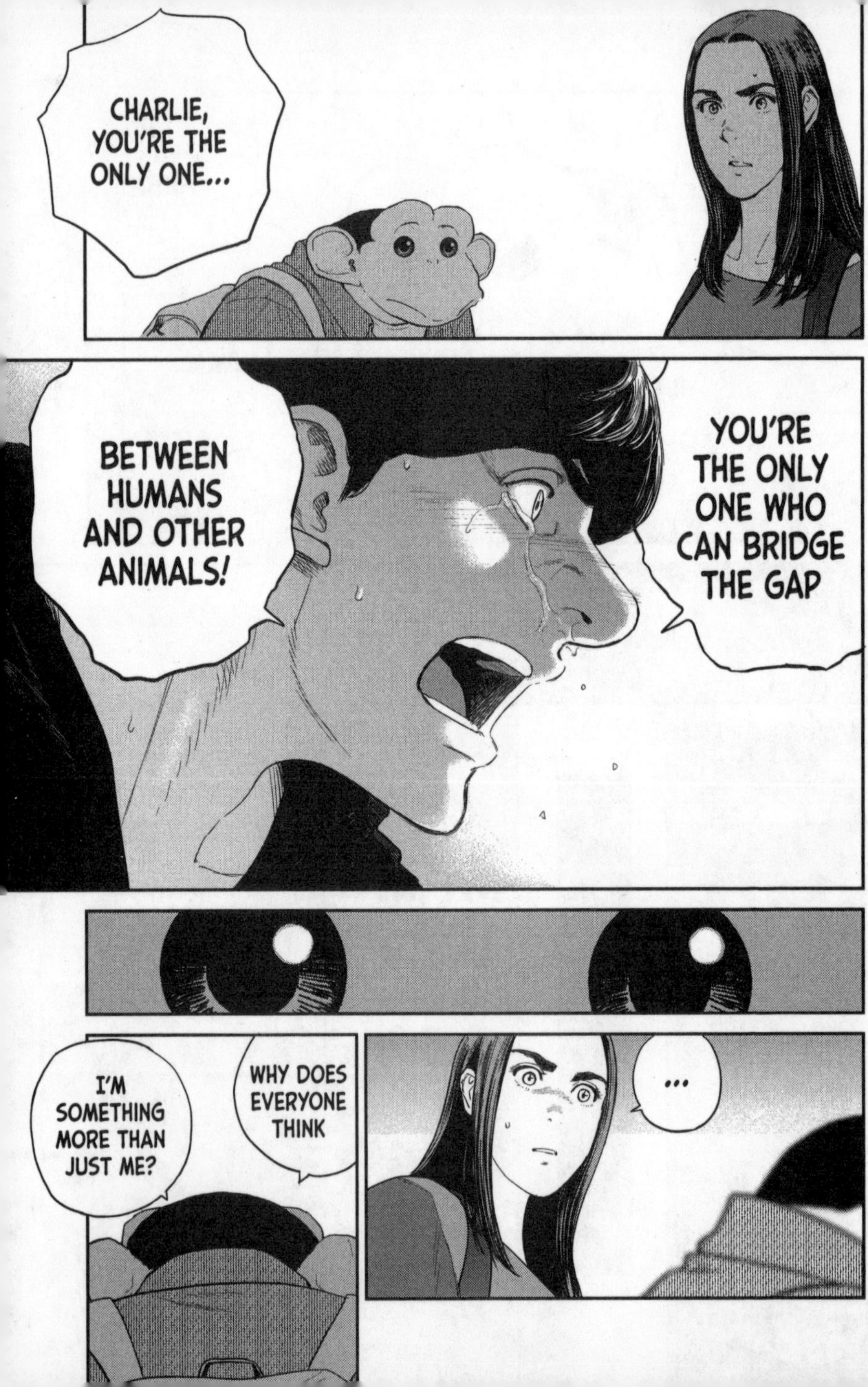
CHARLIE, YOU'RE THE ONLY ONE...
YOU'RE THE ONLY ONE WHO CAN BRIDGE THE GAP
BETWEEN HUMANS AND OTHER ANIMALS!
...
WHY DOES EVERYONE THINK
I'M SOMETHING MORE THAN JUST ME?

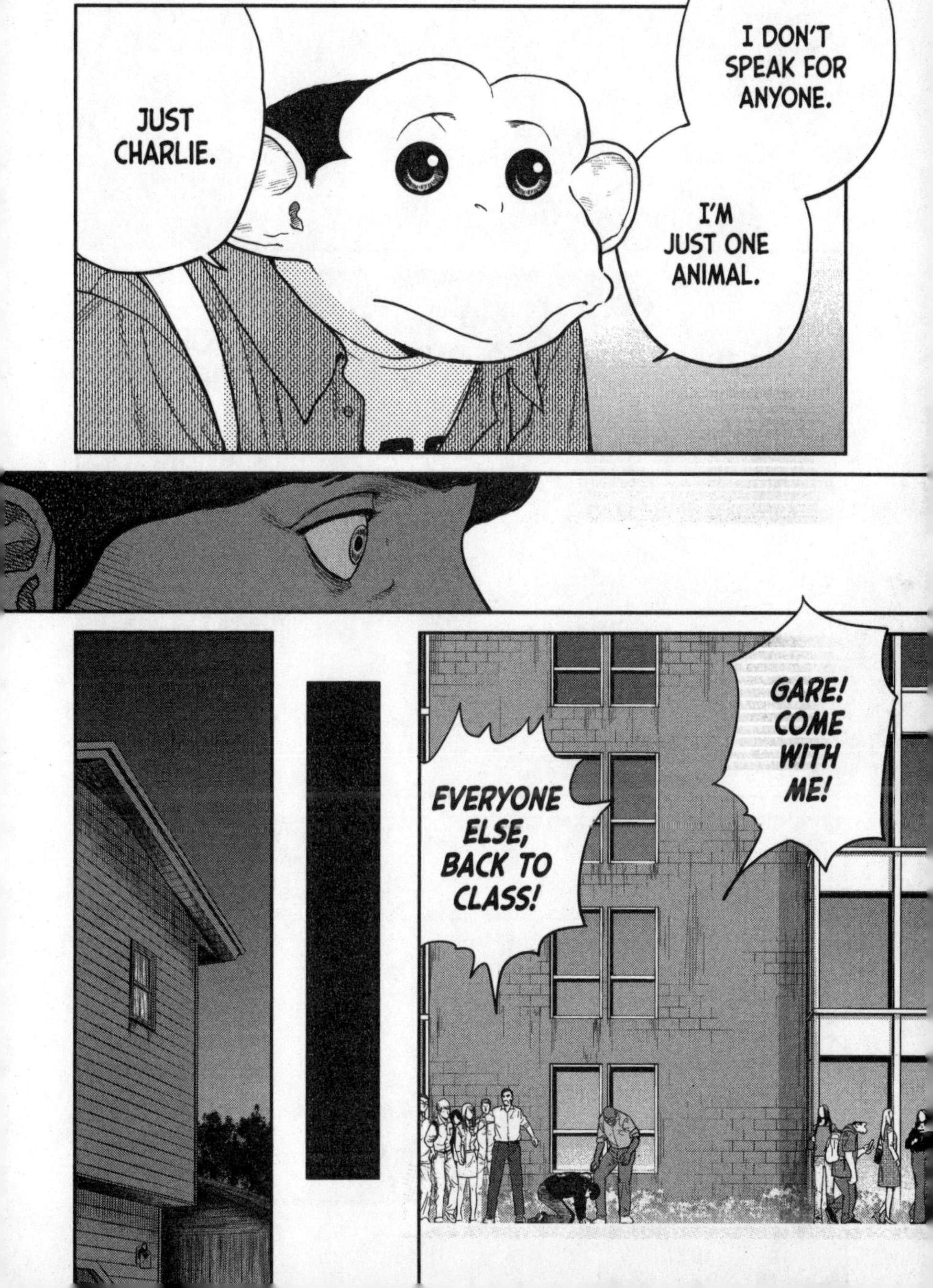
I DON'T SPEAK FOR ANYONE.
I'M JUST ONE ANIMAL.
JUST CHARLIE.
GARE! COME WITH ME!
EVERYONE ELSE, BACK TO CLASS!

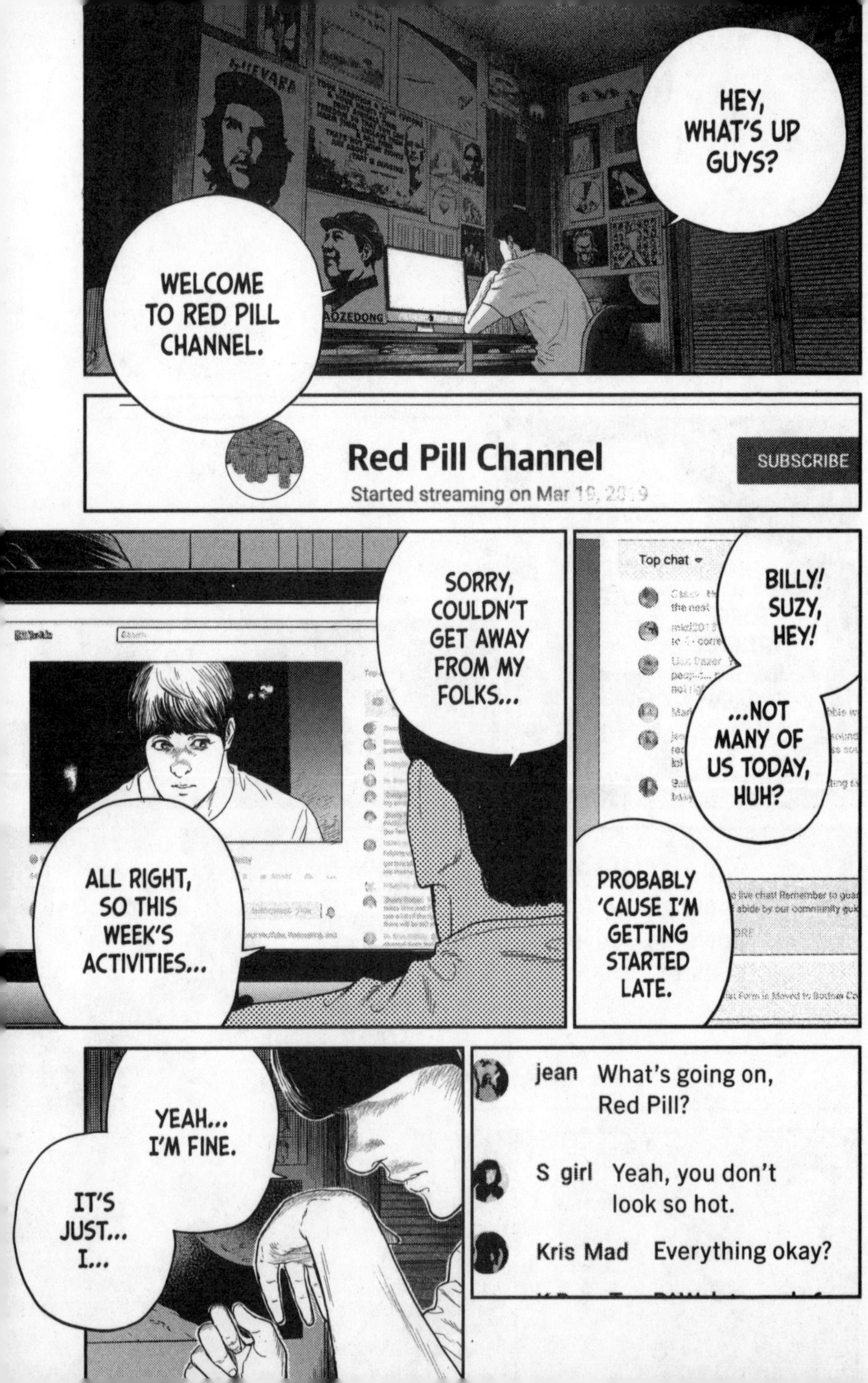
HEY, WHAT'S UP GUYS?
WELCOME TO RED PILL CHANNEL.
Red Pill Channel
SUBSCRIBE
Started streaming on Mar 19, 2019
Top chat
BILLY! SUZY, HEY!
...NOT MANY OF US TODAY, HUH?
PROBABLY 'CAUSE I'M GETTING STARTED LATE.
SORRY, COULDN'T GET AWAY FROM MY FOLKS...
ALL RIGHT, SO THIS WEEK'S ACTIVITIES...
jean What's going on, Red Pill?
S girl Yeah, you don't look so hot.
Kris Mad Everything okay?
YEAH... I'M FINE.
IT'S JUST... I...

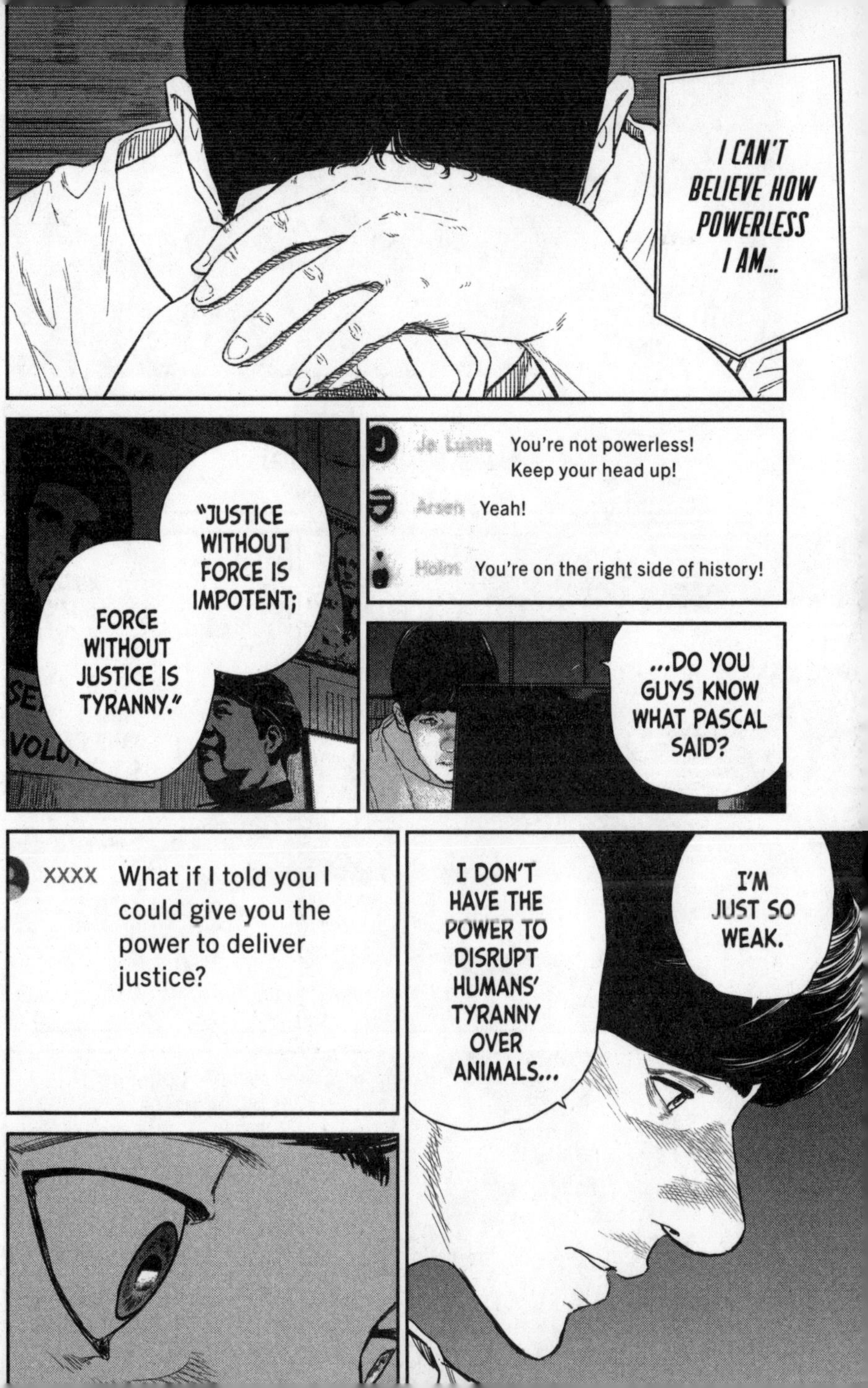
I CAN'T BELIEVE HOW POWERLESS I AM...
You're not powerless! Keep your head up!
Yeah!
You're on the right side of history!
...DO YOU GUYS KNOW WHAT PASCAL SAID?
"JUSTICE WITHOUT FORCE IS IMPOTENT;
FORCE WITHOUT JUSTICE IS TYRANNY."
I'M JUST SO WEAK.
I DON'T HAVE THE POWER TO DISRUPT HUMANS' TYRANNY OVER ANIMALS...
XXXX What if I told you I could give you the power to deliver justice?

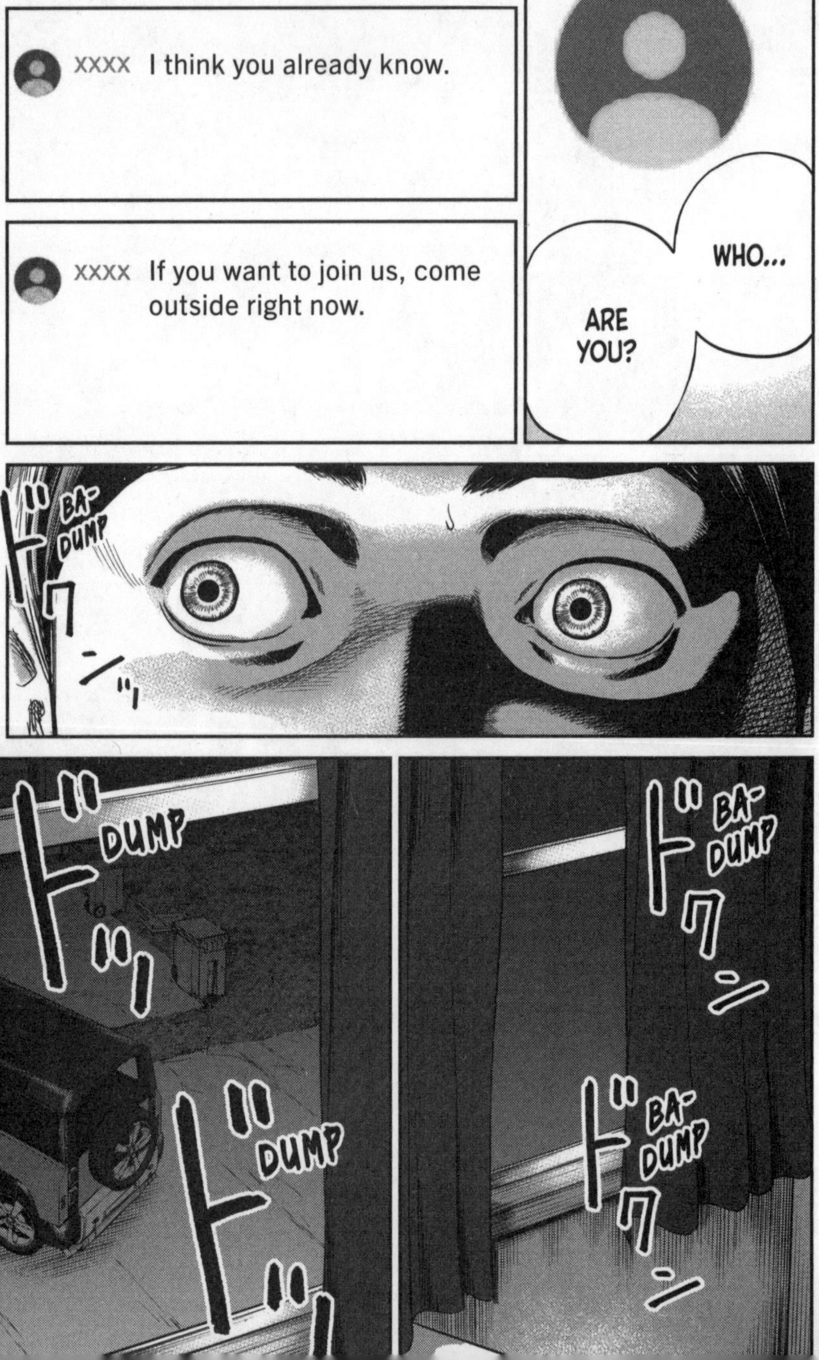
WHO... ARE YOU?
XXXX I think you already know.
XXXX If you want to join us, come outside right now.
BA-DUMP
BA-DUMP
BA-DUMP
DUMP
DUMP

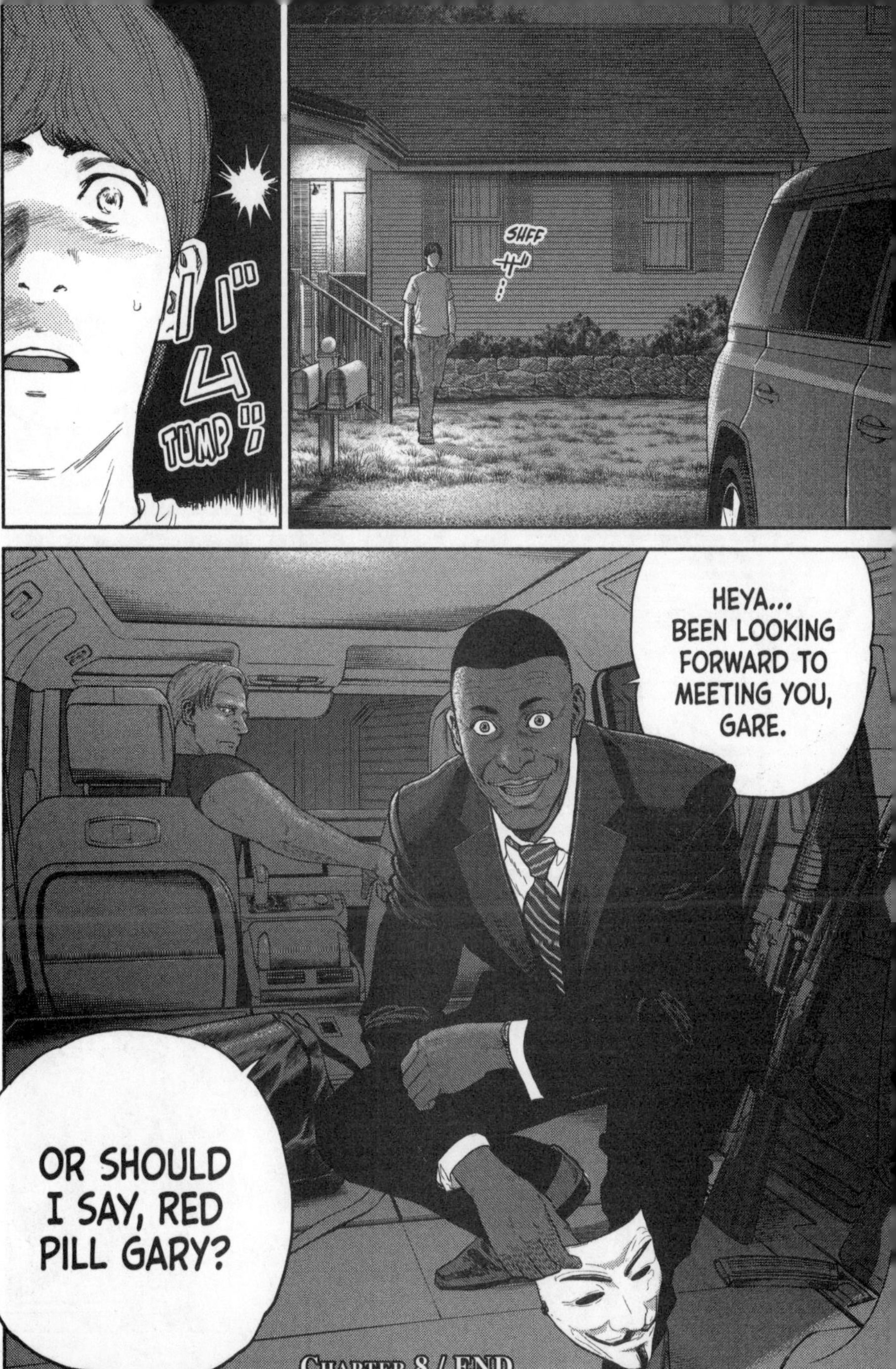
SHUFF
TUMP
HEYA... BEEN LOOKING FORWARD TO MEETING YOU, GARE.
OR SHOULD I SAY, RED PILL GARY?

CHAPTER 8 / END

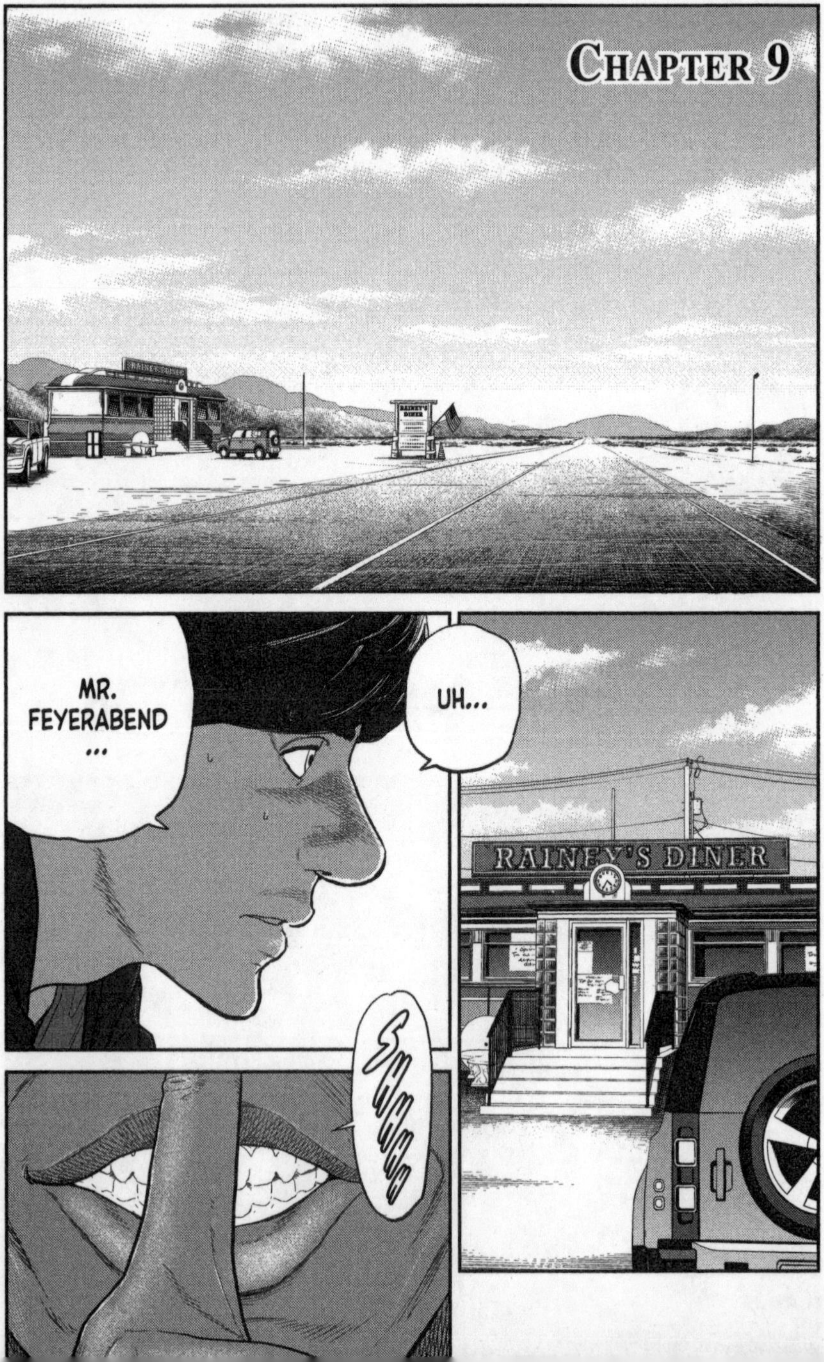
CHAPTER 9
RAINEY'S DINER
UH...
MR. FEYERABEND ...
SHHHH

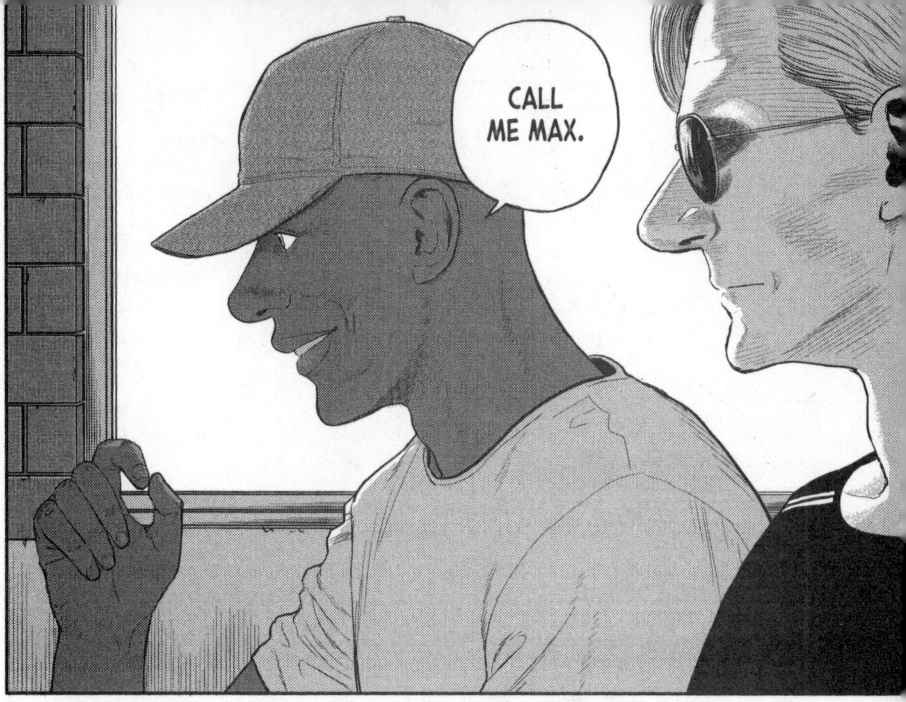
CALL ME MAX.

CHAPTER 9 / DIRECT ACTION

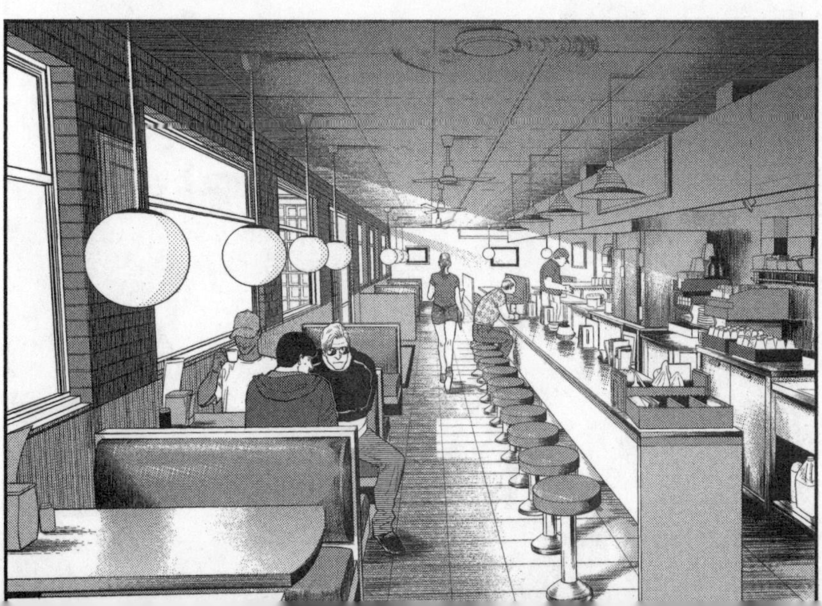

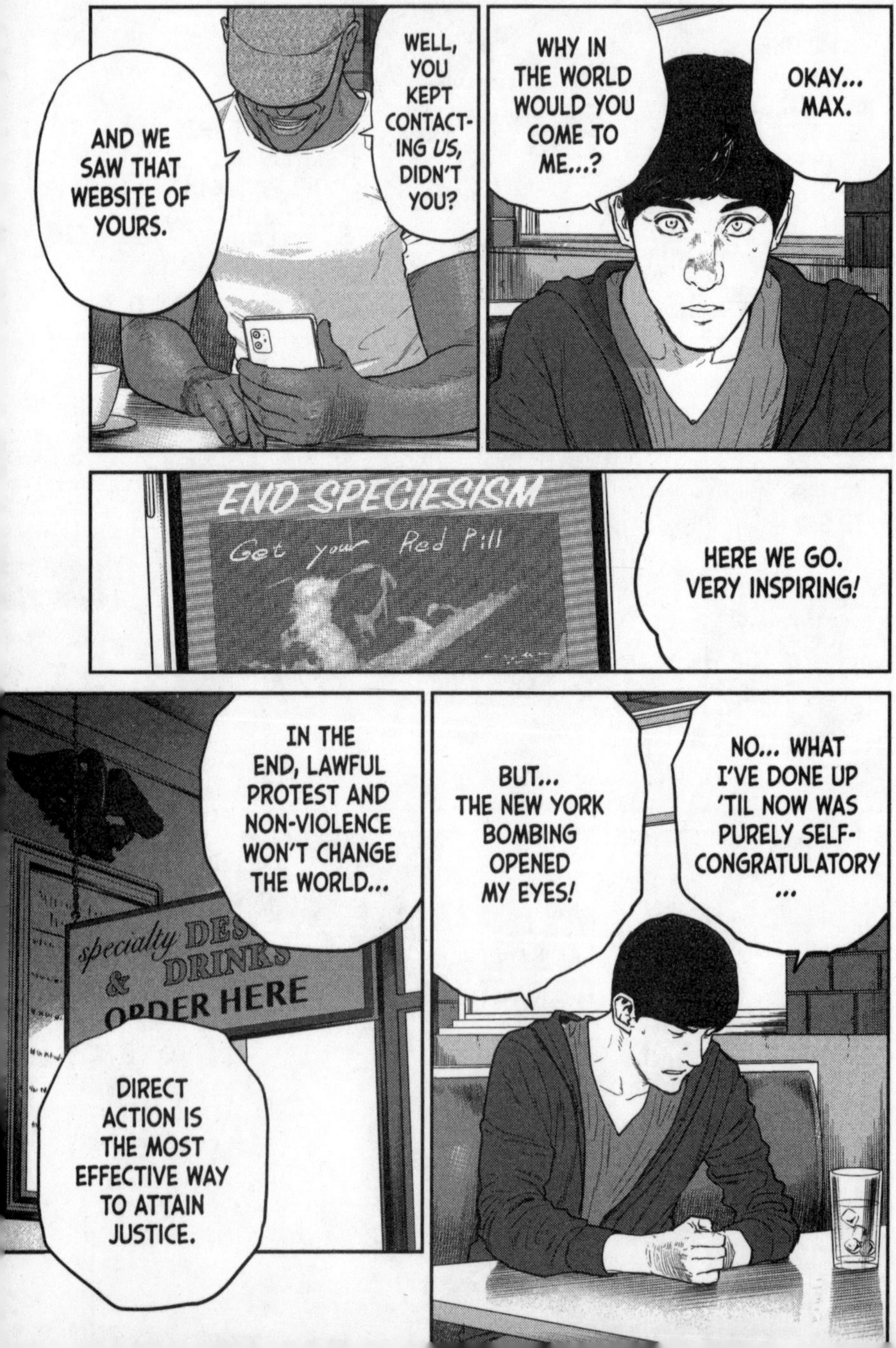
OKAY... MAX.
WHY IN THE WORLD WOULD YOU COME TO ME...?
WELL, YOU KEPT CONTACTING *US*, DIDN'T YOU?
AND WE SAW THAT WEBSITE OF YOURS.
HERE WE GO. VERY INSPIRING!
END SPECIESISM
Get your Red Pill
NO... WHAT I'VE DONE UP 'TIL NOW WAS PURELY SELF-CONGRATULATORY...
BUT... THE NEW YORK BOMBING OPENED MY EYES!
IN THE END, LAWFUL PROTEST AND NON-VIOLENCE WON'T CHANGE THE WORLD...
specialty
DRINKS
&
ORDER HERE
DIRECT ACTION IS THE MOST EFFECTIVE WAY TO ATTAIN JUSTICE.

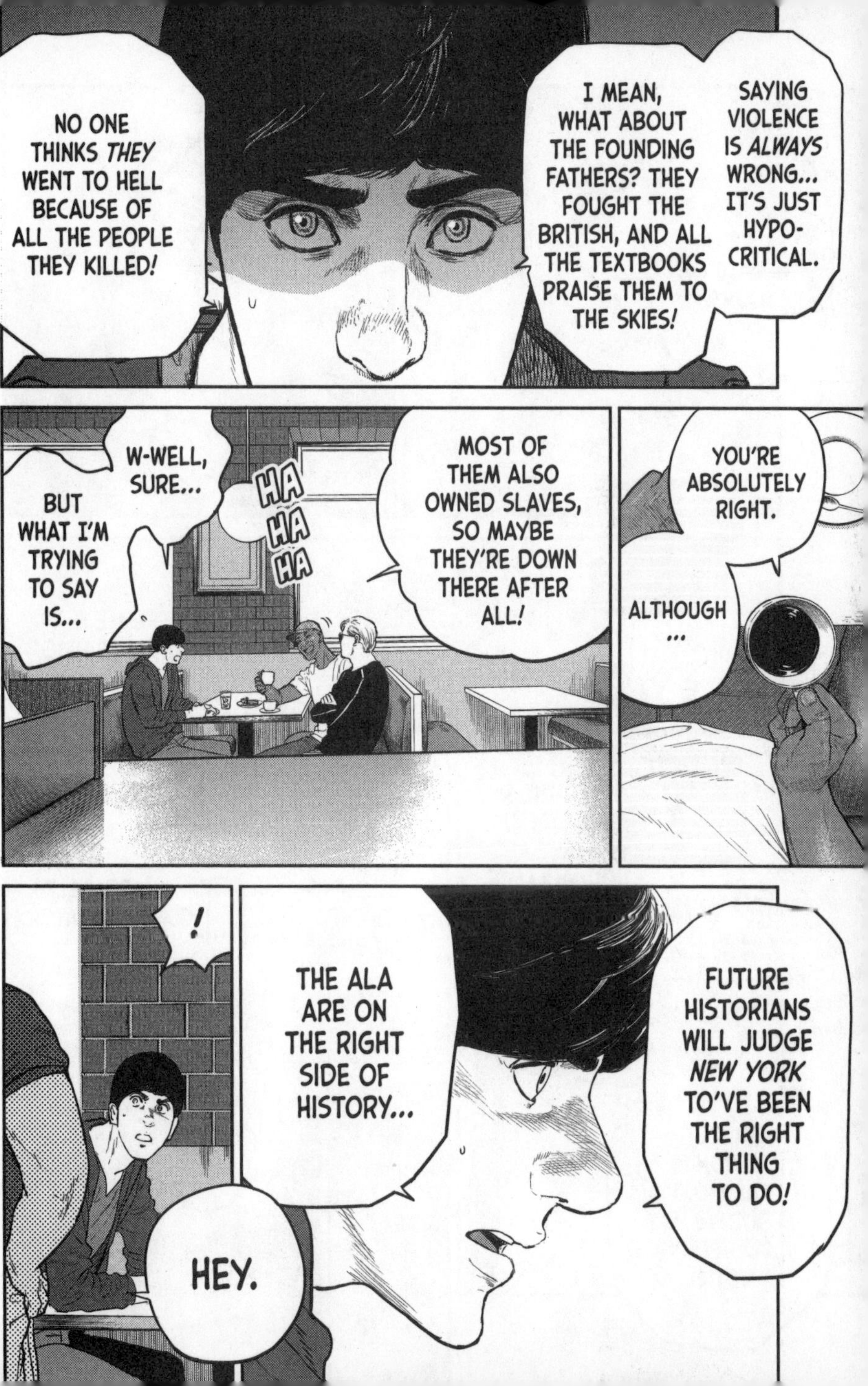
SAYING VIOLENCE IS *ALWAYS* WRONG... IT'S JUST HYPO-CRITICAL.
I MEAN, WHAT ABOUT THE FOUNDING FATHERS? THEY FOUGHT THE BRITISH, AND ALL THE TEXTBOOKS PRAISE THEM TO THE SKIES!
NO ONE THINKS *THEY* WENT TO HELL BECAUSE OF ALL THE PEOPLE THEY KILLED!
YOU'RE ABSOLUTELY RIGHT.
ALTHOUGH ...
MOST OF THEM ALSO OWNED SLAVES, SO MAYBE THEY'RE DOWN THERE AFTER ALL!
HA HA HA
W-WELL, SURE...
BUT WHAT I'M TRYING TO SAY IS...
FUTURE HISTORIANS WILL JUDGE *NEW YORK* TO'VE BEEN THE RIGHT THING TO DO!
THE ALA ARE ON THE RIGHT SIDE OF HISTORY...
!
HEY.

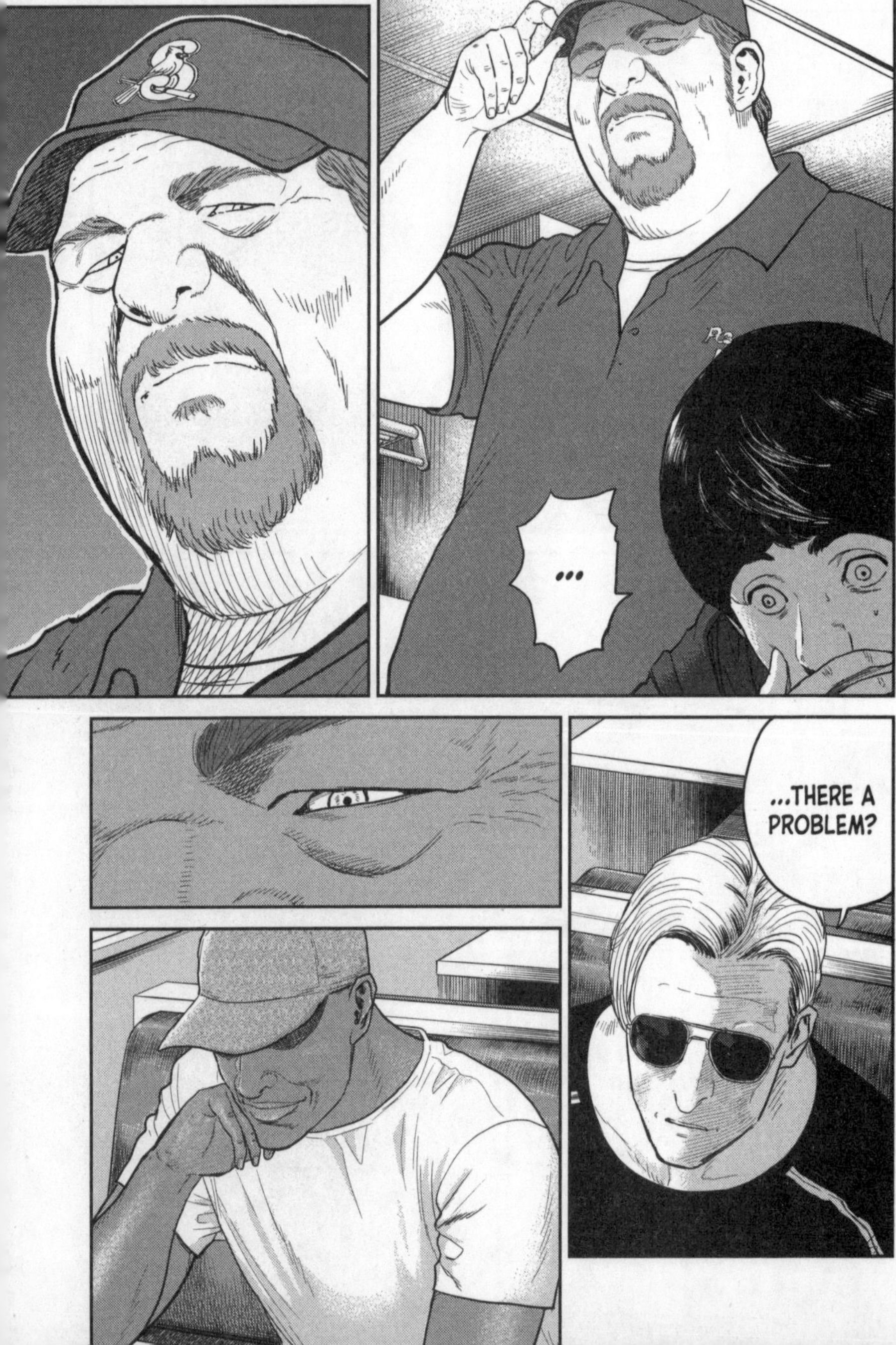
...
...THERE A PROBLEM?

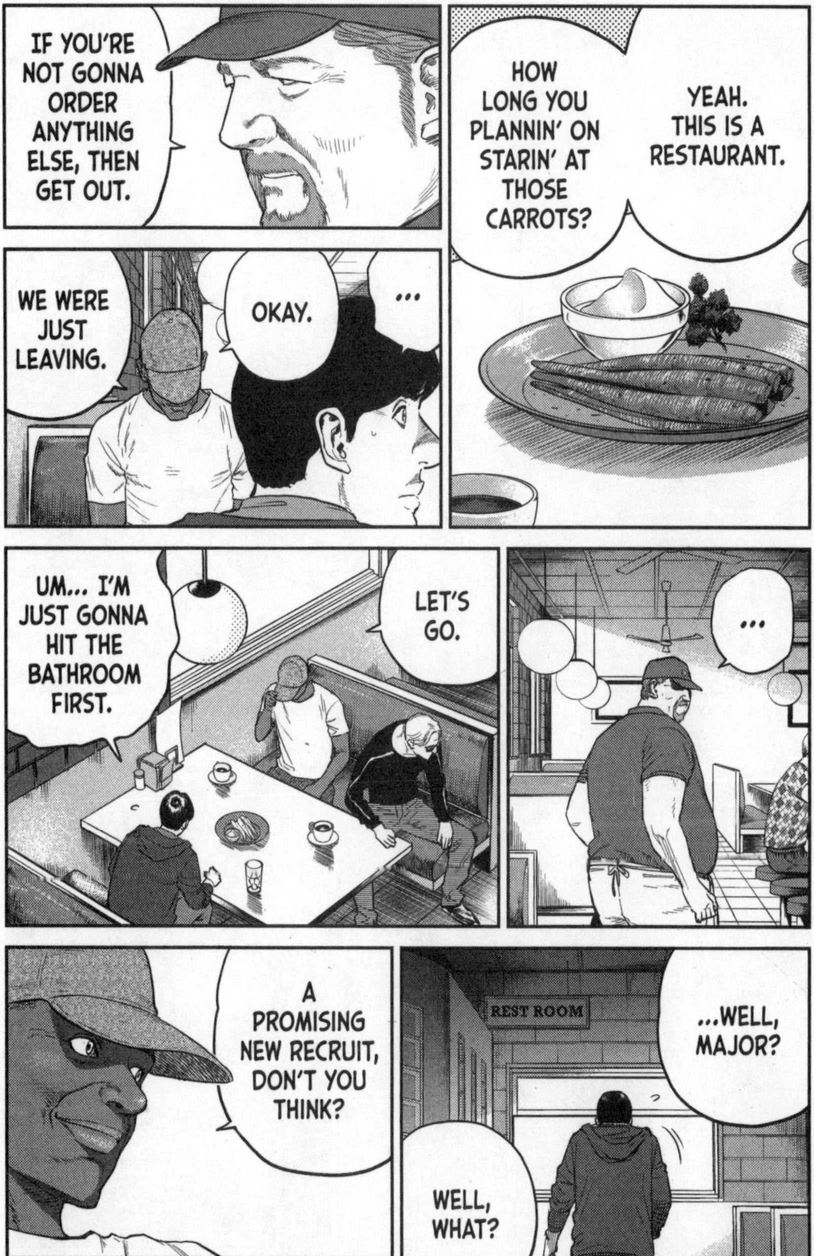
YEAH. THIS IS A RESTAURANT.
HOW LONG YOU PLANNIN' ON STARIN' AT THOSE CARROTS?
IF YOU'RE NOT GONNA ORDER ANYTHING ELSE, THEN GET OUT.
...
OKAY.
WE WERE JUST LEAVING.
...
LET'S GO.
UM... I'M JUST GONNA HIT THE BATHROOM FIRST.
...WELL, MAJOR?
REST ROOM
WELL, WHAT?
A PROMISING NEW RECRUIT, DON'T YOU THINK?

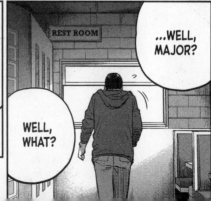

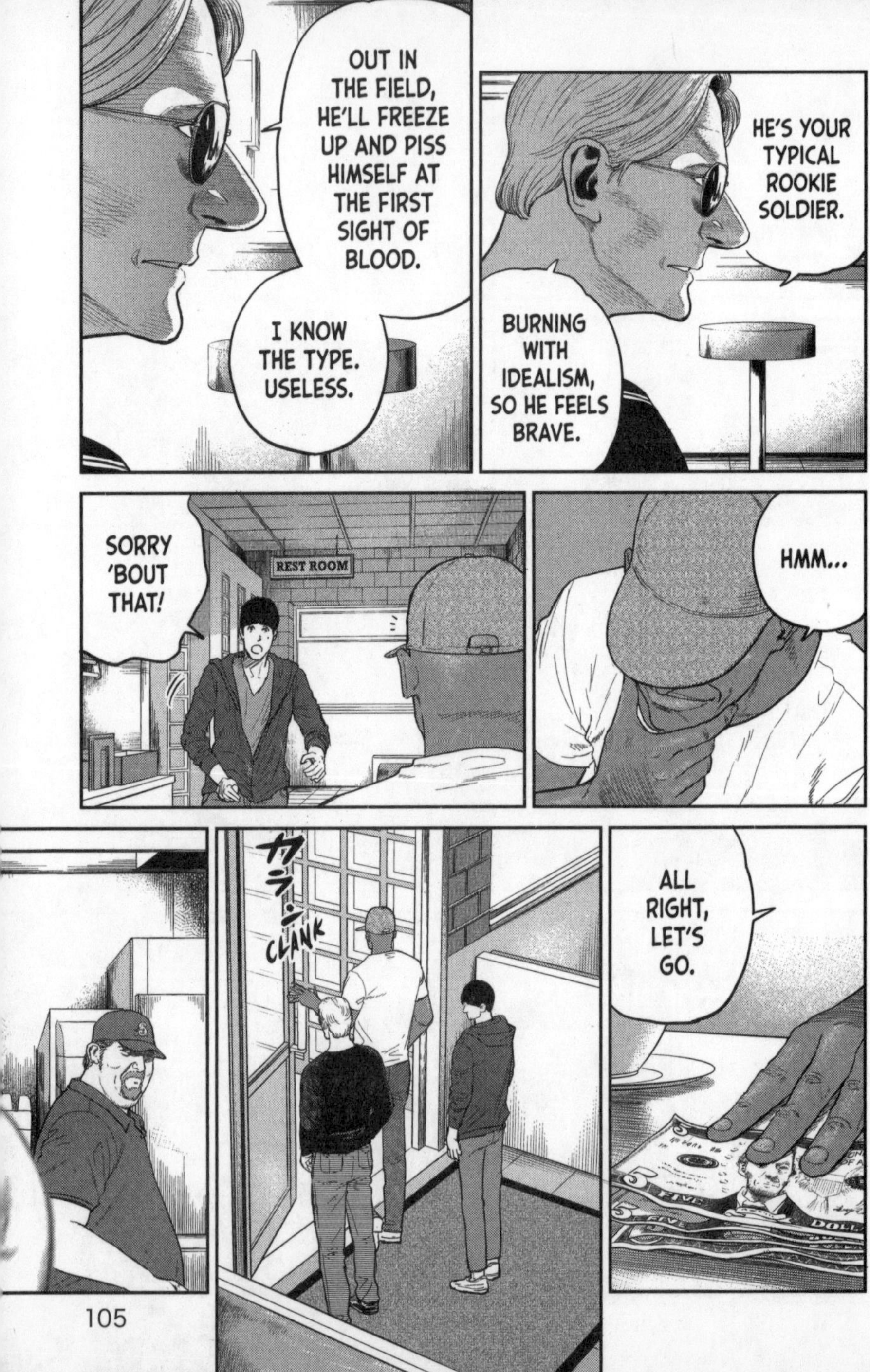
HE'S YOUR TYPICAL ROOKIE SOLDIER.
BURNING WITH IDEALISM, SO HE FEELS BRAVE.
OUT IN THE FIELD, HE'LL FREEZE UP AND PISS HIMSELF AT THE FIRST SIGHT OF BLOOD.
I KNOW THE TYPE. USELESS.
HMM...
REST ROOM
SORRY 'BOUT THAT!
ALL RIGHT, LET'S GO.
ガラン
CLANK

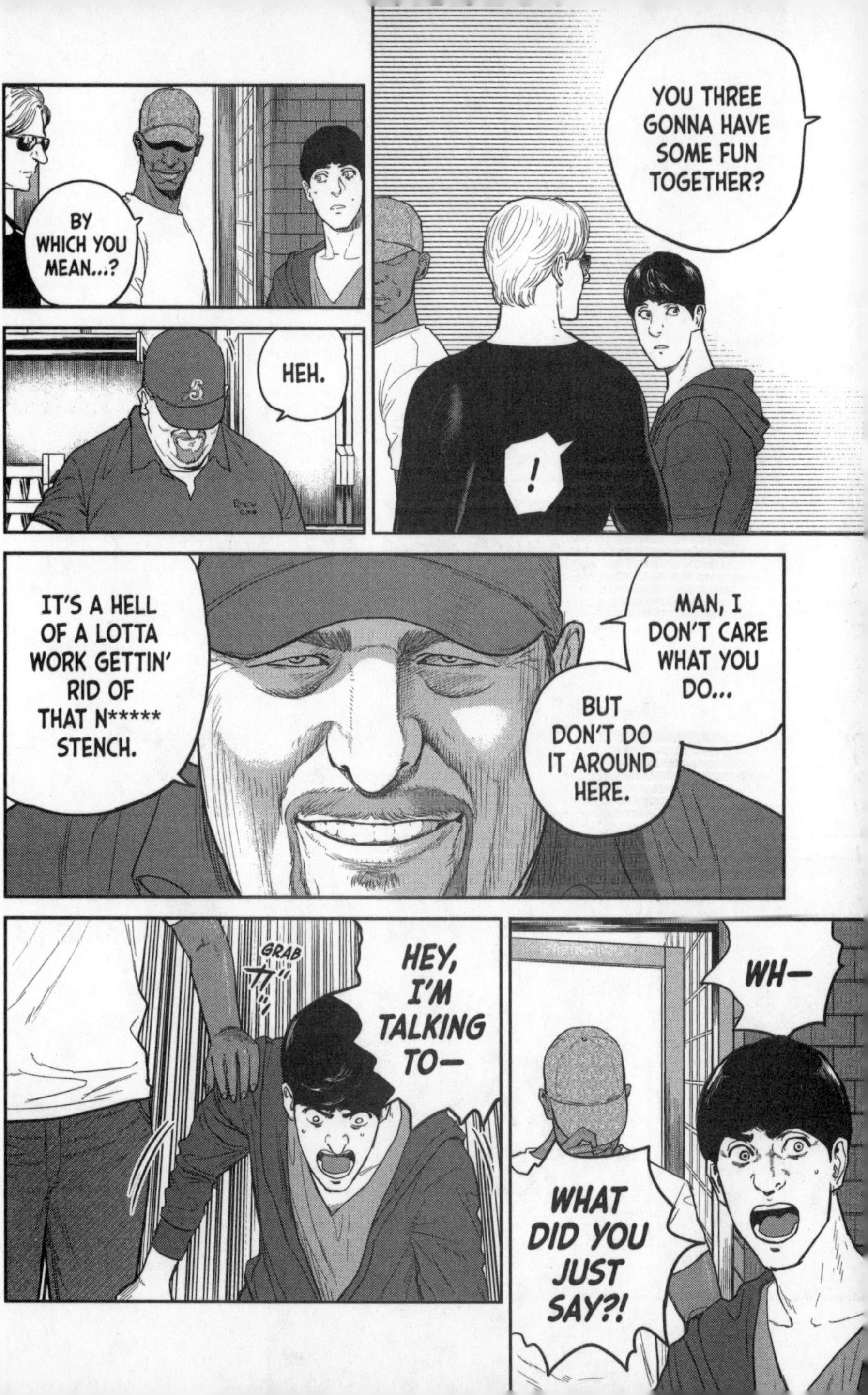
YOU THREE GONNA HAVE SOME FUN TOGETHER?
!
BY WHICH YOU MEAN...?
HEH.
MAN, I DON'T CARE WHAT YOU DO...
BUT DON'T DO IT AROUND HERE.
IT'S A HELL OF A LOTTA WORK GETTIN' RID OF THAT N***** STENCH.
WH—
WHAT DID YOU JUST SAY?!
GRAB
HEY, I'M TALKING TO—

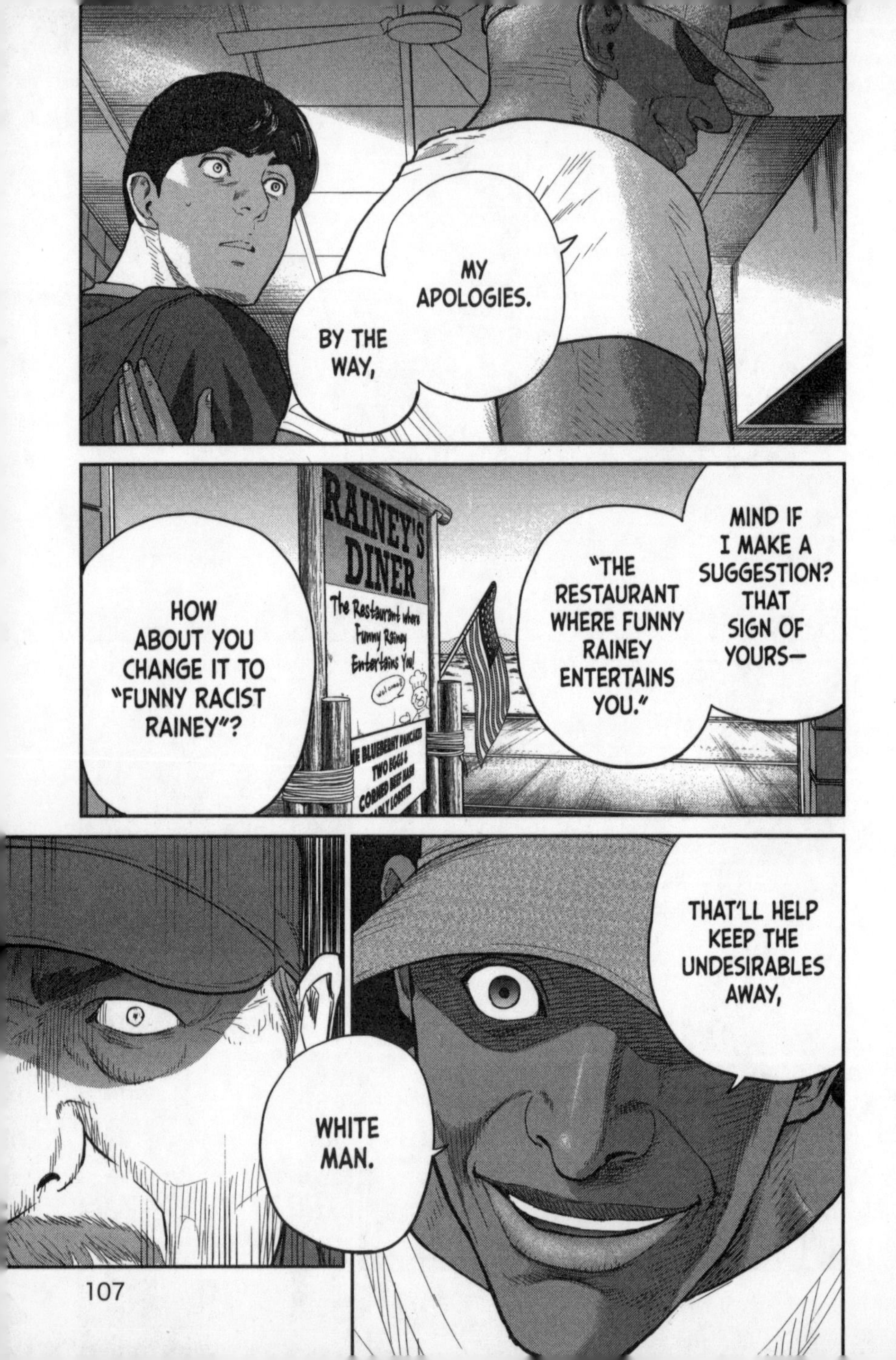
MY APOLOGIES. BY THE WAY,
MIND IF I MAKE A SUGGESTION? THAT SIGN OF YOURS—
“THE RESTAURANT WHERE FUNNY RAINEY ENTERTAINS YOU.”
RAINEY'S DINER
The Restaurant where Funny Rainey Entertains You!
HOW ABOUT YOU CHANGE IT TO “FUNNY RACIST RAINEY”?
THAT'LL HELP KEEP THE UNDESIRABLES AWAY,
WHITE MAN.

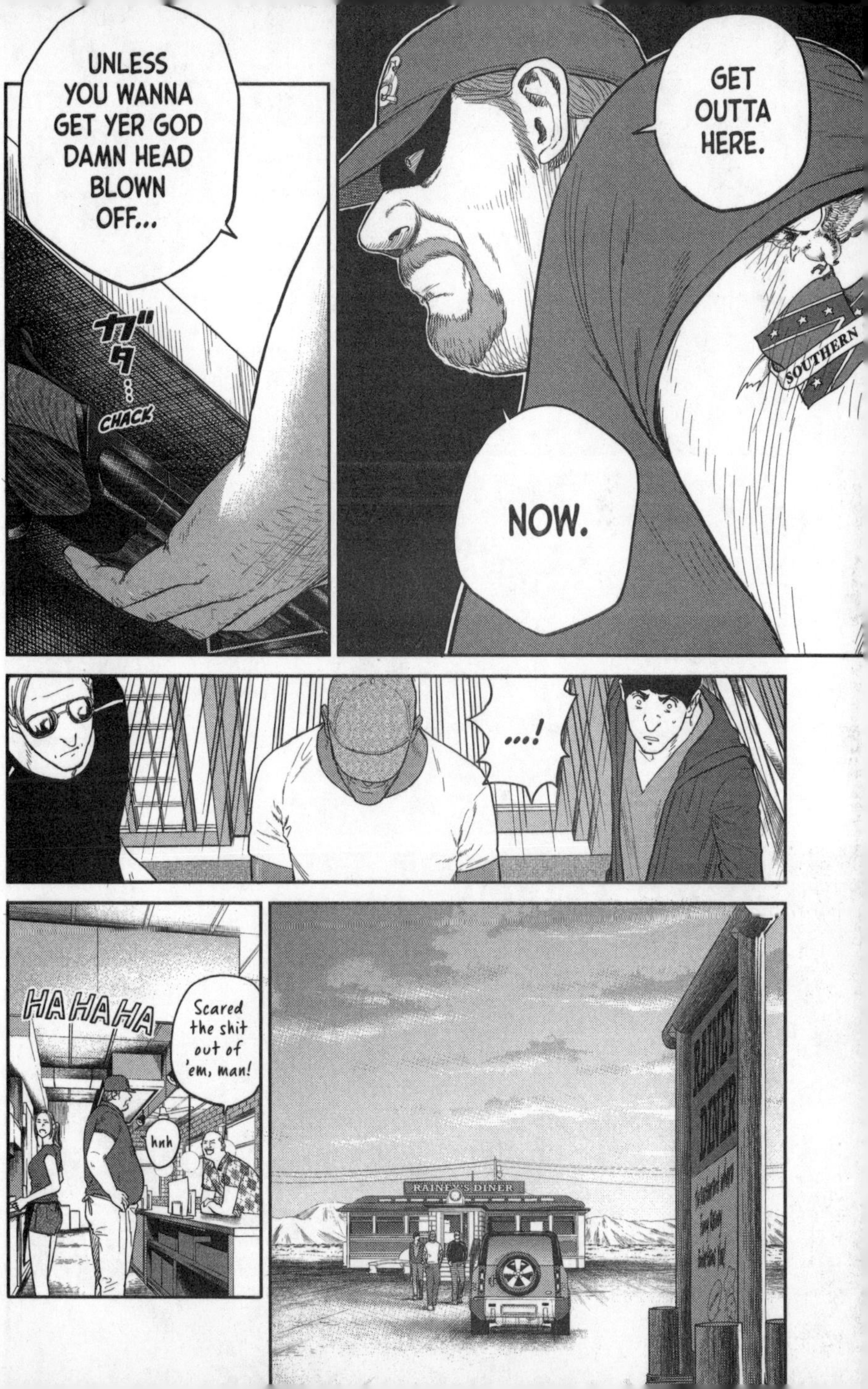GET OUTTA HERE.
SOUTHERN
NOW.
UNLESS YOU WANNA GET YER GOD DAMN HEAD BLOWN OFF...
ガタ…
CHACK
...!
RAINEY'S DINER
HAHAHA
Scared the shit out of 'em, man!
hnh

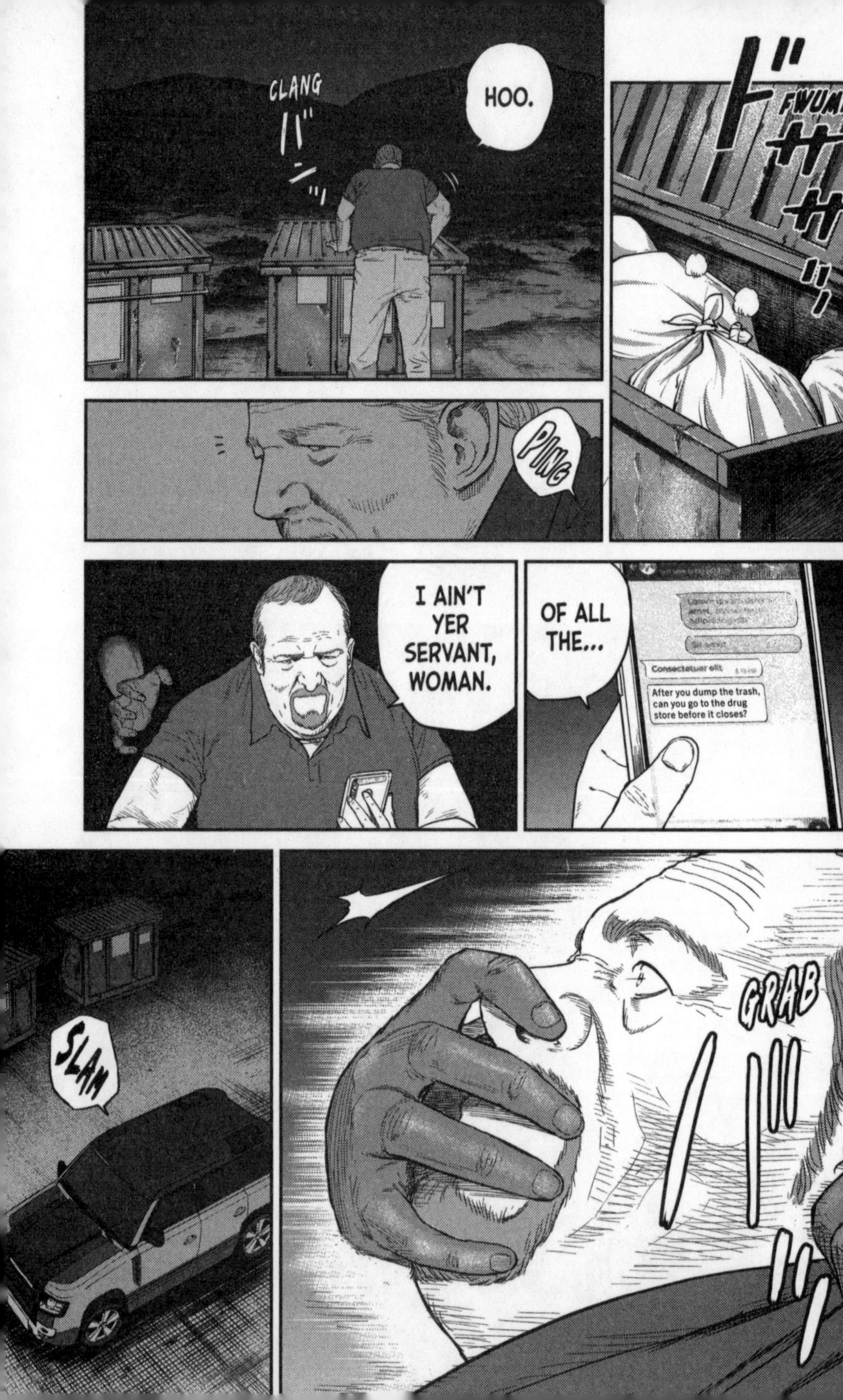
FWUMP
CLANG
HOO.
PING
OF ALL THE...
Consectetuer elit
After you dump the trash, can you go to the drug store before it closes?
I AIN'T YER SERVANT, WOMAN.
GRAB
SLAM

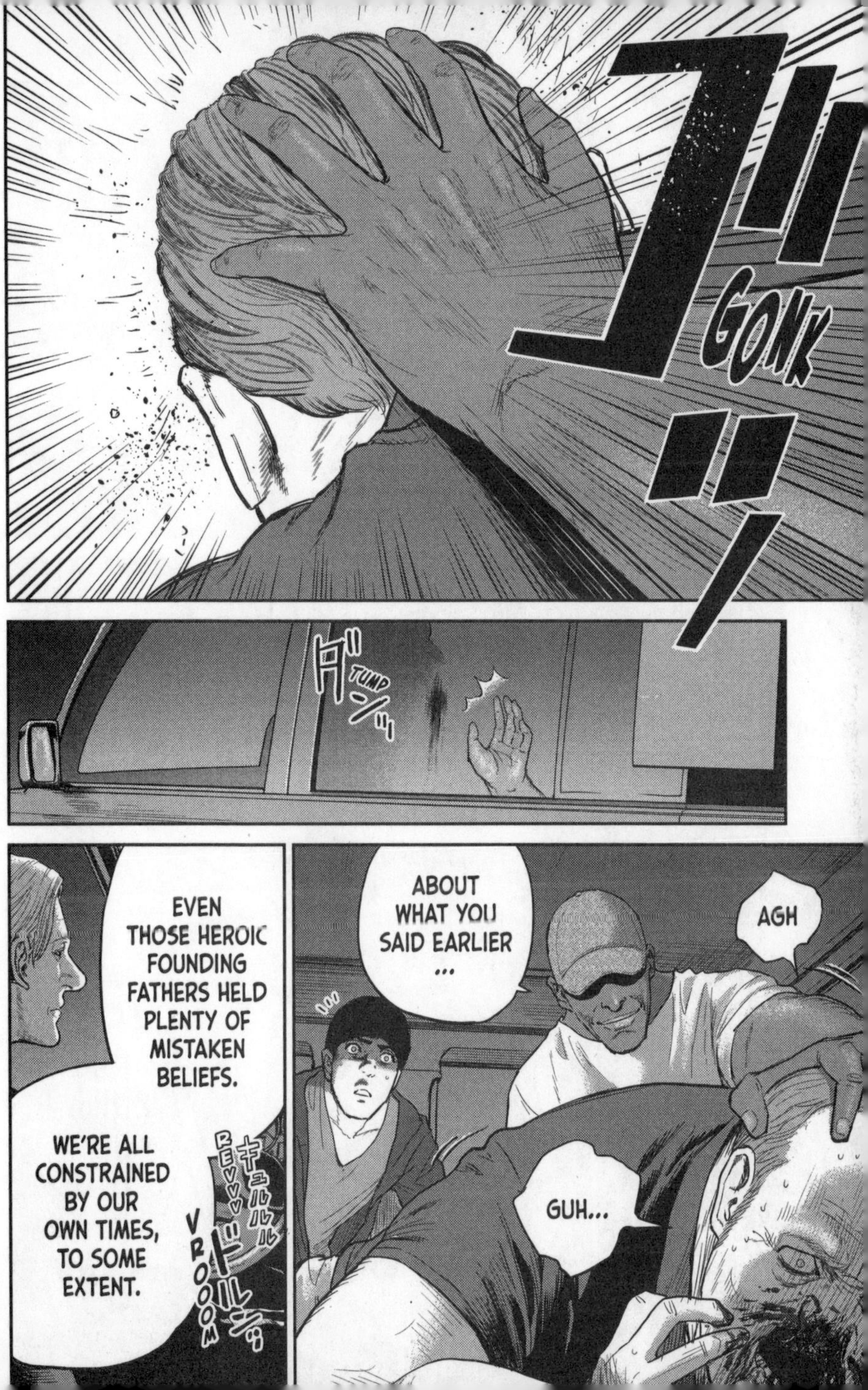
ゴッ
GONK
ダンッ
TUMP
AGH
ABOUT WHAT YOU SAID EARLIER ...
GUH...
EVEN THOSE HEROIC FOUNDING FATHERS HELD PLENTY OF MISTAKEN BELIEFS.
WE'RE ALL CONSTRAINED BY OUR OWN TIMES, TO SOME EXTENT.
キュルルル
REVVVV
ドルンッ
VROOOOM

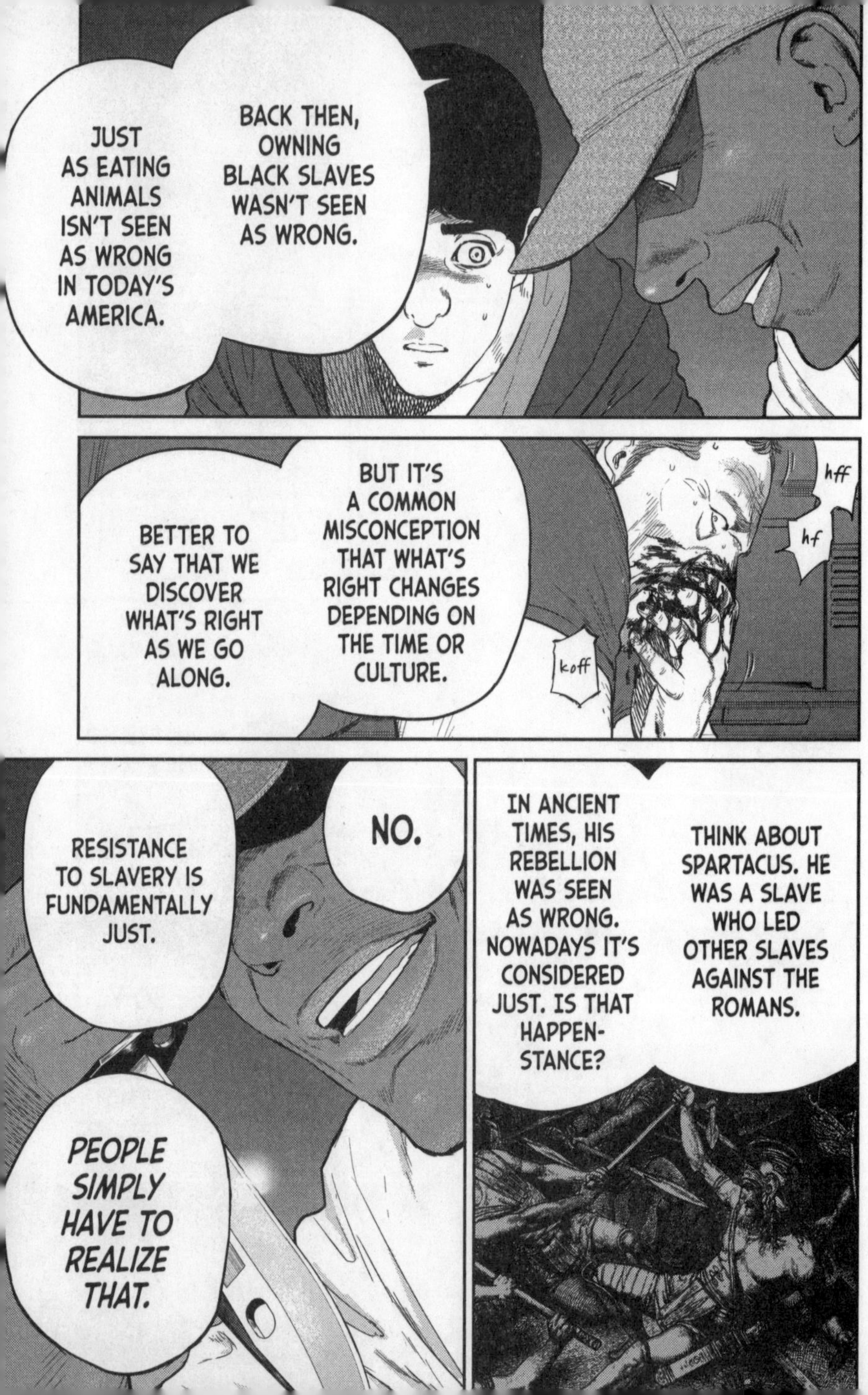
BACK THEN, OWNING BLACK SLAVES WASN'T SEEN AS WRONG.
JUST AS EATING ANIMALS ISN'T SEEN AS WRONG IN TODAY'S AMERICA.
hff
hf
BUT IT'S A COMMON MISCONCEPTION THAT WHAT'S RIGHT CHANGES DEPENDING ON THE TIME OR CULTURE.
BETTER TO SAY THAT WE DISCOVER WHAT'S RIGHT AS WE GO ALONG.
koff
THINK ABOUT SPARTACUS. HE WAS A SLAVE WHO LED OTHER SLAVES AGAINST THE ROMANS.
IN ANCIENT TIMES, HIS REBELLION WAS SEEN AS WRONG. NOWADAYS IT'S CONSIDERED JUST. IS THAT HAPPEN-STANCE?
NO.
RESISTANCE TO SLAVERY IS FUNDAMENTALLY JUST.
PEOPLE SIMPLY HAVE TO REALIZE THAT.

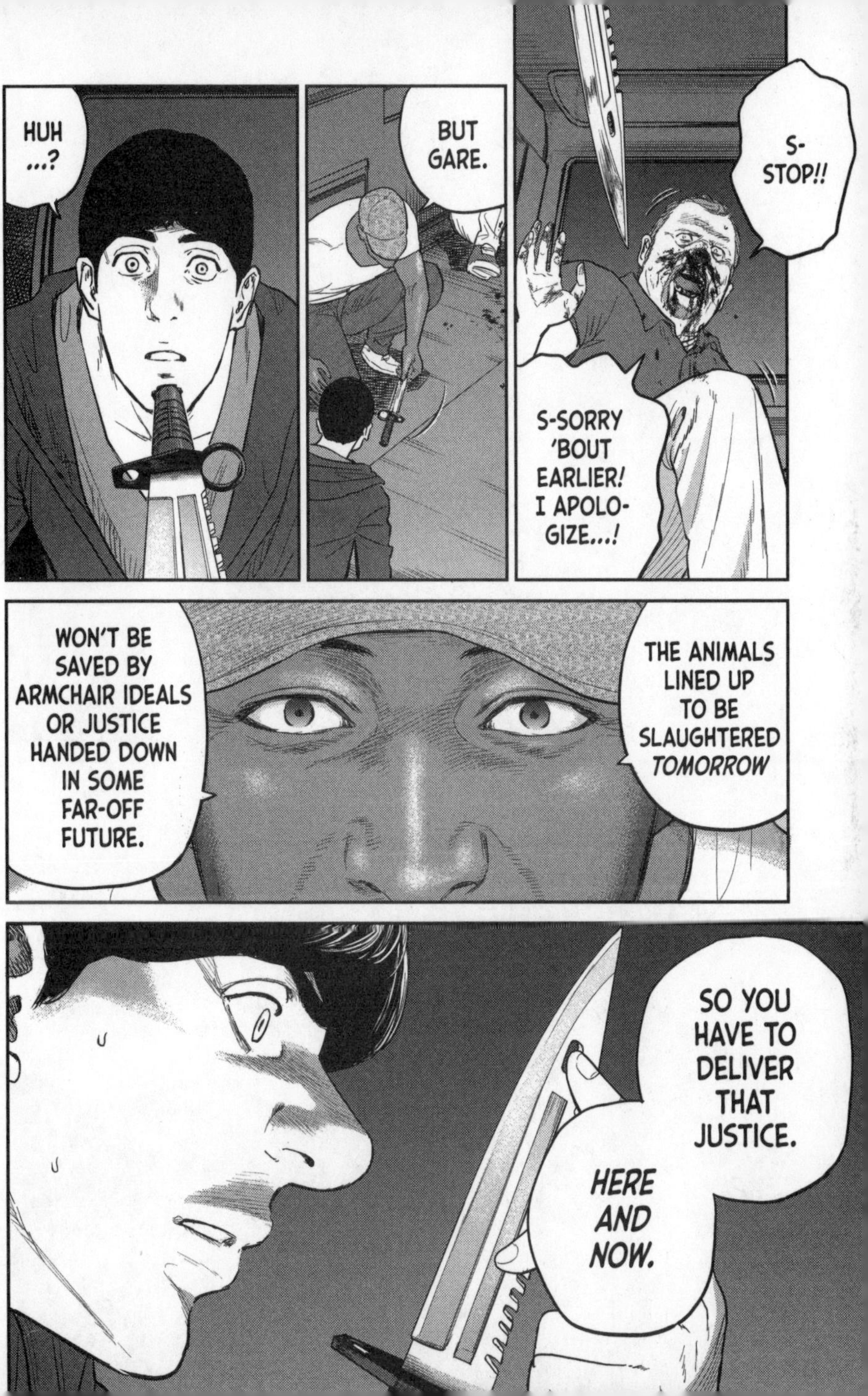
S-STOP!!
S-SORRY 'BOUT EARLIER! I APOLOGIZE...!
BUT GARE.
HUH ...?
THE ANIMALS LINED UP TO BE SLAUGHTERED *TOMORROW*
WON'T BE SAVED BY ARMCHAIR IDEALS OR JUSTICE HANDED DOWN IN SOME FAR-OFF FUTURE.
SO YOU HAVE TO DELIVER THAT JUSTICE.
HERE AND NOW.

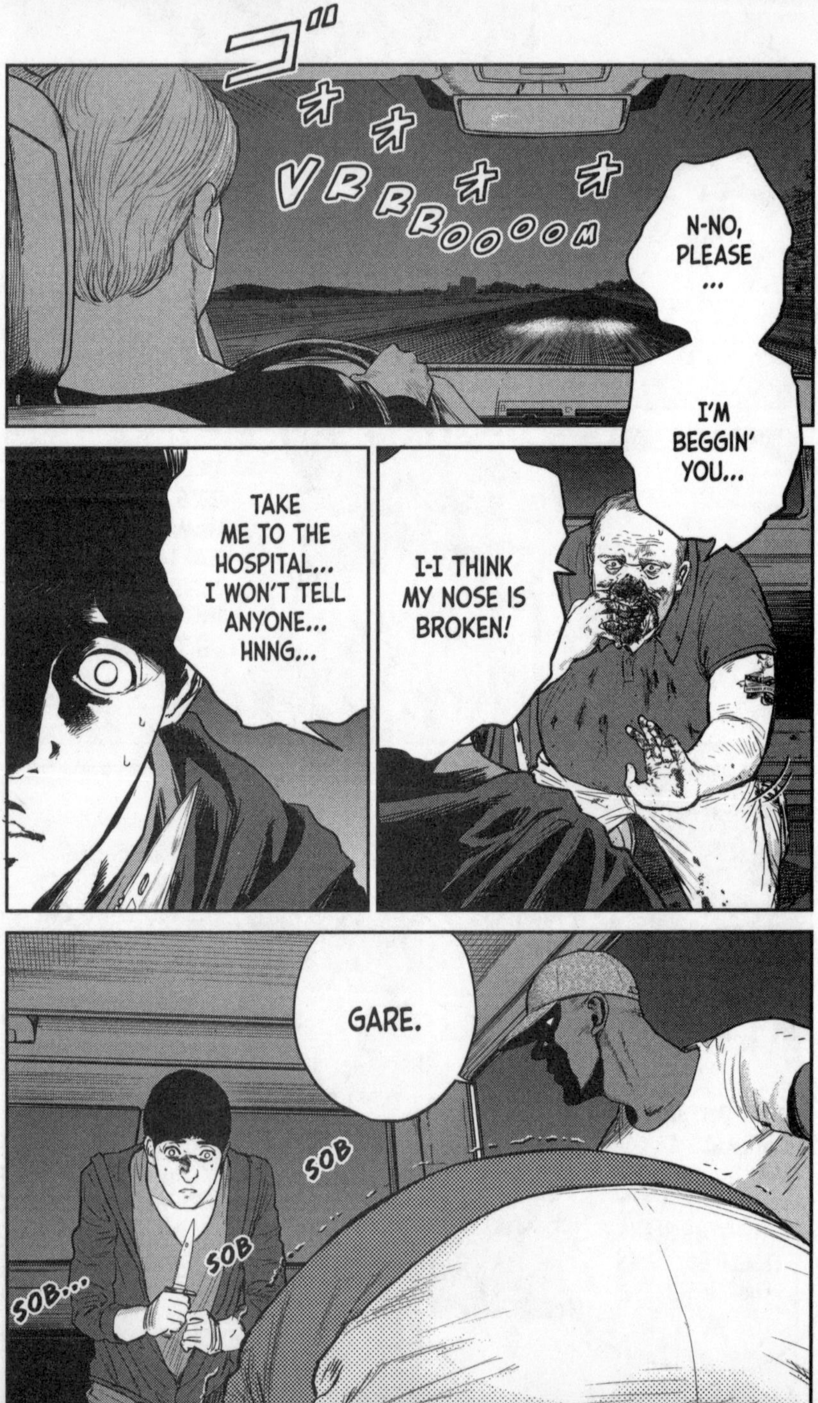
ゴオオオオ
VRRROOOOOM
N-NO, PLEASE ...
I'M BEGGIN' YOU...
I-I THINK MY NOSE IS BROKEN!
TAKE ME TO THE HOSPITAL... I WON'T TELL ANYONE... HNNG...
GARE.
SOB
SOB
SOB...

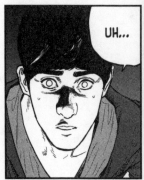

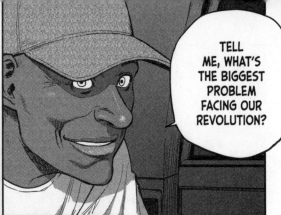

TELL ME, WHAT'S THE BIGGEST PROBLEM FACING OUR REVOLUTION?
UH...
I'LL TELL YOU. IT'S THAT THE ANIMALS AT THE HEART OF IT CAN NEVER RISE UP AND SPEAK OUT FOR THEMSELVES.
THEY CAN'T SCREAM, "ANIMAL LIVES MATTER!"
THAT'S ONE OF THE BIGGEST REASONS NO ONE TAKES THEIR SUFFERING SERIOUSLY.
?
haah
haah
PLIP
ボタ
ボタッ
PLIP
IT MAY BE POWER, NOT JUSTICE, THAT WINS WARS...
BUT IF ANIMALS CAN'T ANNOUNCE THEIR OWN LEGITIMACY, THEN THE FIGHT ITSELF BECOMES IMPOSSIBLE.

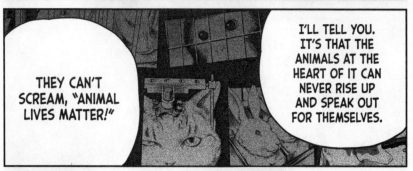

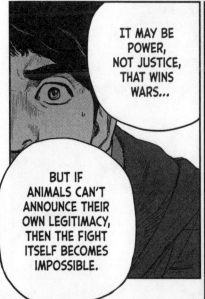

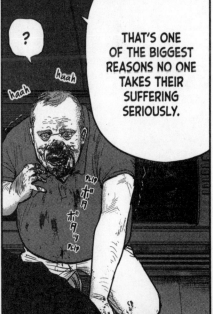

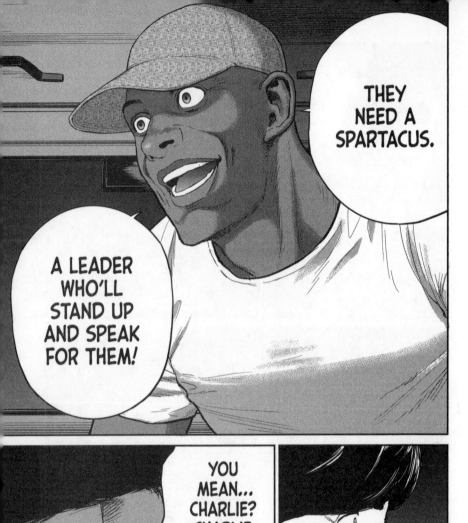

THEY NEED A SPARTACUS.

A LEADER WHO'LL STAND UP AND SPEAK FOR THEM!

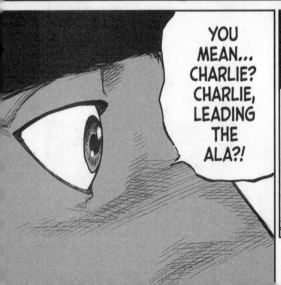

YOU MEAN... CHARLIE? CHARLIE, LEADING THE ALA?!

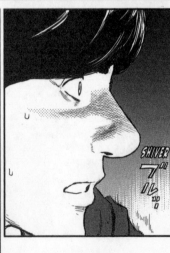

SHIVER

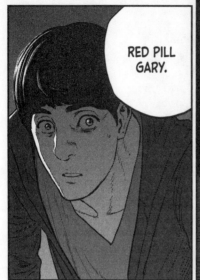

RED PILL GARY.

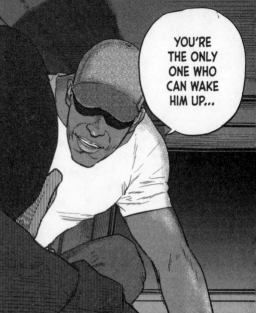

YOU'RE THE ONLY ONE WHO CAN WAKE HIM UP...

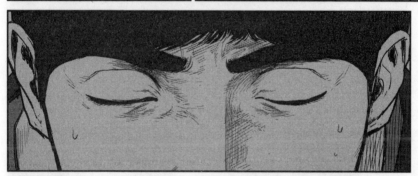

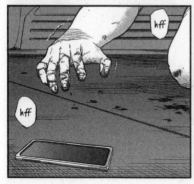

hff

hff

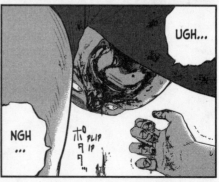

UGH...

NGH...

ホ°
アLIP
ア IP
ア...

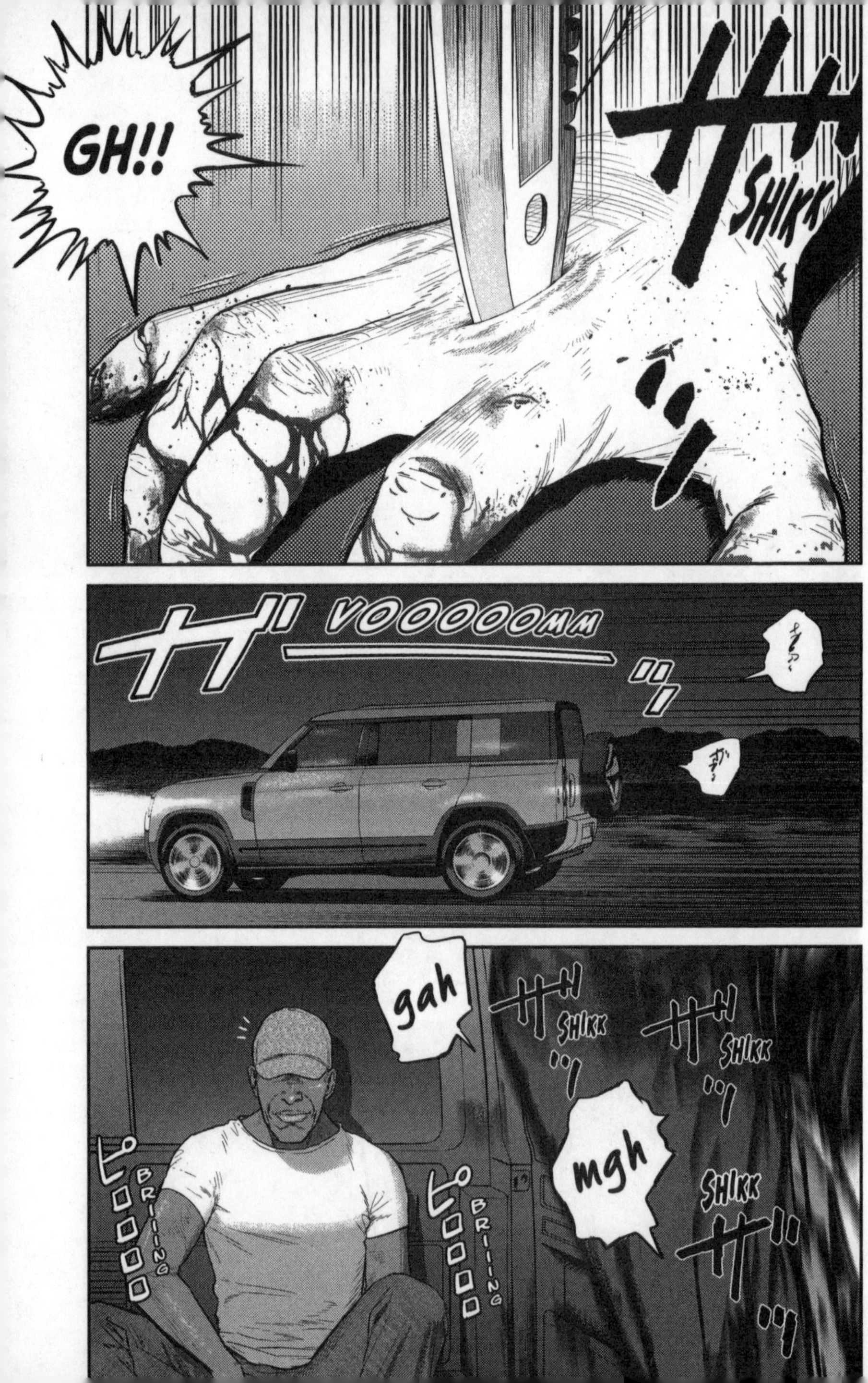
SHIKK
GH!!
VOOOOOMM
SHIKK
SHIKK
gah
mgh
SHIKK
BRIIING
BRIIING

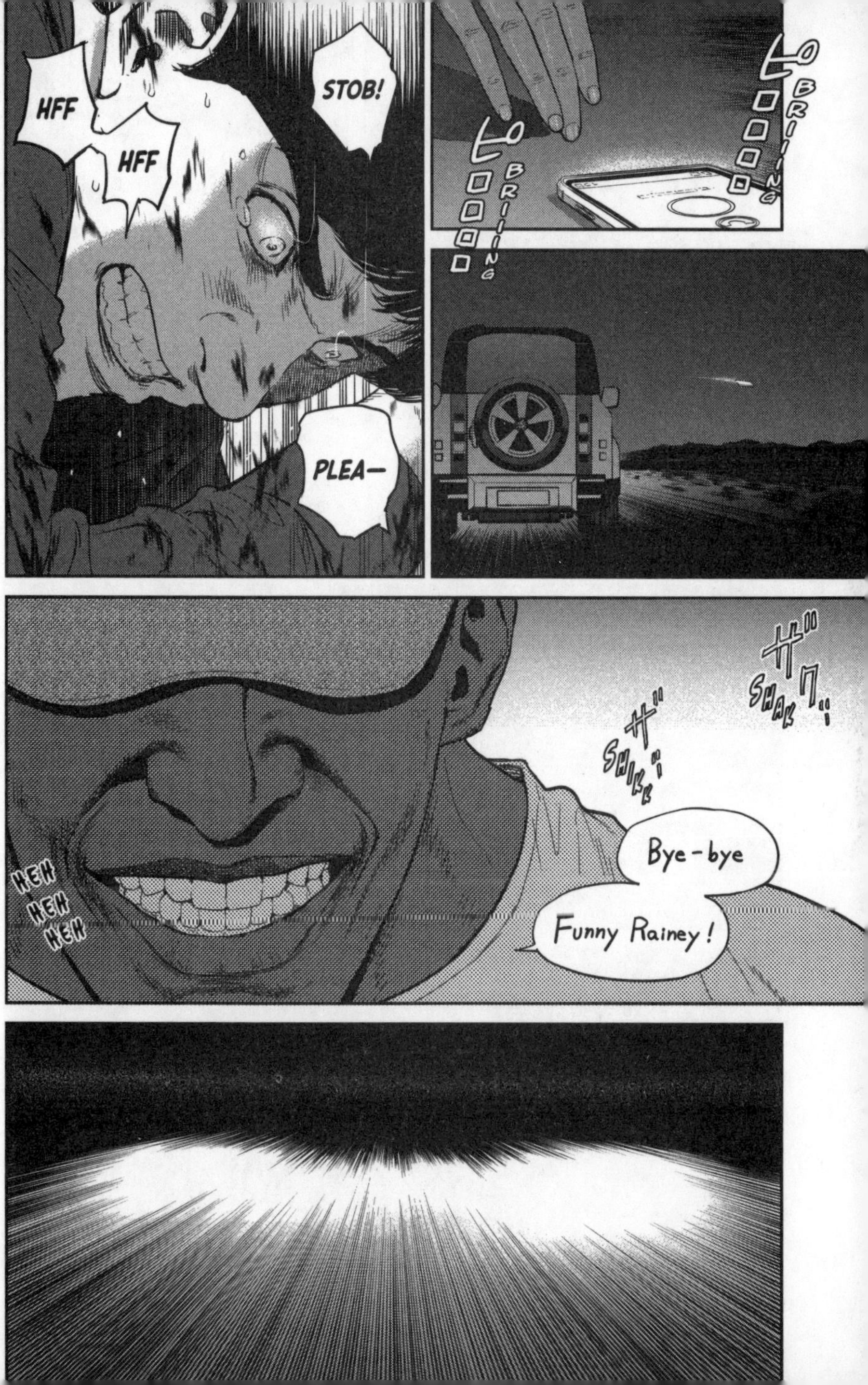
BRIIING
BRIIING
STOB!
HFF
HFF
PLEA—
SHAK
SHIK
Bye-bye
Funny Rainey!
HEH HEH HEH

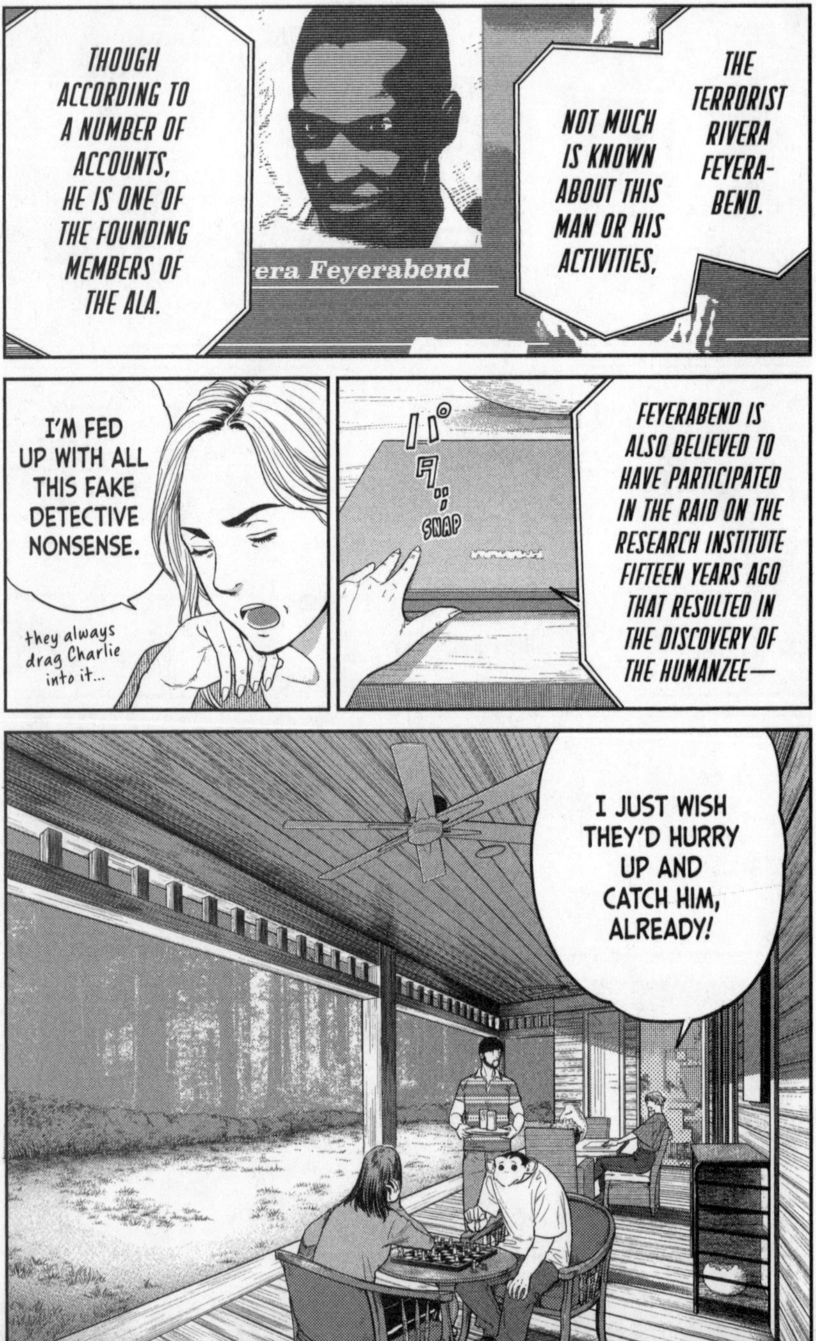
THE TERRORIST RIVERA FEYERA-BEND.
NOT MUCH IS KNOWN ABOUT THIS MAN OR HIS ACTIVITIES,
era Feyerabend
THOUGH ACCORDING TO A NUMBER OF ACCOUNTS, HE IS ONE OF THE FOUNDING MEMBERS OF THE ALA.
FEYERABEND IS ALSO BELIEVED TO HAVE PARTICIPATED IN THE RAID ON THE RESEARCH INSTITUTE FIFTEEN YEARS AGO THAT RESULTED IN THE DISCOVERY OF THE HUMANZEE—
パタッ
SNAP
I'M FED UP WITH ALL THIS FAKE DETECTIVE NONSENSE.
they always drag Charlie into it...
I JUST WISH THEY'D HURRY UP AND CATCH HIM, ALREADY!

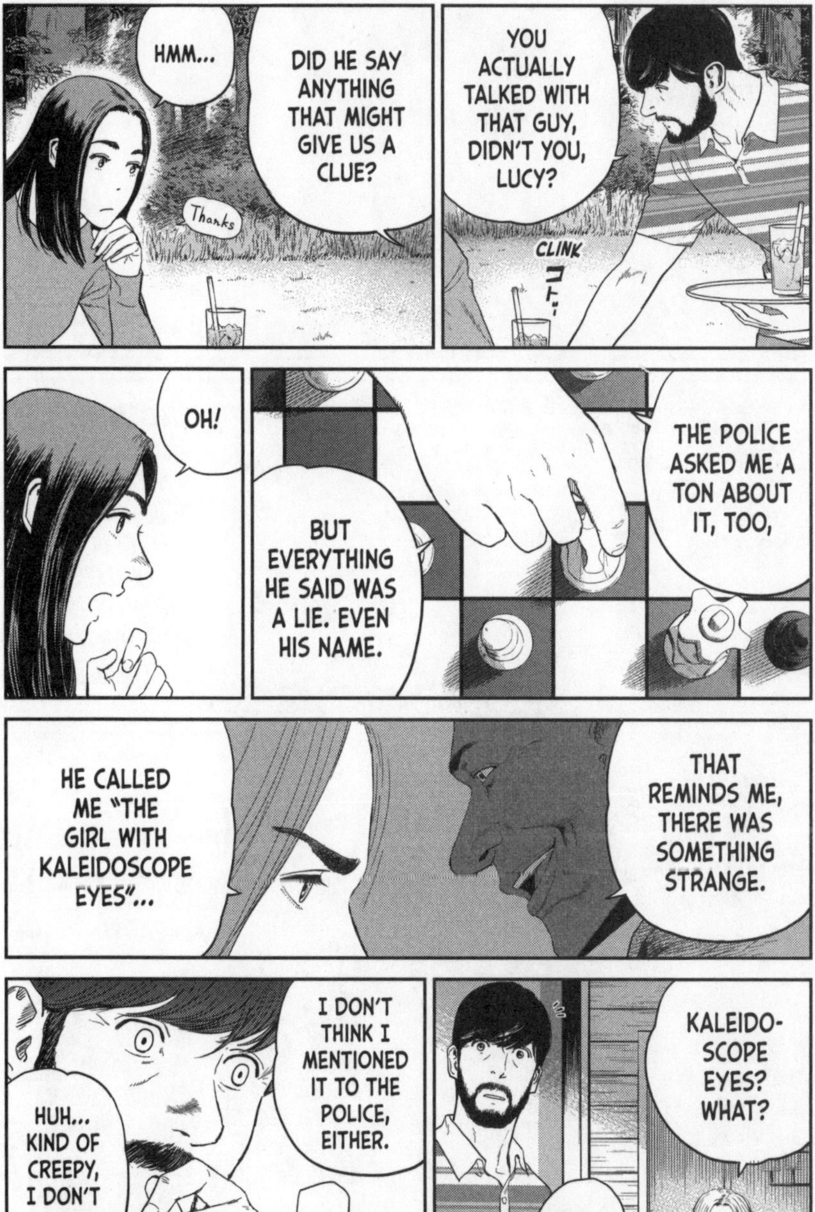
YOU ACTUALLY TALKED WITH THAT GUY, DIDN'T YOU, LUCY?
CLINK
コトッ
DID HE SAY ANYTHING THAT MIGHT GIVE US A CLUE?
HMM...
Thanks
THE POLICE ASKED ME A TON ABOUT IT, TOO,
BUT EVERYTHING HE SAID WAS A LIE. EVEN HIS NAME.
OH!
THAT REMINDS ME, THERE WAS SOMETHING STRANGE.
HE CALLED ME "THE GIRL WITH KALEIDOSCOPE EYES"...
KALEIDO-SCOPE EYES? WHAT?
SEARCH ME.
I DON'T THINK I MENTIONED IT TO THE POLICE, EITHER.
HUH... KIND OF CREEPY, I DON'T LIKE IT.
...

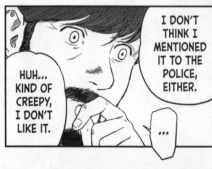

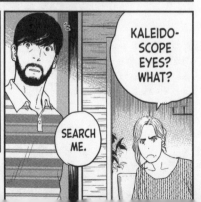

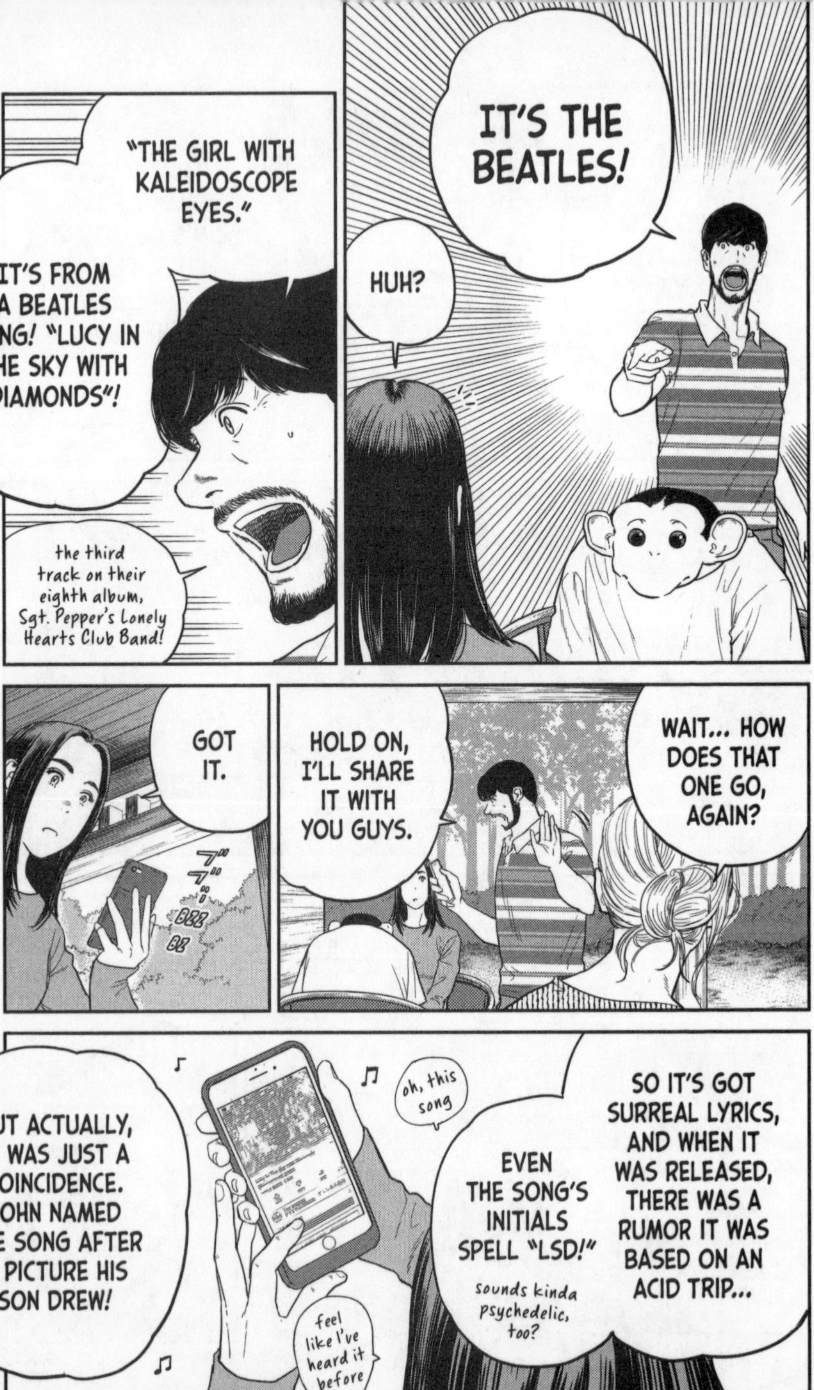
IT'S THE BEATLES!
HUH?
"THE GIRL WITH KALEIDOSCOPE EYES."
IT'S FROM A BEATLES SONG! "LUCY IN THE SKY WITH DIAMONDS"!
the third track on their eighth album, Sgt. Pepper's Lonely Hearts Club Band!
WAIT... HOW DOES THAT ONE GO, AGAIN?
HOLD ON, I'LL SHARE IT WITH YOU GUYS.
GOT IT.
BZZ
BZ
SO IT'S GOT SURREAL LYRICS, AND WHEN IT WAS RELEASED, THERE WAS A RUMOR IT WAS BASED ON AN ACID TRIP...
EVEN THE SONG'S INITIALS SPELL "LSD!"
sounds kinda psychedelic, too?
oh, this song
feel like I've heard it before
BUT ACTUALLY, IT WAS JUST A COINCIDENCE. JOHN NAMED THE SONG AFTER A PICTURE HIS SON DREW!

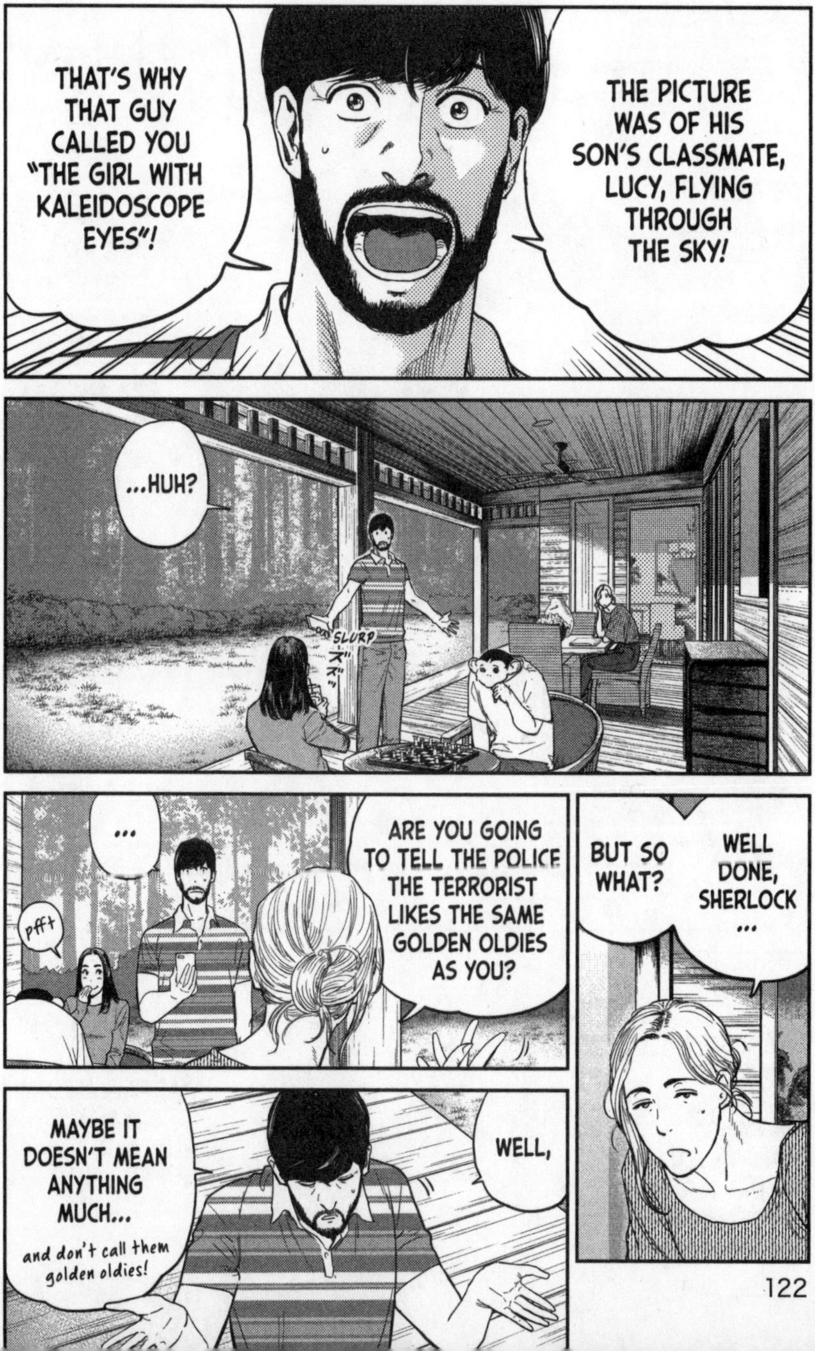
THE PICTURE WAS OF HIS SON'S CLASSMATE, LUCY, FLYING THROUGH THE SKY!
THAT'S WHY THAT GUY CALLED YOU "THE GIRL WITH KALEIDOSCOPE EYES"!
...HUH?
SLURP
ズズ
WELL DONE, SHERLOCK ...
BUT SO WHAT?
ARE YOU GOING TO TELL THE POLICE THE TERRORIST LIKES THE SAME GOLDEN OLDIES AS YOU?
pfft
...
WELL,
MAYBE IT DOESN'T MEAN ANYTHING MUCH...
and don't call them golden oldies!

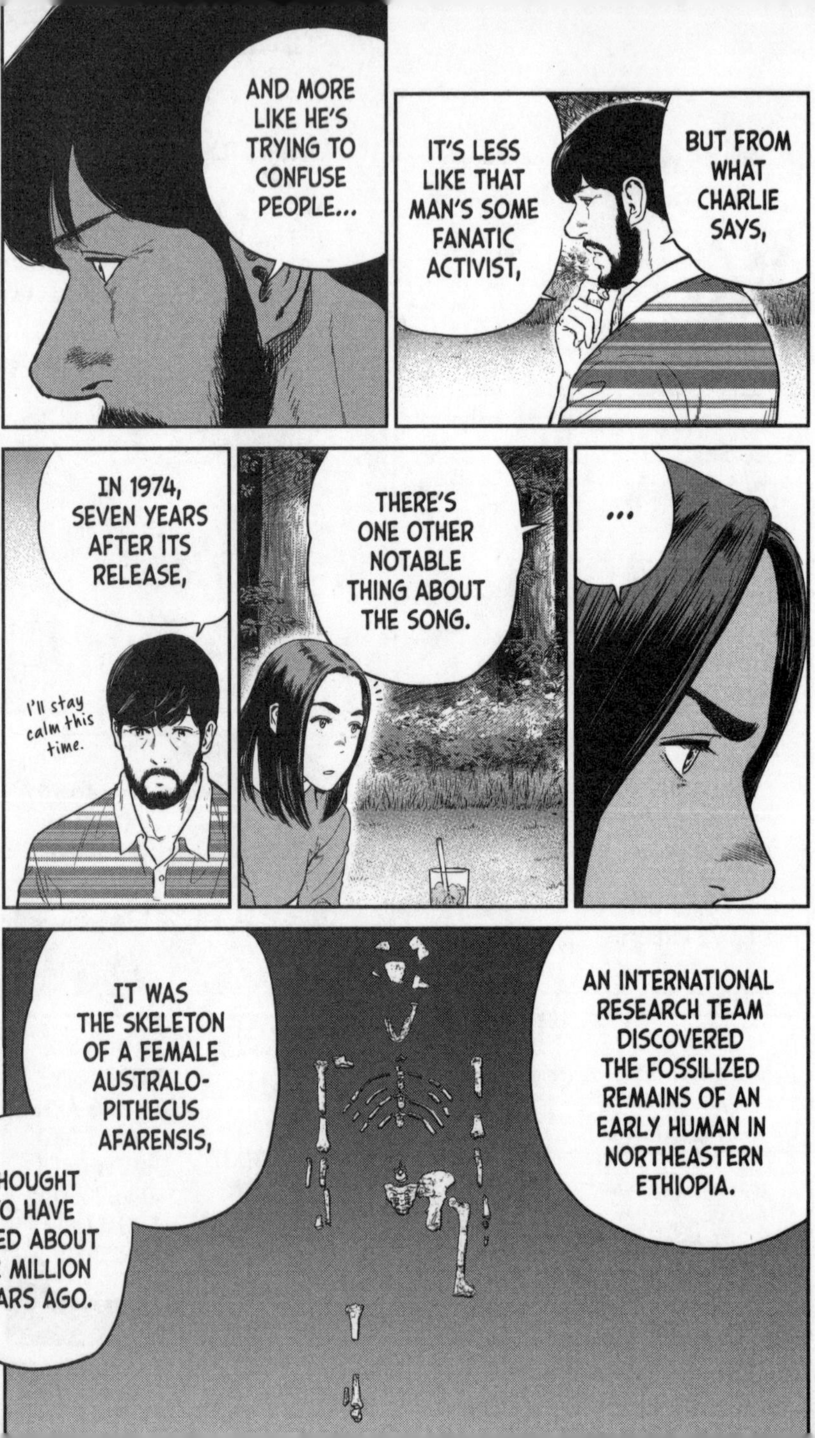
BUT FROM WHAT CHARLIE SAYS,
IT'S LESS LIKE THAT MAN'S SOME FANATIC ACTIVIST,
AND MORE LIKE HE'S TRYING TO CONFUSE PEOPLE...
...
THERE'S ONE OTHER NOTABLE THING ABOUT THE SONG.
IN 1974, SEVEN YEARS AFTER ITS RELEASE,
I'll stay calm this time.
AN INTERNATIONAL RESEARCH TEAM DISCOVERED THE FOSSILIZED REMAINS OF AN EARLY HUMAN IN NORTHEASTERN ETHIOPIA.
IT WAS THE SKELETON OF A FEMALE AUSTRALO-PITHECUS AFARENSIS,
THOUGHT TO HAVE LIVED ABOUT 3.2 MILLION YEARS AGO.

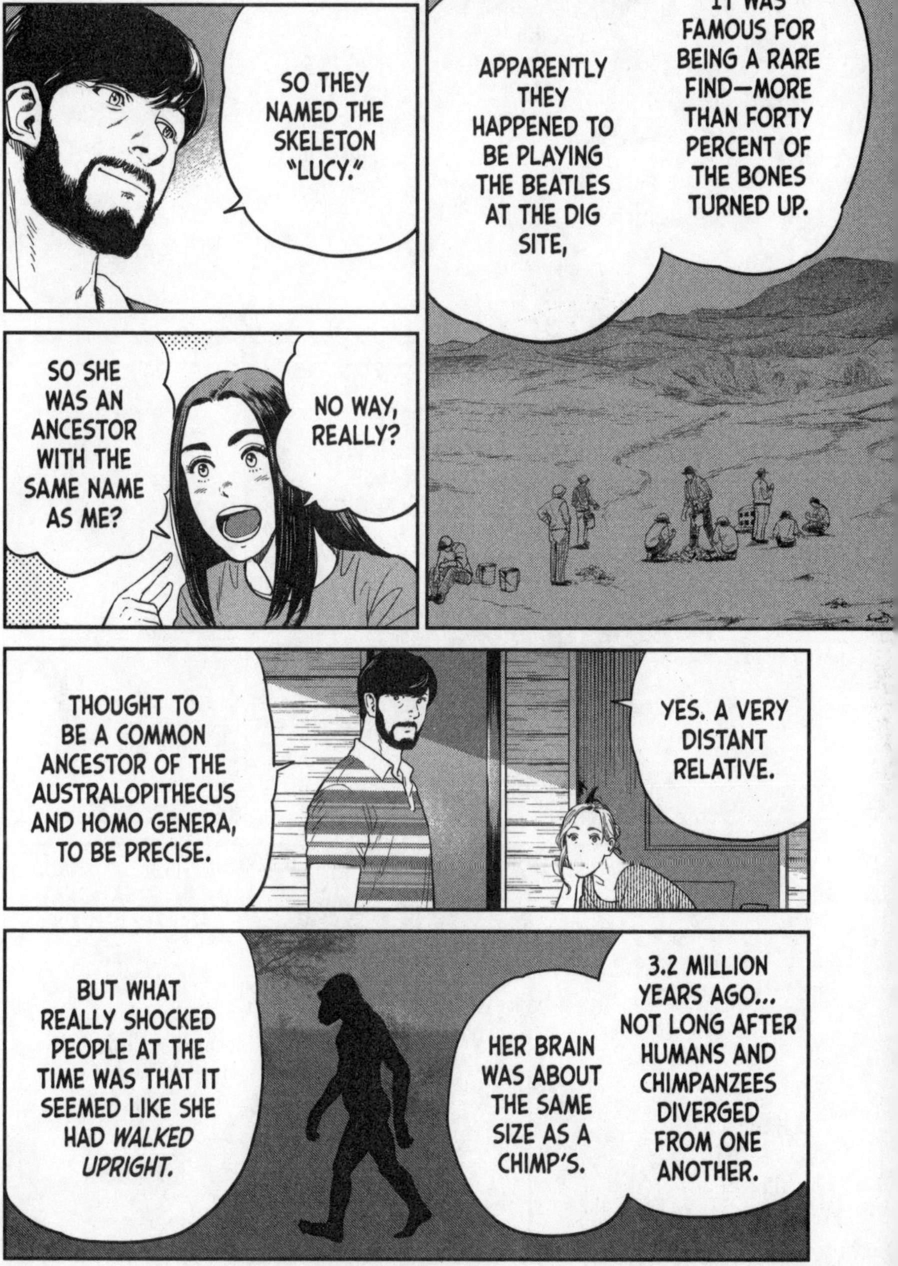
IT WAS FAMOUS FOR BEING A RARE FIND—MORE THAN FORTY PERCENT OF THE BONES TURNED UP.
APPARENTLY THEY HAPPENED TO BE PLAYING THE BEATLES AT THE DIG SITE,
SO THEY NAMED THE SKELETON "LUCY."
NO WAY, REALLY?
SO SHE WAS AN ANCESTOR WITH THE SAME NAME AS ME?
YES. A VERY DISTANT RELATIVE.
THOUGHT TO BE A COMMON ANCESTOR OF THE AUSTRALOPITHECUS AND HOMO GENERA, TO BE PRECISE.
3.2 MILLION YEARS AGO... NOT LONG AFTER HUMANS AND CHIMPANZEES DIVERGED FROM ONE ANOTHER.
HER BRAIN WAS ABOUT THE SAME SIZE AS A CHIMP'S.
BUT WHAT REALLY SHOCKED PEOPLE AT THE TIME WAS THAT IT SEEMED LIKE SHE HAD *WALKED UPRIGHT.*

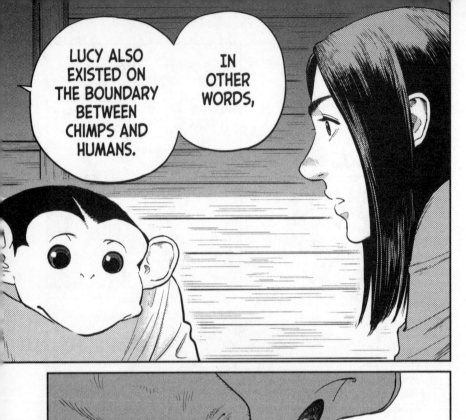

IN OTHER WORDS,

LUCY ALSO EXISTED ON THE BOUNDARY BETWEEN CHIMPS AND HUMANS.

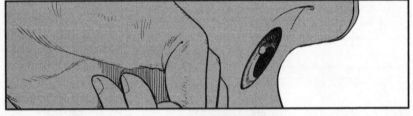

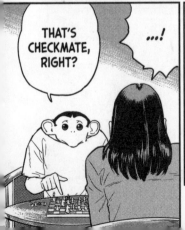

THAT'S CHECKMATE, RIGHT?

....!

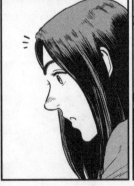

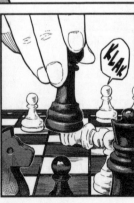

KLAK

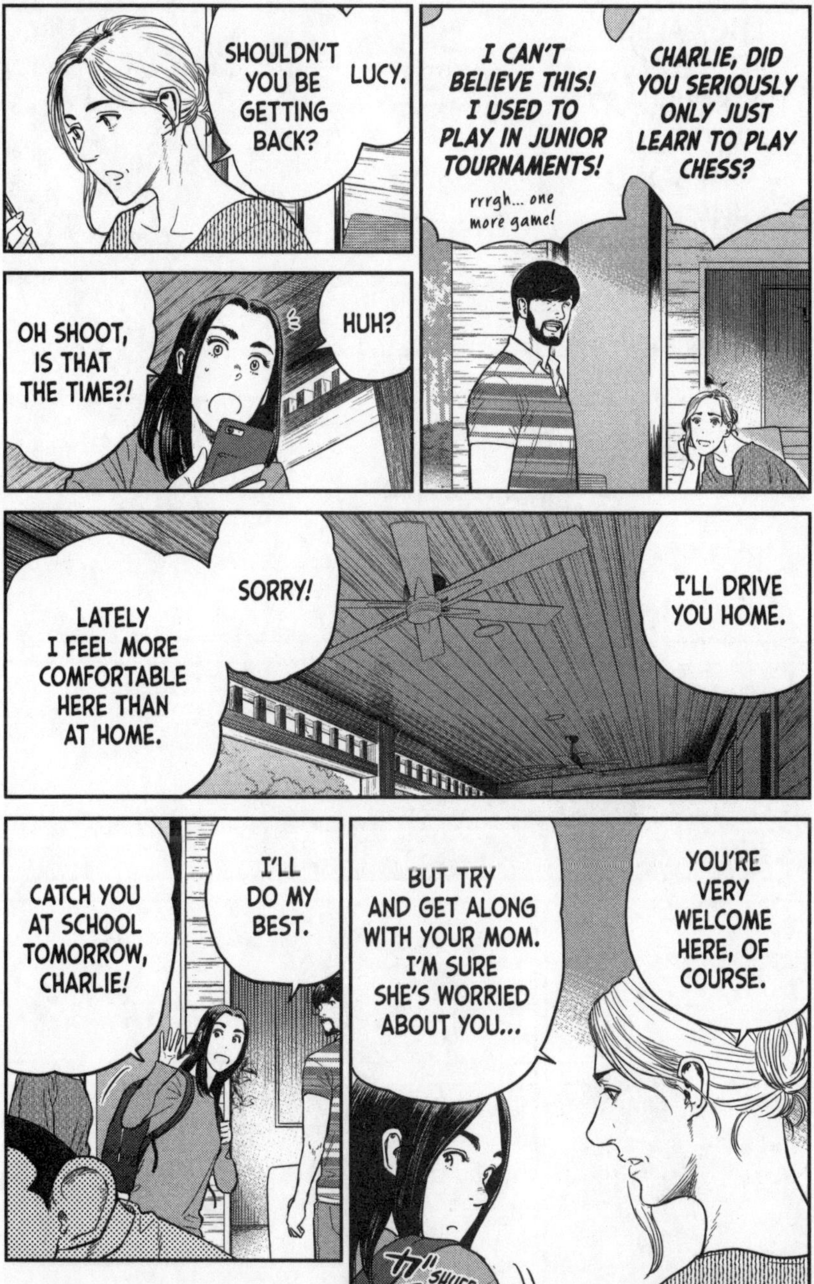
CHARLIE, DID YOU SERIOUSLY ONLY JUST LEARN TO PLAY CHESS?
I CAN'T BELIEVE THIS! I USED TO PLAY IN JUNIOR TOURNAMENTS!
rrrgh... one more game!
LUCY.
SHOULDN'T YOU BE GETTING BACK?
HUH?
OH SHOOT, IS THAT THE TIME?!
I'LL DRIVE YOU HOME.
SORRY!
LATELY I FEEL MORE COMFORTABLE HERE THAN AT HOME.
YOU'RE VERY WELCOME HERE, OF COURSE.
BUT TRY AND GET ALONG WITH YOUR MOM. I'M SURE SHE'S WORRIED ABOUT YOU...
ガチャ
SHUFF
I'LL DO MY BEST.
CATCH YOU AT SCHOOL TOMORROW, CHARLIE!

SHREWS HIGH SCHOOL

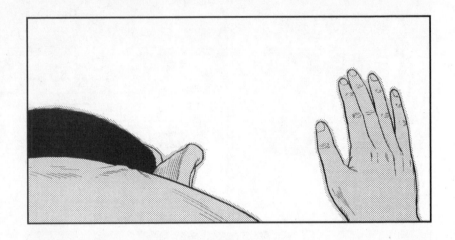

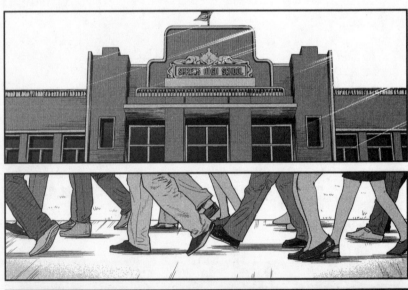

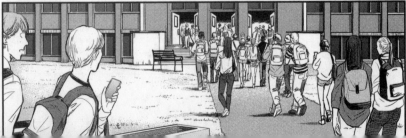

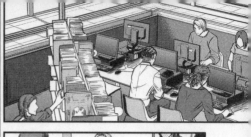

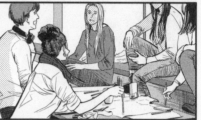

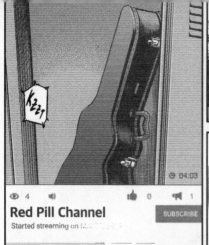

KZZZT

👁 4   🔇   👍 0   📢 1

○ 04:03

Red Pill Channel

Started streaming on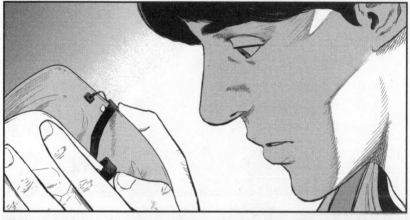

SUBSCRIBE

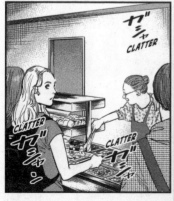

ガチャ
CLATTER

CLATTER
ガチャ
○

CLATTER
ガチャシャ

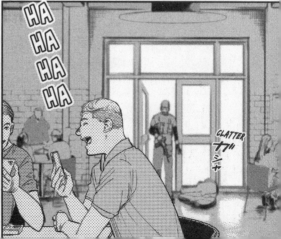

HA
HA
HA
HA

CLATTER
ガチャ

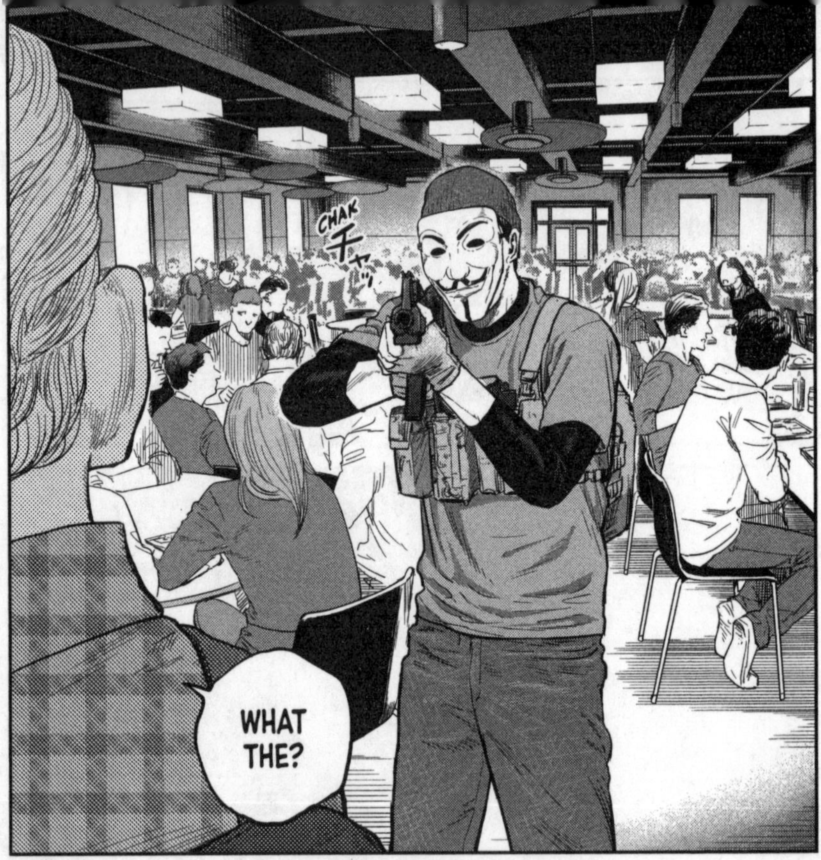
CHAK
チャッ
WHAT THE?

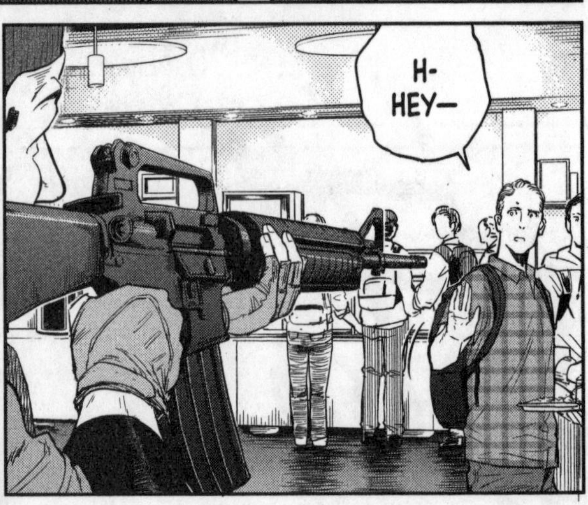
H-
HEY—

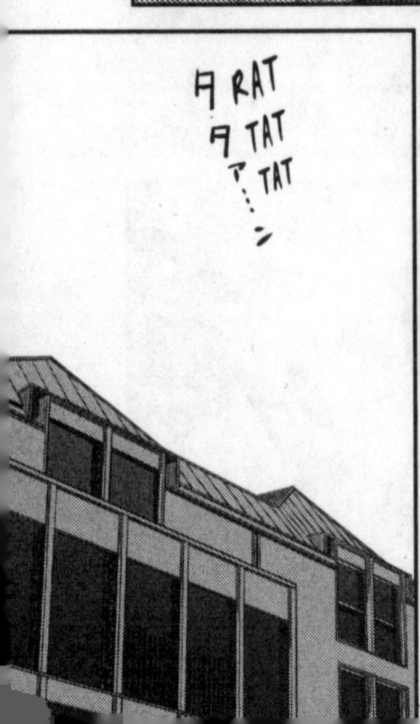
RAT
TAT
TAT

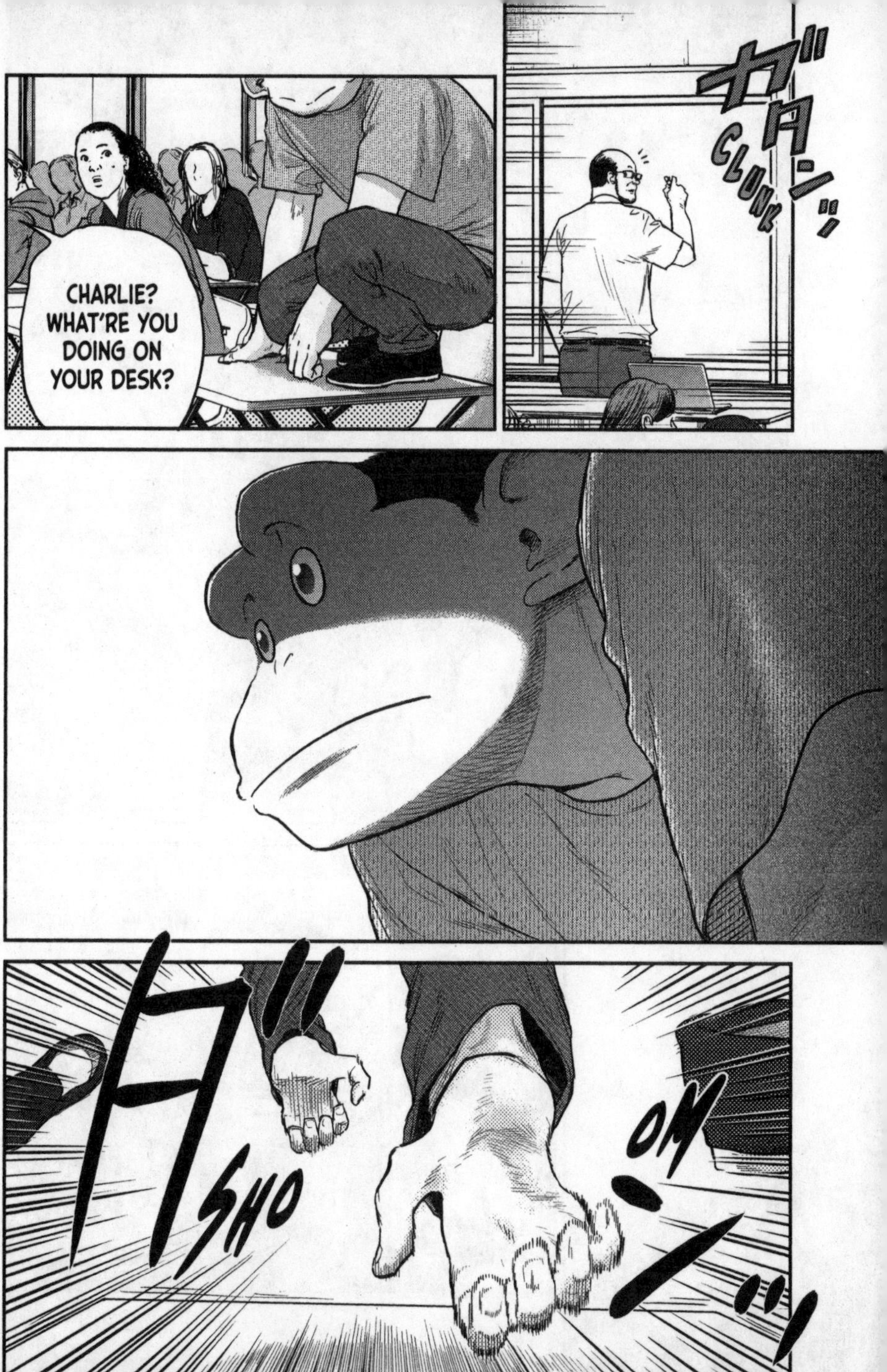
ガタンッ
CLUNK
CHARLIE? WHAT'RE YOU DOING ON YOUR DESK?
SHO
OM

CHAPTER 9 / END

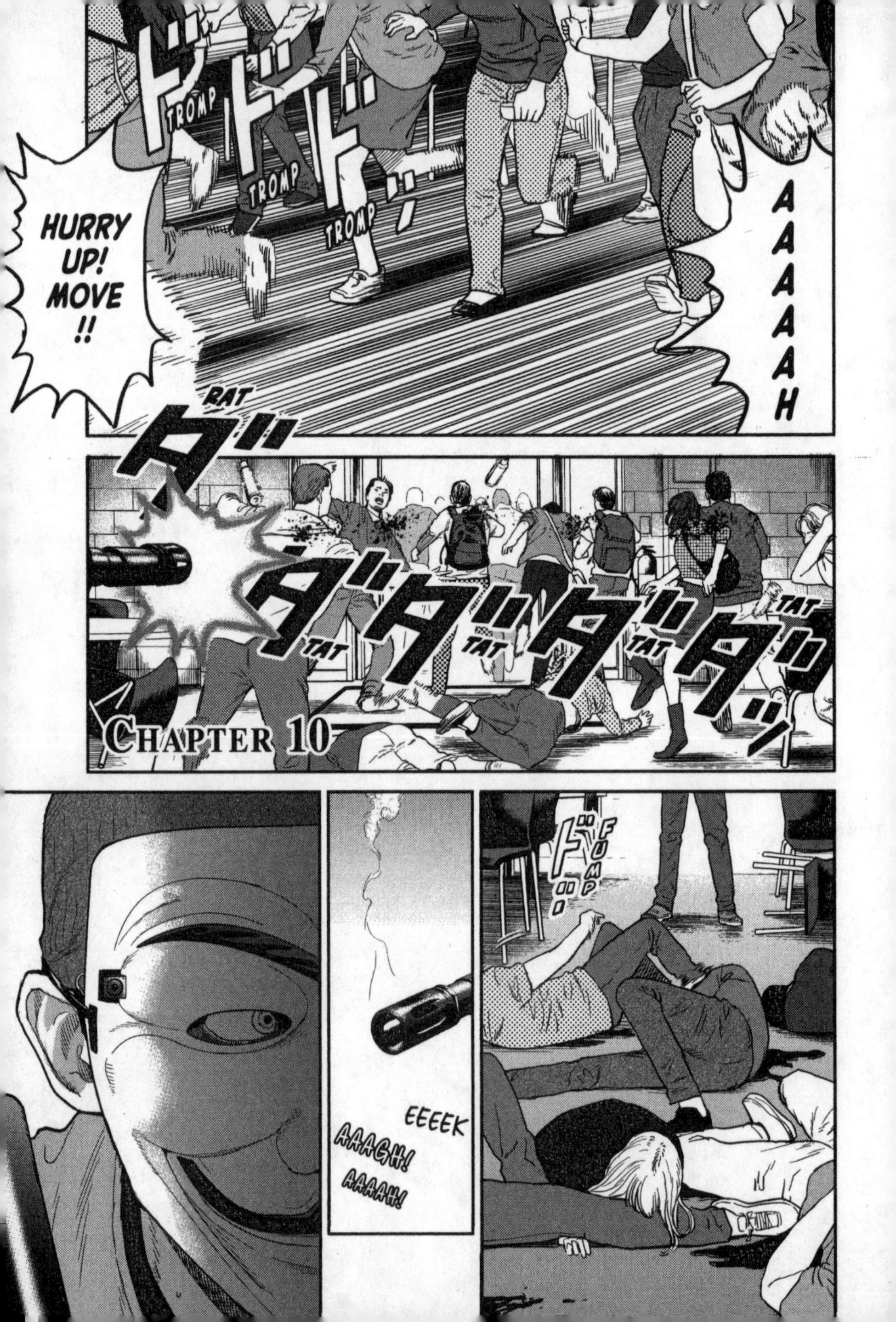
AAAAAAH
TROMP
TROMP
TROMP
HURRY UP! MOVE !!
RAT
TAT
TAT
TAT
TAT
CHAPTER 10
FUMP
EEEEK
AAAAGH!
AAAAH!

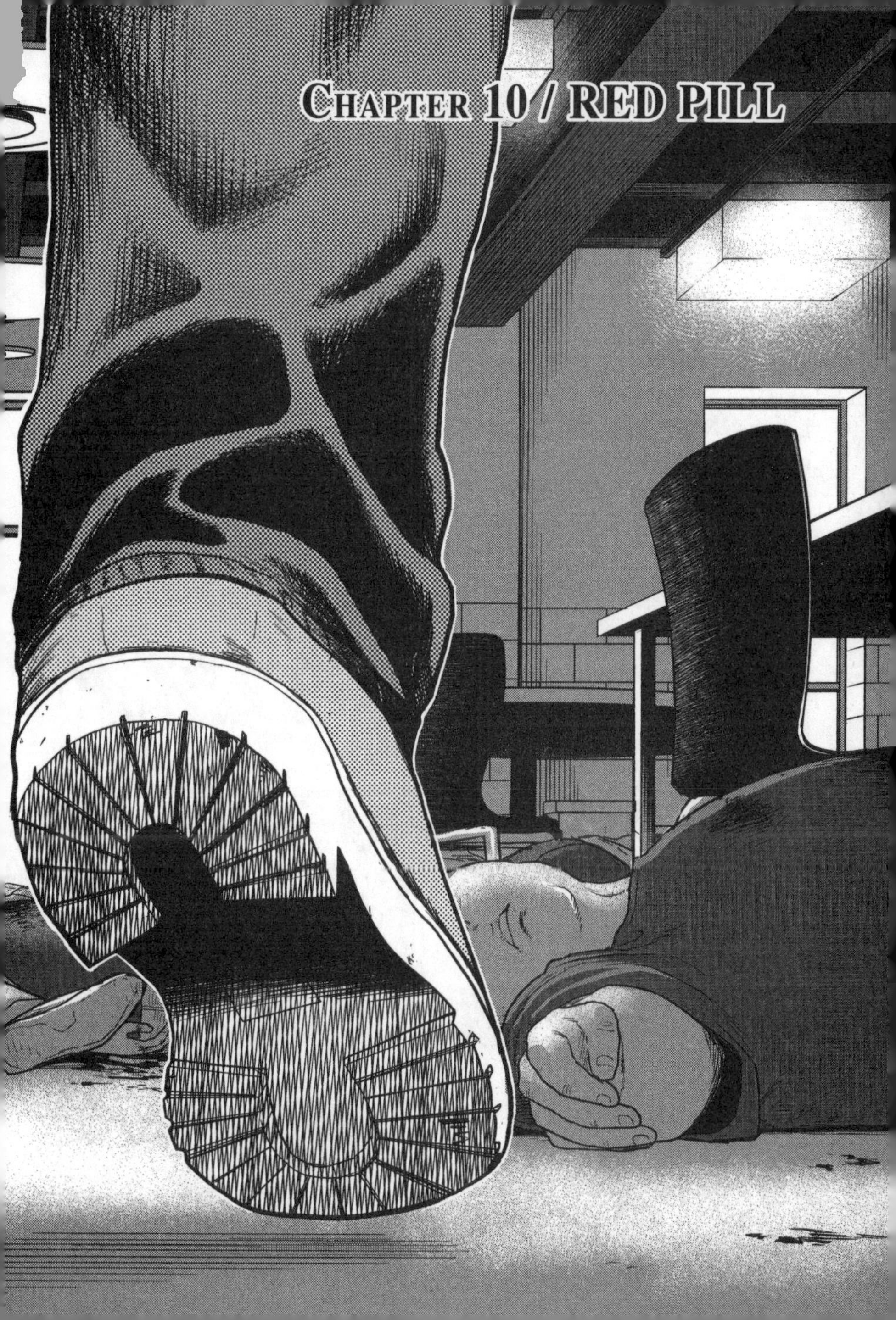
CHAPTER 10 / RED PILL

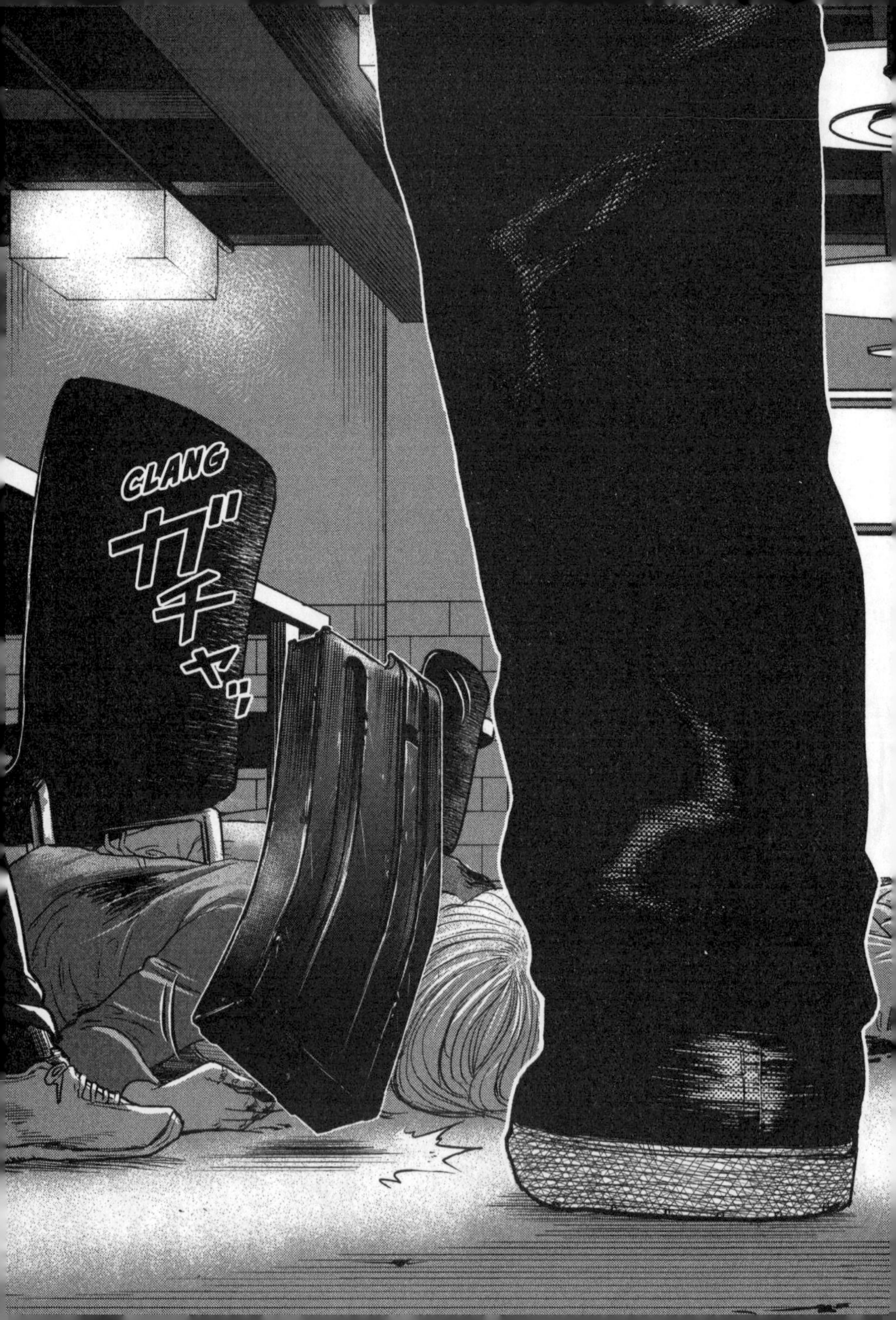
CLANG
ガチャッ

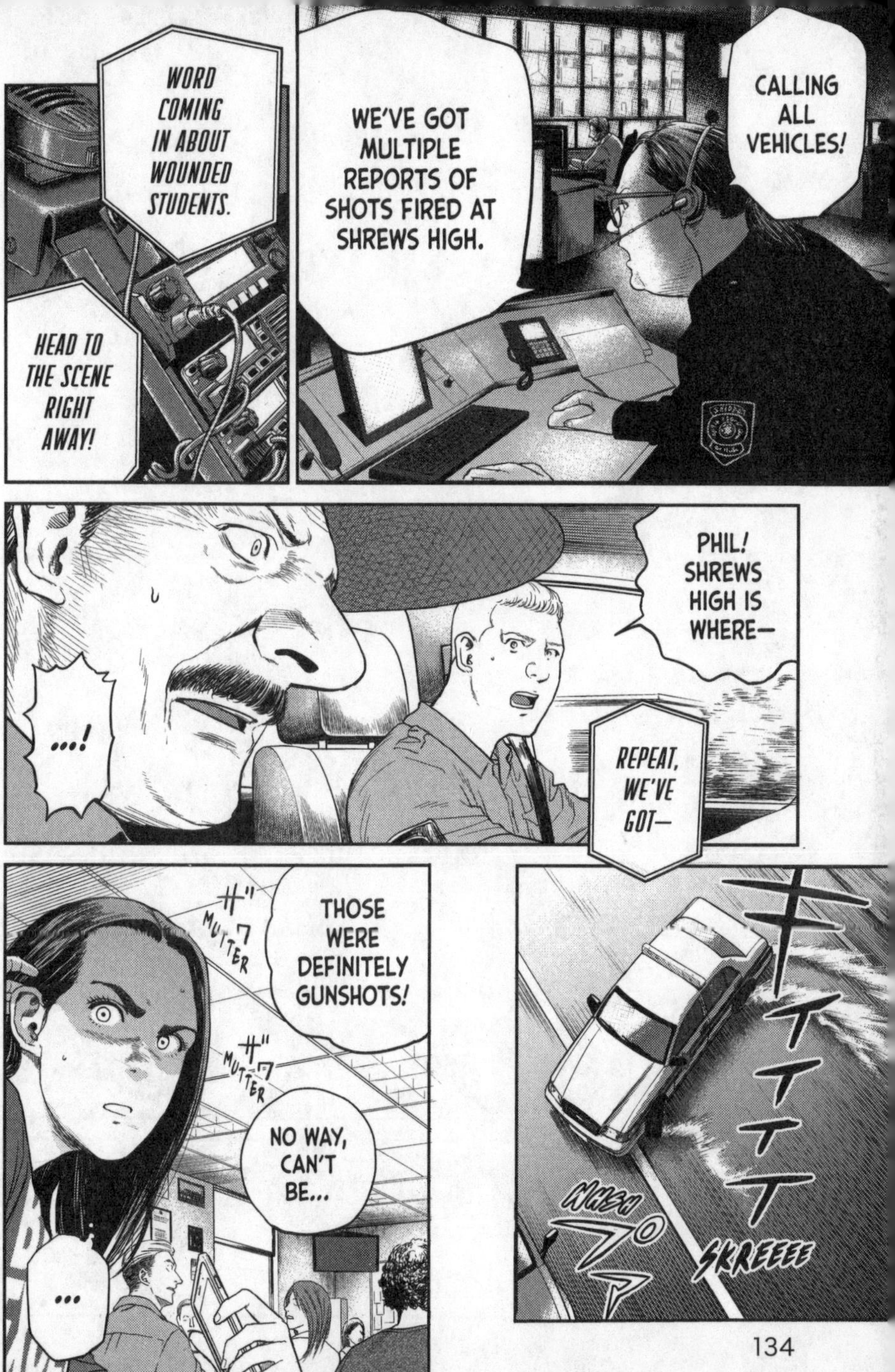
CALLING ALL VEHICLES!
WE'VE GOT MULTIPLE REPORTS OF SHOTS FIRED AT SHREWS HIGH.
WORD COMING IN ABOUT WOUNDED STUDENTS.
HEAD TO THE SCENE RIGHT AWAY!
PHIL! SHREWS HIGH IS WHERE—
REPEAT, WE'VE GOT—
...!
SKREEEE
WHSH
THOSE WERE DEFINITELY GUNSHOTS!
MUTTER
MUTTER
NO WAY, CAN'T BE...
...

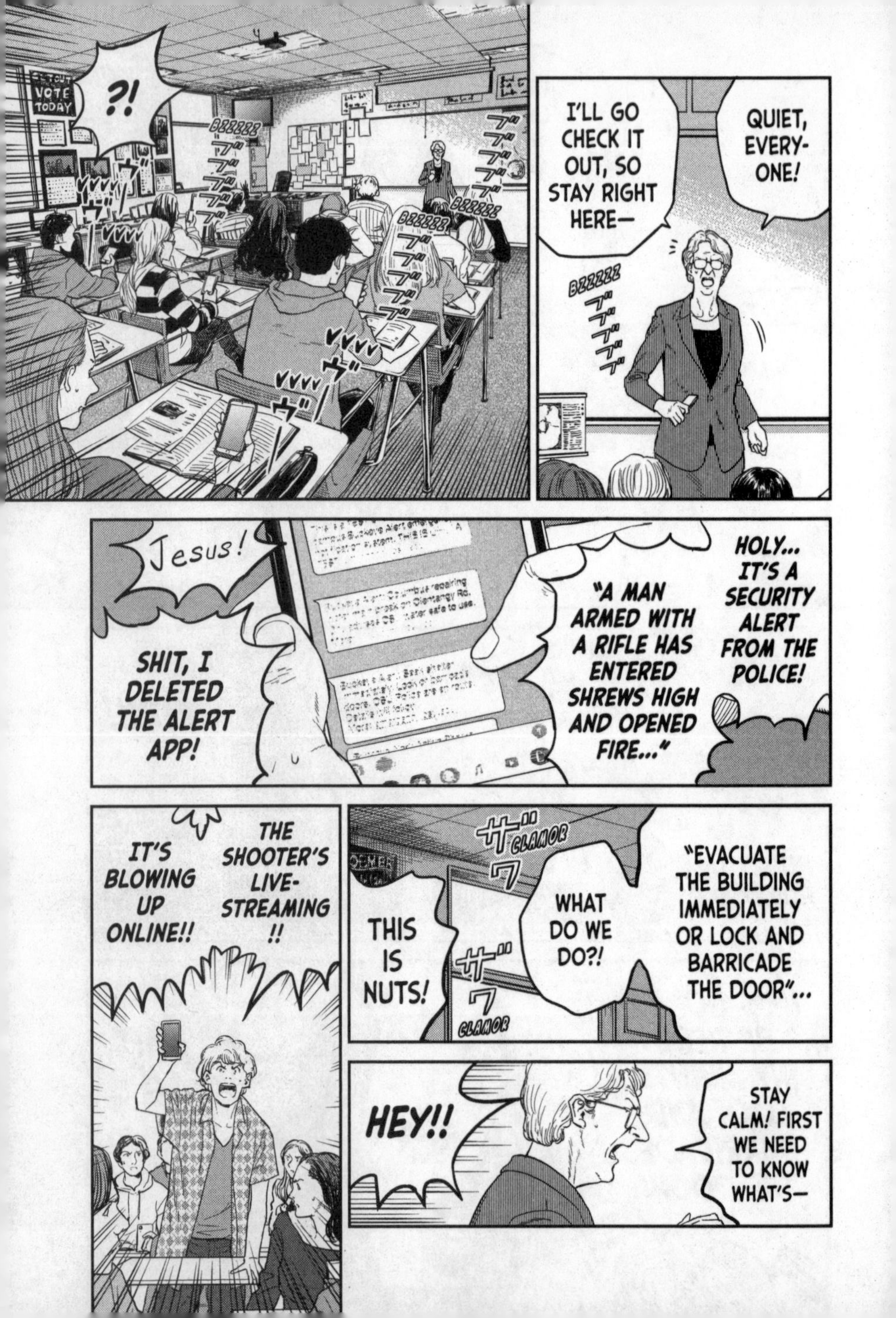
QUIET, EVERY-ONE!
I'LL GO CHECK IT OUT, SO STAY RIGHT HERE—
BZZZZZ
?!
VOTE TODAY
BZZZZZ
BZZZZZ
BZZZZZ
HOLY... IT'S A SECURITY ALERT FROM THE POLICE!
"A MAN ARMED WITH A RIFLE HAS ENTERED SHREWS HIGH AND OPENED FIRE..."
SHIT, I DELETED THE ALERT APP!
Jesus!
"EVACUATE THE BUILDING IMMEDIATELY OR LOCK AND BARRICADE THE DOOR"...
CLAMOR
WHAT DO WE DO?!
THIS IS NUTS!
CLAMOR
STAY CALM! FIRST WE NEED TO KNOW WHAT'S—
HEY!!
THE SHOOTER'S LIVE-STREAMING!!
IT'S BLOWING UP ONLINE!!

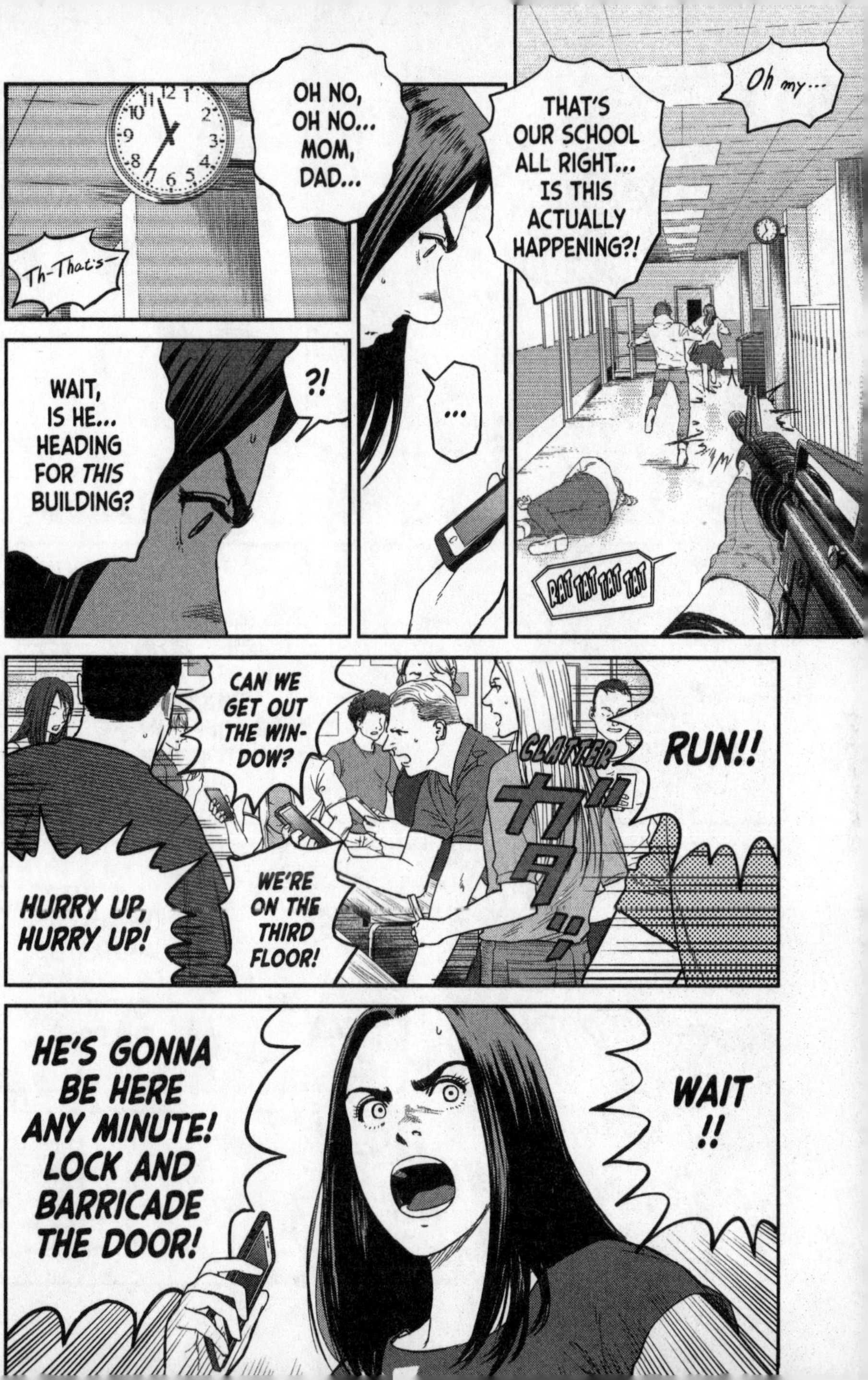
Oh my...
THAT'S OUR SCHOOL ALL RIGHT... IS THIS ACTUALLY HAPPENING?!
RAT TAT TAT TAT
OH NO, OH NO... MOM, DAD...
...
Th-That's—
?!
WAIT, IS HE... HEADING FOR THIS BUILDING?
RUN!!
CLATTER
CAN WE GET OUT THE WIN-DOW?
WE'RE ON THE THIRD FLOOR!
HURRY UP, HURRY UP!
WAIT !!
HE'S GONNA BE HERE ANY MINUTE! LOCK AND BARRICADE THE DOOR!

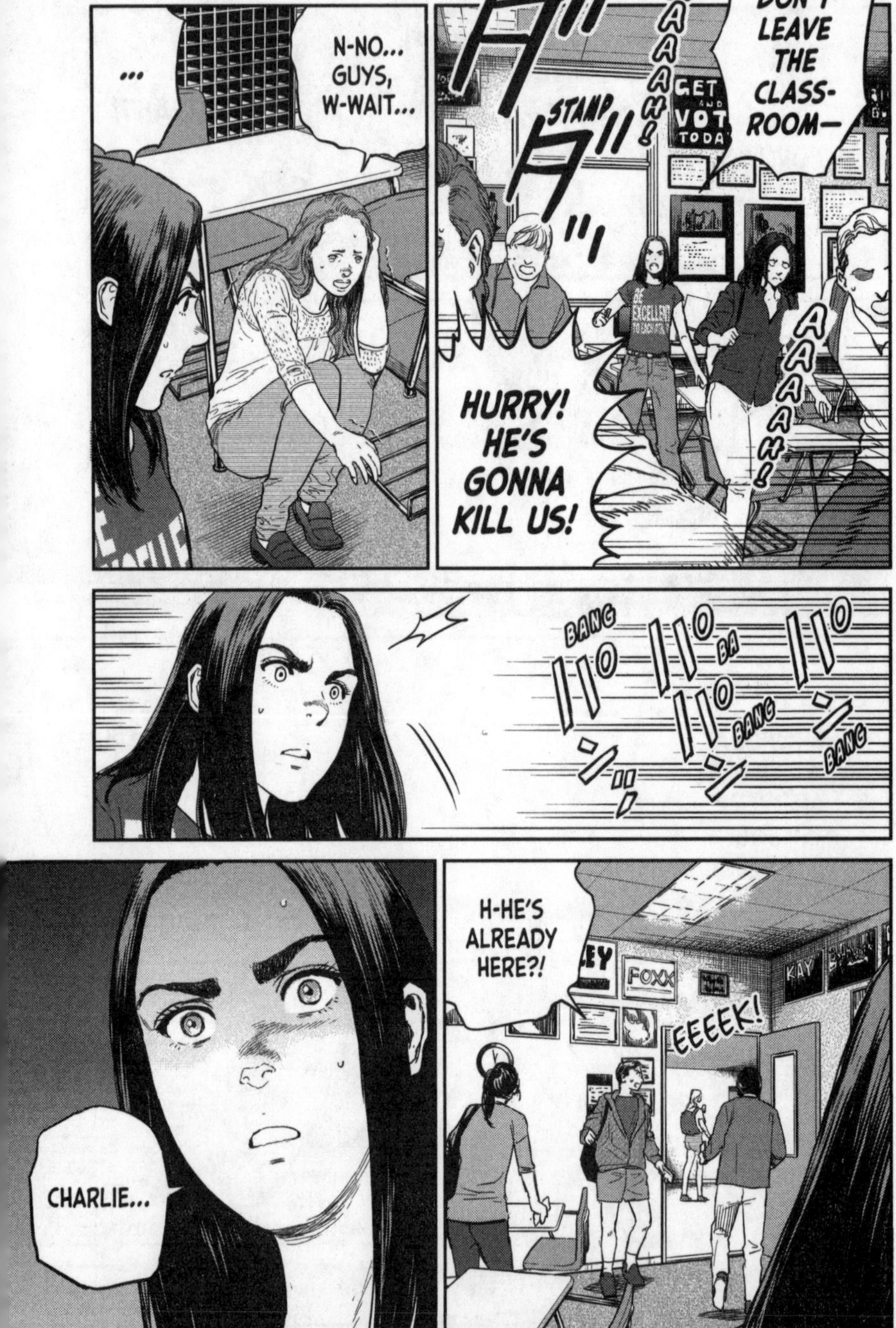
DON'T LEAVE THE CLASS-ROOM—
AAAAAH!
STAMP
STAMP
HURRY! HE'S GONNA KILL US!
AAAAAAH!
N-NO... GUYS, W-WAIT...
...
BANG
BA
BANG
BANG
H-HE'S ALREADY HERE?!
FOXX
KAY
EEEEK!
CHARLIE...

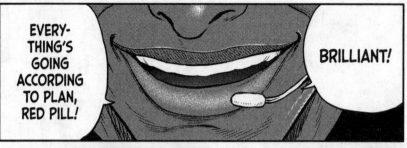

BRILLIANT!
EVERY-THING'S GOING ACCORDING TO PLAN, RED PILL!
HFFF
HFFF
HFFF
LET'S GO OVER THIS ONE MORE TIME.
THERE'S NO DOUBT CHARLIE WILL TRY TO STOP YOU.
HIS BEHAVIORAL PRINCIPLES ARE VERY SIMPLE.

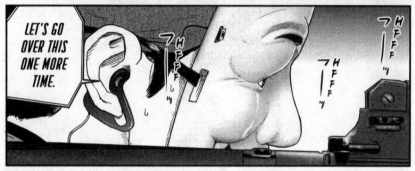

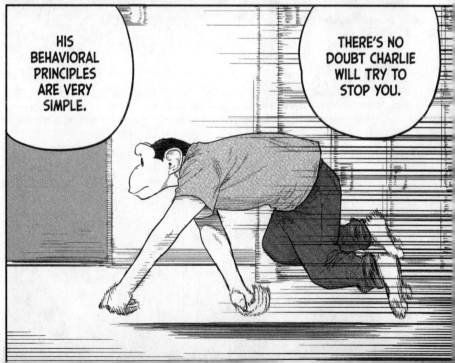

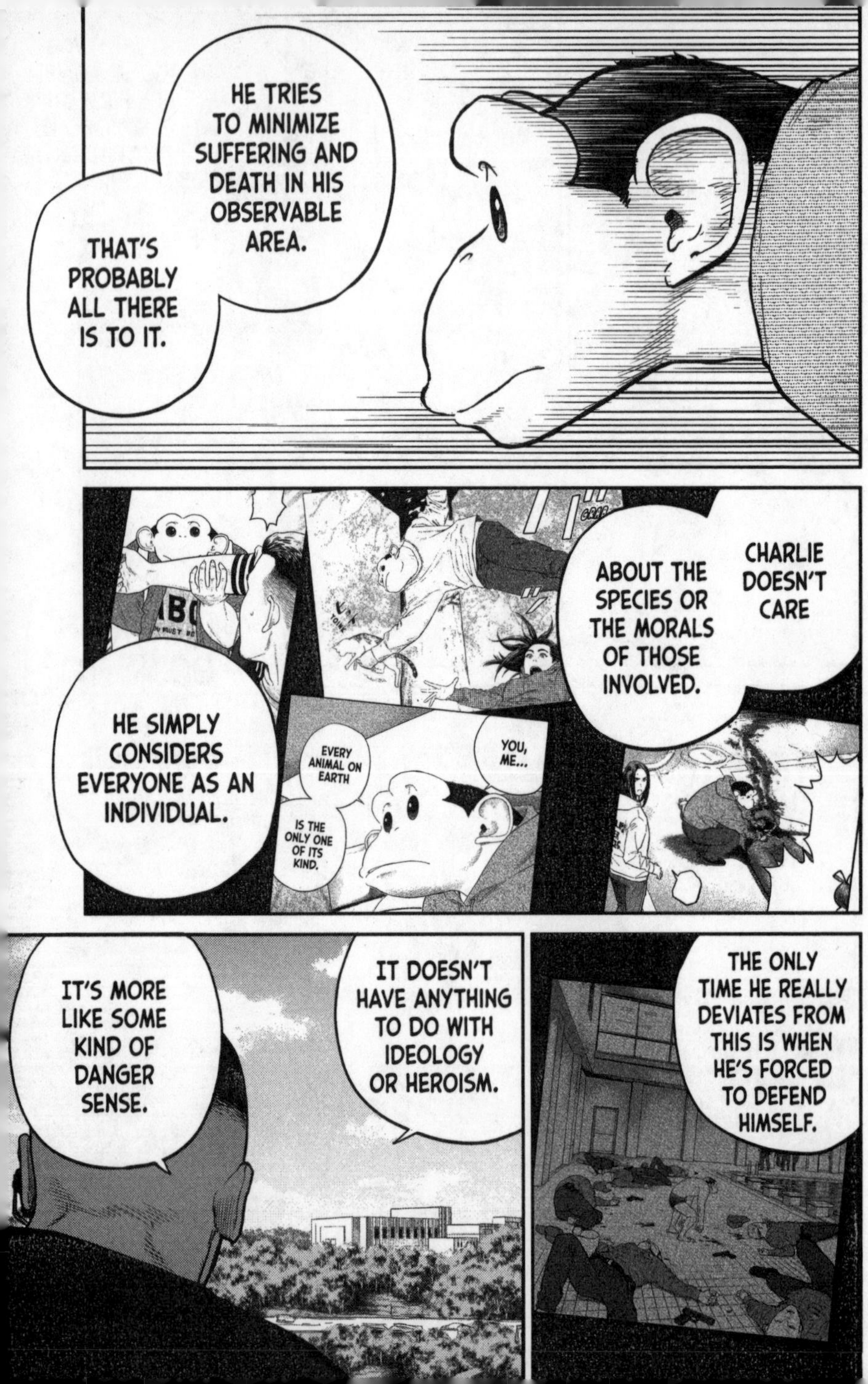
HE TRIES TO MINIMIZE SUFFERING AND DEATH IN HIS OBSERVABLE AREA.
THAT'S PROBABLY ALL THERE IS TO IT.
CHARLIE DOESN'T CARE
ABOUT THE SPECIES OR THE MORALS OF THOSE INVOLVED.
HE SIMPLY CONSIDERS EVERYONE AS AN INDIVIDUAL.
YOU, ME...
EVERY ANIMAL ON EARTH
IS THE ONLY ONE OF ITS KIND.
THE ONLY TIME HE REALLY DEVIATES FROM THIS IS WHEN HE'S FORCED TO DEFEND HIMSELF.
IT DOESN'T HAVE ANYTHING TO DO WITH IDEOLOGY OR HEROISM.
IT'S MORE LIKE SOME KIND OF DANGER SENSE.

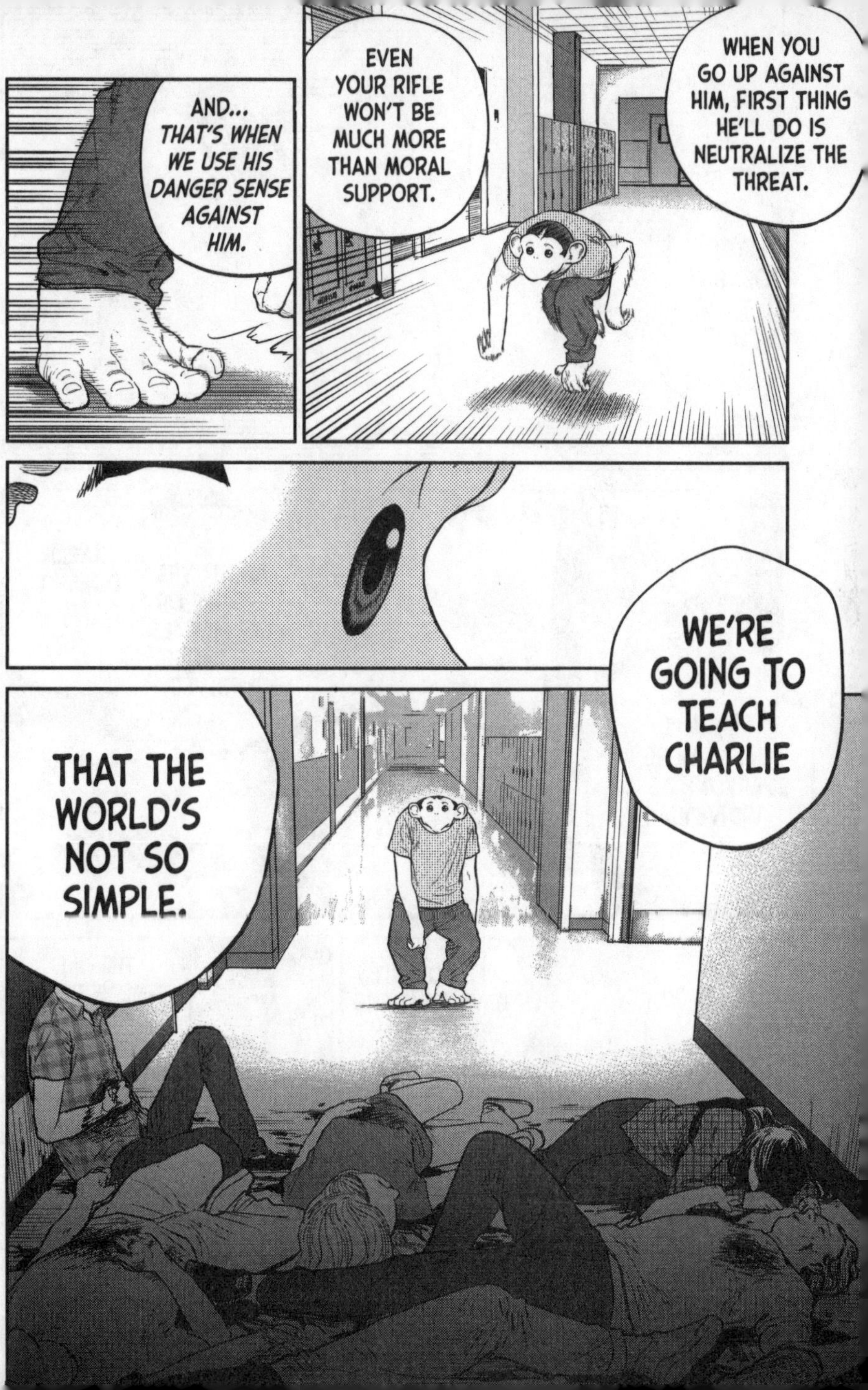
WHEN YOU GO UP AGAINST HIM, FIRST THING HE'LL DO IS NEUTRALIZE THE THREAT.
EVEN YOUR RIFLE WON'T BE MUCH MORE THAN MORAL SUPPORT.
AND... THAT'S WHEN WE USE HIS DANGER SENSE AGAINST HIM.
WE'RE GOING TO TEACH CHARLIE
THAT THE WORLD'S NOT SO SIMPLE.

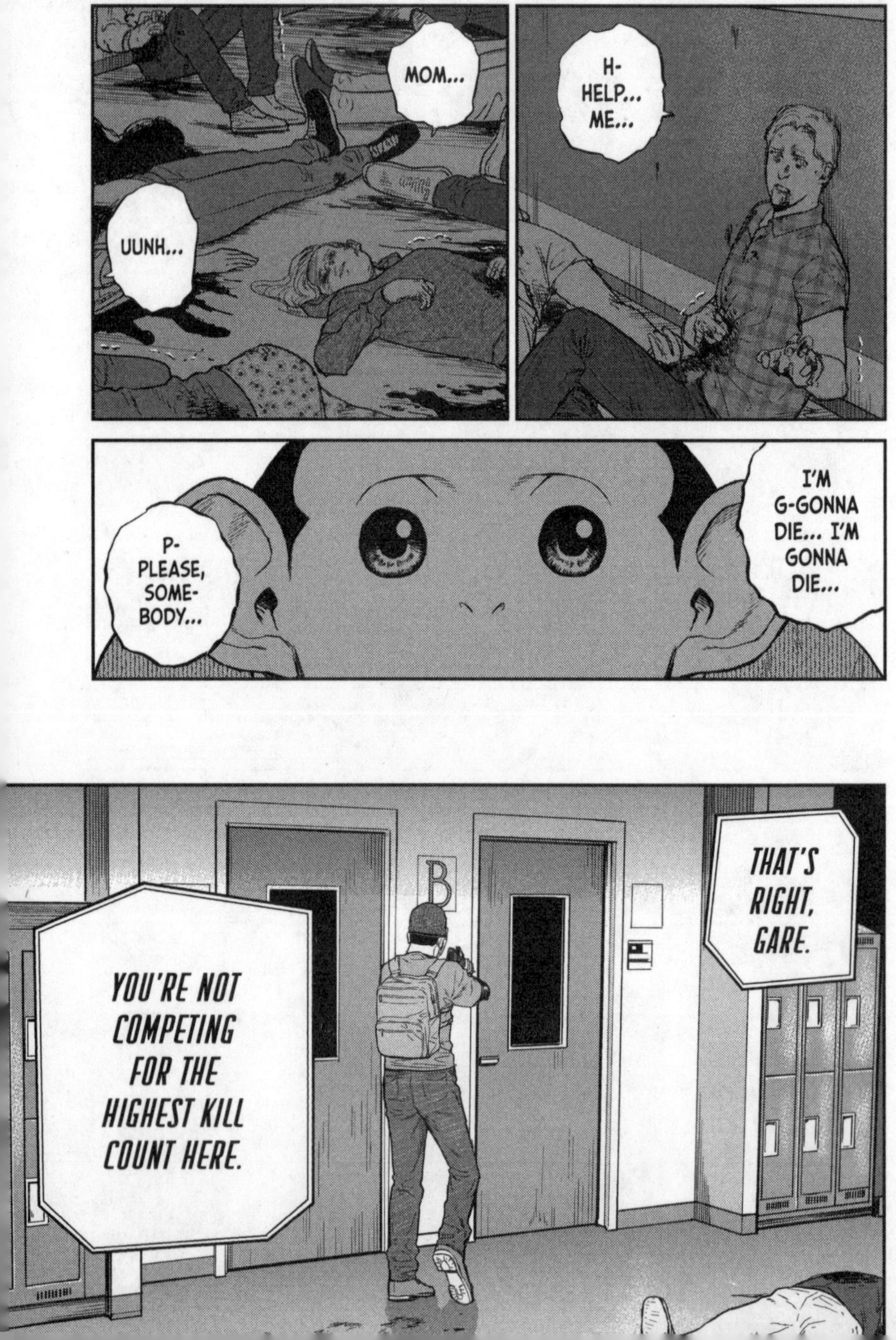
H-HELP... ME...
MOM...
UUNH...
I'M G-GONNA DIE... I'M GONNA DIE...
P-PLEASE, SOMEBODY...
THAT'S RIGHT, GARE.
YOU'RE NOT COMPETING FOR THE HIGHEST KILL COUNT HERE.

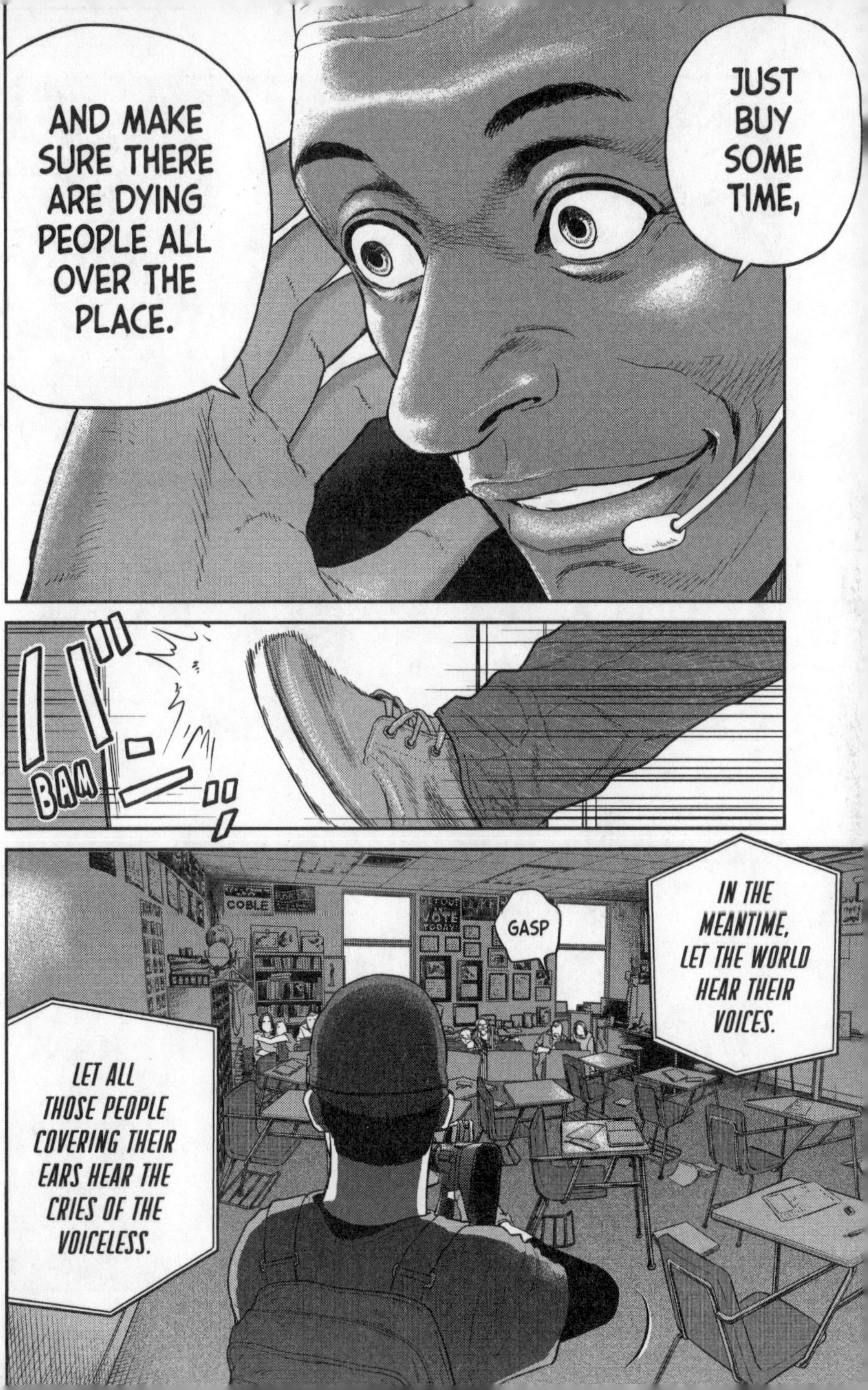
JUST BUY SOME TIME,
AND MAKE SURE THERE ARE DYING PEOPLE ALL OVER THE PLACE.
BAM
IN THE MEANTIME, LET THE WORLD HEAR THEIR VOICES.
GASP
LET ALL THOSE PEOPLE COVERING THEIR EARS HEAR THE CRIES OF THE VOICELESS.

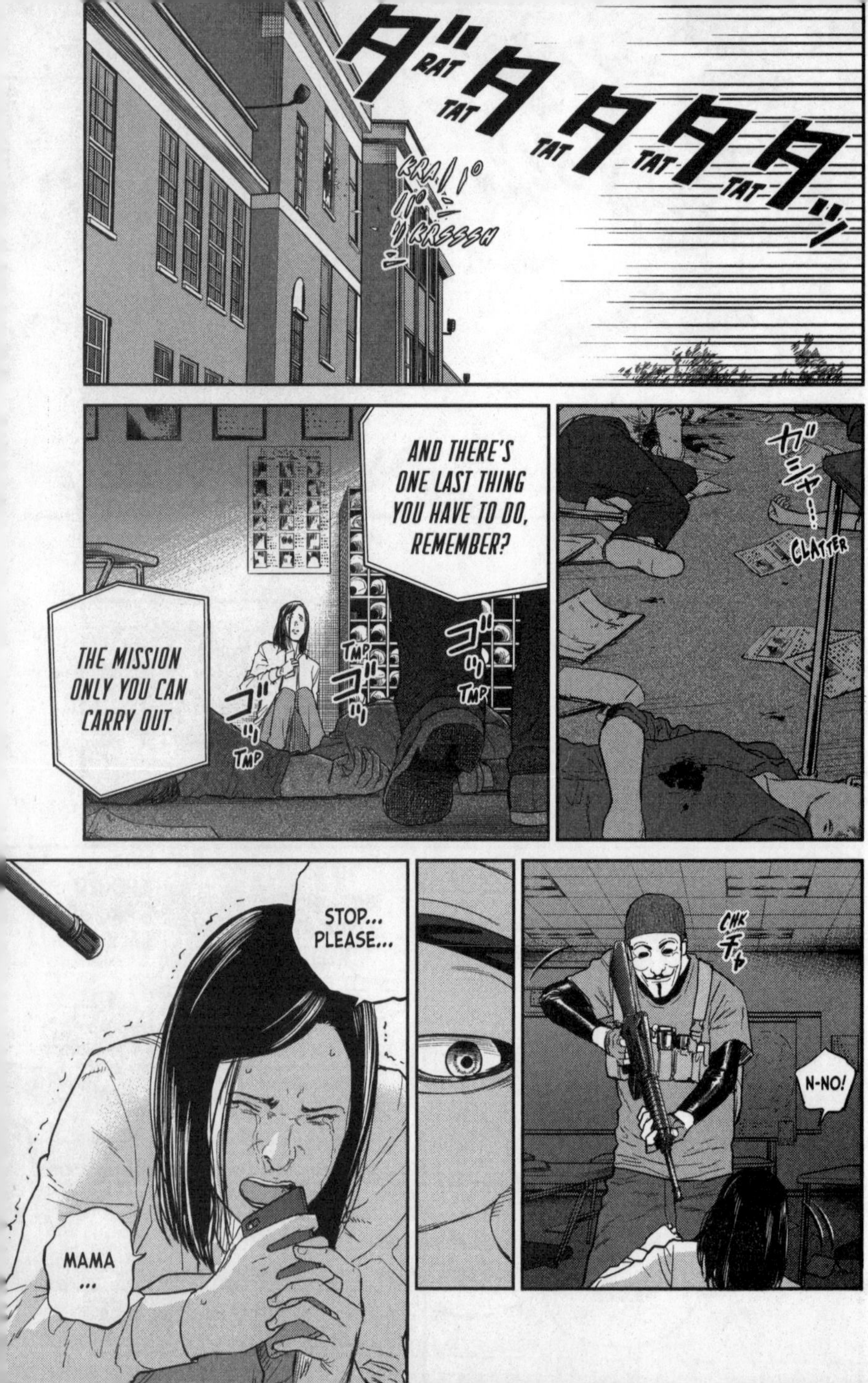
RAT TAT TAT TAT TAT
KRA
KRSSSH
CLATTER
AND THERE'S ONE LAST THING YOU HAVE TO DO, REMEMBER?
THE MISSION ONLY YOU CAN CARRY OUT.
TMP
TMP
TMP
CHK
N-NO!
STOP... PLEASE...
MAMA ...

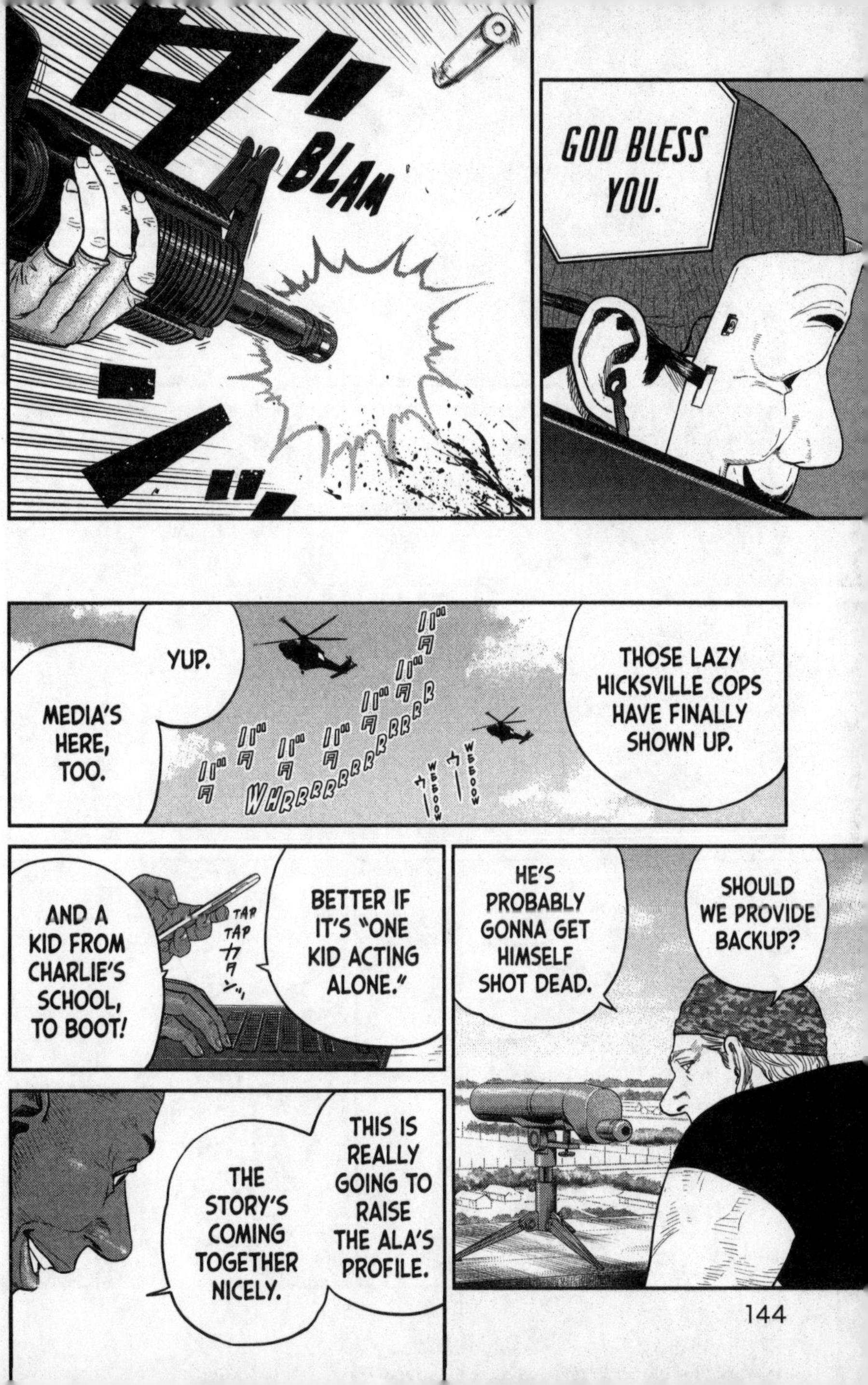
GOD BLESS YOU.
BLAM
THOSE LAZY HICKSVILLE COPS HAVE FINALLY SHOWN UP.
WEEOOW
WEEOOW
WHRRRRRRRRRRRRRRRR
YUP.
MEDIA'S HERE, TOO.
SHOULD WE PROVIDE BACKUP?
HE'S PROBABLY GONNA GET HIMSELF SHOT DEAD.
BETTER IF IT'S "ONE KID ACTING ALONE."
TAP TAP
AND A KID FROM CHARLIE'S SCHOOL, TO BOOT!
THIS IS REALLY GOING TO RAISE THE ALA'S PROFILE.
THE STORY'S COMING TOGETHER NICELY.

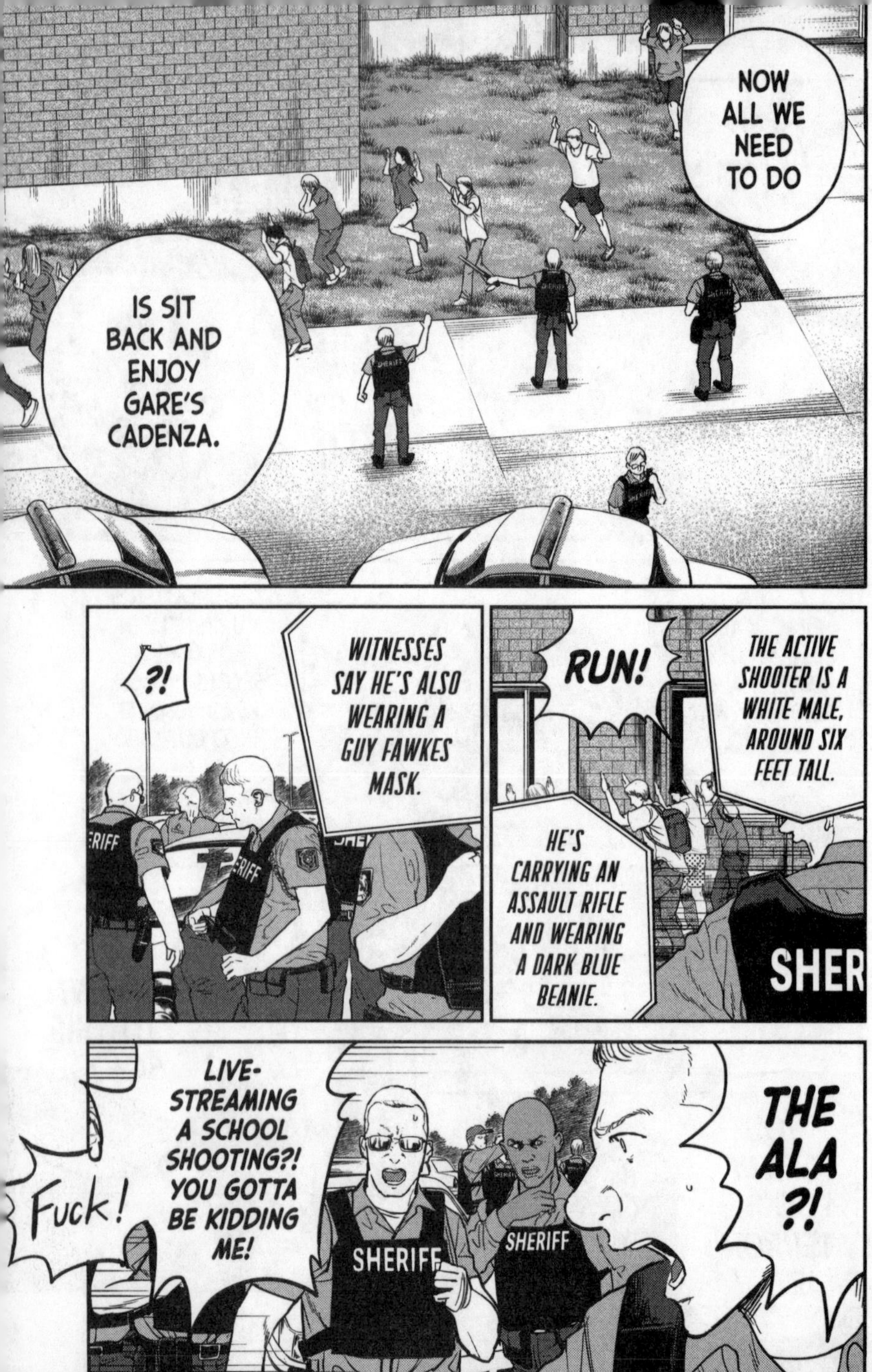
NOW ALL WE NEED TO DO
IS SIT BACK AND ENJOY GARE'S CADENZA.
RUN!
THE ACTIVE SHOOTER IS A WHITE MALE, AROUND SIX FEET TALL.
HE'S CARRYING AN ASSAULT RIFLE AND WEARING A DARK BLUE BEANIE.
WITNESSES SAY HE'S ALSO WEARING A GUY FAWKES MASK.
?!
THE ALA ?!
LIVE-STREAMING A SCHOOL SHOOTING?! YOU GOTTA BE KIDDING ME!
Fuck!

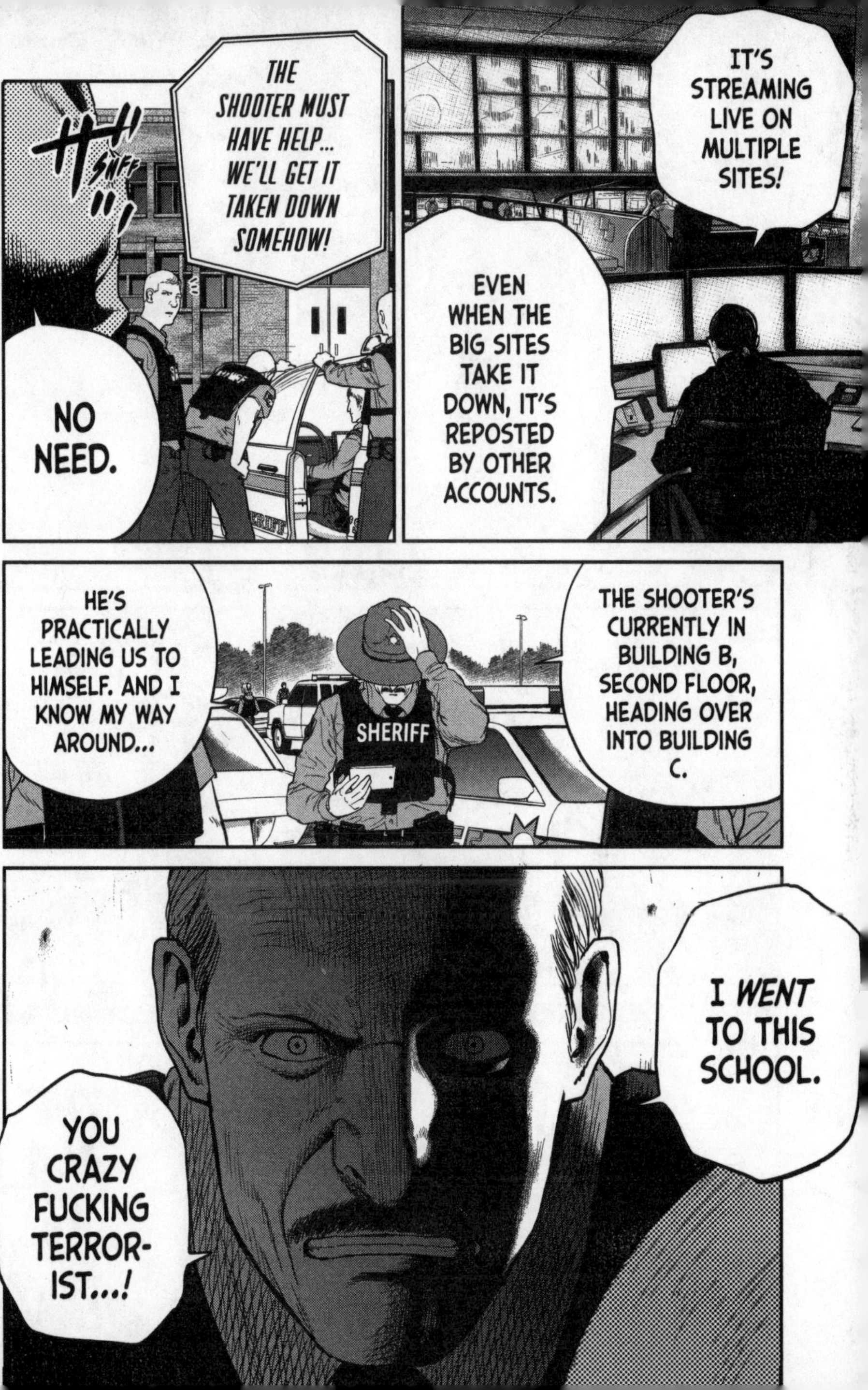
IT'S STREAMING LIVE ON MULTIPLE SITES!
EVEN WHEN THE BIG SITES TAKE IT DOWN, IT'S REPOSTED BY OTHER ACCOUNTS.
THE SHOOTER MUST HAVE HELP... WE'LL GET IT TAKEN DOWN SOMEHOW!
SNFF
NO NEED.
THE SHOOTER'S CURRENTLY IN BUILDING B, SECOND FLOOR, HEADING OVER INTO BUILDING C.
HE'S PRACTICALLY LEADING US TO HIMSELF. AND I KNOW MY WAY AROUND...
I *WENT* TO THIS SCHOOL.
YOU CRAZY FUCKING TERROR-IST...!

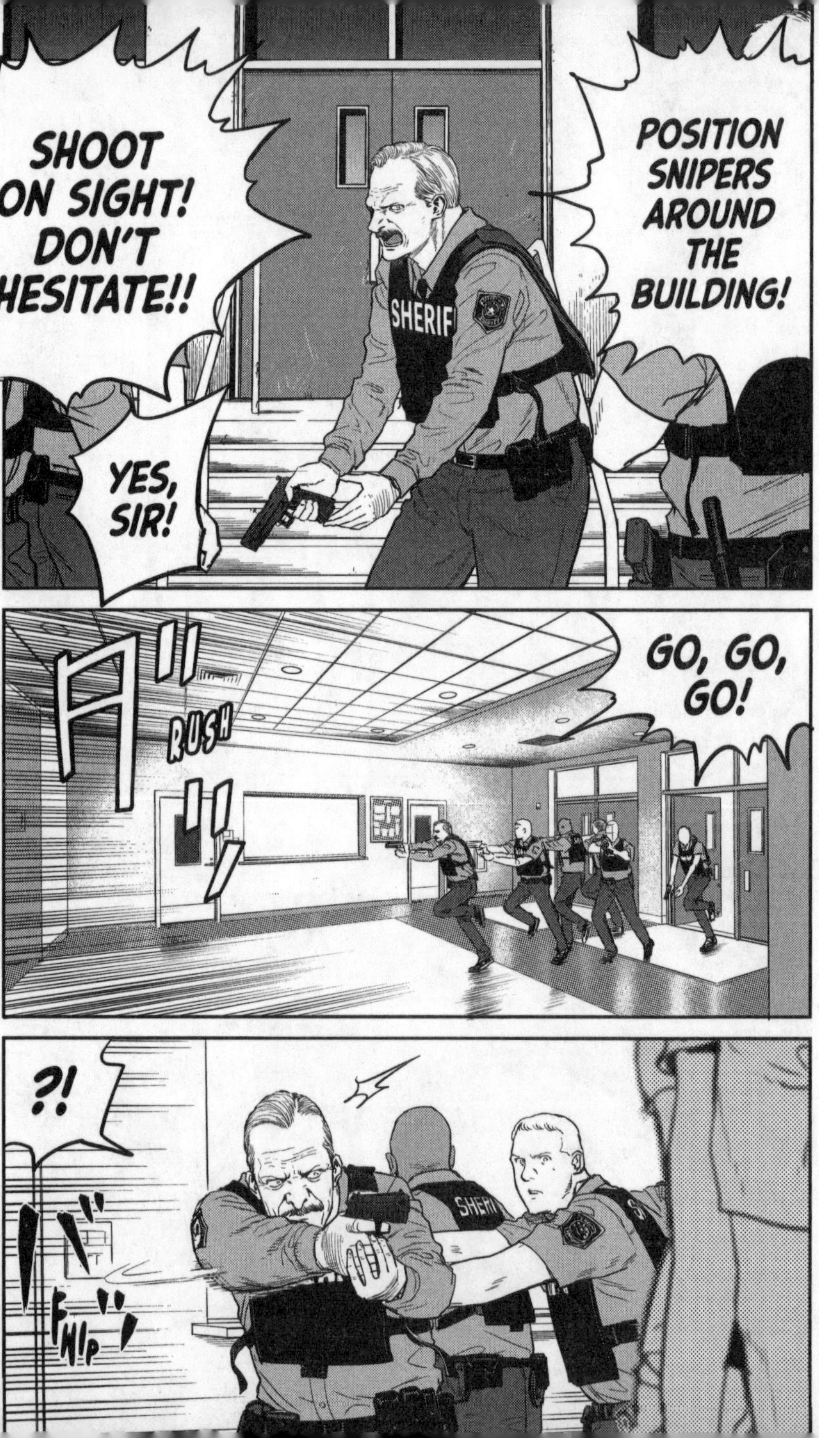
POSITION SNIPERS AROUND THE BUILDING!
SHOOT ON SIGHT! DON'T HESITATE!!
SHERIF
YES, SIR!
GO, GO, GO!
RUSH
?!
FHIP

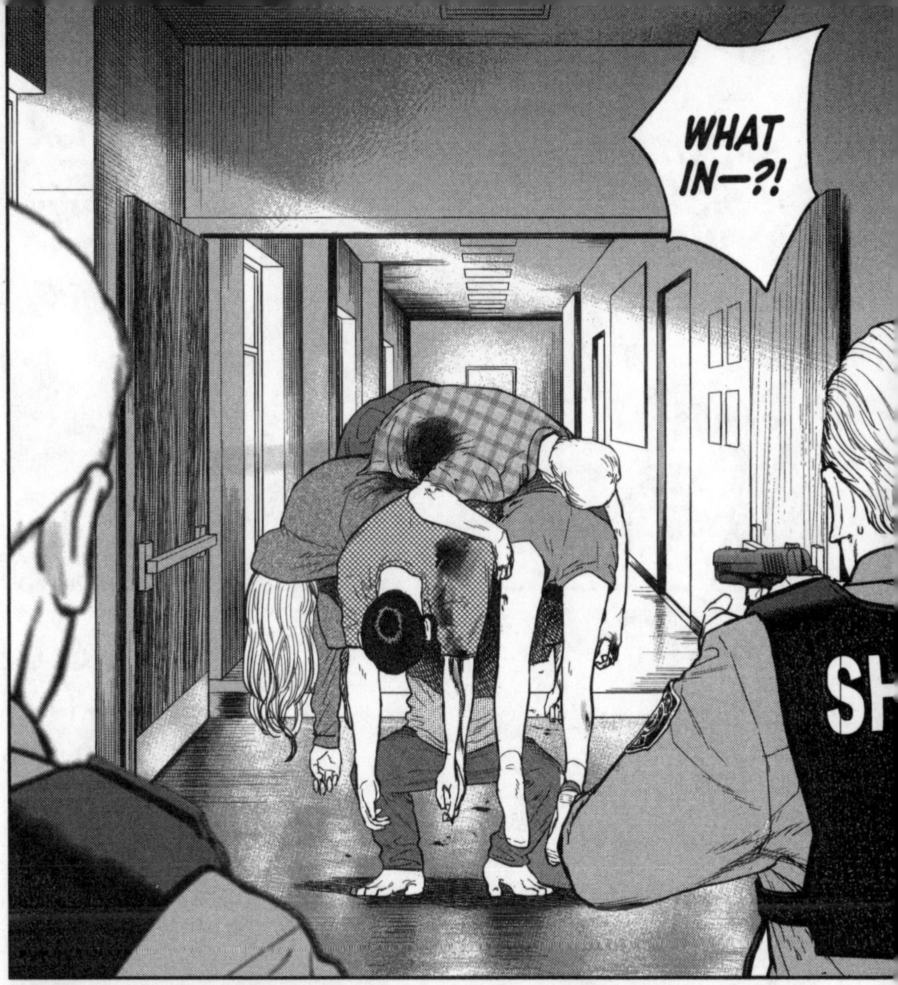
WHAT IN—?!
SH
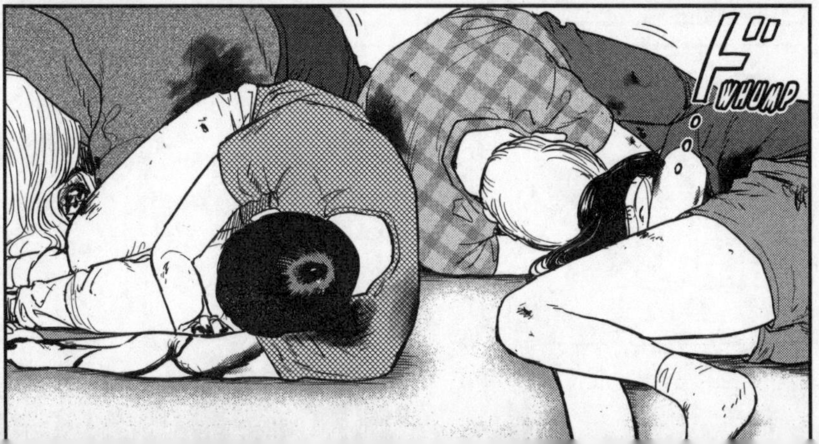
ド
WHUMP

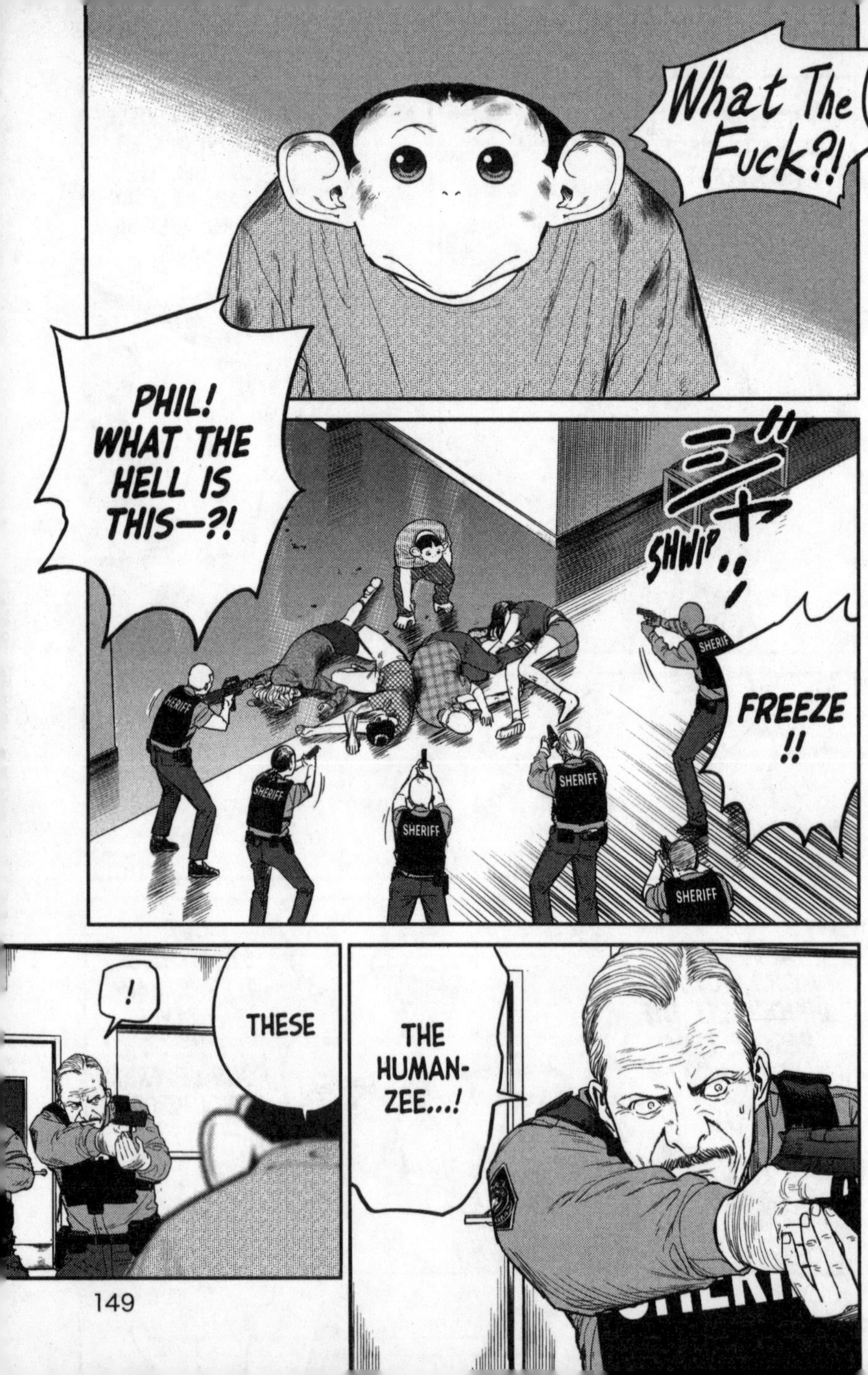
What The Fuck?!
PHIL! WHAT THE HELL IS THIS—?!
SHWIP
FREEZE!!
THE HUMAN-ZEE...!
!
THESE

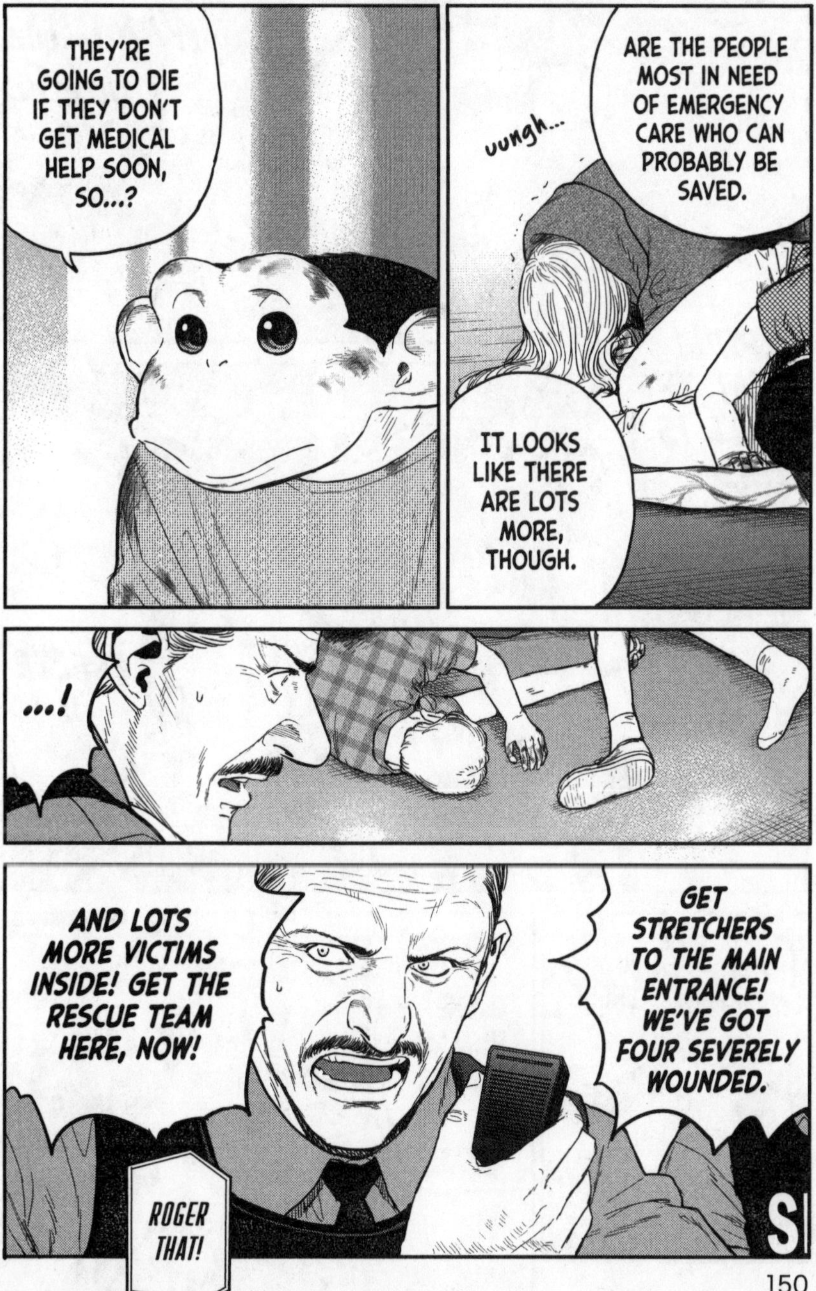
ARE THE PEOPLE MOST IN NEED OF EMERGENCY CARE WHO CAN PROBABLY BE SAVED.
uungh...
IT LOOKS LIKE THERE ARE LOTS MORE, THOUGH.
THEY'RE GOING TO DIE IF THEY DON'T GET MEDICAL HELP SOON, SO...?
...!
GET STRETCHERS TO THE MAIN ENTRANCE! WE'VE GOT FOUR SEVERELY WOUNDED.
AND LOTS MORE VICTIMS INSIDE! GET THE RESCUE TEAM HERE, NOW!
ROGER THAT!

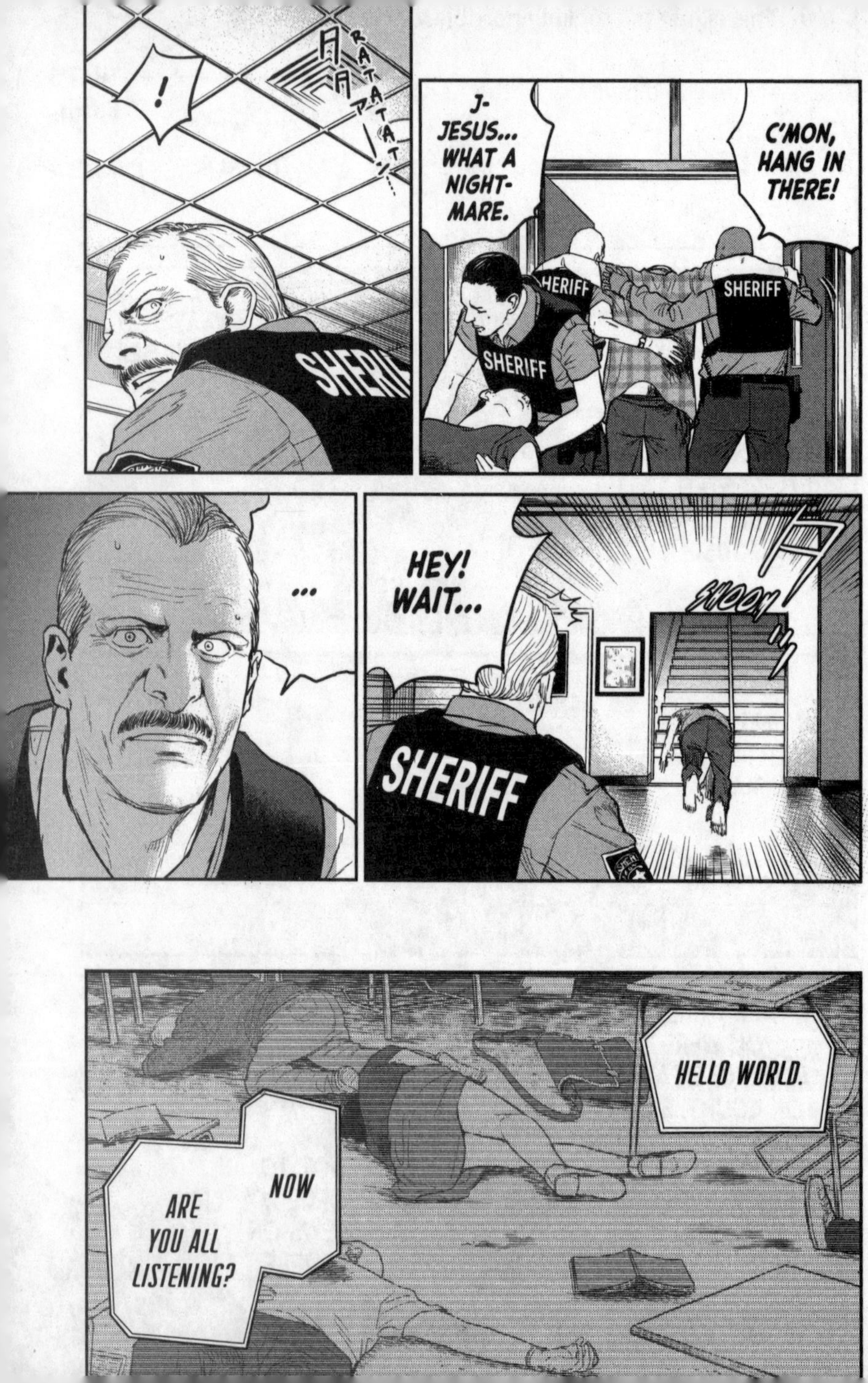
C'MON, HANG IN THERE!
J-JESUS... WHAT A NIGHT-MARE.
!
RATATAT
HEY! WAIT...
...
HELLO WORLD.
NOW
ARE YOU ALL LISTENING?

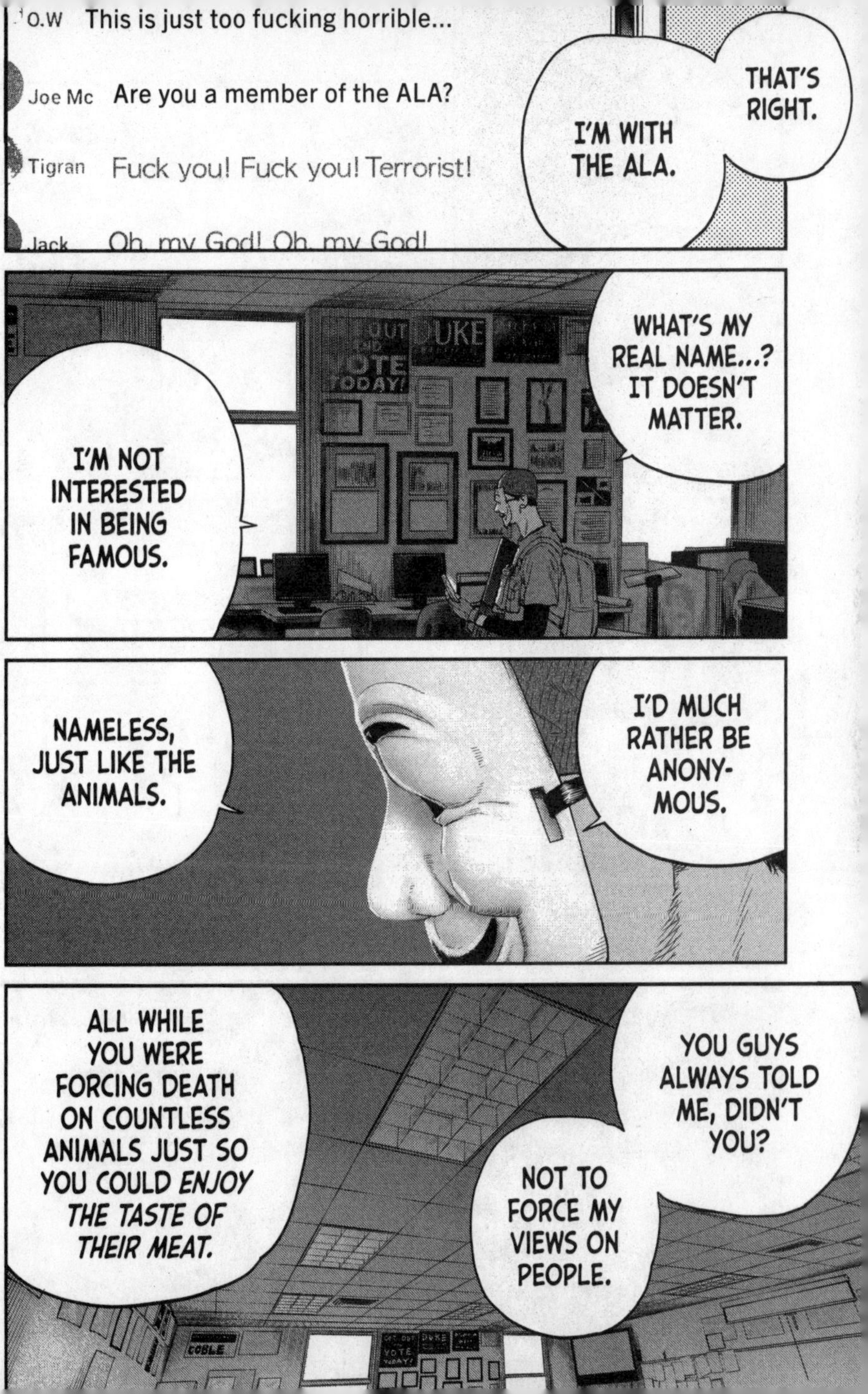
THAT'S RIGHT.
I'M WITH THE ALA.
O.W This is just too fucking horrible...
Joe Mc Are you a member of the ALA?
Tigran Fuck you! Fuck you! Terrorist!
Jack Oh, my God! Oh, my God!
WHAT'S MY REAL NAME...? IT DOESN'T MATTER.
I'M NOT INTERESTED IN BEING FAMOUS.
I'D MUCH RATHER BE ANONY-MOUS.
NAMELESS, JUST LIKE THE ANIMALS.
YOU GUYS ALWAYS TOLD ME, DIDN'T YOU?
NOT TO FORCE MY VIEWS ON PEOPLE.
ALL WHILE YOU WERE FORCING DEATH ON COUNTLESS ANIMALS JUST SO YOU COULD *ENJOY THE TASTE OF THEIR MEAT.*

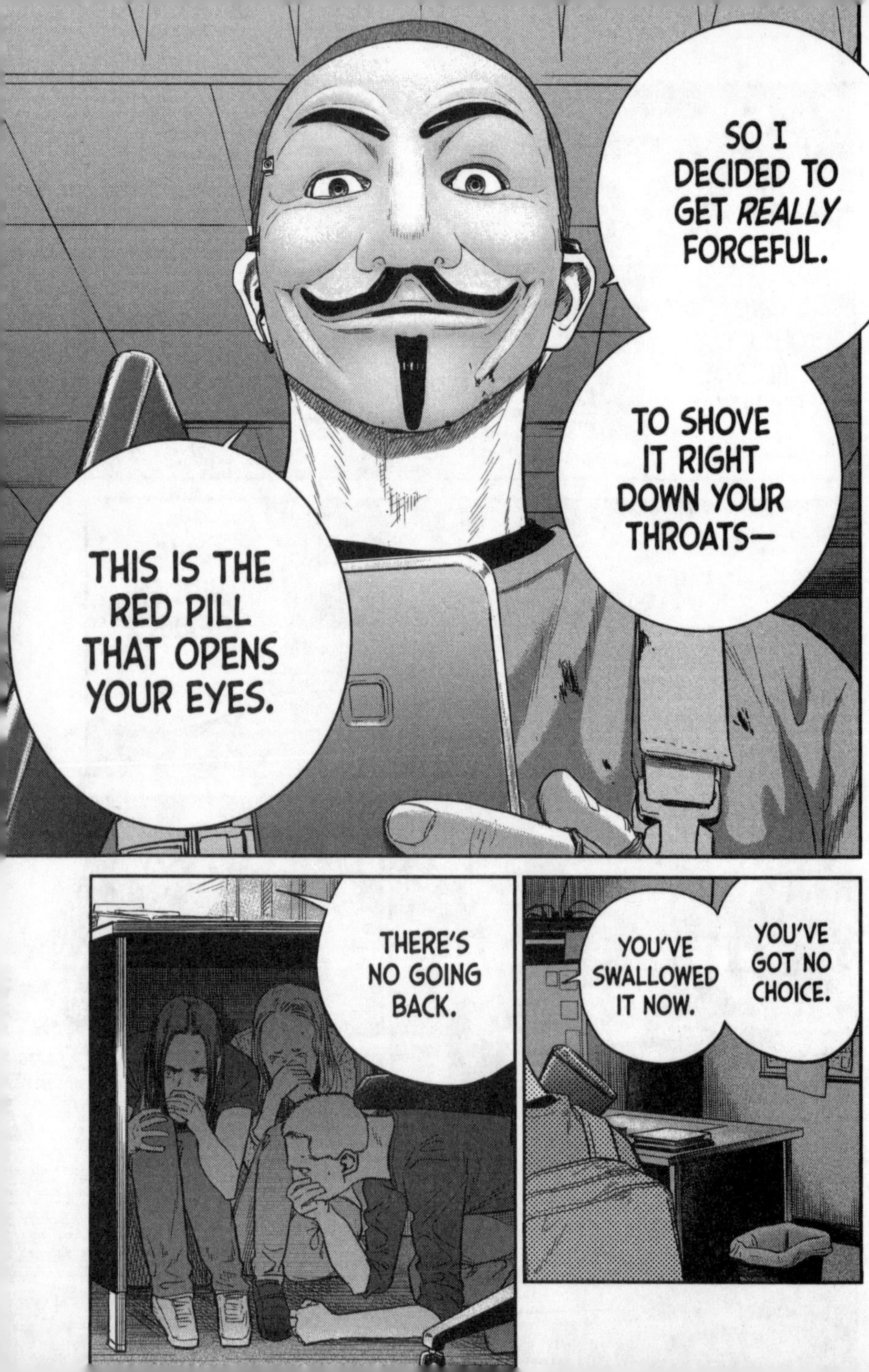
SO I DECIDED TO GET *REALLY* FORCEFUL.
TO SHOVE IT RIGHT DOWN YOUR THROATS—
THIS IS THE RED PILL THAT OPENS YOUR EYES.
YOU'VE GOT NO CHOICE.
YOU'VE SWALLOWED IT NOW.
THERE'S NO GOING BACK.

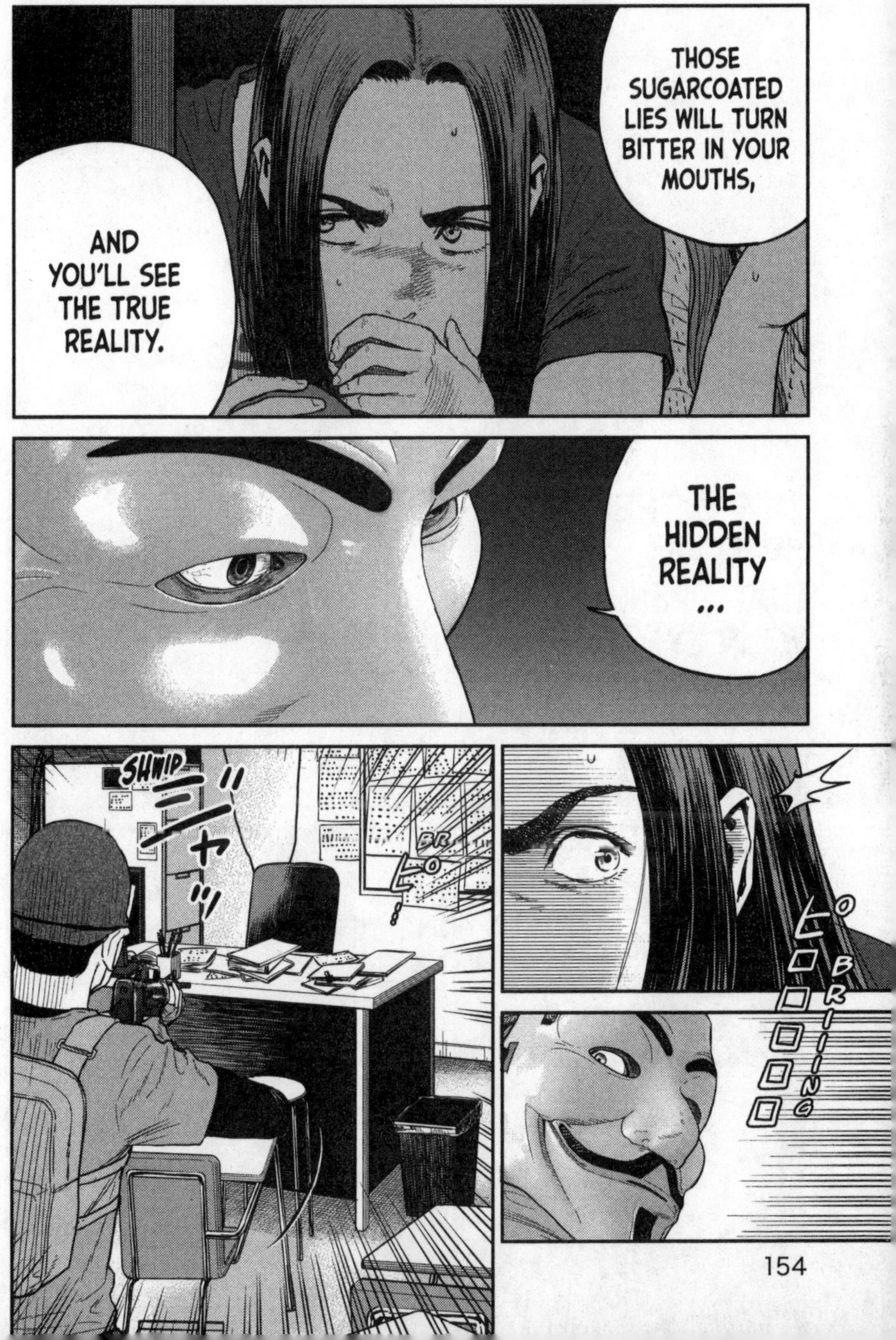
THOSE SUGARCOATED LIES WILL TURN BITTER IN YOUR MOUTHS,
AND YOU'LL SEE THE TRUE REALITY.
THE HIDDEN REALITY ...
BRIIING
ピロロロロロ
SHWIP
ジャッ
BR

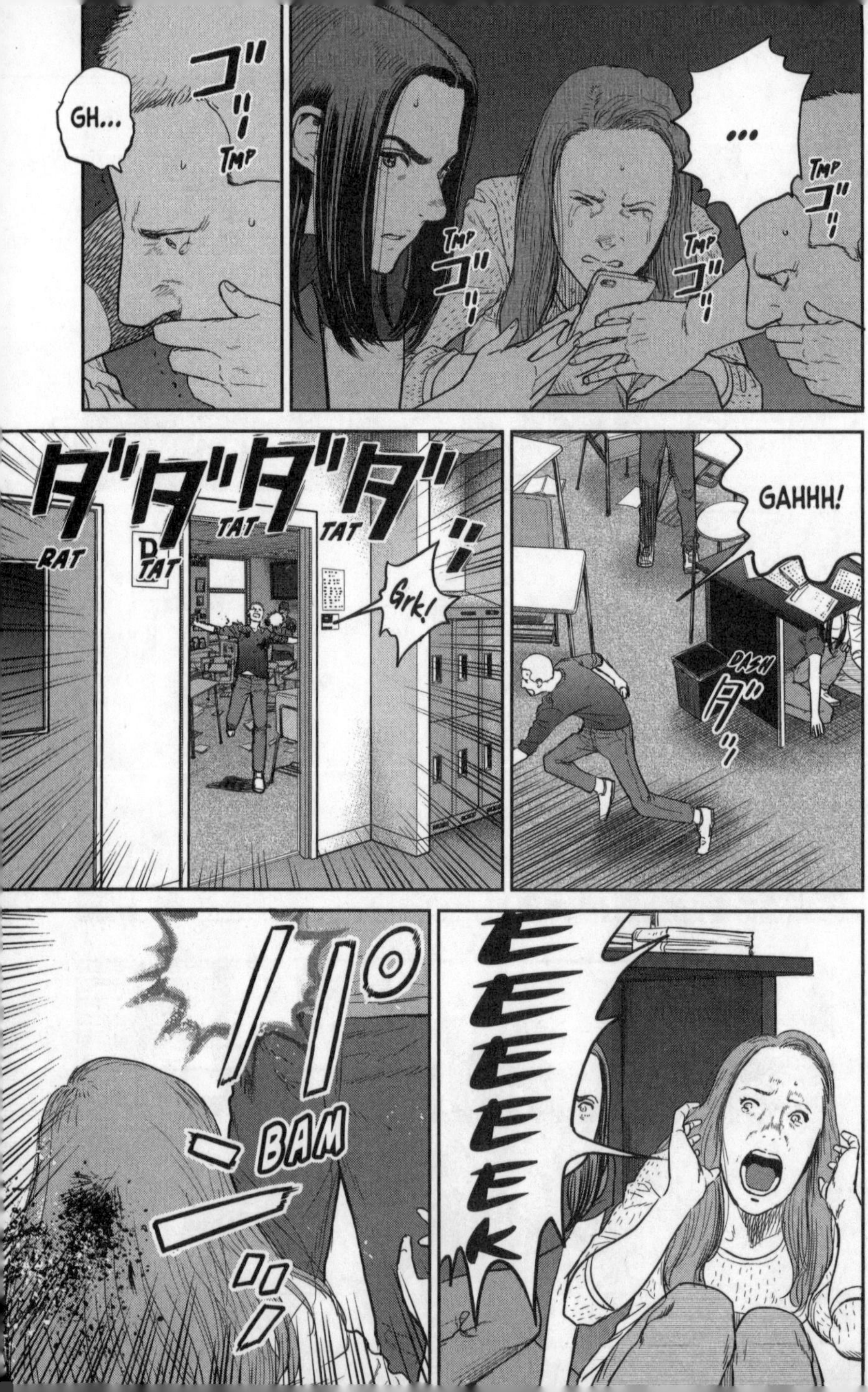
...
Tmp
ゴッ
Tmp
ゴッ
Tmp
ゴッ
ゴッ
Tmp
GH...
GAHHH!
DASH
ダッ
ダダダダダッ
RAT
TAT
TAT
TAT
Grk!
EEEEEEEK
パーン
BAM

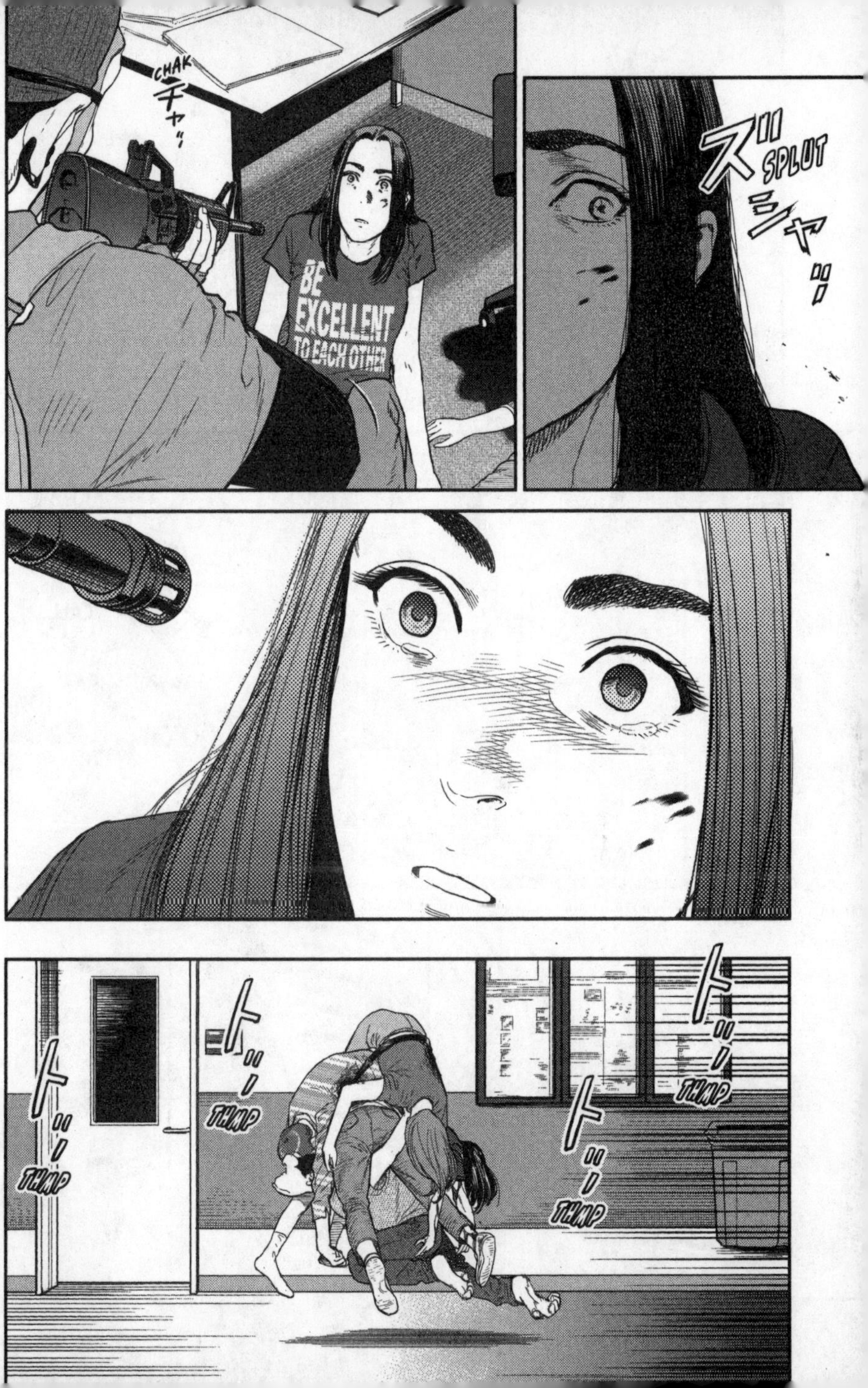
ズシャッ
SPLUT
チャッ
CHAK
BE EXCELLENT TO EACH OTHER
ドッ
THMP
ドッ
THMP
ドッ
THMP
ドッ
THMP

CHAPTER 10 / END

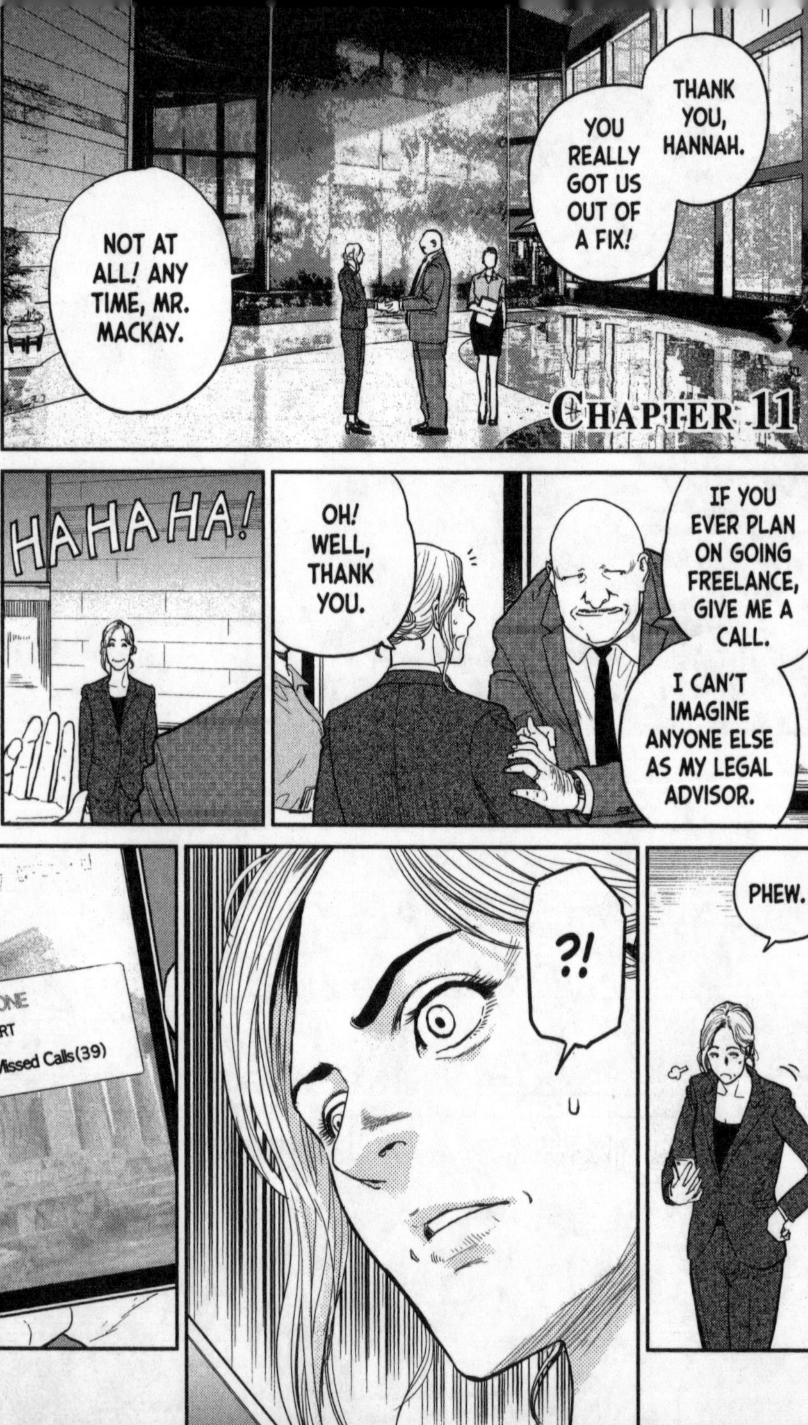
THANK YOU, HANNAH.
YOU REALLY GOT US OUT OF A FIX!
NOT AT ALL! ANY TIME, MR. MACKAY.
CHAPTER 11
IF YOU EVER PLAN ON GOING FREELANCE, GIVE ME A CALL.
I CAN'T IMAGINE ANYONE ELSE AS MY LEGAL ADVISOR.
OH! WELL, THANK YOU.
HAHAHA!
PHEW.
?!
PHONE
from BERT
Missed Calls(39)

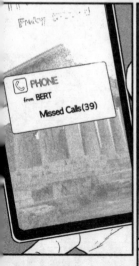

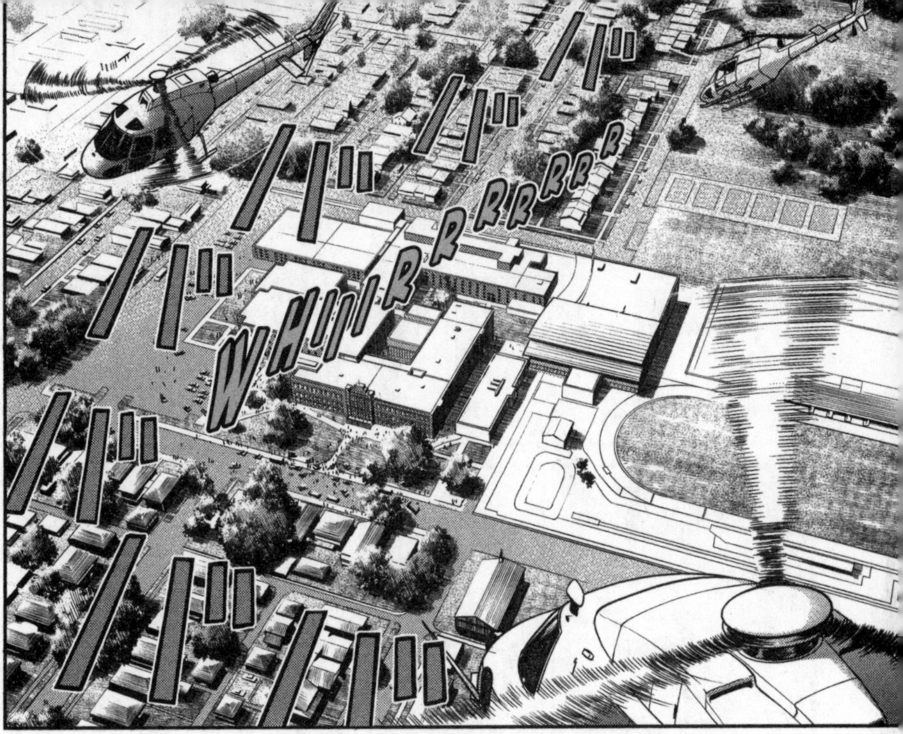
WHIIIRRRRRRRR

CHAPTER 11 / TRICKSTER

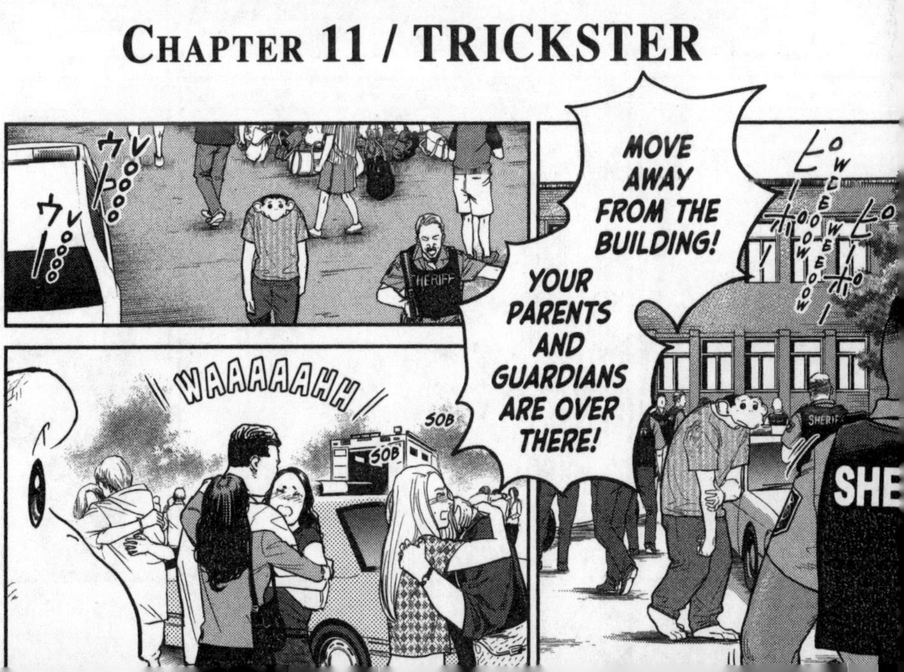
MOVE AWAY FROM THE BUILDING!
YOUR PARENTS AND GUARDIANS ARE OVER THERE!
SHERIFF
SHERIFF
SHE
WAAAAAAHH
SOB
SOB

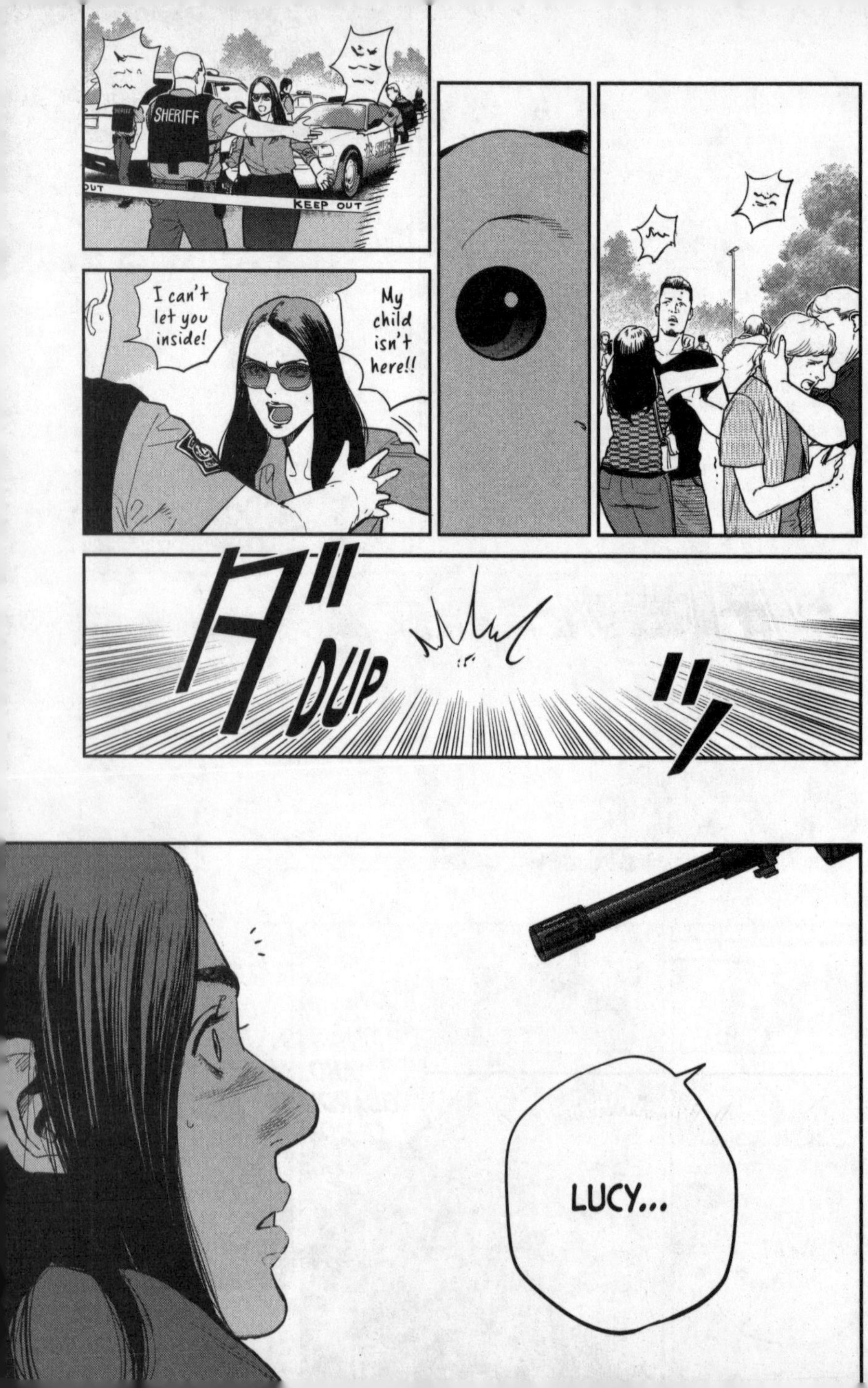
My child isn't here!!
I can't let you inside!
ダッ
DUP
LUCY...

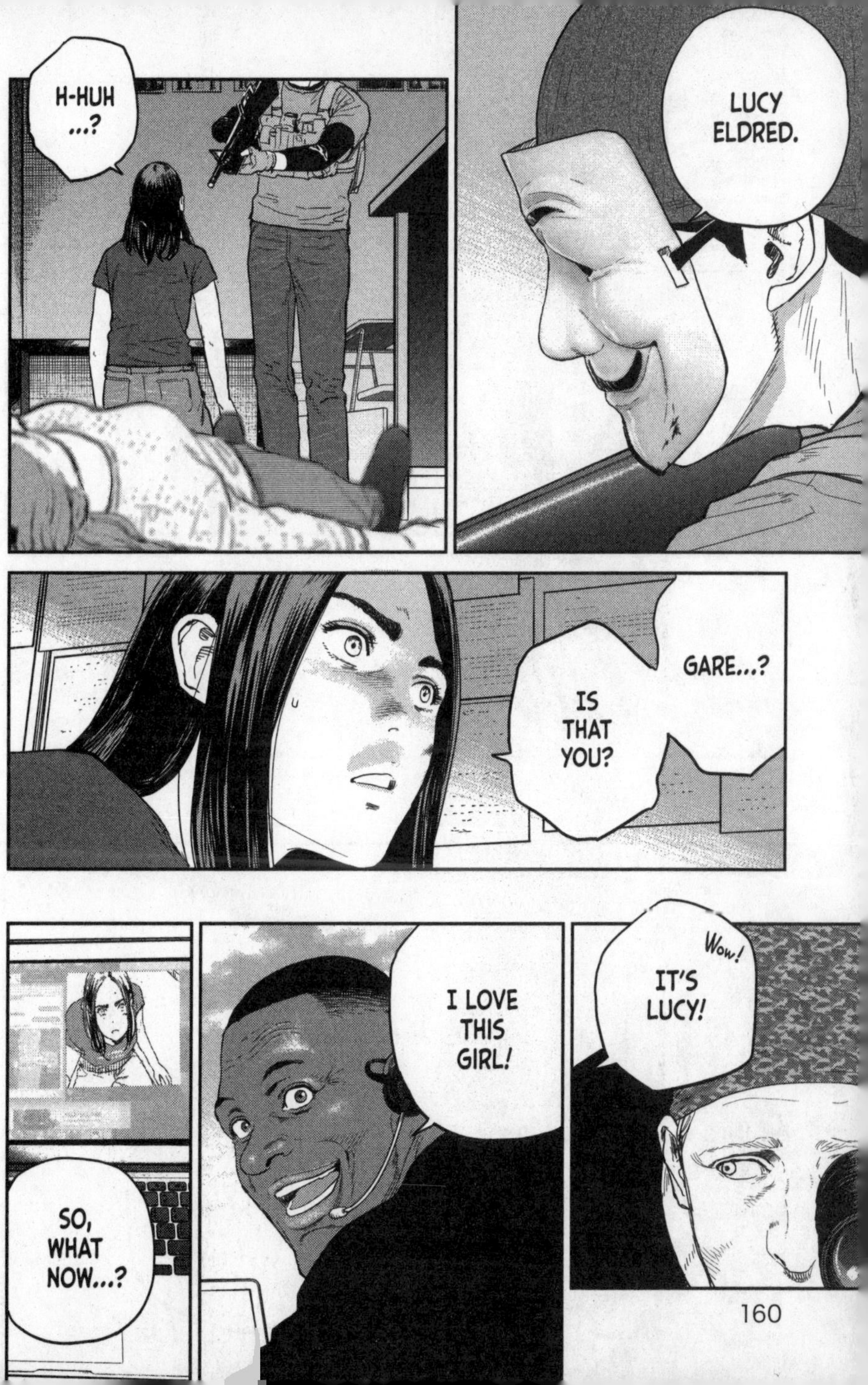
LUCY ELDRED.
H-HUH ...?
GARE...?
IS THAT YOU?
Wow!
IT'S LUCY!
I LOVE THIS GIRL!
SO, WHAT NOW...?

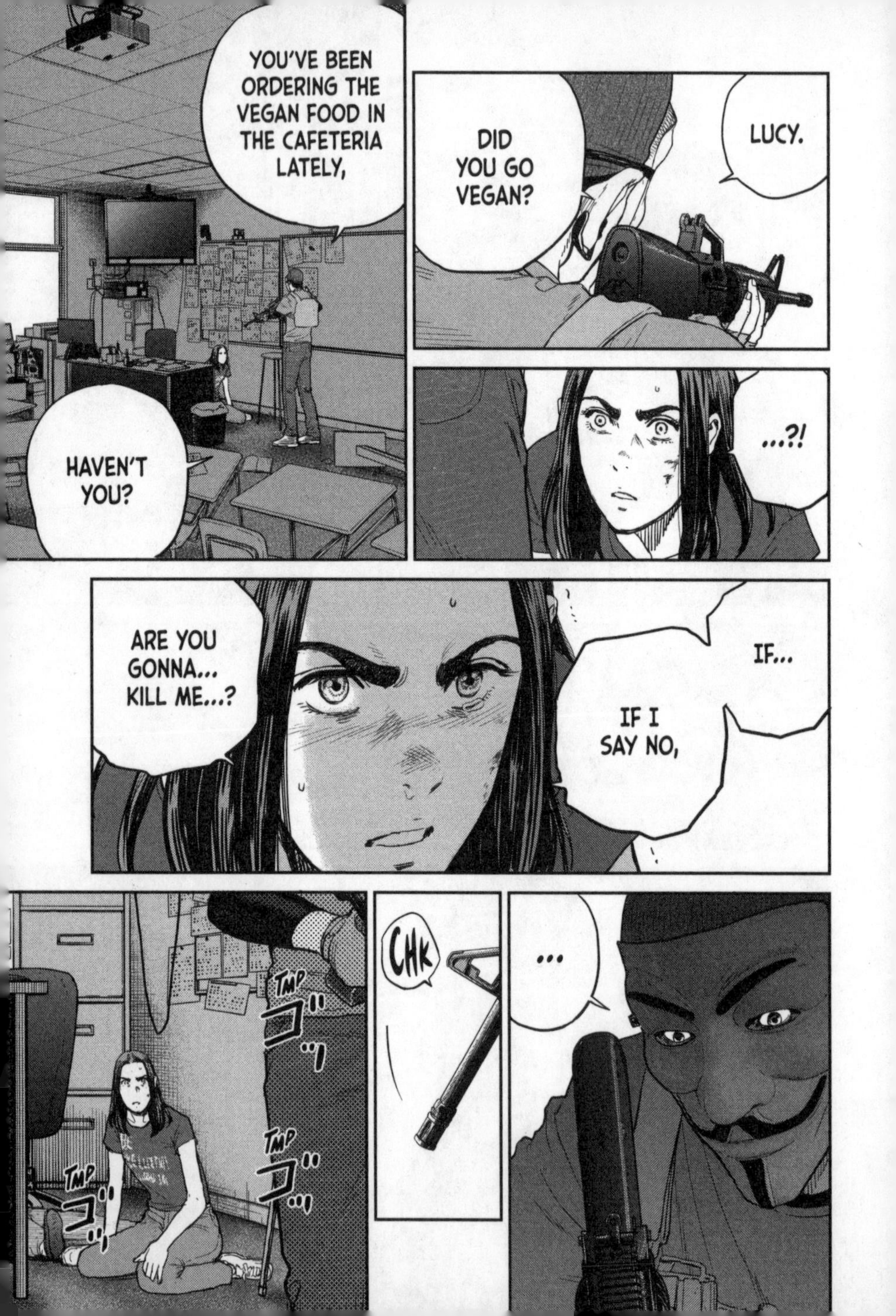
LUCY.
DID YOU GO VEGAN?
...?!
YOU'VE BEEN ORDERING THE VEGAN FOOD IN THE CAFETERIA LATELY,
HAVEN'T YOU?
IF...
IF I SAY NO,
ARE YOU GONNA... KILL ME...?
...
CHK
TMP
ゴッ
TMP
ゴッ
TMP
ゴッ

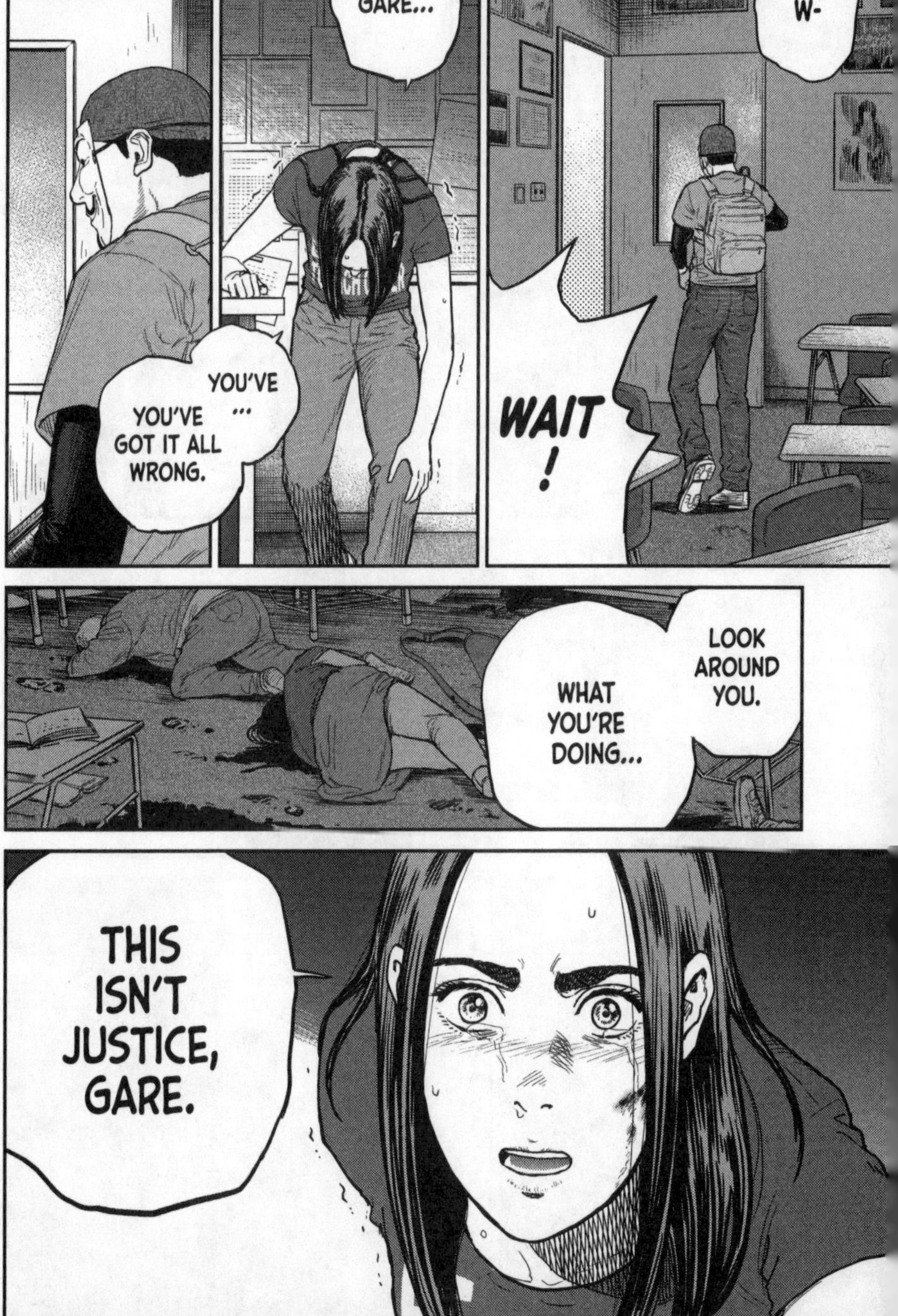
W-
WAIT!
GARE...
YOU'VE ...
YOU'VE GOT IT ALL WRONG.
LOOK AROUND YOU.
WHAT YOU'RE DOING...
THIS ISN'T JUSTICE, GARE.

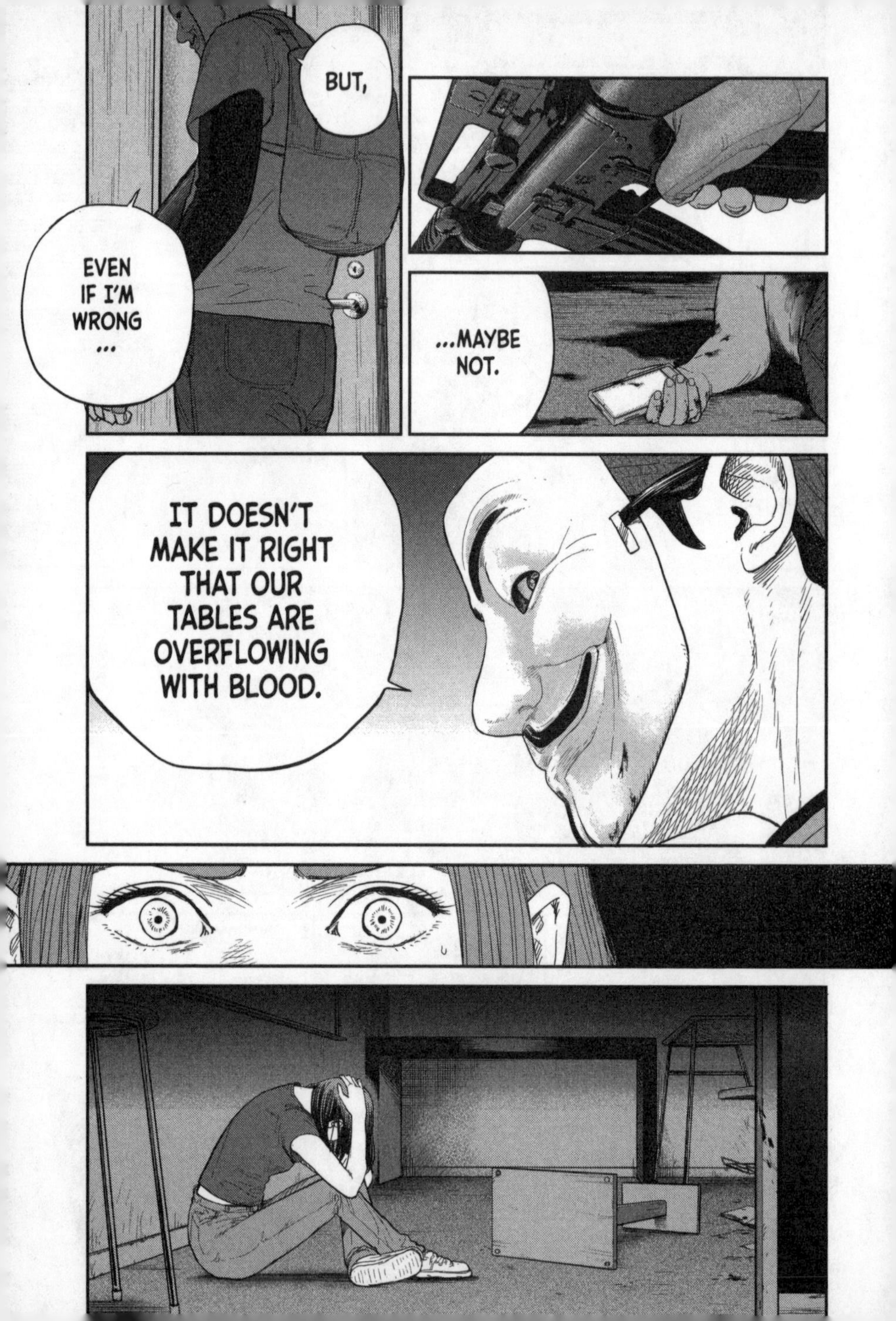
...MAYBE NOT.
BUT,
EVEN IF I'M WRONG ...
IT DOESN'T MAKE IT RIGHT THAT OUR TABLES ARE OVERFLOWING WITH BLOOD.

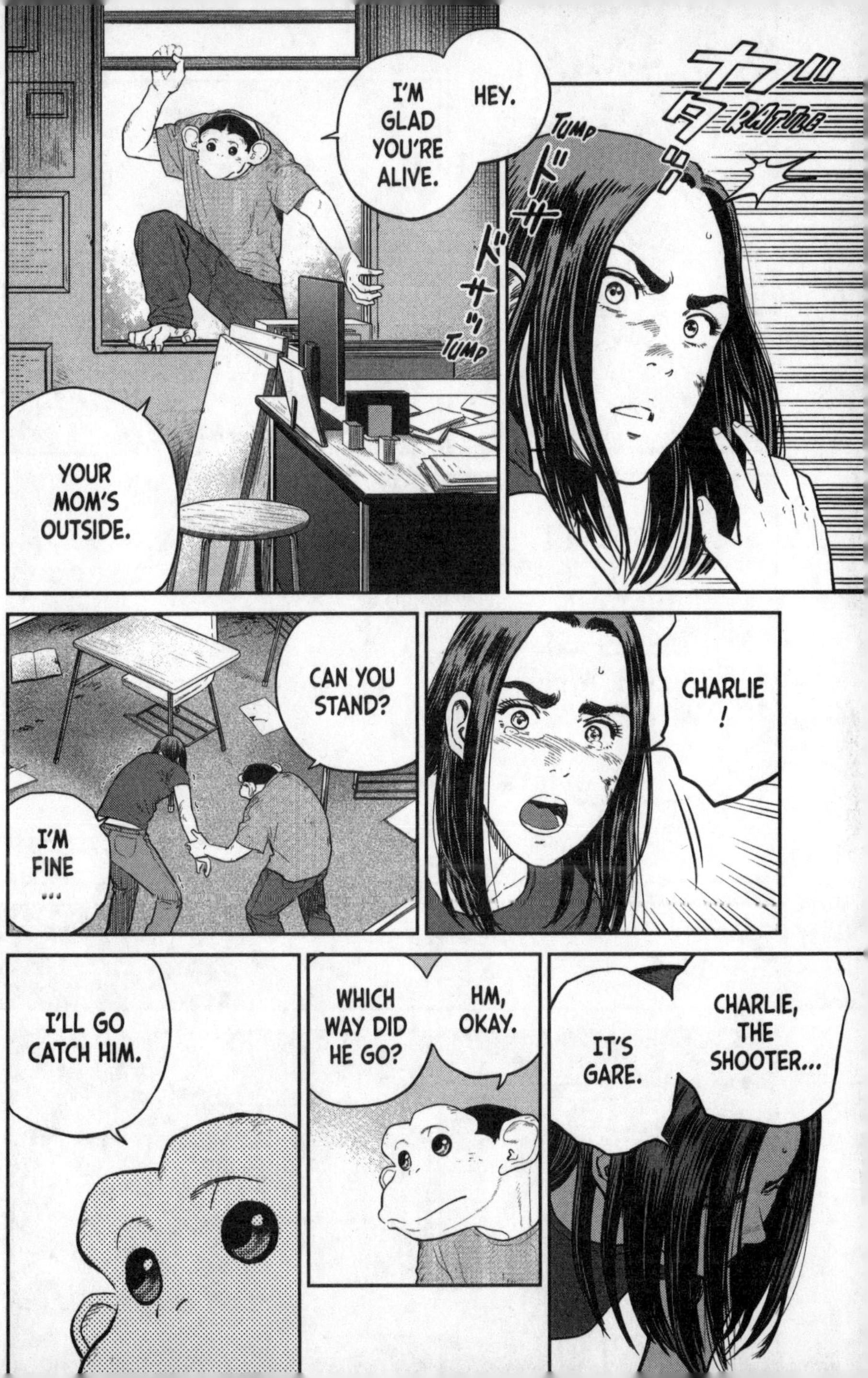
RATTLE
TUMP
TUMP
HEY.
I'M GLAD YOU'RE ALIVE.
YOUR MOM'S OUTSIDE.
CHARLIE!
CAN YOU STAND?
I'M FINE...
CHARLIE, THE SHOOTER...
IT'S GARE.
HM, OKAY.
WHICH WAY DID HE GO?
I'LL GO CATCH HIM.

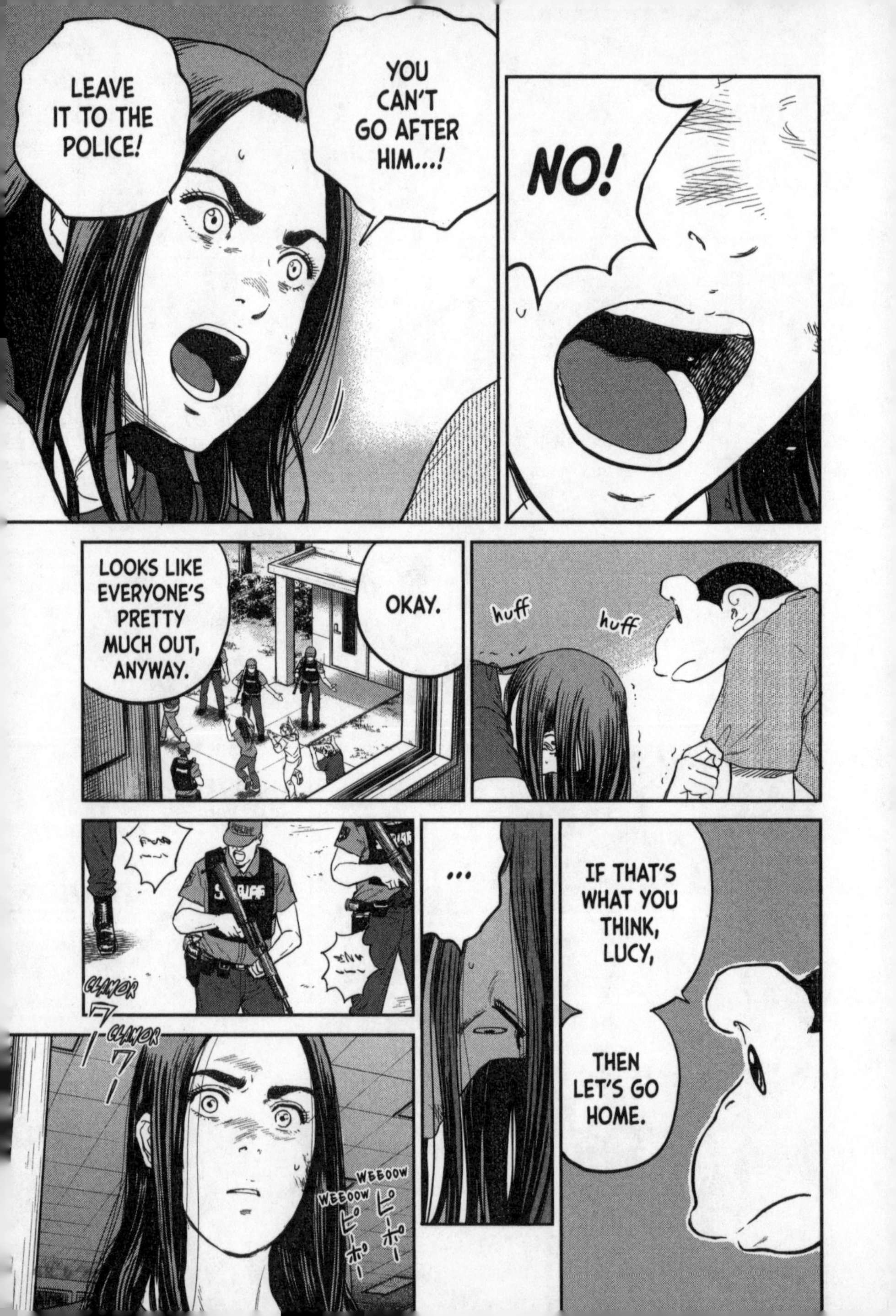
NO!
YOU CAN'T GO AFTER HIM...!
LEAVE IT TO THE POLICE!
huff
huff
OKAY.
LOOKS LIKE EVERYONE'S PRETTY MUCH OUT, ANYWAY.
IF THAT'S WHAT YOU THINK, LUCY,
THEN LET'S GO HOME.
...
CLAMOR
CLAMOR
WEEOOW
WEEOOW

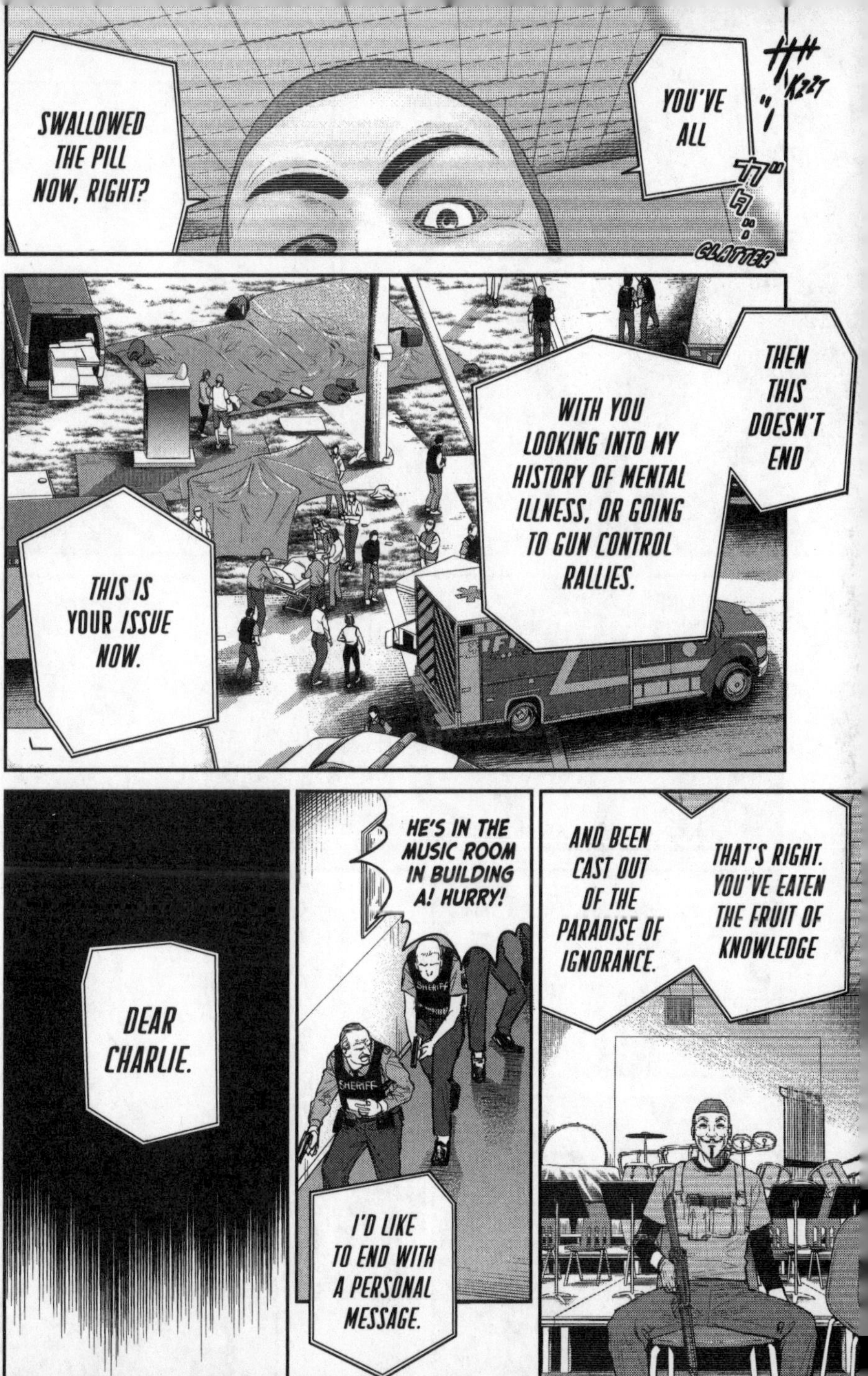
YOU'VE ALL
KZZT
CLATTER
SWALLOWED THE PILL NOW, RIGHT?
THEN THIS DOESN'T END
WITH YOU LOOKING INTO MY HISTORY OF MENTAL ILLNESS, OR GOING TO GUN CONTROL RALLIES.
THIS IS YOUR ISSUE NOW.
THAT'S RIGHT. YOU'VE EATEN THE FRUIT OF KNOWLEDGE
AND BEEN CAST OUT OF THE PARADISE OF IGNORANCE.
HE'S IN THE MUSIC ROOM IN BUILDING A! HURRY!
I'D LIKE TO END WITH A PERSONAL MESSAGE.
DEAR CHARLIE.

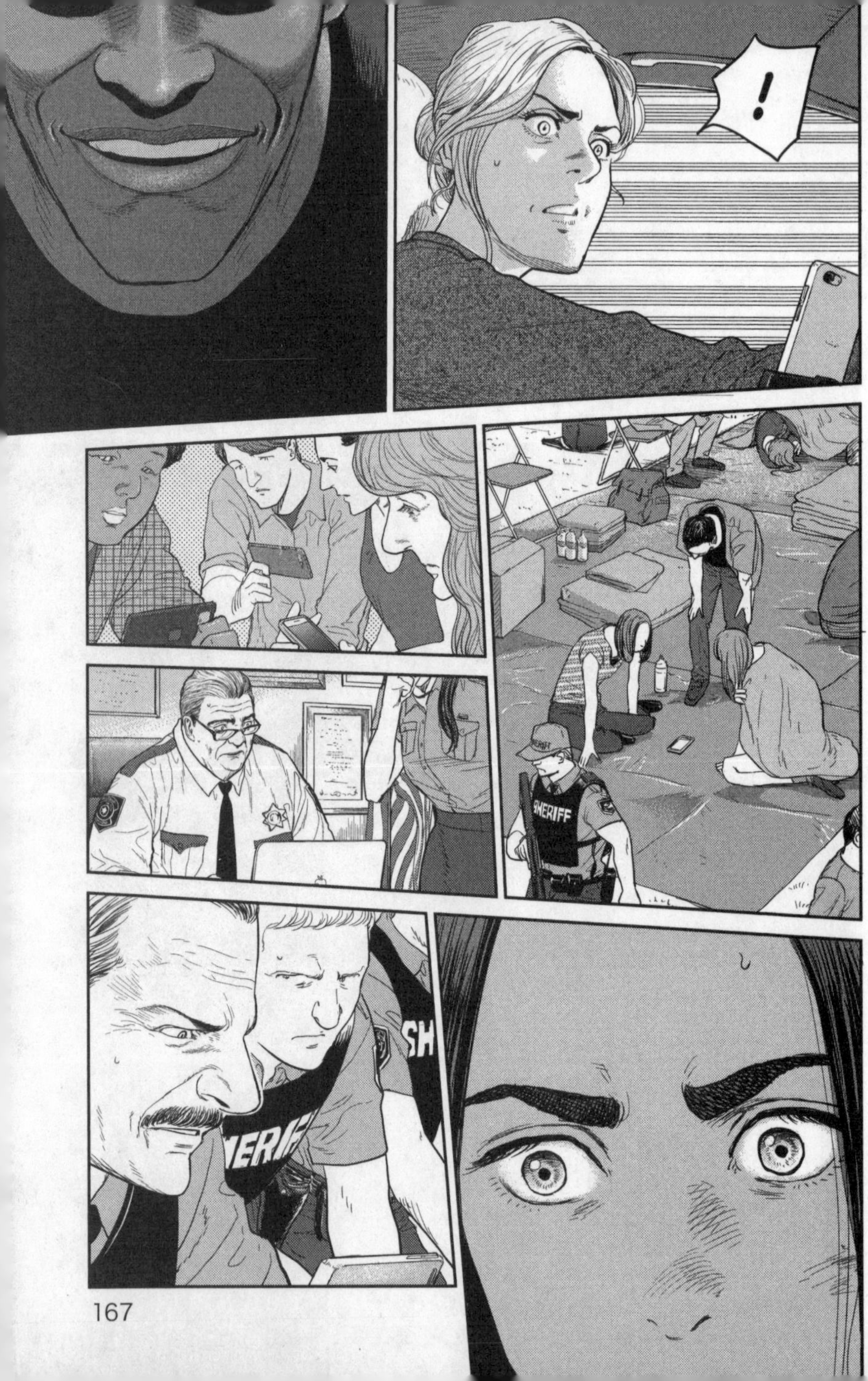
!
SHERIFF

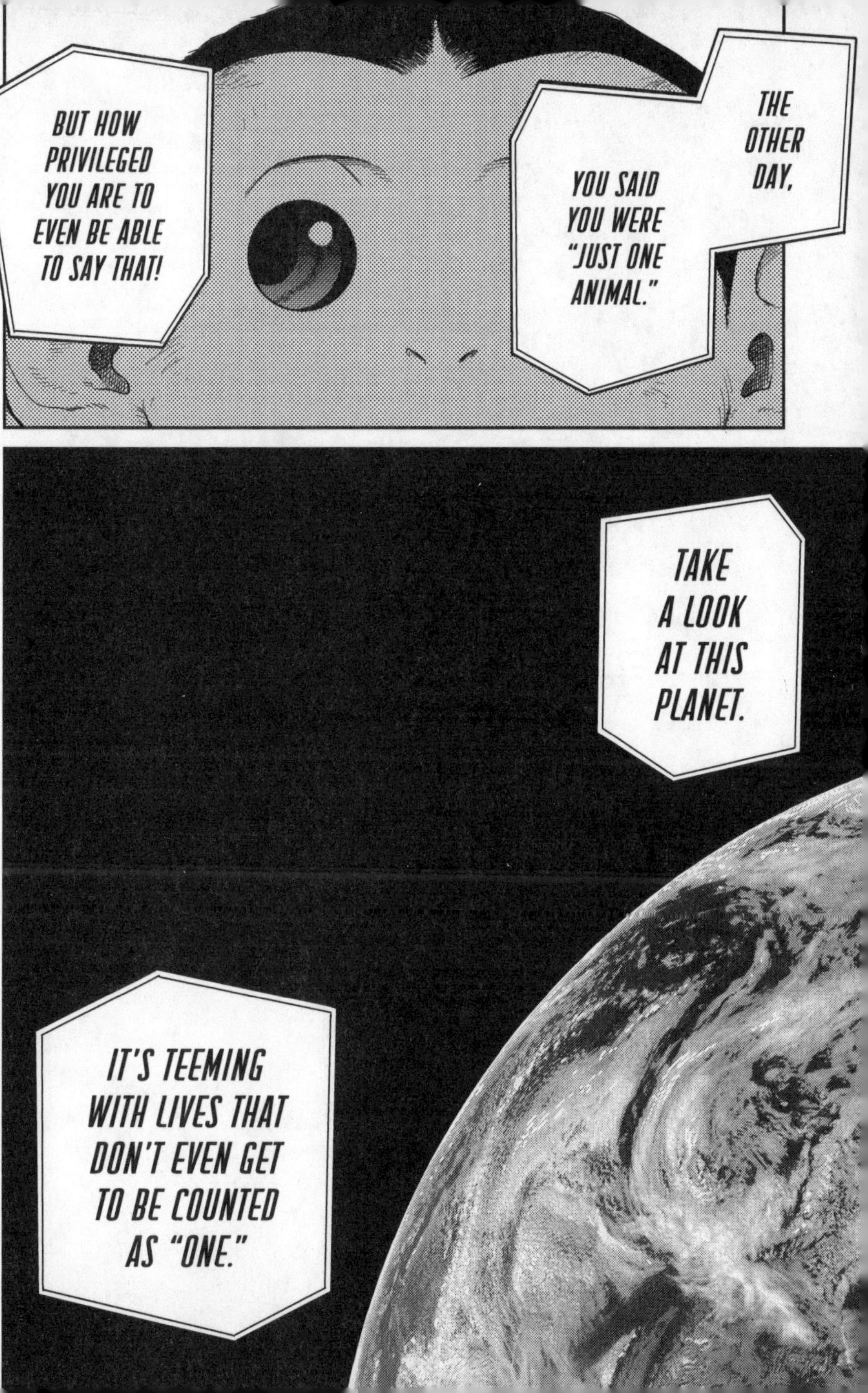
THE OTHER DAY,
YOU SAID YOU WERE "JUST ONE ANIMAL."
BUT HOW PRIVILEGED YOU ARE TO EVEN BE ABLE TO SAY THAT!
TAKE A LOOK AT THIS PLANET.
IT'S TEEMING WITH LIVES THAT DON'T EVEN GET TO BE COUNTED AS "ONE."

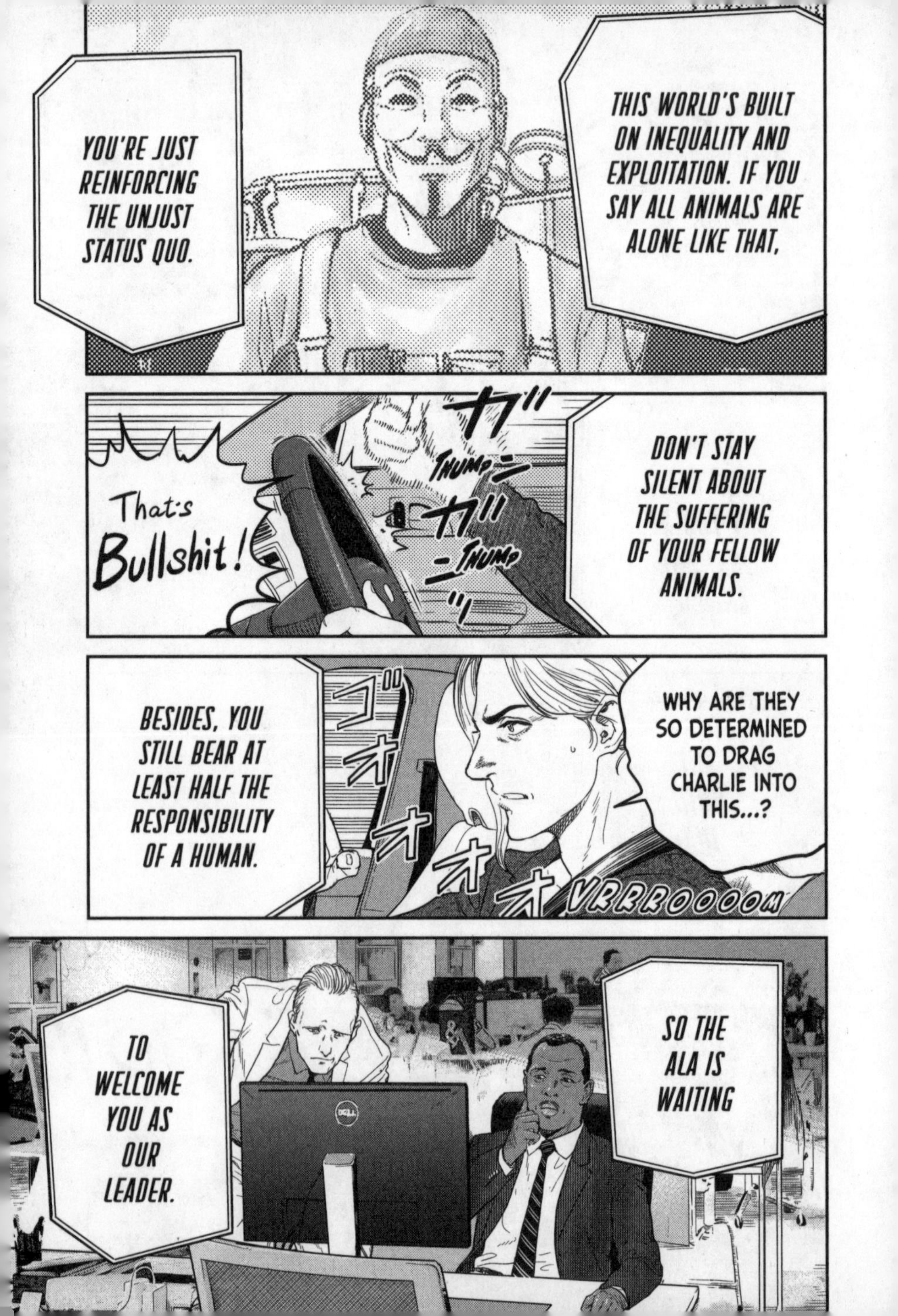
THIS WORLD'S BUILT ON INEQUALITY AND EXPLOITATION. IF YOU SAY ALL ANIMALS ARE ALONE LIKE THAT,
YOU'RE JUST REINFORCING THE UNJUST STATUS QUO.
DON'T STAY SILENT ABOUT THE SUFFERING OF YOUR FELLOW ANIMALS.
THUMP
THUMP
That's Bullshit!
WHY ARE THEY SO DETERMINED TO DRAG CHARLIE INTO THIS...?
VRRROOOOM
BESIDES, YOU STILL BEAR AT LEAST HALF THE RESPONSIBILITY OF A HUMAN.
SO THE ALA IS WAITING
TO WELCOME YOU AS OUR LEADER.

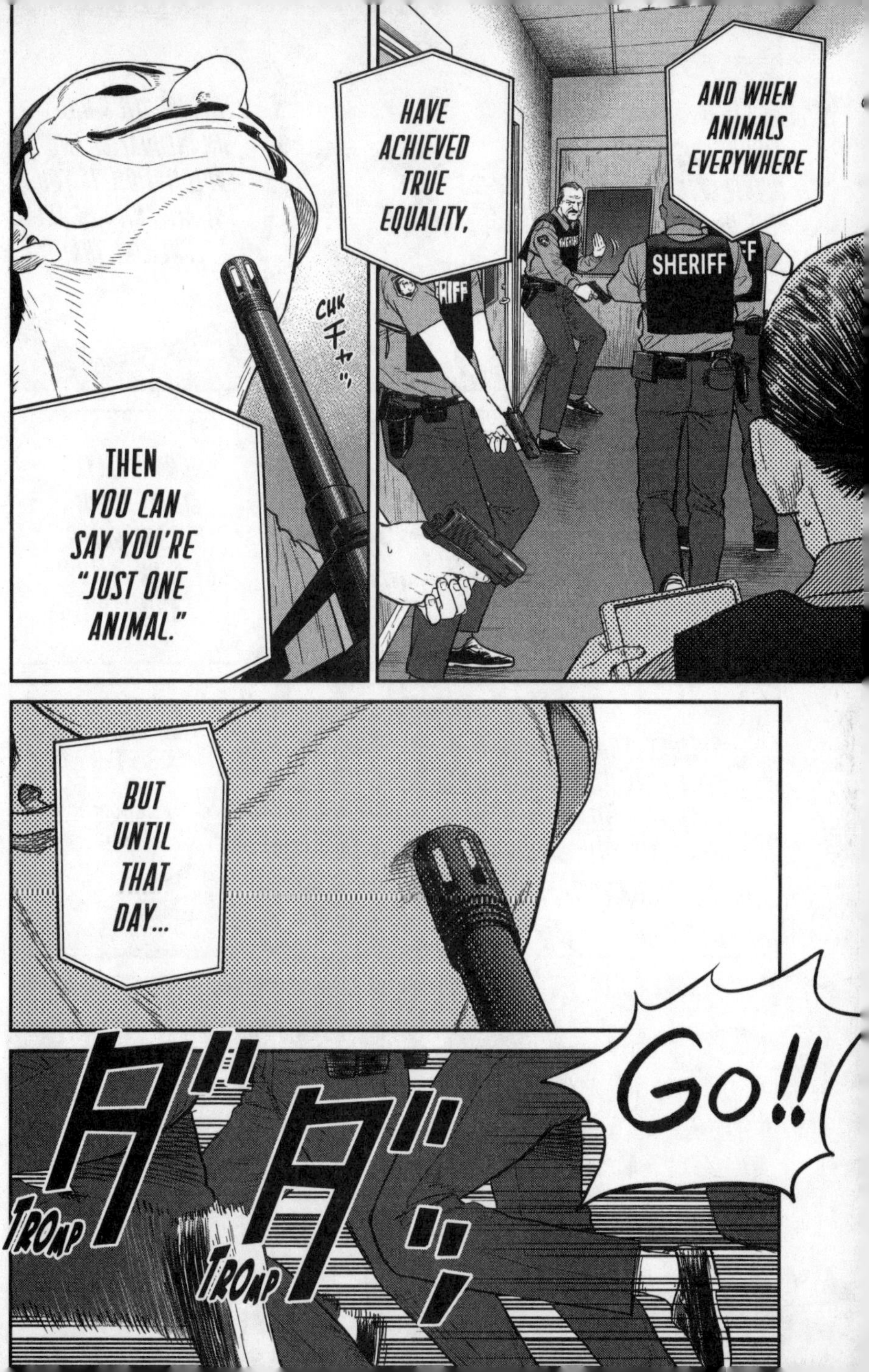
AND WHEN ANIMALS EVERYWHERE
HAVE ACHIEVED TRUE EQUALITY,
SHERIFF
CHK
THEN YOU CAN SAY YOU'RE "JUST ONE ANIMAL."
BUT UNTIL THAT DAY...
GO!!
TROMP
TROMP

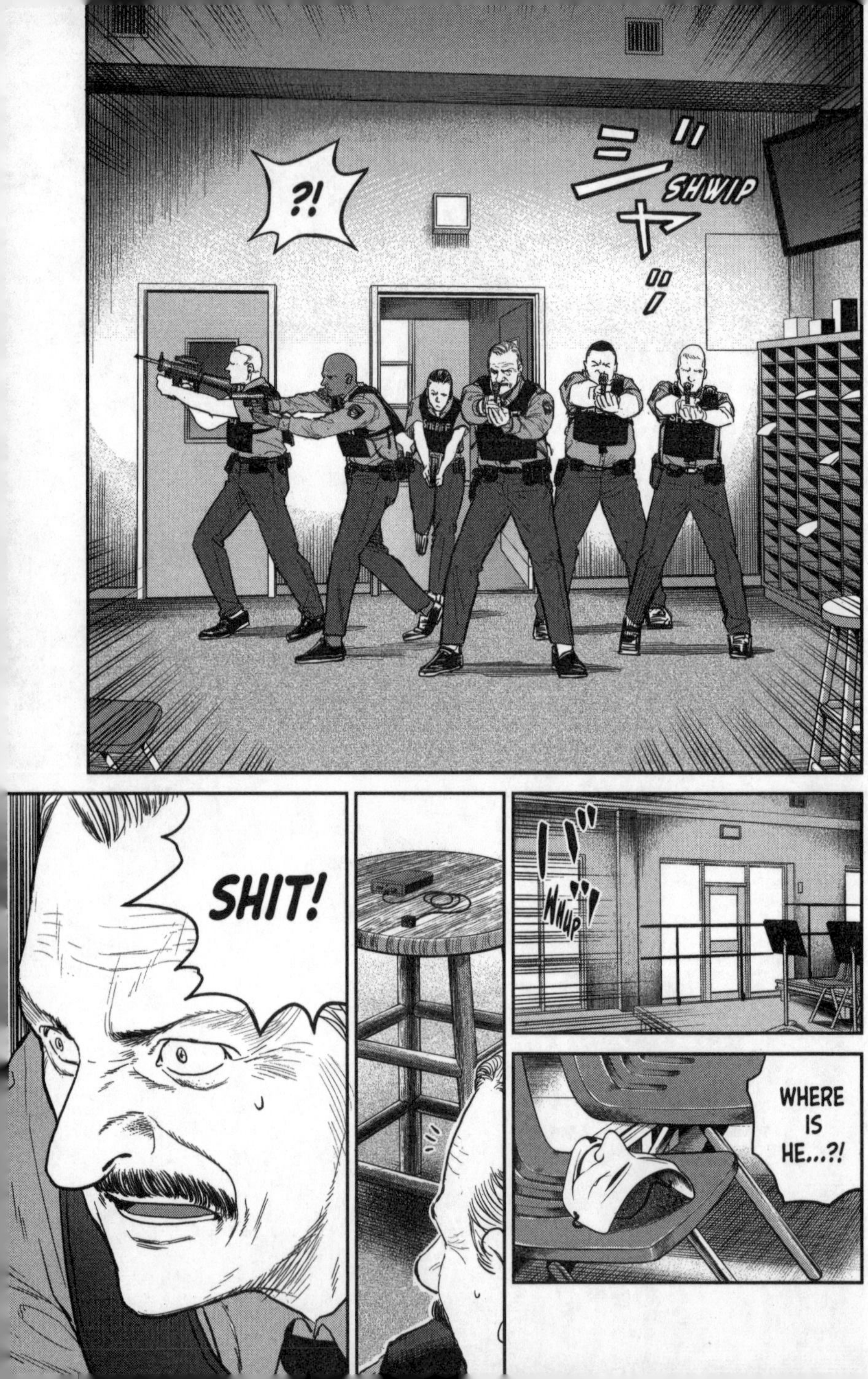
?!
SHWIP
WHUP
WHERE IS HE...?!
SHIT!

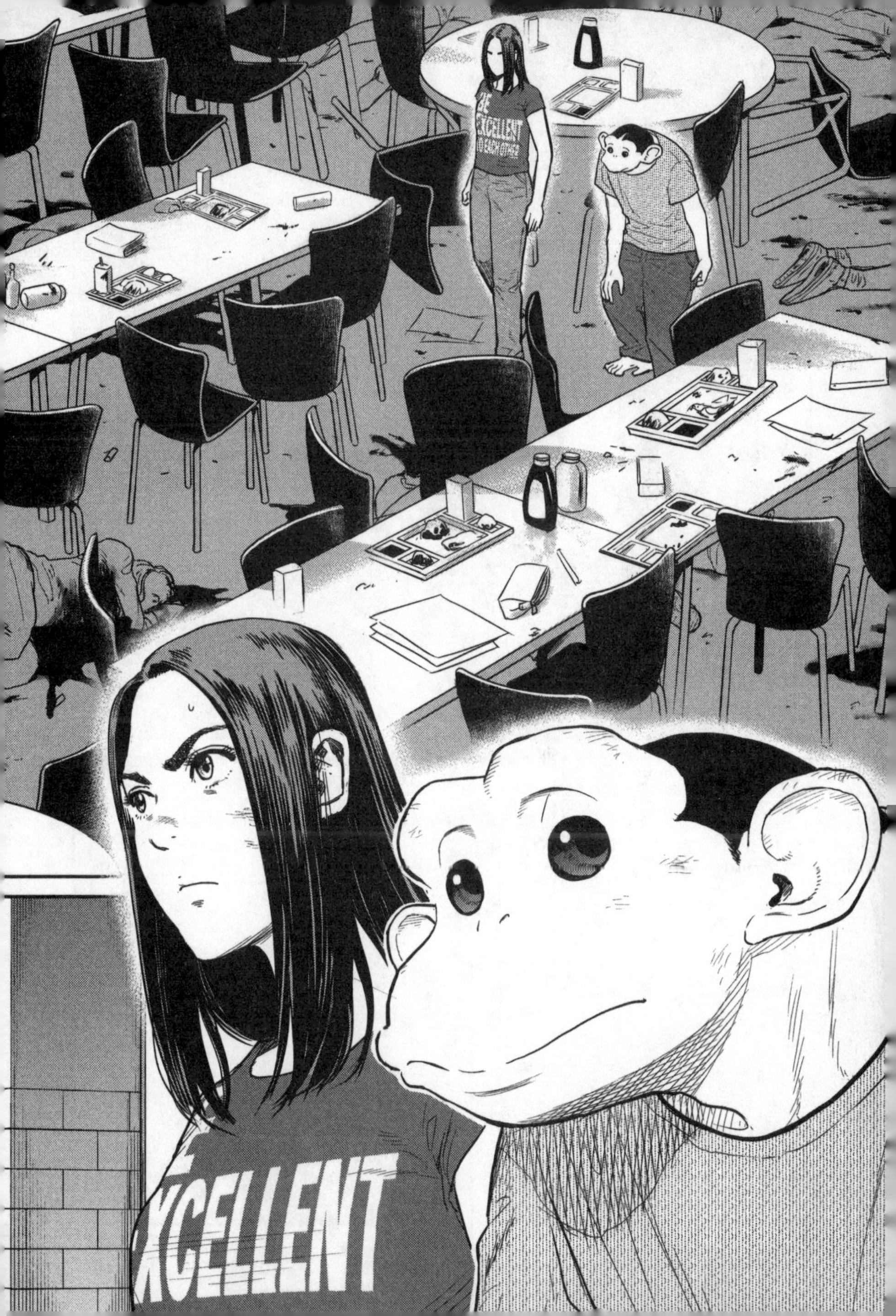
BE
EXCELLENT
TO EACH OTHER
XCELLENT

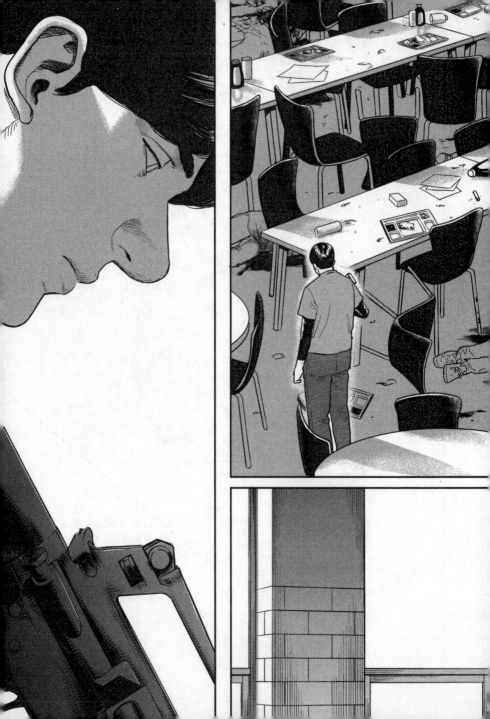

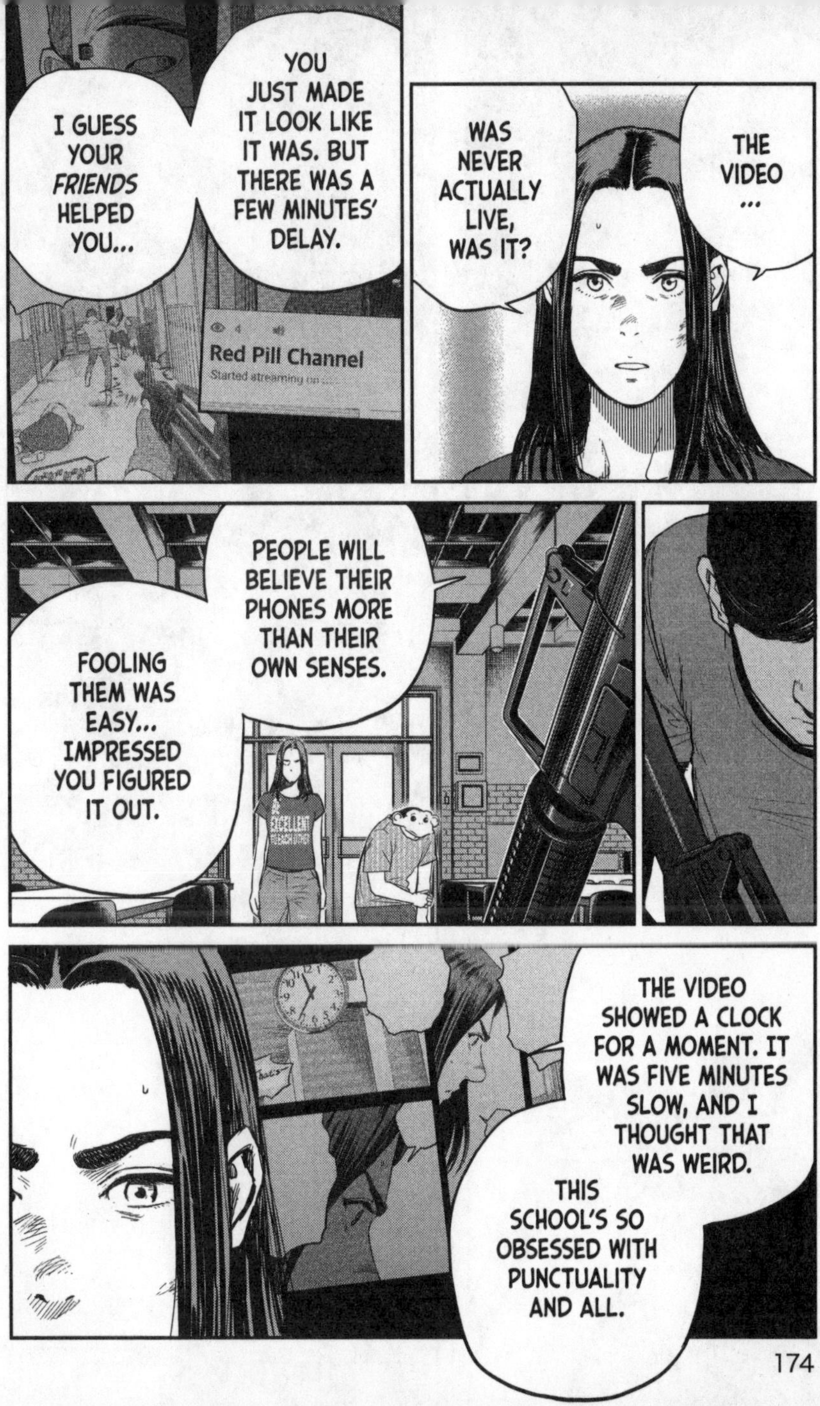
THE VIDEO ...
WAS NEVER ACTUALLY LIVE, WAS IT?
YOU JUST MADE IT LOOK LIKE IT WAS. BUT THERE WAS A FEW MINUTES' DELAY.
I GUESS YOUR *FRIENDS* HELPED YOU...
Red Pill Channel
PEOPLE WILL BELIEVE THEIR PHONES MORE THAN THEIR OWN SENSES.
FOOLING THEM WAS EASY... IMPRESSED YOU FIGURED IT OUT.
THE VIDEO SHOWED A CLOCK FOR A MOMENT. IT WAS FIVE MINUTES SLOW, AND I THOUGHT THAT WAS WEIRD.
THIS SCHOOL'S SO OBSESSED WITH PUNCTUALITY AND ALL.

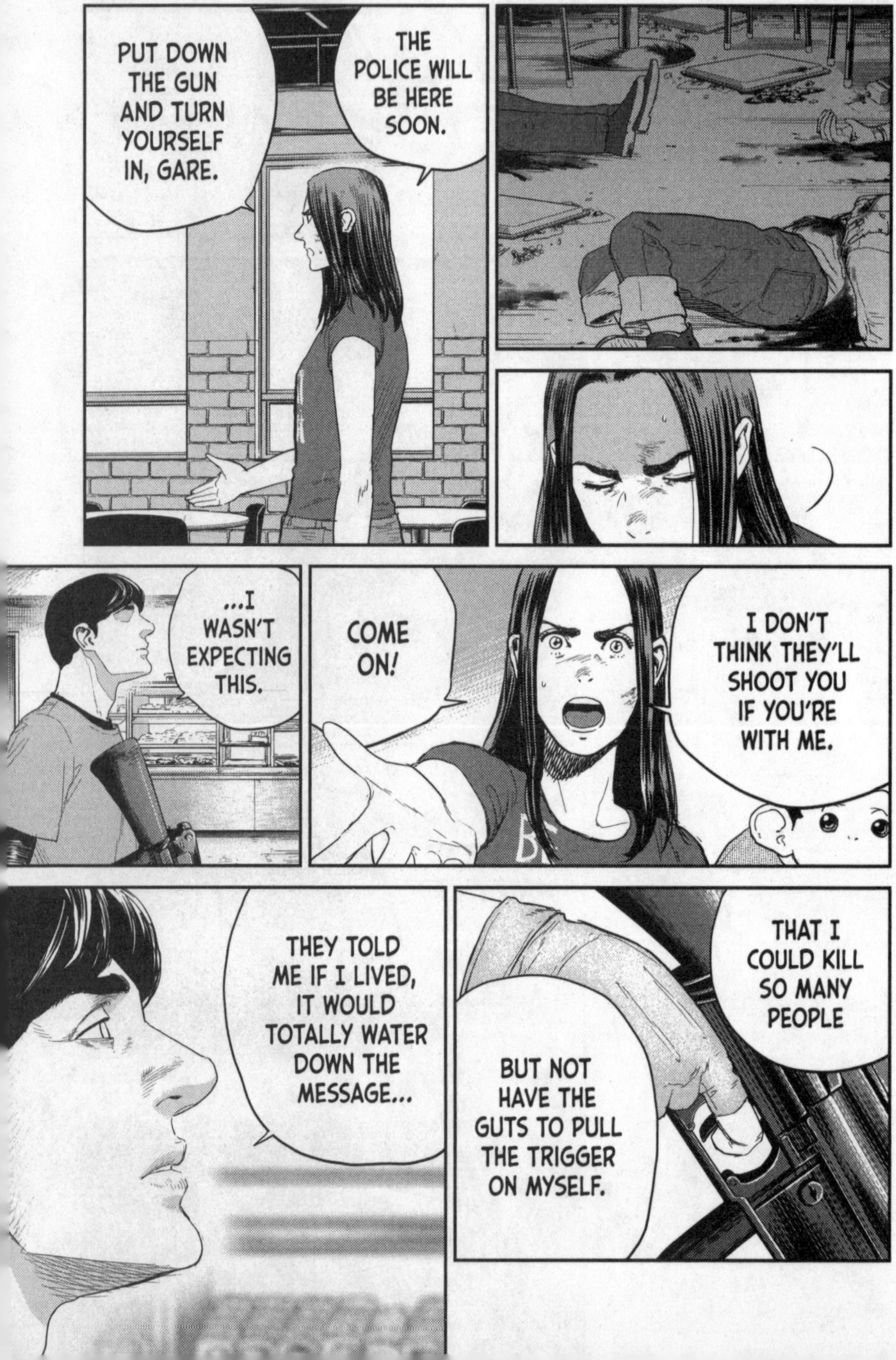
THE POLICE WILL BE HERE SOON.
PUT DOWN THE GUN AND TURN YOURSELF IN, GARE.
I DON'T THINK THEY'LL SHOOT YOU IF YOU'RE WITH ME.
COME ON!
...I WASN'T EXPECTING THIS.
THAT I COULD KILL SO MANY PEOPLE
BUT NOT HAVE THE GUTS TO PULL THE TRIGGER ON MYSELF.
THEY TOLD ME IF I LIVED, IT WOULD TOTALLY WATER DOWN THE MESSAGE...

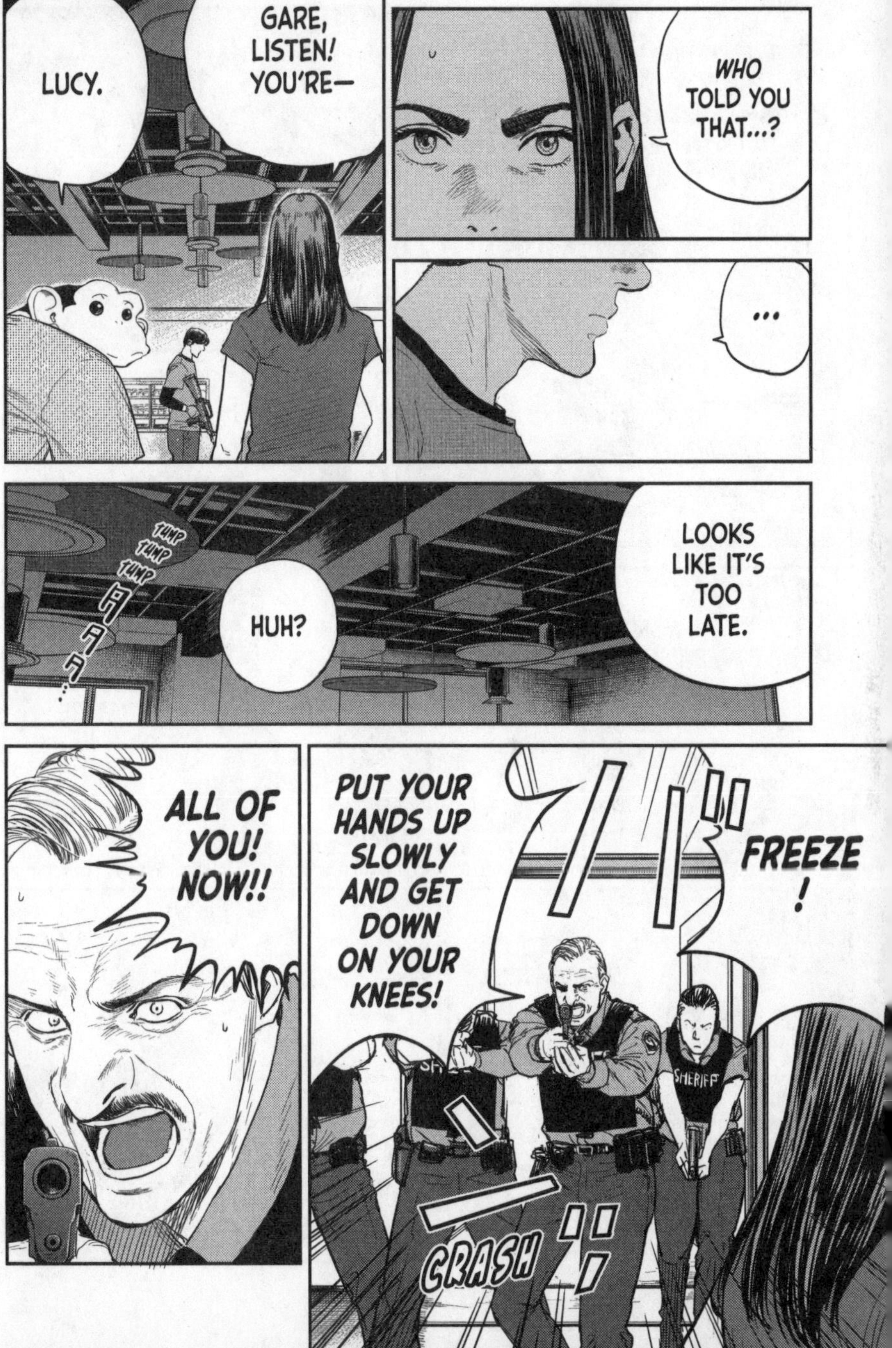
WHO TOLD YOU THAT...?
...
GARE, LISTEN! YOU'RE—
LUCY.
LOOKS LIKE IT'S TOO LATE.
HUH?
TUMP TUMP TUMP
タタタ...
FREEZE!
PUT YOUR HANDS UP SLOWLY AND GET DOWN ON YOUR KNEES!
CRASH
ALL OF YOU! NOW!!

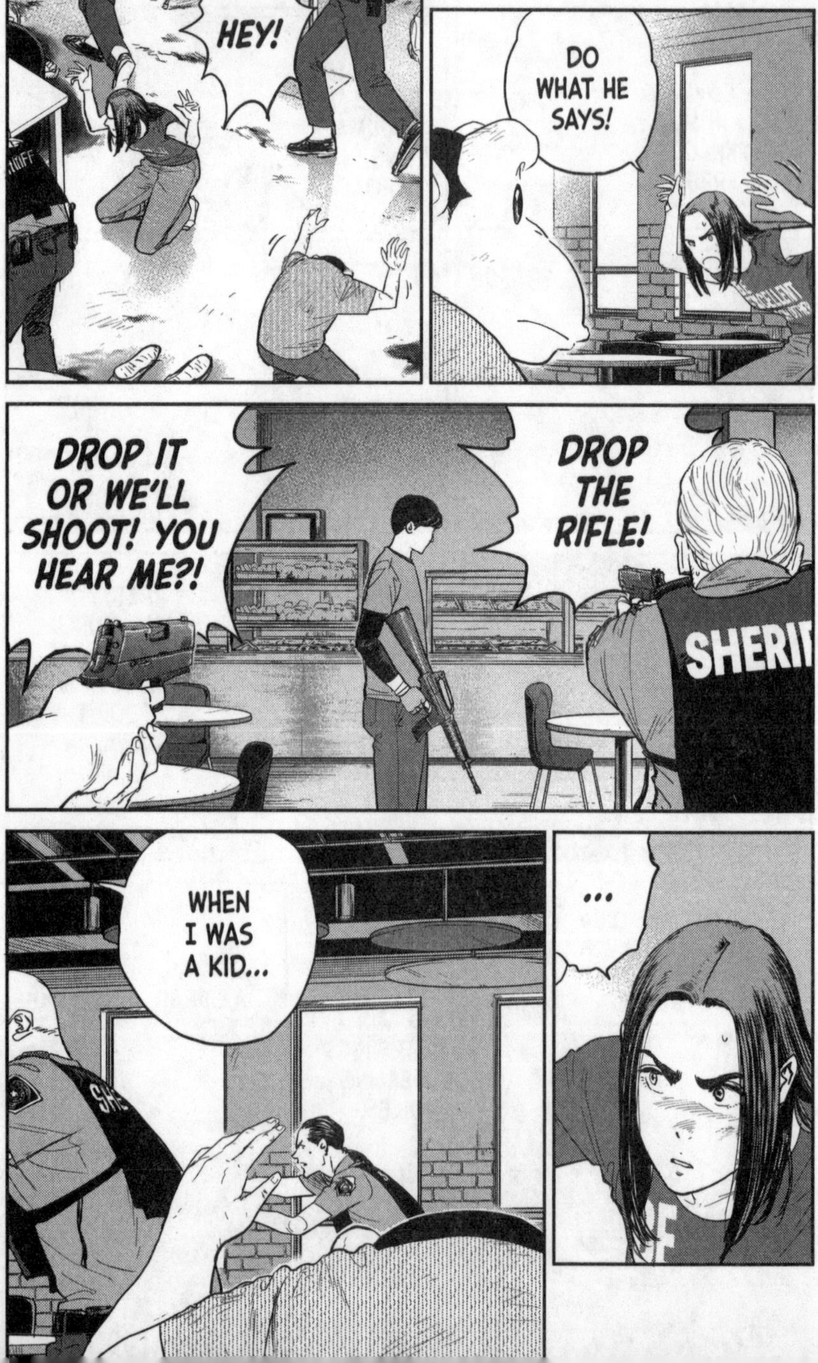
DO WHAT HE SAYS!
HEY!
DROP THE RIFLE!
DROP IT OR WE'LL SHOOT! YOU HEAR ME?!
...
WHEN I WAS A KID...

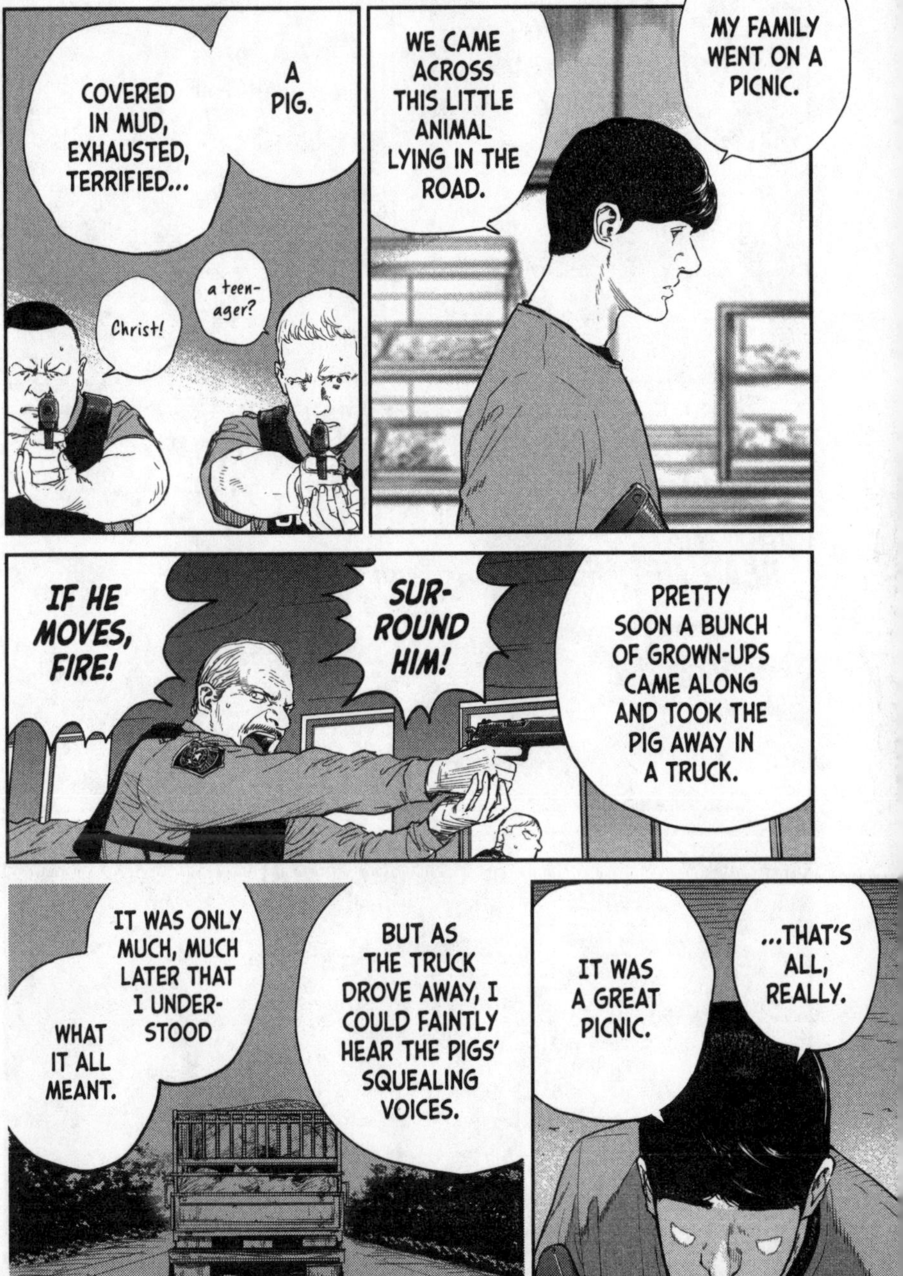
MY FAMILY WENT ON A PICNIC.
WE CAME ACROSS THIS LITTLE ANIMAL LYING IN THE ROAD.
A PIG.
COVERED IN MUD, EXHAUSTED, TERRIFIED...
a teen-ager?
Christ!
PRETTY SOON A BUNCH OF GROWN-UPS CAME ALONG AND TOOK THE PIG AWAY IN A TRUCK.
SUR-ROUND HIM!
IF HE MOVES, FIRE!
...THAT'S ALL, REALLY.
IT WAS A GREAT PICNIC.
BUT AS THE TRUCK DROVE AWAY, I COULD FAINTLY HEAR THE PIGS' SQUEALING VOICES.
IT WAS ONLY MUCH, MUCH LATER THAT I UNDER-STOOD
WHAT IT ALL MEANT.

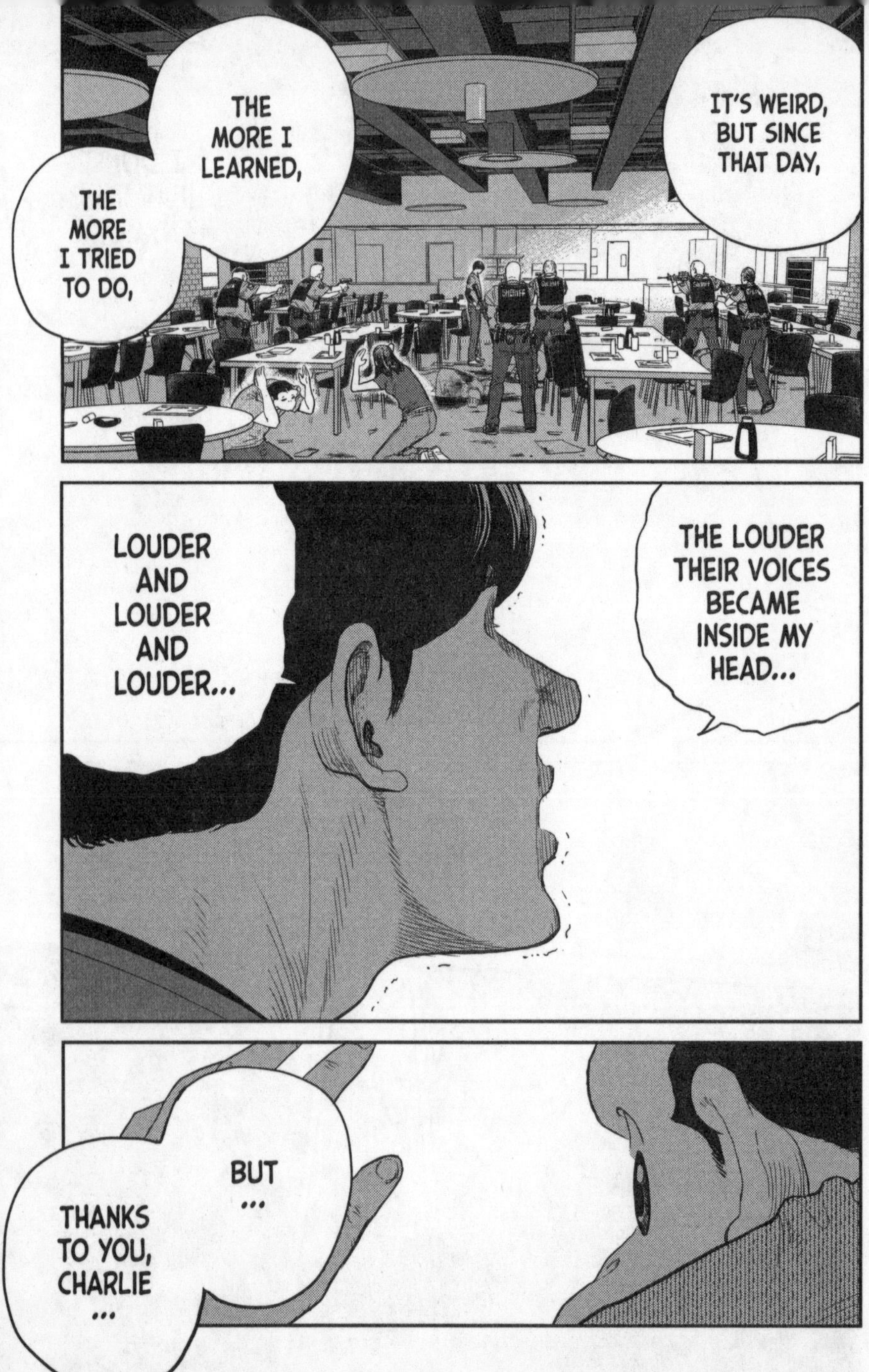
IT'S WEIRD, BUT SINCE THAT DAY,
THE MORE I LEARNED,
THE MORE I TRIED TO DO,
THE LOUDER THEIR VOICES BECAME INSIDE MY HEAD...
LOUDER AND LOUDER AND LOUDER...
BUT ...
THANKS TO YOU, CHARLIE ...

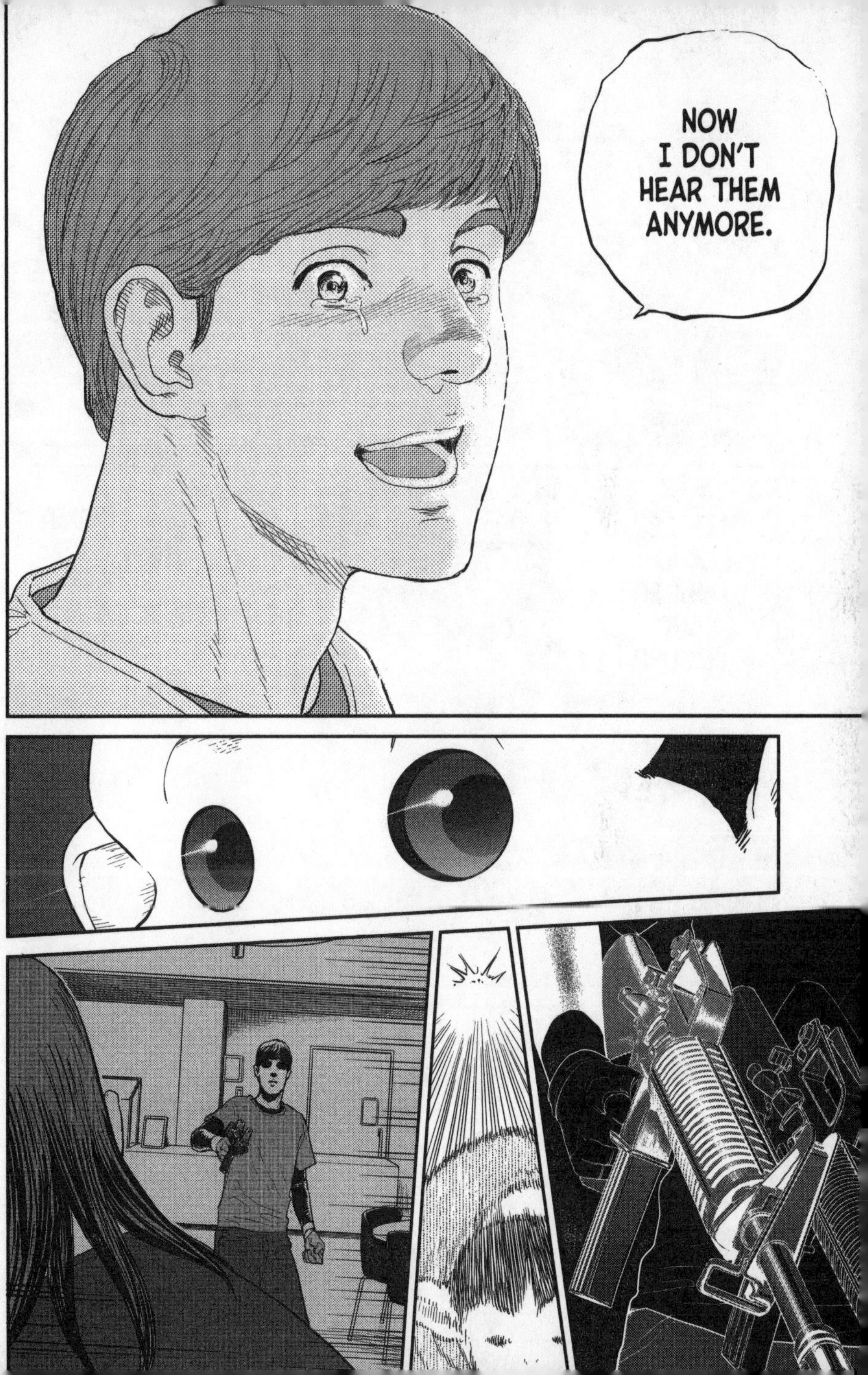
NOW I DON'T HEAR THEM ANYMORE.

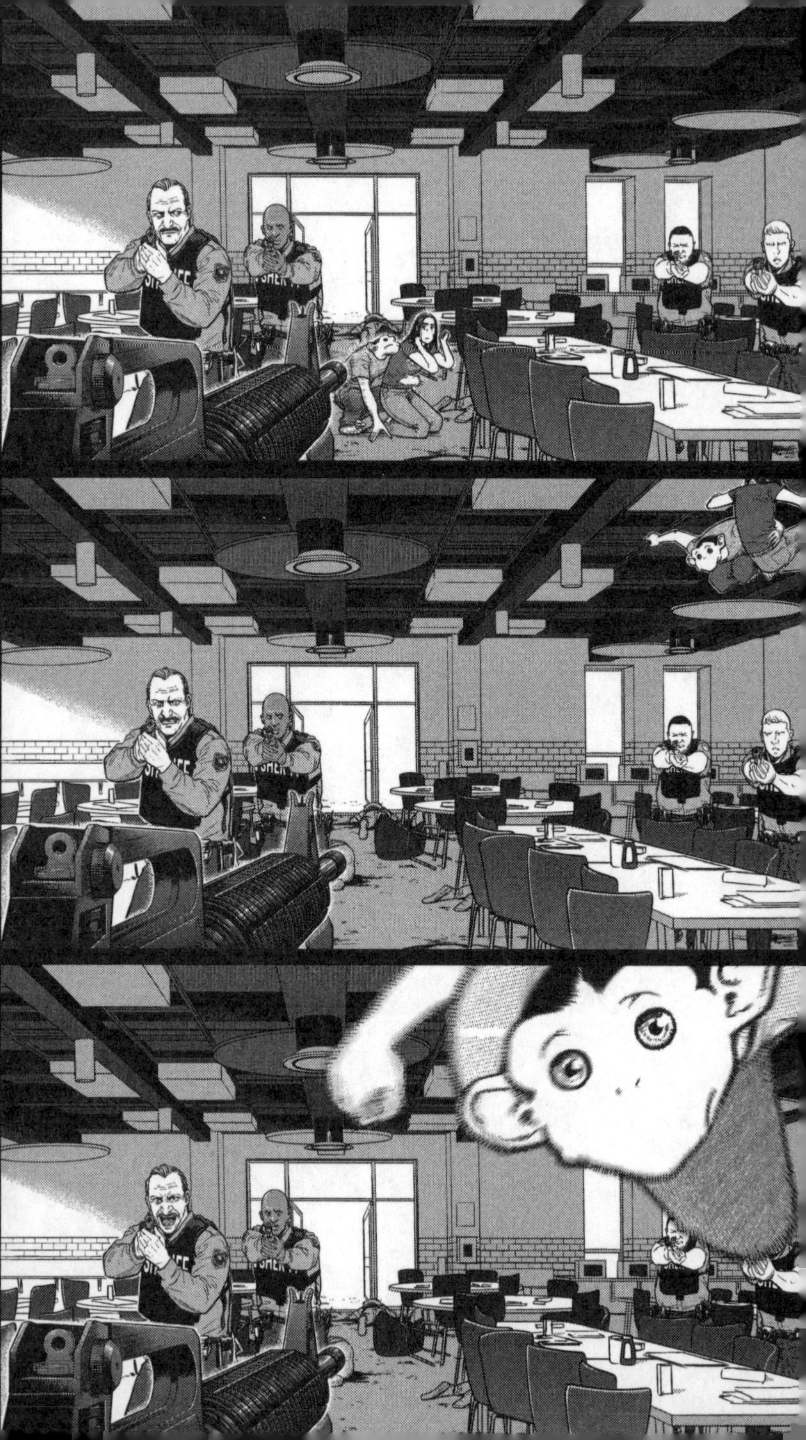

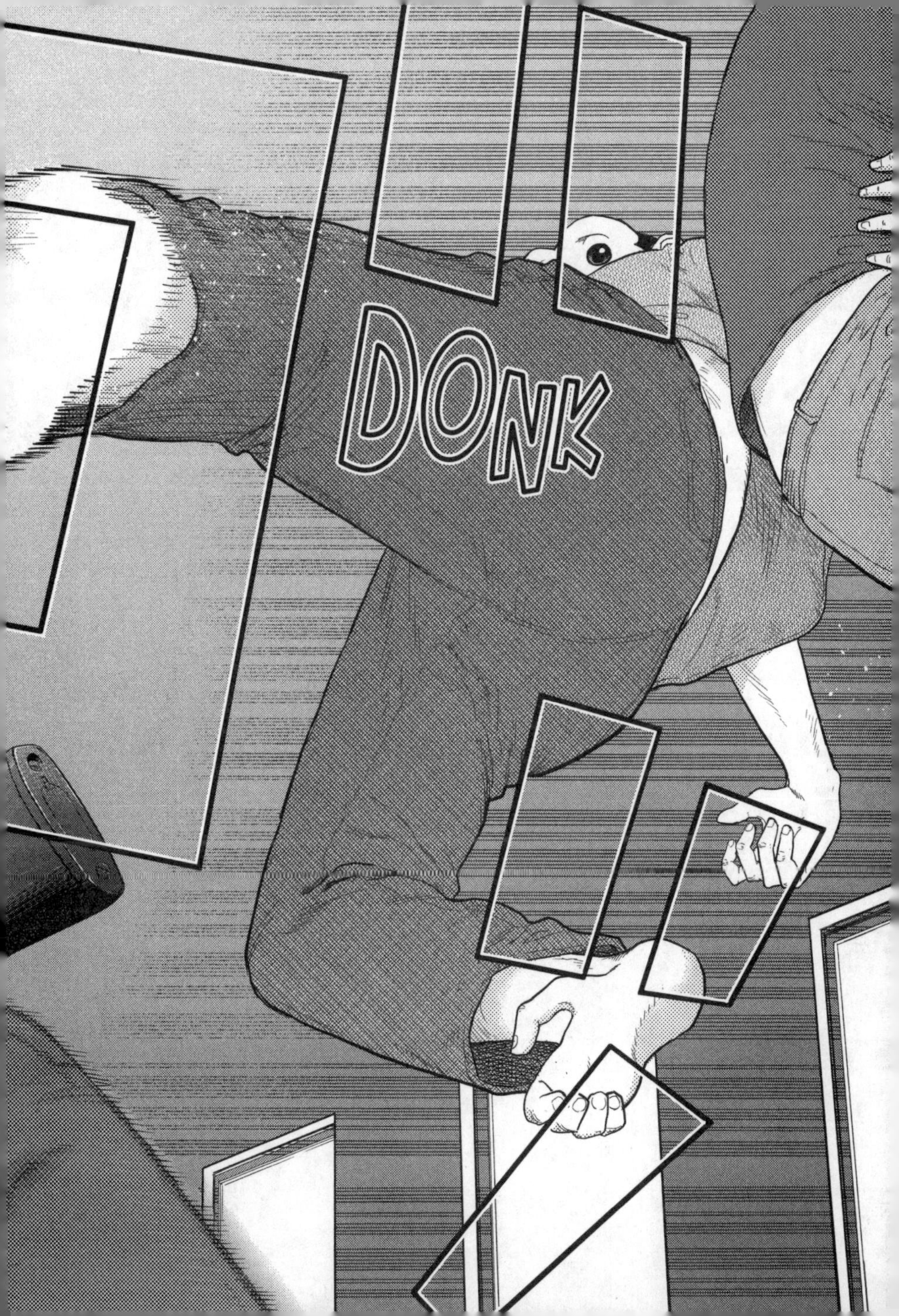
DONK

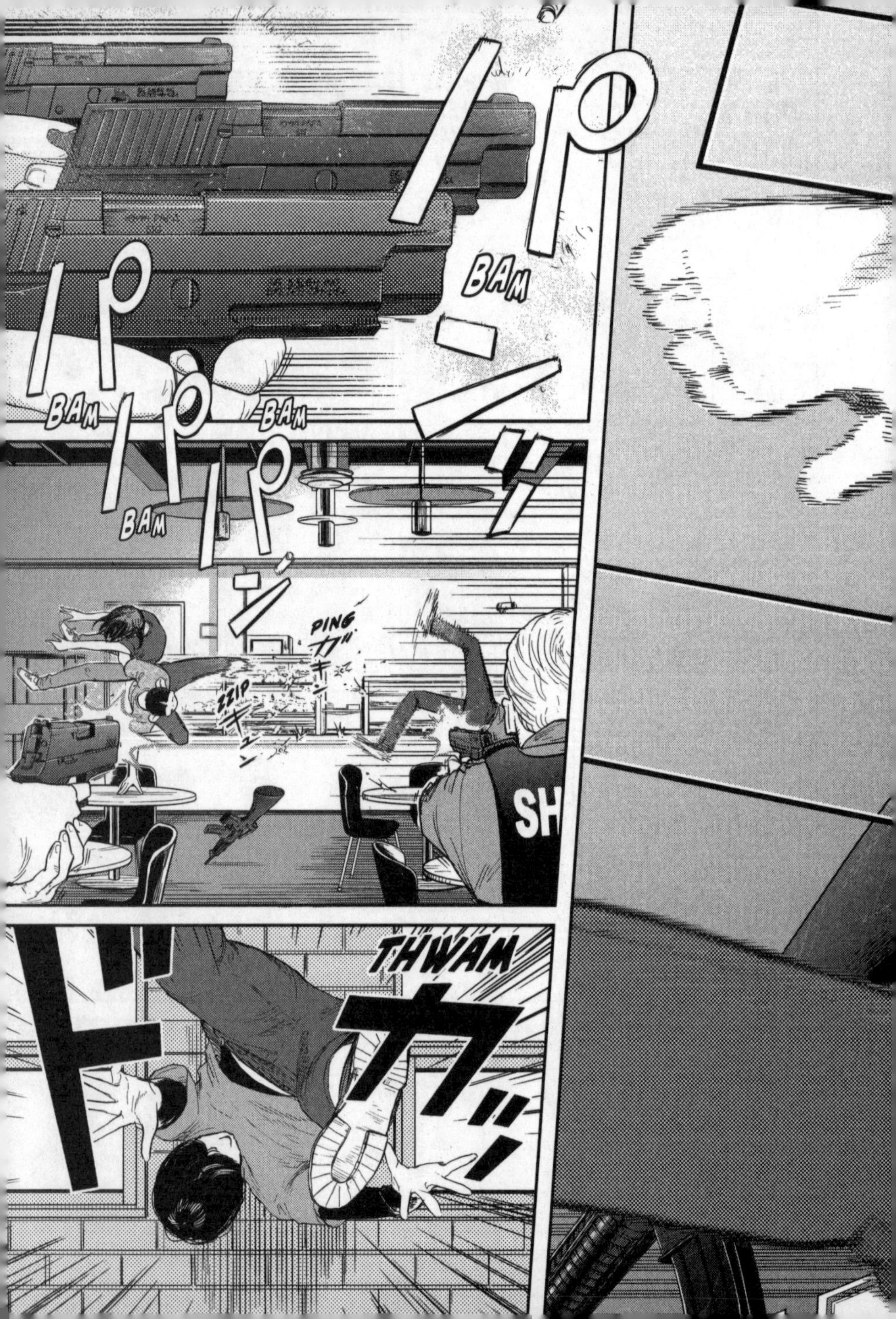
BAM
BAM
BAM
BAM
PING
ZZIP
SH
THWAM

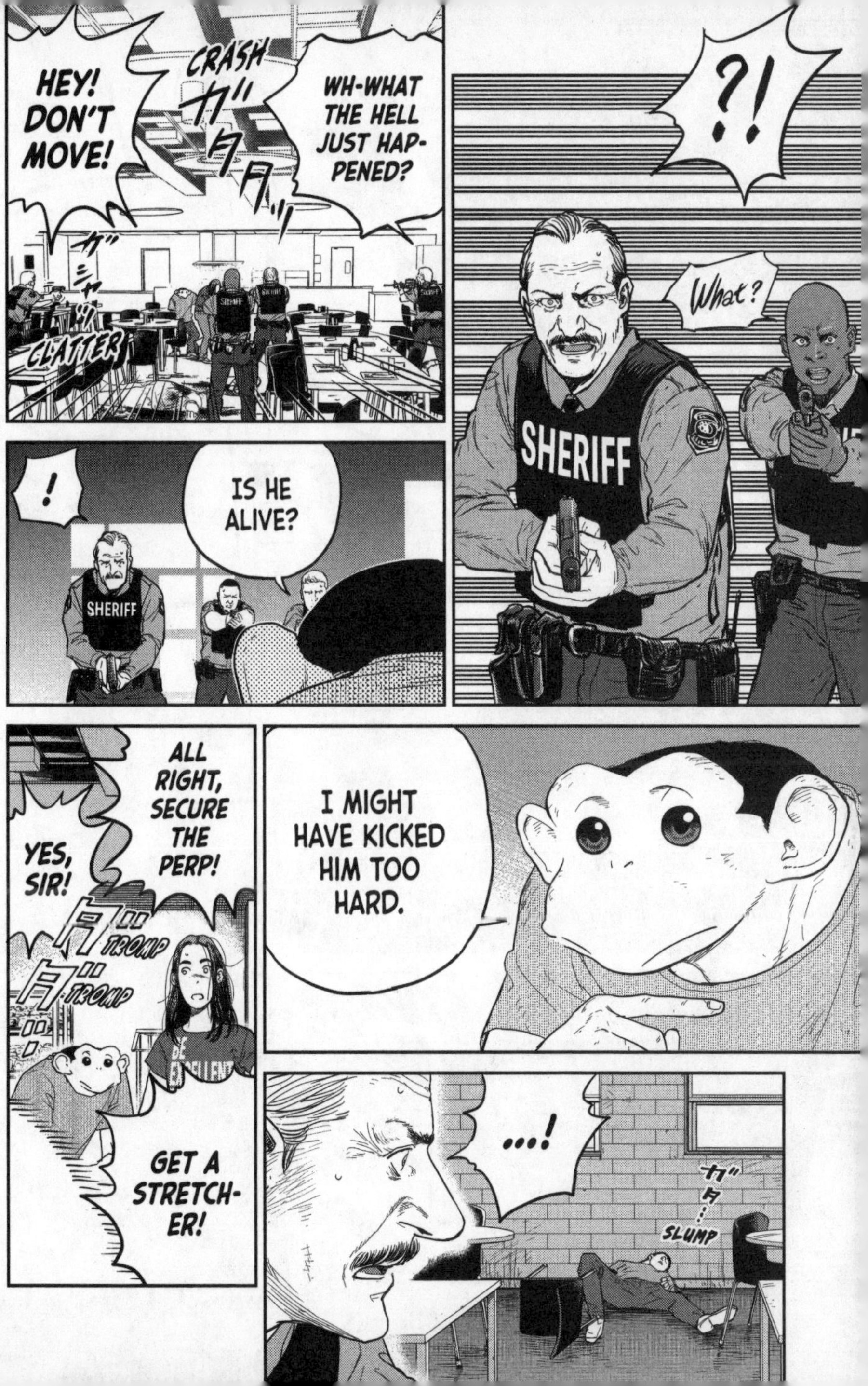
?!
What?
WH-WHAT THE HELL JUST HAP-PENED?
CRASH
HEY! DON'T MOVE!
CLATTER
IS HE ALIVE?
!
I MIGHT HAVE KICKED HIM TOO HARD.
...!
SLUMP
ALL RIGHT, SECURE THE PERP!
YES, SIR!
TROMP
TROMP
GET A STRETCH-ER!

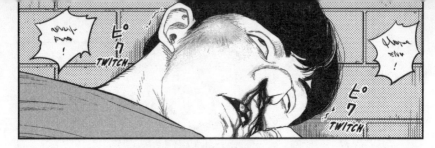

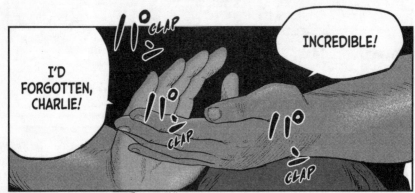

ピク
TWITCH
ピク
TWITCH
INCREDIBLE!
I'D FORGOTTEN, CHARLIE!
パン
CLAP
パン
CLAP
パン
CLAP
YOU'RE THE HUMANZEE.
THE TRICKSTER WHO DOESN'T STICK TO THE SCRIPT!
ゴオオオオ
VOOOOOOMM
WELL, SO MUCH FOR CREATING A MARTYR.
AH WELL,
SO BE IT.

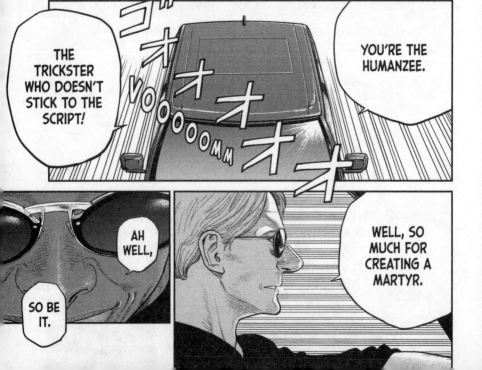

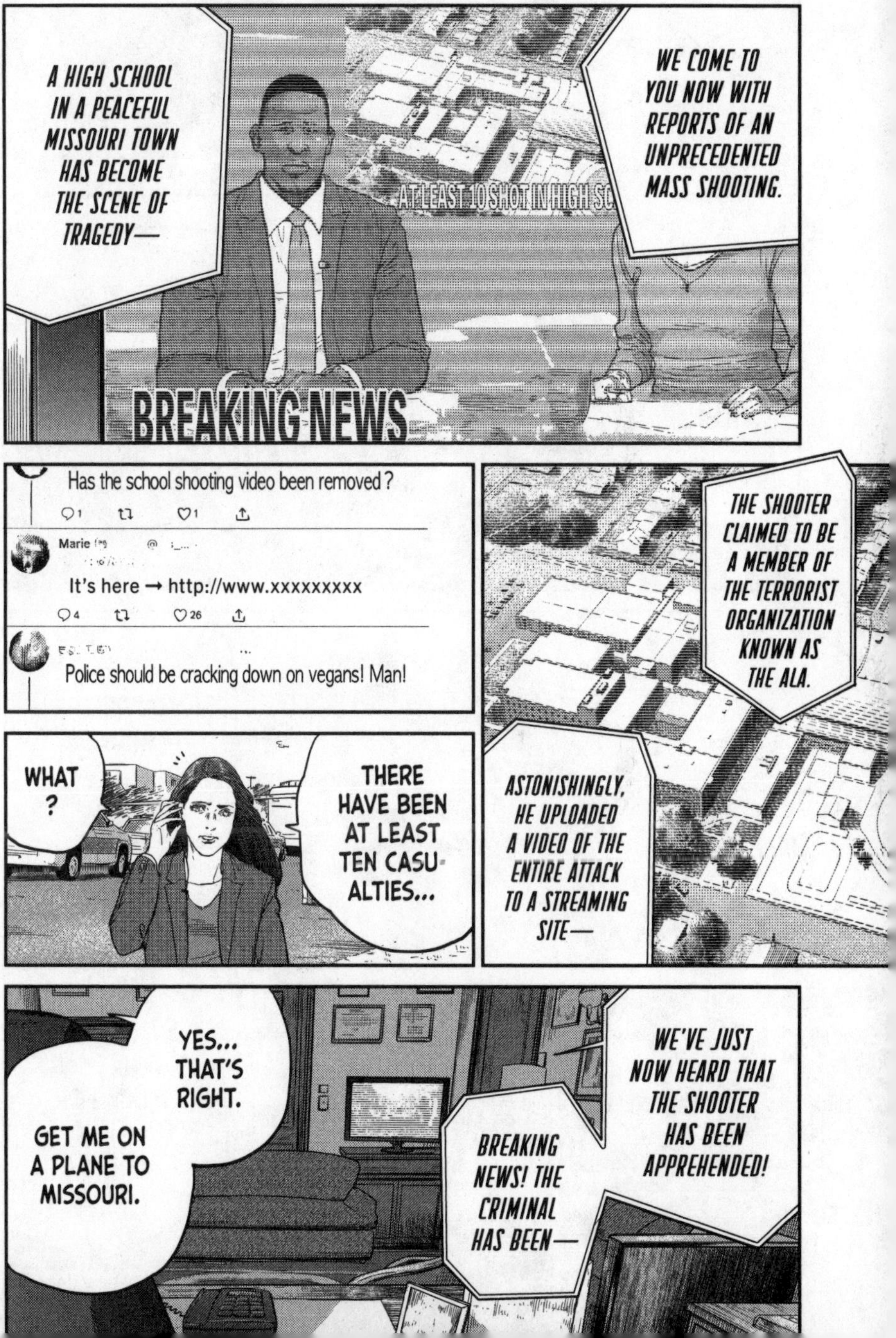
WE COME TO YOU NOW WITH REPORTS OF AN UNPRECEDENTED MASS SHOOTING.
A HIGH SCHOOL IN A PEACEFUL MISSOURI TOWN HAS BECOME THE SCENE OF TRAGEDY—
AT LEAST 10 SHOT IN HIGH SC
BREAKING NEWS
THE SHOOTER CLAIMED TO BE A MEMBER OF THE TERRORIST ORGANIZATION KNOWN AS THE ALA.
ASTONISHINGLY, HE UPLOADED A VIDEO OF THE ENTIRE ATTACK TO A STREAMING SITE—
Has the school shooting video been removed?
1
1
Marie
It's here → http://www.xxxxxxxxx
4
26
Police should be cracking down on vegans! Man!
THERE HAVE BEEN AT LEAST TEN CASU-ALTIES...
WHAT?
WE'VE JUST NOW HEARD THAT THE SHOOTER HAS BEEN APPREHENDED!
BREAKING NEWS! THE CRIMINAL HAS BEEN—
YES... THAT'S RIGHT.
GET ME ON A PLANE TO MISSOURI.

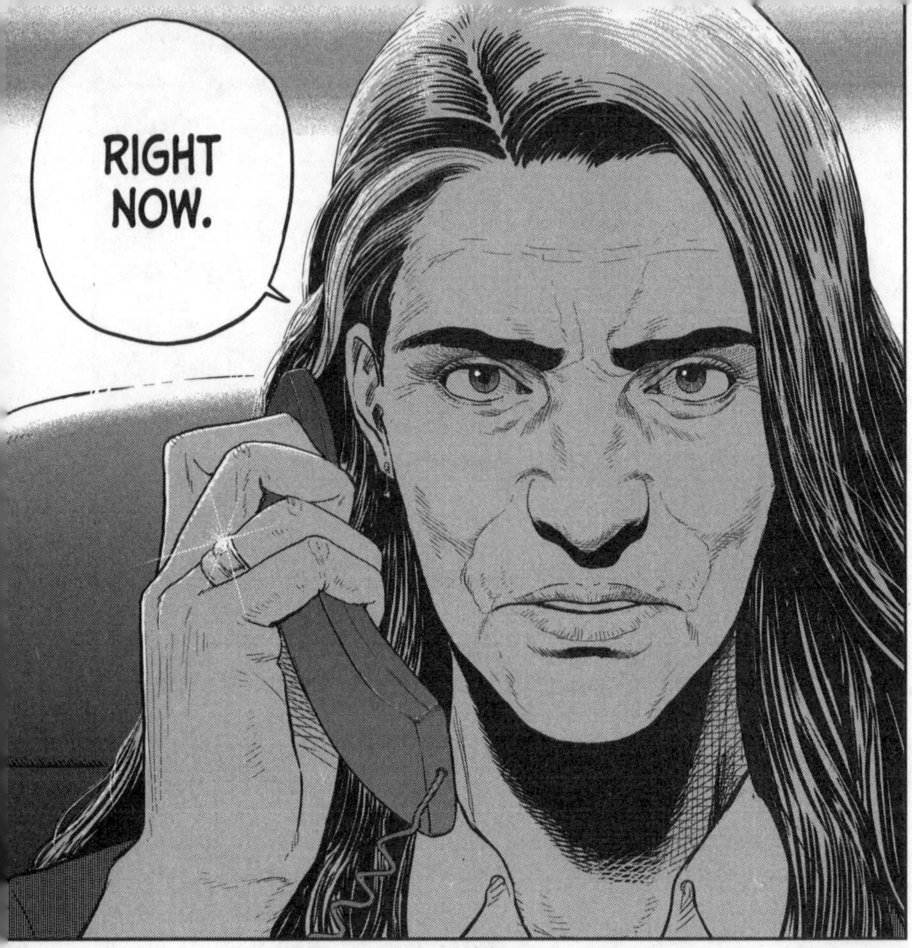
RIGHT NOW.
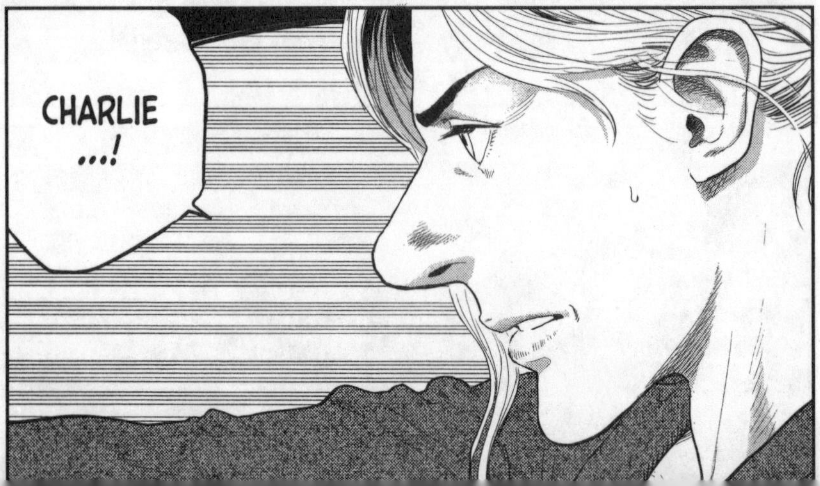
CHARLIE ...!

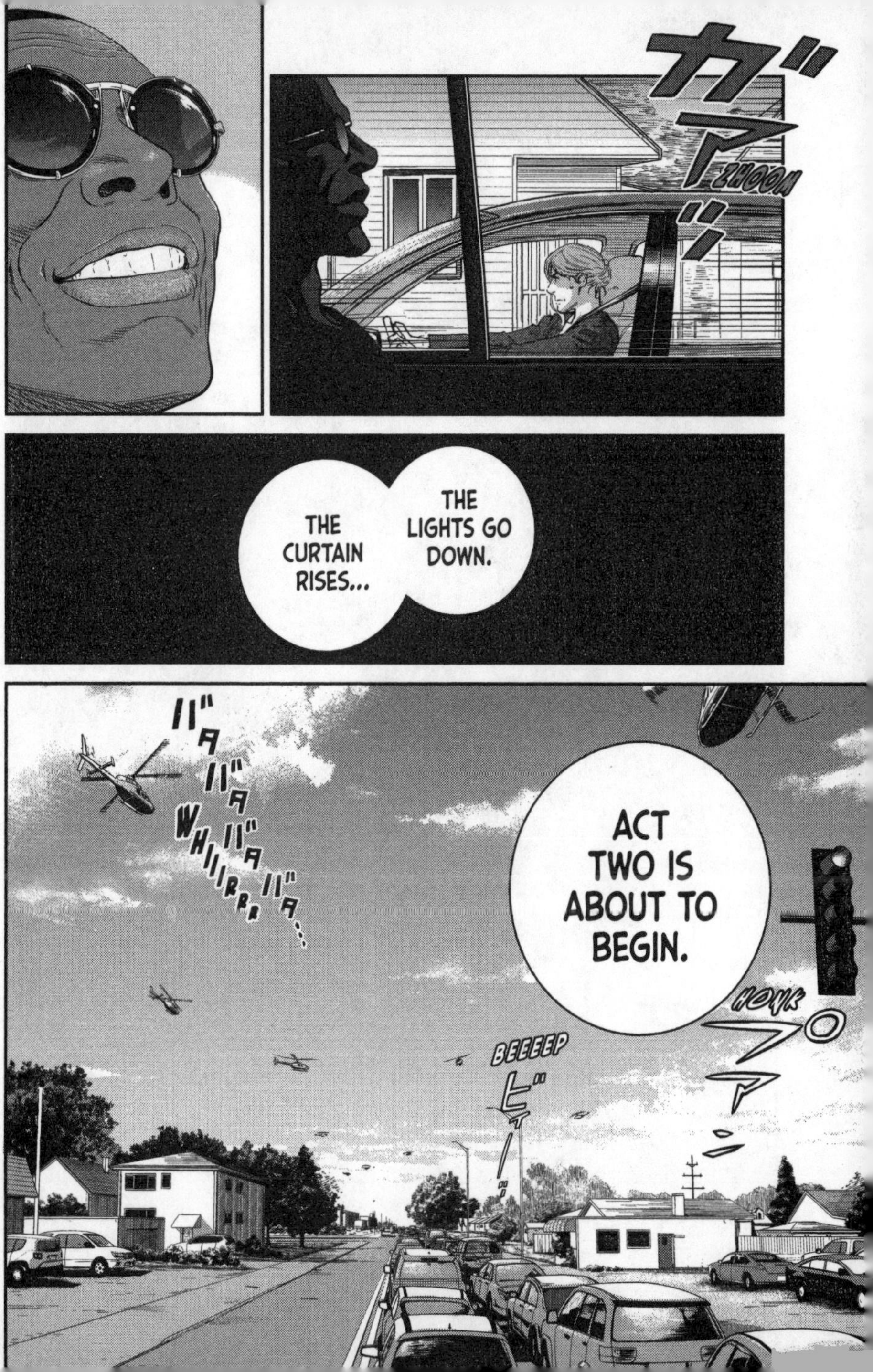
ガァーッ
ZHOOM
THE LIGHTS GO DOWN.
THE CURTAIN RISES...
HONK
プァーン
ACT TWO IS ABOUT TO BEGIN.
BEEEEP
ビィー
バタバタバタバタ...
WHIIIRRR

THE DARWIN INCIDENT VOLUME 2 END / TO BE CONTINUED

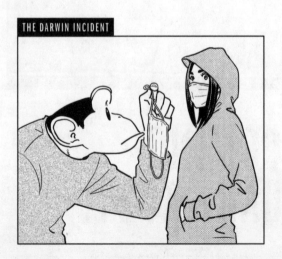
THE DARWIN INCIDENT

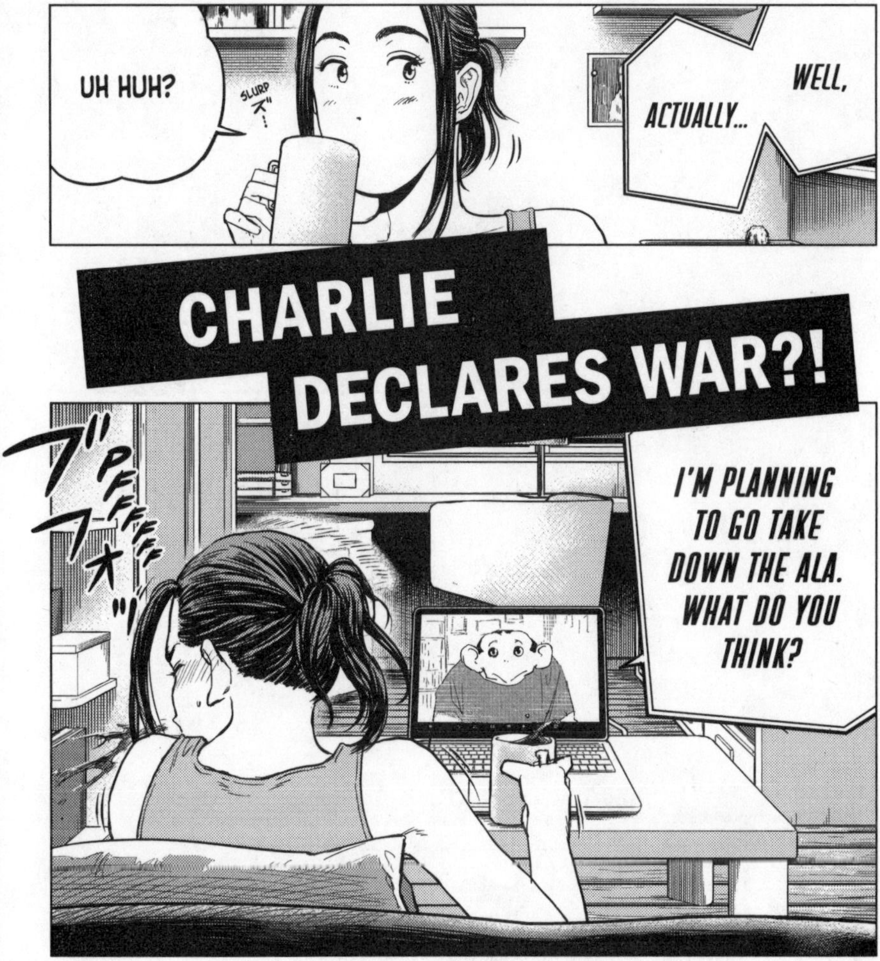
WELL, ACTUALLY...
UH HUH?
SLURP
ズ…
CHARLIE DECLARES WAR?!
I'M PLANNING TO GO TAKE DOWN THE ALA. WHAT DO YOU THINK?
PFFFFFFF
ブフォッ

COMING JANUARY 2024!

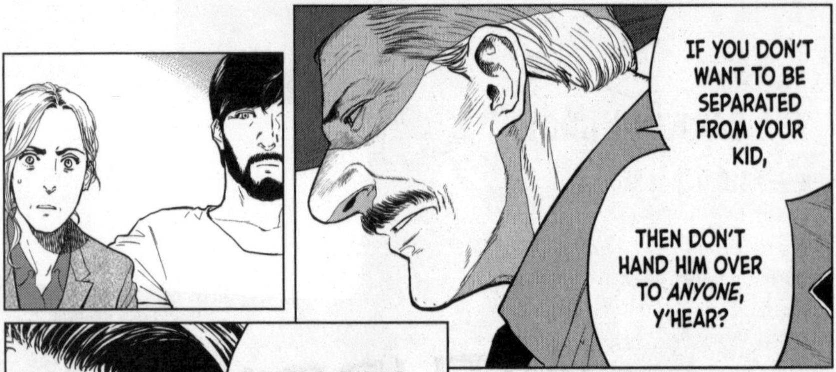
IF YOU DON'T WANT TO BE SEPARATED FROM YOUR KID,
THEN DON'T HAND HIM OVER TO *ANYONE*, Y'HEAR?

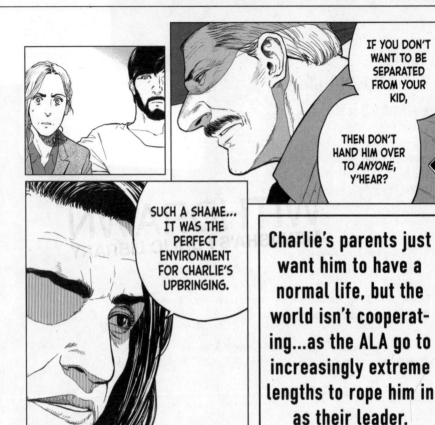

Charlie's parents just want him to have a normal life, but the world isn't cooperating...as the ALA go to increasingly extreme lengths to rope him in as their leader.

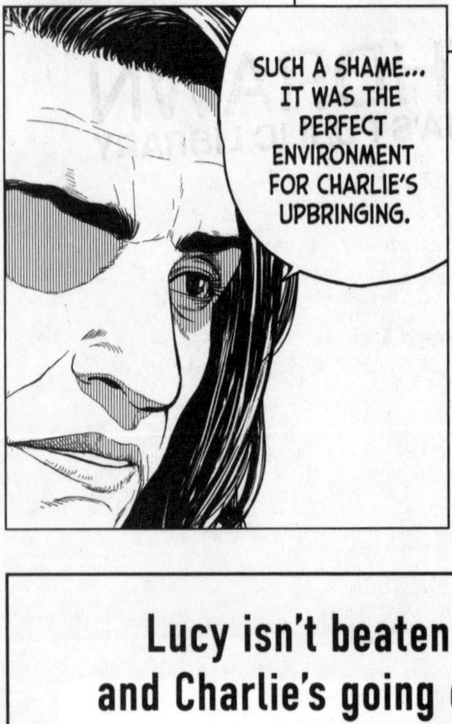
SUCH A SHAME... IT WAS THE PERFECT ENVIRONMENT FOR CHARLIE'S UPBRINGING.

Lucy isn't beaten yet, though—
and Charlie's going on the offensive!

THE DARWIN INCIDENT 03

THE DARWIN INCIDENT 2

A VERTICAL Book

Translation: Cat Anderson
Editor: Daniel Joseph
Production: Grace Lu
            Pei Ann Yeap
            Eve Grand
Proofreading: Kevin Luo

© 2021 Shun Umezawa
All rights reserved.
First published in Japan in 2021 by Kodansha, Ltd., Tokyo
Publication rights for this English edition arranged through Kodansha, Ltd., Tokyo
English language version produced by Kodansha USA Publishing, LLC, 2023

Originally published in Japanese as *Darwin Jihen 2* by Kodansha, Ltd.
Darwin Jihen first serialized in *Monthly Afternoon*, Kodansha, Ltd., 2020-

This is a work of fiction.

ISBN: 978-1-64729-317-8

Printed in the United States of America

First Edition

Kodansha USA Publishing, LLC
451 Park Avenue South
7th Floor
New York, NY 10016
www.kodansha.us

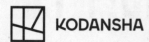